REVELATION'S

BATTLE PLANS

Your Marching Orders from Today to the Last Day

I0825831

CARL WESLEY ANDERSON

Praise for *Revelation's Battle Plans*

"Revelation's Battle Plans *is a masterfully crafted work that reflects Carl's deep love for Jesus and his passion for unveiling the truths of Scripture. I was particularly impressed with his scholarly precision. With a pastoral heart, Carl brings clarity to the rich symbolism of the Book of Revelation, always pointing to Jesus as the central figure of history and eternity.*

"His victorious Kingdom perspective offers hope, strength, and encouragement for Believers that may be navigating uncertain times.

"Though perspectives on the end-times may differ, Carl's commitment to sound scholarship and his Christ-centered approach make this book an important tool in cracking the code of the Book of Revelation.

"His blend of historical insight, theological depth, and practical application allows readers to engage with Revelation as a guide to faith and triumph, rather than fear and confusion.

"Carl's work is a gift to the Body of Christ, offering a fresh lens through which to see the ultimate victory of God's Kingdom and our role within it."

—**Ray Goolsby, Pastor & Life Coach,** Bethel Leadership Network

"I thank God for my friend Carl Wesley Anderson and this powerful book, Revelation's Battle Plans. *Carl combines brilliant theological insight with the humility of a man who hears God's voice and dares to obey it. I'm so grateful for his friendship and the depth of revelation he brings to the Church through this work, especially in such a crucial time as this day we live in.*

"I'm genuinely excited to dive into the deep waters of Revelation alongside Carl, knowing the Lord is using him to help awaken, equip, and arm the Bride. Carl is no "Titanic," (prideful and obstinate to the Lord's voice); he's a BATTLESHIP in these last days.

"This book is a weapon against darkness and a refuge for those searching for direction, anchored in the hope-filled assurance of King Jesus' return and our victorious destiny as His Church."

—**Troy Brewer, Senior Pastor & Prophet,** OpenDoor Church

"Brother Carl fills these pages with a heartfelt love for Jesus, a passion for prayer, and a courageous spirit of perseverance. He also brings to modern evangelicals what the Church taught consistently for well over a millennium: amillennialism, or as Carl puts it, NOW-Millennialism! This now-millennial perspective paired with an approach to the Book of Revelation called 'idealism' enables Carl to not just talk to us about the end times, but apply end-times truths to our generation. And whether we are the last generation, or still one of a thousand yet to live, I join with my brother and pray, 'Even so, come, Lord Jesus!'"

—**Dave Olson,** Lead Pastor, SkyWater Church, Shakopee, MN

"Revelation's Battle Plans *is both inspiring and instructing, not only to be kept close at all times as an indispensable handbook, but also as a source of comfort and encouragement at difficult times. Our Lord Jesus warned us about the trials and tribulations of the end of times and His Second Coming, with direct revelations and with different parables.*

"In essence He admonishes us to be ready, to be prepared, not be caught asleep, nor badly equipped, nor distracted by passing and unnecessary concerns. Carl gives us strong tools that we can make our own and adapt to our circumstances as individual Believers and as members of a community of faith, so that we will be ready and prepared, as Jesus commanded, at the time when whatever has to come will come.

"Carl makes reference to the universal Body of true Believers and followers of Christ as an army ready to fight and that will fight. During my short spell in the navy for my national service at the height of the Cold War, the possibility of a sudden, total and devastating conflict was a daily reality. One way to keep everyone on his toes, what was technically called 'status of readiness', was to call for general alarms at the least predictable moments.

"The time and manner of response of everyone, from the top admiral to the newly recruited seaman, determined the status of readiness. To achieve the highest levels everyone had to be trained, equipped, informed, and ready to answer quickly and effectively to any general alarm.

*"*Revelation's Battle Plans *equips the army of the Lord to know well the Commander-in-Chief, to discern friends and foes, to learn how to fight effectively, to be prepared and stay prepared, not in fear, not in anxiety, but with hopeful expectations and keeping our eyes, attention and hearts focused on Jesus, the Captain of the army of the Lord, at all times."*

—**Giancarlo Elia, Catch the Fire,** London, England

"I am blown away and completely refreshed as you draw out the Father's plan for the church to engage in warfare with our enemy and to bring Saving Grace to the entire earth. What a somber warning to not lose heart when all seems lost, but to always trust in the Lord who never fails us!

"Such an important message for the church today! Thank you, brother! This book is a gift!"

—**Pastor Jeff Orluck,** Hope Community

"In Revelation's Battle Plans *Carl Wesley Anderson profoundly intertwines deep, Scriptural insights from the Book of Revelation, unveiling in a very practical way its' teachings. He brings a heartfelt examination of human nature and Divine love. This book is essential for anyone seeking to understand the delicate balance of judgment and mercy in God's plan. As we navigate our turbulent times, this work serves as both a profound reminder of God's steadfastness and an urgent call to repentance and hope. A truly transformative and powerful read!"*

—**Adam F. Thompson,** Prophetic International Author and Ministry Voice of Fire Ministries.

"Demystifying what is often misunderstood and wrongly applied has been Carl's goal in writing his most recent book, Revelation's Battle Plans. *I strongly recommend reading his book if you desire to gain a high-level, mountain-top view, leaving behind the clutter and noise of misunderstandings that are often associated with the biblical Book of Revelation. Well done, Carl, keep on writing!"*

—**Michael Motsinger,** Senior Pastor—Elder Care-Focused Ministries

"Carl Wesley Anderson's book Revelation's Battle Plans *offers a visual perspective on the Book of Revelation, approaching this often misunderstood apocalyptic text not as mystic prophecy to be passively decoded, but as a dynamic call to action for Believers.*

"Carl builds his analysis on a compelling foundation: The Revelation, like the parables of the Gospels, communicates through symbolic language employed to transform understanding rather than simply inform. He explains to readers how to approach Revelation's vivid imagery as an apocalyptic genre.

"While Anderson's military metaphor might not resonate with all theological perspectives, his emphasis on active faith rather than speculative interpretation offers valuable insight for the reader seeking deeper engagement with this challenging biblical text.

"If we critique our contemporary postmodern culture we see that our habit of passively consuming visual media—from films to memes to news broadcasts—has conditioned us to approach the Revelation of Saint John as grand spectacle rather than as a spiritual battle plan requiring response.

"Revelation's Battle Plans *would particularly benefit readers unconvinced of sensationalist end-times calculations as to who is 666 and look instead for a practical, faith-building approach to Revelation that connects it to contemporary spiritual life.*

"To illustrate his idealistic view he has many interesting testimonies from well-known to little-known Believers who have battled for the faith and we can expect have received their crowns."

—**Gary Schreiner,** Bible Teacher based in Switzerland

"Revelation's Battle Plans *is more than just a book—it's a wake-up call to the Church. Carl writes with prophetic clarity and spiritual urgency, calling Believers to rise up, suit up, and step into their God-given assignments. In a time where confusion and fear often dominate the narrative, this book brings strategic hope, grounded in Scripture and guided by the Holy Spirit.*

"What I love most is that no matter your theological view on the end times—whether pre-, mid-, or post-tribulation—we are all called to be ready for the

return of Jesus, whenever and however He comes. This book urges us to get ready and don't fall for the Enemy's tactics.

"As a Christian leader navigating both the battlefield of culture and the frontlines of faith, I found these pages filled with direction, encouragement and divine insight. This isn't theory—it's a call to action. For anyone who longs to live with boldness and purpose in these end times, this book is your spiritual briefing."

—**Stephanie van der Horst,** Director, Family 7 Television Network, the Netherlands

"If you have an interest in eschatology and in the Book of Revelation, I recommend you read Revelation's Battle Plans *by Carl Wesley Anderson. The majority of Evangelicals today are locked into a dispensational interpretation of eschatology and the Book of Revelation and often aren't very knowledgeable regarding other views and their biblical basis.*

"In Revelation's Battle Plans *Carl presents another view along with its biblical basis and does so with grace and sensitivity. Carl does not come across in a dogmatic way and acknowledges that he is still learning.*

"If you have an interest in the Book of Revelation, I believe you will find Carl's explanation of the poetic structure of Revelation and the 7 parallel visionary cycles (verses a chronological interpretation) interesting and will expand your understanding and appreciation for the Book of Revelation. I also appreciate how Carl focused on King Jesus the Lord of Sabaoth as the predominant theme of the Book of Revelation.

"If you find you disagree with something Carl has written, please don't dismiss the entire book. I appreciate Carl's gracious attitude towards those who differ from him and challenge you to have the same attitude towards this book. While I embrace much of what Carl wrote in this book, I don't embrace everything, and I'm okay with that, as is Carl."

—**Pastor Mark A. Johnson,** Crossroads Church

"Carl Wesley Anderson has been my friend since the mid-1990s. His consistency and devotion to Jesus are remarkable. At a young age, he was prophetically called out in a stadium in Germany. He spent many years traveling the world, teaching the Bible, and inspiring countless people through his exceptional media ministry.

"A notable example is his outstanding television series, Love Speaks. Carl's ability to document and articulate church history, revivals, and the various aspects the Church needs to hear is a tremendous asset to the Body of Christ and future generations.

"My friend Carl has heroically overcome cancer and continues to be a global voice that sheds light on the prophetic implications of our times by pointing to the times and seasons of previous moments and how they relate to us today.

"The work Carl has done in his latest book is crafted intelligently and filled with tremendous insights on eschatology. Although Carl and I come from different perspectives, every time I read his work or watch one of his programs, I am profoundly blessed by his brilliant insights and the revelatory aspects of the Word of God.

"I honor Carl's tireless service to the Lord Jesus Christ, bringing life and joy to so many!"

—**Joseph Z,** Author, Broadcaster, Prophetic Voice

"You will find yourself in the midst of end time reality, spiritual warfare and eschatological mystery as you read Carl's book. Every page is filled with historical heroes of faith, telling their stories to inspire you to do the same.

"Jesus Christ is the center character leading and supporting His people through tough times and eventually Home. This is a challenging book and will require you to reflect and think, but it will also bring peace and joy as you prepare for your journey toward the End of Days.

"The author has continued his theme of "Love Speaks"—a work that reveals 21 ways to hear God's voice—with "Love Leads"—a work to help you navigate your life in these turbulent times."

—**Helmar W. Heckel,** BS, MDiv, Dmin

"Carl's insights in this book helped me gain a clearer understanding of these perspectives and how they relate to the events unfolding in the Book of Revelation. He also shows us how to approach Revelation from different Vantage Points, offering fresh insights on this often complex Book.

"This is an excellent resource for anyone wanting to prepare for the Last Battle, and a great study tool for small groups, with plenty of thought-provoking questions and answers. Bravo!"

—**Yvonne Carroll,** The Well Ministry, The Netherlands

"I first met Carl when he was a student at ACTS Bible School. At the time he was a new Christian and had a lot to learn, which he did! Now some 30+ years later, he is not only a student of the Bible, but a Teacher of it as well. He ministers in many overseas countries and is a successful TV Producer with his films being shown on many International Networks.

"Then, too, he is an author, and his newest book is on the biblical Book of Revelation. We have talked together quite a lot about his views on the End Times. While I personally take a different approach on some of what he has written, we both agree on the return of Christ and the need to be ready and prepared for His soon return.

"Well done, Carl."

—**Alan Langstaff,** Kairos Ministries

"This is a challenging book in many ways. For those like me (and I know I am by no means alone), who have dared to admit to sitting-on-the-fence regarding the Book of Revelation, Section 2 will be a genuine challenge, but also an exciting one as he introduces us to a different way of considering this extraordinary section of Scripture.

"On re-reading Section 2 about Revelation, I realized that as a teacher and trainer on biblical dream interpretation, I look at dreams in a manner similar to the poetic parallelism outlined by Carl. As a result, I relaxed and continued to read with a reduced level of inadequacy!

"The 3 other Sections of Carl's book are typical of his written and film work;

the passion, the enthusiasm, the love for Christ, His Church, His Word and His Kingdom is tangible and inspiring. I love the practicality; this is where we are; this is what we need to know and this is what we need to understand and follow up in faith. A timely reminder to us all, thank you!"

—**Tony Cooke,** The Dream Academy, England

"Why should you read Carl Wesley Anderson's book? Because you will benefit greatly, as I did, to gain insights I have not learned in my 40 years of ministry. You will learn so much about this important and very timely subject so many steer away from. Yes, there are many complexities and mysteries about the Book of Revelation. Carl Wesley Anderson runs to this challenge and makes it so interesting. You've got to read his book!

—**Londa Lundstrom,** Evangelist, Pastor

"I would like to give a high recommendation to read Revelation's Battle Plans *which has an insightful approach to the Book of Revelation. As a Christian leader who trained over 6,000 Pastors last year I appreciate practical applications for Believers. It is not just another end-time theology book, but one that can be taught to others.*

"This book serves as a tool for understanding the symbolism in Revelation and preparing for the Last Battle. The overarching message is one of hope, urging Believers to remain vigilant in prayer and to prepare for Christ's return. I look forward to sharing insights from the book with others."

—**Rev. Dr. Paul Marzahn,** President and General Overseer of International Ministerial Fellowship

"What I appreciate about Carl Wesley Anderson's new book and episodic documentary series, Revelation's Battle Plans, *is that it serves as a guide for followers of Jesus Christ, preparing them for these uncertain times. Many of us have forgotten that we are in a spiritual war that has existed since the Garden of Eden, and we are now closer than ever to the Return of Christ.*

"Having listened to Carl through his films and books, I can attest to the presence of the Lord in both his life and his work. He delivers a powerful message in Revelation's Battle Plans *for those willing to hear it: we must advance the Kingdom of God rather than fall back. While numerous interpretations of the Book of Revelation exist, what sets this endeavor apart is its focus on our personal preparation of heart, soul, and mind. This book, along with its episodic documentary series, will greatly encourage and equip you for the Last Battle against the deceptions and persecution facing Believers."*

—**Timothy Mahoney,** President, Founder of THINKING MAN FILMS, director and producer of the Patterns of Evidence film series, and Heroic Pictures, The American Miracle: Our Nation is No Accident

"We never truly move beyond the fundamentals of our faith, which makes it vital to encounter fresh teaching that brings them into sharper focus. For many Believers, fear has too often replaced hope, and confusion has diminished confidence in reading the Book of Revelation.

"Carl Wesley Anderson offers a Christ-centered, hope-filled contribution that redirects us to the core truth: all of history, and every book of Scripture, revolves around the person of Jesus Christ.

"In his writing, you can hear the excitement and passion that God has given Carl to share this message: when Christ is clearly seen, fear loses its power, the enemy is exposed, and God's people gain clarity about the task set before them.

"My prayer is that readers will engage with this fresh approach, deepen their longing for Christ and His return, and receive practical, faith-filled direction to endure and advance until the Kingdom consumes the whole Earth.

—**Pastor Joshua Mitchell,** CHRISTchurch, Apple Valley, Minnesota

"For several years, a group of diverse pastors in my city met each week to pray for our city. One of the pastors gave me a book, Warfare, *written by the U.S. Marine Corps Staff. He had observed God at work in our city because of our prayers. He said, "You will appreciate this book because you understand prayer and warfare."*

"Carl Wesley Anderson's book on Revelation is needed for the Church to understand God's battle plans and Satan's battle plans.

"This book is practical in revealing tactical plans for defeating the Enemy, Satan, now and finally. John the Revelator said the LORD wanted "…to show to His servants things that must soon take place."

"Carl's book will make the Book of Revelation relevant and practical for every Believer."

—**Jim Munson,** Pastor/Teacher

"Revelation's Battle Plans *by Carl Wesley Anderson deeply resonates with my own convictions about the end times. In a world filled with speculation along with competing theories, what sets this book apart is Carl's clear teaching gift. He doesn't sensationalize Revelation, but instead he unfolds it. With biblical precision and spiritual insight, he reveals God's heart for His Church and equips Believers with essential end-time battle plans where we need to stand firm. God calls us to be overcomers, we reject false teaching, and resist all cultural distractions, while remaining faithful to Christ alone.* Revelation's Battle Plans *is not just a study of prophecy. This book is a spiritual strategy for every Believer who desires to endure, overcome, and reign with Christ. This book is a timely and necessary message for the Church today."*

—**Jennifer Weiss,** host of the Grace Grit Glory Show

"Then I saw Heaven open wide—and oh!
a white horse and its Rider.

The Rider, named Faithful and True,
judges and makes war in pure righteousness.

His eyes are a blaze of fire, on His head many crowns.

On His robe and thigh is written, King of kings, Lord of lords."[1]

1 A selection from Revelation 19, The Message Translation.

"A mighty fortress is our God,
a bulwark never failing;
Our helper He amid the flood,

of mortal ills prevailing:
For still our ancient foe,
Does seek to work us woe;
His craft and power are great,
and armed with cruel hate,
On earth is not his equal.

"Did we in our own strength confide,
our striving would be losing,
were not the right Man on our side,
the Man of God's own choosing:
You ask who that may be?
Christ Jesus, it is He;
Lord Sabaoth His name,
from age to age the same,
and He must win the battle." —Martin Luther[2]

---

2 Martin Luther, A Mighty Fortress is Our God, verses 1 and 2. Composed in 1528.

"Imagine that leader of all the enemy, in that great plain of Babylon, sitting on a sort of throne of smoldering flame, a horrible and terrifying sight. Watch him summon countless devils together, to send them to different cities until the whole world is covered, without forgetting any province or locality, any class or individual. We cannot be passive in this battle but must learn to face evil with spiritual wisdom and strength."

—Ignatius of Loyola[3]

"One of our great allies at present is the Church itself. Do not misunderstand me. I do not mean the Church as we see her spread through all time and space and rooted in eternity, terrible as an army with banners. That, I confess, is a spectacle which makes our boldest tempters uneasy. But fortunately, it is quite invisible to these humans."—C.S. Lewis[4]

---

3 Ignatius of Loyola, Jesuit Founding Priest and Spanish Saint, 1491-1556.
4 C.S. Lewis, The Screwtape Letters, Quote from Preface, The Centenary Press, 1945.

© 2015, 2026 Carl Wesley Anderson

FIRST EDITION

All rights reserved. This book is protected by the copyright laws of the United States of America. This book may not be copied or reprinted for commercial gain or profit. The use of short quotations or occasional page copying for personal or group study is permitted and encouraged. Permission will be granted upon request.

Unless otherwise identified, Scripture quotations are taken from the NEW AMERICAN STANDARD BIBLE, copyright © 1960, 1962, 1963, 1968, 1971, 1973, 1975, 1977, 1995 by The Lockman Foundation. Used by permission. Emphasis within Scripture is the author's own. Please note that Born to Blaze Ministries publishing style capitalizes certain pronouns in Scripture that refer to key pronouns like End Times, the Last Battle, Believers, the Last of the Last Days, Vantage Points, and others.

With special thanks to my former spouse, Sarah Elizabeth Anderson, for all her time and wisdom in helping me organize the original manuscript in 2015.

Edited by Ron Olson.

Cover and Interior Design by Suzann Beck, BeckHaus Design, Inc.

Revelation Island & custom Cycle Illustrations by Heidi Stohr

Born to Blaze Ministries Publishing, Apple Valley, Minnesota, U.S.A.

Printed in the United States of America.

Email Contact: Carl@borntoblaze.com

https://www.BornToBlaze.com

Our Vision: "To Empower & Equip Believers as Witnesses for the Savior, to Call People to Repentance, & to Inspire Passionate Discipleship as We Prepare for Christ's Return"

SUBSCRIBE to Carl's YouTube Channel, www.youtube.com

Search "Carl Wesley Anderson Born to Blaze Ministries"

SPEAKING: http://BornToBlaze.com/invite-carl

FACEBOOK Follow: https://www.facebook.com/carlwesleyandersonjunior/

INSTAGRAM Follow: @Born2Blaze

For instant access to all of our discipleship tools, including books, the Love Speaks MASTERCLASS (online training course for individuals & small group study), the Love Speaks Documentary Film Series (including Special Director's Cuts), or to subscribe to our latest "Listener Updates e-Letter," please visit us at http://www.LoveSpeaks.Today

---

ISBN: 978-0-9762910-7-7

Library of Congress Control Number: 2025945922

TABLE OF CONTENTS

Foreword

Revelation's Battle Plans
By Dr. Bill Hamon

Carl has traveled the nations preaching the truths found in this book.

He has investigated and filmed (for his new documentary film series based on this book) at many of the places where battles were fought by great men and women of God to bring restoration truth to Christ's Church.

Martin Luther was the first restoration General to lead the battle that moved the Church out of the Dark Age of religious dead works and formalism, and this battle was called the Protestant Movement (1517).

There have been nine major restoration movements during the period of the second reformation (1517–2007). The Saints Movement in 2007 was the end of the Second Reformation. Then the Third Reformation began in 2008 with its first major Movement being the Army of the Lord.

One of the main reasons I am writing this Foreword is because I am a pioneer General in the Army of the Lord. I wrote a book in 2016 called *God's Weapons of War*. It is the first book teaching the Church how to do corporate warfare. I have led 23 nations and numerous churches in corporate warfare.

Carl, in his book on *Revelation's Battle Plans*, lists many practical weapons to use in God's Battle Plans for these Last Days (see especially Sections 3 & 4).

If you are not familiar with Acts 3:21, which declares that the restoration of all things spoken by the mouth of the Prophets since the world began, must be fulfilled before Jesus can return from heaven. It declares that Jesus is held in the heavens until the fulfillment of all prophetic scriptures.

One of the last things that must take place is the Army of the Lord fighting and advancing God's *WWIII*.

That's one reason Carl's book, *Revelation's Battle Plans*, is so valuable for the Church at this time.

In 1984, God commissioned me to raise up a company of Prophets. They were to *make ready a people and...prepare the way* for Jesus' Second Coming as the conquering warrior King. Just as John the Baptist (one Prophet) prepared the way and made ready a people for Jesus' First Coming as Israel's Messiah and the world's Redeemer.

During the last 40 years, my Christian International Ministries and I have trained over 500,000 in prophetic ministry. A certain number of these have proven to be Prophets. Both John the Prophet and the end-time company of Prophets fulfill the prophecy in Malachi 4:5-6.

In all 15 of my books, I usually put this illustration in the introduction of the book. Whenever you have a plate full of fried chicken, you will find there is some bone that you cannot chew. You eat the meat but set the bones aside. In any book you read, you may find something you think is bone and cannot eat it.

Don't throw the book out, but go ahead and read the rest of the book. You will probably find some meaty truths. When you go back and evaluate the bone, it may really be bone or tough meat that you simply could not chew at the time of first reading.

I would suggest that unless you have made an in-depth study of Pre-Mill, Post-Mill, or A-millennialism, you can always skip over that chapter and read first the previous chapters on understanding the Book of Revelation and the subsequent chapters with practical Battle Plans and Strategies. Then come back to the Millennium teaching to learn more of Carl's perspective.

On New Years 2024 I said to the Lord, "I am now 90 years old and 70 years of ministry. I am still alive on planet earth and able to minister. What do you have left for me to do?" He said, "I want you to raise up a company of warriors as you raised up a company of Prophets."

Carl is one of those many warriors and has a good attitude about this book. He feels you do not have to believe every detail. You can disagree on some points and still be friends with him with mutual love and respect in the areas he teaches.

Thank you, Carl, for your vision and dedication to God and to His work!

By: Bishop (Dr.) Bill Hamon, Bishop, Christian International Apostolic-Global Network, Author of: The Eternal Church, Prophets & Personal Prophecy, Prophets & the Prophetic Movement, Prophets, Pitfalls, & Principles, Apostles/Prophets & the Coming Moves of God, The Day of the Saints, Who Am I & Why Am I Here, The Final Reformation & Great Awaking, 70 Reasons for Speaking in Tongues, and How Can These Things Be? God's Weapons of War, Your Highest Calling, The Final Reformation & Great Awakening

Prologue

From a Hopeless End to an Endless Hope

> *"And I heard a loud voice from the Throne, saying, 'Behold, the Tabernacle of God (the Father) is among men, and HE shall dwell among them, and they shall be His people, and God Himself shall be among them"* (Revelation. 21:3).

The "greatest generation" is the generation of soldiers in God's army who will still be alive and fighting when the final invasion of Heaven to Earth commences with the physical return of the world's true King, Jesus the Messiah, and His Father & Spirit! According to Bishop Bill Hamon, World War III has, at least in a spiritual sense, already commenced (which would make ours or the rising generation "the greatest generation").[5]

This is the true and scriptural "war to end all wars," as it is fought in the realms of the Spirit alongside actual battles in the natural realms. It is the final clash of Kingdoms, with Jesus, depicted as the Warrior Lamb, defeating forever Satan, depicted as a Dragon & Beasts *(see Revelation chapters 5, 12-14, 19 and 20:7-9)*.

The Bible begins in Genesis 1-3 with a Divine love story: the Father creates man and woman in His very own image and likeness, places them in a lush garden with a river and the Tree of Life, and enjoys personal fellowship with them. After Adam and Eve's disobedience through the deception of the serpent, that fellowship was broken and the door to the Tree of Life was shut.

The Bible closes in Revelation 22 with the climax of the love story: the Father Himself descends with His Son and Spirit to live in the New Heavens and New Earth in the lush garden with the river. He clothes His crowning

5 Dr. "Bishop" Bill Hamon, God's Weapons of War: Arming the Church to Destroy the Kingdom of Darkness, Chosen Books, 2018. Bishop Hamon believes World War III, spiritually began in 2016.

of creation with eternal bodies and eternal life and fellowship. The serpent will be forever vanquished. The Tree of Life is forever present and all who are there have access. The Divine romance is eternally enjoyed!

The Last Battle will soon commence. And from what appears to many people like a "hopeless end" in a Last Battle, will actually dawn an "endless hope" for those who love the Father, His Son, and the Holy Spirit!

Even so, come, LORD Jesus. Amen.

Author's Introduction

Every Eye Will See Him

"Behold, He is coming with the clouds, and every eye will see Him, even those who pierced Him; and all the tribes of the earth will mourn over Him. Even so. Amen" (Revelation 1:7).

The Ultimate Cosmic Chess Match

Many Believers are wondering just *when* the End will come, and *how* will it come? This book will answer both of those questions by discovering answers in the words of Jesus Himself from the Gospels and in the last book of the Bible: the Revelation of Jesus Christ.

These are extraordinary times in which we live, and times like these demand a special response. You are doing well in reading a book like this and seeking to understand more fully these times and discover the *when and how.*

This book was born out of a deep desire in my heart to help enable every follower of Jesus to identify with their calling as a soldier in God's last-days army, and walk closer with Him as part of "The Church Militant."

Some of the imagery of the army of God going to battle comes from Psalm 110:3, one of David's Psalms that speaks prophetically of our *"present, evil age" (Galatians 1:4)* which we find ourselves living in and having to battle against sin and forces of darkness. It reads in the Expanded Bible Translation,

> *"Your people will join [freely offer themselves to] You on Your day of battle [the day of Your ARMY]. You have been dressed in holiness [splendor of holiness] from birth [the womb of the dawn]"* (Psalm 110:3).

As you'll soon read, I also wanted to reveal a most wonderful approach to studying the Book of Revelation. Revelation reveals the battle plans of the LORD throughout Salvation-History, and the battle plans of the Enemy, too.

NOTE: this book is not a verse-by-verse commentary on Revelation. It will, however, give you an approach of understanding and studying Revelation on your own, in order to grasp the relevance of John's visions for your own life.

My idea to write this came in prayer one day when the LORD spoke to me and called me to write it as He said to me,

"Carl, you bring Revelation!"

I said, "Yes, LORD!"

Revelation is a beautiful and relevant Book!

It was relevant to the 1st Century.

It was relevant to every epoch of history since.

And it is relevant today & tomorrow.

It deserves a fresh reading.

I have developed a unique way of looking at the many visions of John the Revelator as if they showed us an ultimate "Chess Game" of Salvation-History, complete with two opposing Kings and their own armies.

What if you could know the strategies of the Enemy in advance?

The black king is Satan, who is trying to bring a checkmate against King Jesus and deploying his dark forces through governments, religious leaders, and common soldiers. The white King is, of course, King Jesus, and is deploying His own government: the 5-fold ministry of Apostles, Prophets, Evangelists, Pastors and Teachers, along with His own authority and power in the other white pieces on the board fighting against the dark forces.

Let me ask you a question: WHAT IF you could know the strategies and moves of the Enemy in advance? What if you could play your game of chess with King Jesus at the head of your forces, and plan 12 moves in advance to checkmate the opposing king?

That is exactly what the Book of Revelation, and ONLY the Book of Revelation, brings to you. You and I are the victorious army on the battlefield, and at the end of it all: CHECKMATE.

King Jesus, with us alongside Him, wins!

A War Was Declared Upon Me

Scripture teaches me that the day I surrendered my life to Jesus Christ, I enlisted in His supernatural army, and a war was declared against me. I suddenly recognized I had a real spiritual Enemy who hated my commitment to Christ and was going to deploy every tactic at his disposal to attempt to delay or stop my advancement and growth in grace.

Whether I was ready or not, I had to learn to fight the Enemy and counter his moves in the Cosmic chess match.

I had entered into a spiritual struggle, a war, of the clashing of kingdoms that is just as real to any natural army fighting a natural war against an enemy. I soon learned about the term, Spiritual Warfare, and how real it is. And there are many battles to fight in this war.

For example, in 2014, at the age of just 44, I was attacked with a very serious stage of cancer: metastatic melanoma. I say "attacked" because I do not believe sickness and disease comes from God. I believe disease is part of the Fall of man, and in some cases can also be a weapon against us from Satan, the enemy of God and Believers.

As I prayed about my initial grim diagnosis, the LORD indeed confirmed this and spoke to me in a still, small voice:

> *"The Enemy is trying to kill you before your time. You must be as aggressive in fighting him as he is in attacking you."*

That particular battle for my very life would go on to last about 5 years before my healing was fully realized.

A long battle in the war had been declared upon me.

It was a very difficult battle with many victories and defeats.

Many days I felt like giving up. But I didn't give up. I praised the LORD in spite of it. I worshipped King Jesus knowing He would see me through. And I have obtained healing for my body and I am still here today to write this encouraging book to you.

I willingly serve *Christus Victor!* (Latin for, *Christ is the Conqueror!*)

The Timing of This Book: from 2015 to 2025

Believe it or not, I wrote the original manuscript of this book during the actual year leading up to my own battle with cancer, and finished it during the first year of very intense cancer treatments in 2015.

One day I was praying over this manuscript. I had it spread out in sections and chapters, all over the floor of my study. Suddenly the LORD said to me,

> *"Carl, put this book away and hide it from the Enemy. It is not time to publish this yet. The world is going to get darker, and there is coming a time of more intense spiritual battles, pressures from the Enemy to walk away from the true faith, compromises, world-wide shakings, massive natural disasters, and an increase of fear, apathy and complacency upon people.*
>
> *"THAT will be the time to publish.*
>
> *"Instead,* (and it was as if the LORD shown a spotlight on another pile of pages in the middle of my floor) *I want you to publish THAT."*

It was another book I had also been writing about hearing His voice called, *Love Speaks: 21 Ways to Recognize God's Multi-Faceted Voice.*

> *"Start with THAT book! Publish it. Impart faith for hearing My voice in the midst of days of increasing uncertainty. Teach My people how to hear My voice more clearly and more often."*

So that was in the year 2015. *Revelation's Battle Plans* would have to wait.

I obeyed and moved forward with publishing *Love Speaks* in 2016, followed by creating a 21-Episode TV Series and a full MASTERCLASS on the themes of hearing God's voice.[6]

The documentary film series took me seven years to create, from 2017 to 2024, and to date has been broadcast to over 170 Nations.

So why NOW publish this book and create a new film series?

Earlier in 2024, I was walking through a very dark and lonely valley, full of shadows and sadness.

My Good Shepherd was speaking to me as He gently led me through that valley of shadows. I asked Him, "What do I do next?" (as I had just finished my seven-year assignment as a Media Missionary to create, *Love Speaks* for international broadcast).

He quickly answered:

> *"Carl, NOW is the time to rewrite and publish* Revelation's Battle Plans! *And create a new documentary film series, too! Teach My people about the coming Last Battle and how to practically prepare for it BEFORE it comes."*

And so, here it is: *Revelation's Battle Plans.*

Over the past 10 years or so since I originally wrote this book, many, many

6 In faith, I obeyed the LORD and published, "LOVE SPEAKS" as well as creating a whole world-wide Media Platform to bring this message of hearing God's voice in many new ways. This Platform includes the Paperback, a Kindle Edition, an Audio Book, a 21-Episode TV Series that has been broadcast on the world's largest Christian Networks, and a MASTERCLASS. You can access all these Resources on our website, https://www.lovespeaks.today

historical events have happened to confirm the acceleration of timing we seem to be at in the world today.

When I turn on the news every day, there seems to be an increase of evil far worse than previous times. And there is an uncertainty now in many cultures about Christians experiencing persecution and becoming marginalized. This is disturbing. "Christians have come to be seen no longer as merely irrelevant," shared Mark Thompson, Principal of Moore College in Sydney, Australia, "but are seen as a threat to the culture. People are not just bored with us but angry at us."[7]

Here are just a few of the events of the past 10 years that were all written about in various chapters of this book (before they took place), which fill our newspapers every day and are causing even Believers to experience anxiety and fear.

— The intensification and acceleration of evil and growing spiritual darkness.

— An acceleration and growing intensity of natural disasters like earthquakes, hurricanes, flooding, tornados, tsunamis and volcanic eruptions.

— An identity crises of youth, rampant sexual sin, and a horrifying, worldwide increase of human trafficking.

— Growing and specific persecution against Christians from various governments and world religions, like Islam, including imprisonments and suffering. Horrific public martyrdoms are taking place and being broadcast on social media.

— Wars and rumors of wars in various territories, including the Middle East.

— COVID-19 and the current threat of other killer viruses and further governmental lockdowns.

7 Mark Thompson, Principal of Moore College, in a recent address to the bible school students on the theme of the world that the new generation of ministers are facing, 2013.

What on earth is going on? Let's make a key point: God is not the author of evil, Satan is, as he continuously opposes God, God's ways and God's people: the Church.

The Book of Revelation reveals these kinds of evil events as the "Enemy's Battle Plans" as he wages war against the Church around the world. But you will soon learn that we, as His Body, are the Triumphant Church of the Last of the Last Days, and ultimately WE win the final war with Christ as Conqueror, following HIS Battle Plans! Checkmate!

Our Focus in Every Chapter: King JESUS: the LORD of SABAOTH

The Commander-in-Chief of our spiritual army is none other than our LORD Jesus Christ, dressed in holy array and known also as, *The LORD of Heaven's Armies or, The LORD of Hosts (James 5:4 and Isaiah 1:9).*

> *"God is our refuge and strength, always ready to help in times of trouble.*
>
> *So we will not fear when earthquakes come and the mountains crumble into the sea.*
>
> *"Be still, and know that I am God!"*
>
> *"The LORD of Heaven's Armies is here among us; the God of Israel is our fortress."* —A selection from Psalm 46.

Let's also remember how the Apostle Paul encouraged Timothy.

> *Take [with me] your share of the hardships and suffering [which you are called to endure] as a good (first-class) soldier of Christ Jesus"* (2 Timothy 2:3, Amplified).

"Let us first take note that in the Bible there are 240 references to God as LORD of Hosts," writes Bishop Bill Hamon, "Hosts refers to a group of people prepared for war."[8]

8 Dr. (Bishop) Bill Hamon, God's Weapons of War: Arming the Church to Destroy the Kingdom of Darkness, Chosen Books, 2018, pgs. 72-73.

So, prepare to assume the stance of the first-class warrior in God's Last Days army, and believe afresh that *the time is near,* and prepare to endure every hardship which may be on your path.

Here is a significant proposal: Scripture teaches that there is a Last Battle to prepare for just prior to the Second Coming, and this book will help you feel a new urgency to prepare now!

As to the actual year or a date for the Second Coming, this book does not address that whatsoever.

I truly believe that the return of King Jesus will be based on a set of *conditions* that exist on the earth at that time, *rather than on a specific date* in the future. The conditions themselves are dependent upon the free-will choices of men, women, and children in the Kingdom in every new generation.

To Be Forewarned is to be Forearmed

I believe the Book of Revelation, along with the teachings of Jesus Himself about the Last Days, gives us a clear set of Battle Plans that reveal the truth of the battles of all the ages of Salvation-History (since Revelation was first written) and the coming Last Battle at the return of Jesus Christ, which all Believers of the final generation will face.

The Battle Plans of Revelation reveal that this Last Battle is actually the *next event* on the end times timetable and *the final climax of all of recorded history* as it relates to Jesus Christ, His Church, and the ultimate defeat of all evil and spiritual darkness.

Which then brings up some questions.

First, WHEN will the End come? Just where are we in Salvation-History in relation to the End Times timetable? How do I know that we are in the time of Christ's return? What are the greatest signs of the ages which Jesus gave us, and the Book of Revelation reveals, that could potentially be fulfilled in our own generation? **(Answered in Section 1.)**

Question: Where is this coming Last Battle found in Scripture?

Answer: Only in the Book of Revelation.

Thus, you may be asking, how can I really understand the Book of Revelation and develop my own faith in its teachings? How is it a useful tool and how do I read it? How can I interpret it and apply it, by faith, to my life today? **(These questions are answered in Section 2.)**

You will learn in Section 2 that one of the real gems of this book is that I bring you an understanding of Revelation as apocalyptic literature, with the original context of the time in which it was written.

The original audience understood it to be not full of literal numbers, symbols and pictures, nor chronological in time or order of events. Instead, they understood John the Revelator's visions as holding deeper spiritual realities and structured in an ancient form of prophetic writing known as parallelism (and what are known as Chiasms). There are (at least) seven cycles of both judgment and salvation which run parallel to each other and encompass the entire Church Age in Revelation!

And when you learn how this Hebrew way of writing is meant to be interpreted, you can truly understand and appreciate passages that seem puzzling to those who haven't learned how to understand them in the rich symbolism they bring (like Revelation chapter 20 and the subject of the Millennium).

So when will the End come? And what will it look like?

Then you might logically ask, if I know what's coming soon, just what will it look like? Revelation gives us a strategic understanding of the tactics of the Enemy so we can learn how to counter-attack him. You'll get a unique walk-through of some stories of Salvation-History to understand how our Enemy has always been fighting us, and thus learn how he will fight us in the Last Battle.

If you're wondering: how is Revelation relevant to me today and in the future, to show me the reality of the spiritual conflict and Cosmic Chess Game I am fighting in? **(Answered in Section 3.)**

Finally, knowing the Last Battle is coming, how do I practically prepare for it? How do I endure to the end IN that Battle? And how can I hear my own unique Marching Orders to follow the LORD wherever He leads me, and know for certain my special place IN that Battle and becoming part of the pure, spotless Bride of Christ? **(Answered in Section 4.)**

In All Things, Charity

My hope for you as you read all 4 Sections of this book: admire the person of Jesus Christ, our Captain, BEFORE you learn the strategies of the Enemy.

The author John, in Revelation, saw first the image of the resurrected Christ in the midst of the candlesticks *(chapter 1)*, followed by an incredible vision of the Father, the Son, the Holy Spirit, the redeemed people of God and all of nature and creation at the very center of the universe *(chapter 4)*!

Always remember, in the Book of Revelation, before you start reading of the visions of Satan and His helpers as hideous, evil beasts influencing the world for selfish sinful degradation, you see the visions of the glorious Father, Son, Holy Spirit, angels, redeemed creation and the victorious army of God at the center of time and space and history!

In other words, see King Jesus first in every circumstance of every day of battle!

We are both His Church Militant (His Army on Earth) and Church Triumphant (His Army in Eternity) of the Last of the Last Days!

I am praying that you will learn to appreciate the fresh approach to prophecy contained in this book and see Jesus revealed in the interpretations of texts given long ago which had relevance to their particular audience and have relevance to us as the audience today and in the future.

And on that note of "interpretations" of texts and of some of the creative ideas postulated in this book on themes of Eschatology (theological studies concerned with the final events in the history of the world), may I quote from a German Lutheran theologian? His name was Rupertus Meldenius and he first wrote this in a tract on Christian Unity during the Thirty Years War of 1618 to 1648,

> *"In Essentials: Unity, In Non-Essentials: Liberty, In All Things: Charity."*

So all the Scriptures and beliefs about the life, death, resurrection and ascension of Jesus Christ would be part of our "essentials" and we must be unified in them.

Eschatology (including subjects like the timing of the Rapture, the Millennial Reign, and the approach to the study of the Book of Revelation) would fall outside of that category. So I simply ask that you maintain an open heart, an open mind, and "liberty" as you read this book.

Allow for spontaneous moments of instruction from your Teacher, the Holy Spirit. You may be saying (a LOT): *"I never read that Scripture in that way before,"* or *"I never thought of it that way before. Holy Spirit, is that true?"*

Thus, I believe we, as the Church, are actually being prepared now to advance *INTO* the "Greatest Tribulation" (also known as the Last Battle in the Book of Revelation) with faith and courage.

After all, who wants to follow a retreating army? The Captain of our salvation is calling to His troops with these words,

THE ARMY WILL ADVANCE!

But wait...what about the timing of the Rapture?

Will there be a Rapture *before* the Last Battle?

Perhaps you have read a book, seen a movie or heard a modern-day leader teach that there is coming soon, (maybe any day now), a "pre-tribulation Rapture" to remove all Christians on the earth BEFORE the coming Final Battle, so that they do not have to go through the persecution and tribulation accompanying that Battle.

I pose the following question here and answer it fully in my 1st Appendix.

Question: Are you ready for the Rapture?

Answer: Yes or No...

Follow-up question: WHAT IF GOD ISN'T?

What's that, Carl? Maybe HE isn't ready?

Hey, you know what? You may not have heard or thought of this idea before, because most people living in the last 200 years here in the West have had a predominant teaching that the Rapture happens *next* on the timetable of unfolding events, *before* the final events of the End.

I believe that the modern Church needs to reopen her thinking to just the opposite possibility.

The Rapture, as Paul taught it in 1 Thessalonians, might just happen *at the end* of the coming events, and the Church is not being called *away* to Heaven in retreat before the Last Battle.

Instead, is it possible that the Rapture actually happens at the very *END* of the coming final conflict as *the start* of the Second Coming of Christ and His resurrection of the dead and the Final Judgment?

IF this is really true, what are the implications for me—today?

I propose this alternative theory in **Appendix 1**.

You may want to pause reading here and turn to **Appendix 1** to read and learn more of the importance of this theory.

This means I believe the timing of the Rapture happens at *the end* of the Last Battle, and not *before* it happens.

I also believe the Book of Revelation teaches we are approaching the very end of the Millennial Reign, which ends with the Last Battle.

What's that, Carl?

Did you say we are nearing *the end* of the Millennial Reign/the Millennium? As in, right now (and not something yet coming in the future)?

This other subject has kept Believers in various interpretations since the early Church Fathers. In fact, in about 155 A.D., Justin Martyr was writing to a friend that he believed in a literal 1,000 year reign just after the Second Coming and resurrection of the dead, though he also included this phrase, "but on the other hand, many who belong to the pure and pious faith, and are true Christians, *think otherwise.*"[9]

Many believe, (like Irenaeus, Justin Martyr and others did), that when Jesus returns, He will usher in a literal 1,000 year period of time of the Kingdom of God flourishing on the earth with Jesus reigning from a rebuilt Jerusalem. And people tend to be in one of two schools of thought that are called, 'Pre-Mill' (Premillennial) and 'Post-Mill' (Postmillennial).

But as you will soon learn, I personally think otherwise.

Something unique you will learn in this book in **Chapter 7** is that **my approach is "NOW-Mill"** (or a NOW-Millennial approach commonly referred to as **"A-Mill" or Amillennial** by other Theologians).

Question: What is the relevance of this? Why does it matter what I believe about the Millennium?

The Answer: It's very relevant and it matters because Revelation gives us the Battle Plans that indeed, at the very close of our own generation (if we are the final generation to see the Second Coming) there is a Last Battle to prepare for, spiritually.

In this Last Battle, the Enemy with his army of darkness will be let loose with full forces of spiritual wickedness and rampant evil, to attempt to silence the witness of the Church and deceive the Nations.

I personally believe the Scriptures indicate that persecution and suffering for our faith will be rampant and worldwide for a short season. The Enemy will try to turn many away from real faith, and apostacy will abound. *(See Revelation 11, 20 and 2 Thessalonians 2.)*

9 Justin Martyr's "Dialogue with Trypho" written approx.. 155 to 160 A.D.

THE NOW-MILLENNIUM: *Timing of the Rapture*

Special things to note within this Diagram,

1. The Millennial Reign of Christ potentially began at the victory of the Cross/Resurrection (when Satan's powers to deceive the Nations were curbed for the entire Church Age). In the Old Testament, he did such a good job of deception that every Nation was deceived, and even many people of the Nation of Israel itself fell into the worship of idols and turned their hearts away from Yahweh.

2. In Chapter 3, you will learn of my view of how to interpret the Book of Revelation as an *Idealist*. An Idealist view allows for a broad understanding and interpreting the Book so it has relevance to every generation, including our own. John the Revelator writes,

   "These are the ones who are coming out of the great tribulation" (Revelation 7:14).

Some other translations give us more light on this phrase, "the great tribulation" by saying "the great testing" or, "great hardship" or, "great persecution."

I personally believe we, as the Church, have been IN this "tribulation, testing, hardship, and persecution" from the *beginning* of the Book of Acts, with the arrest and imprisonment of Peter and John, followed closely by the martyrdom of Stephen.

We see throughout Acts and the life of Paul that suffering/tribulation and the victorious spread of the Good News of the Gospel go hand in hand. Satan can resist and try to block the progress of the Church, but ultimately the Kingdom of God keeps advancing. Satan is not allowed to stir up a worldwide rebellion against the Church. At least, not yet.

Thus, the "Great Tribulation" that John sees has progressively been in motion for nearly 2,000 years and counting.

In this sense, we are IN "the Great Tribulation" right now, today. During the time of the Last Battle, it will be "the Greatest Tribulation" that the Church has ever undergone. I realize this may be a sobering thought for you.

Yet there is good news. God's glory will be a strong canopy of protection over the Church and revivals will also happen (with the Church underground in many places) as the light of Christ burns ever more brightly. We are to become the pure Bride of Christ in that last hour. And you and I need to be ready with oil in our lamps and know what is coming. *(See Isaiah chapters 4 and 60, Matthew 25:1-13, and Revelation 19.)*

And of course, at the end of the day, if you and I are not fully on the same page as to all of the perspectives I share, we can still walk in Agape love, (Charity) with one another. Amen.

"Jesus wants a bride who is eager for His presence, in love with Him, and longing for Him to come, and seeing in His return, the only hope for her to be fulfilled at last!" shared my English friend, Rev. Eric Delve one day. "There is this prayer in the Book of Revelation, **Even So, Come, LORD Jesus!** When the Church is truly saying this with all of her heart, He will come."[10]

To summarize my hope for you as you read and learn Revelation's Battle Plans for your life:

— Exalt King Jesus first and foremost in every Section!
— Allow for moments of, "I never thought of it this way before!"

10 Rev. Eric Delve, one of the fathers of modern evangelism in the UK, from a conversation with me.

— Pray through those moments and develop fresh convictions!
— Let convictions lead to repentance, faith and fresh preparation!
— Tune your ears to hear God's personal marching orders for you!
— Learn practical wisdom from the Father to conform your life closer to Him!

Are You Ready?

In Matthew 25, Jesus tells the parable of the ten virgins, urging His people to be different from the world: to keep oil in their lamps (stay on the alert); to *stay awake and watch and prepare themselves, with urgency,* for Him to come at any moment. Here is a portion of that parable.

> *"But at midnight there was a shout, 'Behold, the bridegroom! Come out to meet him.' The* **bridegroom came**, *and* **those who were ready** *went in with him to the wedding feast; and the door was shut.* **BE ON THE ALERT** *then, for you do not know the day nor the hour"*(Matthew 25: 6,10,13).

He calls us His people, metaphorically *"virgins"* and we are His pure, spotless Bride that is making herself ready *(Revelation 19:7)*.

To *keep oil in your lamp* means you have a personal responsibility to be wise and prudent with your spiritual resources, and to fall in love more and more with Jesus Christ, the Father, and the Holy Spirit every day, even as you choose to remain uncompromising and faithful.

Jesus is not after your obedience.

Jesus is not after your obedience. He is after your heart. When He has that and you are in close fellowship with Him, moment by moment, you will walk in obedience out of that relationship!

To not keep oil in your lamp means you will be unprepared for the Last Day on Earth (as we know it).

The Titanic is About to Sink: *Are You Wearing Your Eternal Life Jacket?* On a recent ministry trip to Belfast, Northern Ireland, I had a day off in-between preaching gigs, and decided to tour the world-famous Titanic Museum. Titanic set sail on her maiden (and only) voyage on the 10th of April, 1912. Just two days later, at about 11:40 pm on the 12th of April, she struck a massive iceberg and sank in the icy waters of the North Atlantic Ocean.

I remember the feeling of awe and wonder in the opening areas of the displays, showing how that massive ship was first assembled and prepared for her voyage. They even have a full stateroom and other displays set up so you can experience just how magnificent she was.

Then awe turned to utter horror as the night of the sinking was so vividly displayed. I could almost hear the screams of terror as countless people were plunged into the icy-cold waters of the sea, and swallowed up in despair and sudden death.

I brought home a souvenir coffee cup, showing the Titanic sailing in all her splendor, with the words that they used for marketing that voyage, "The World's Largest and Safest Ship."

I drink a cup of coffee every week in that mug, just to remind myself of the utter totality of the pride of man in the building of that ship, and of the person who once boasted, "God Himself could not sink this ship."

I am reminded when I drink that coffee of 1 John 2.

> *"For all that is in the world, the lust of the flesh, the lust of the eyes and the boastful pride of life is not from the Father, but is from the world. And the world is passing away, and also its lusts; but the one who does the will of God abides forever"* (1 John 2:16-17).

Pride cost many lives that night. Up to 64 life boats could have been placed on board, saving all. But instead, only 20 were installed, because the ship "looked better" that way. Over 1500 people perished that could have been saved.

In its sinking, I seem to see a kind of parable for the End Times. In a sense, we could say that this very world in which we live, and which is also under a curse from her Creator, will one day sink like the Titanic. To put it another way: this ship is going down (meaning, the earth itself will experience God's wrath and all evil will be judged).

And did you know, speaking of the Titanic, God had sent at least two prophetic warnings from two very different sources to warn the people that this ship was going to sink?

My friend, Troy Brewer, has written a very stirring book recently, and I got to hear him preach a whole sermon on this event.[11] Years before Titanic had launched, two different writers had published fictional books with exact details of the events of April 12, 1912!

And in a very real sense, when disasters such as this one happen, which was caused by the earth itself (the iceberg), each one is a warning signal from the LORD that ultimately, Judgment Day is coming.[12]

God's bowls of wrath are nearly filled to the brim from centuries of His longsuffering towards evil, and are about to be poured out at the Second Coming of Jesus Christ. The earth as we know it will be burned up in fervent heat in judgment, only to be recreated into a *new heavens and new earth, wherein only righteousness will dwell.* (See Revelation chapters 15-16, 2 Peter 3:10, and Revelation chapters 21 and 22).

To the Believer and Follower of Jesus Christ: this book will encourage you to know that it is possible to be as the Tribe of Issachar, to both, *understand the times and know the best course to take (1 Chronicles 12:32).* You, too, can develop confident insight into what Scripture teaches about the Last of the Last Days, and know which course to take for your own walk of faith, with your own personal Marching Orders.

"The world is now drawing nearer to the time of the end," wrote author Jessie Pen-Lewis, "characterized by the deception depicted in the Apocalypse as being world-wide; when there will be deception of nations, and *individuals,* on such a vast scale that the deceiver will practically have the whole earth under his control.

"To understand why the deceiver will be able to produce the world-wide deception depicted in the Apocalypse, which will permit the supernatural

11 Troy Brewer, "Numbers That Prophesy: Hearing God Through Historic Headlines and Numbers That Preach," Destiny Image Publishing, 2024.

12 For more details, turn to the chapter in this book called, "Earth's Trauma" which gives a fuller understanding of this startling phrase as we learn about this truth from the Book of Revelation.

powers to carry out their will, and drive nations and men into active rebellion against God, we need clearly to grasp what the Scriptures say."[13] And this book will teach you what the Scriptures say and help prepare you!

You and I, as Believers, will be the very *survivors whom the LORD shall call* to survive the iceberg and be rescued through our **Eternal Life Jackets and Eternal Life Boats** as the ship sinks! Joel prophesied so many years ago of those of us who will SURVIVE.

> *"And I will display wonders on the sky and on the earth, blood, fire, and columns of smoke. The sun will be turned into darkness and the moon into blood, before the great and awesome day of the LORD comes. And it will come about that whoever calls on the name of the LORD will be delivered. For on Mount Zion there will be those who ESCAPE, as the LORD has said, even among the SURVIVORS whom the LORD calls"* (Joel 2:30-32).

One of my favorite stories on the Titanic is that of a wealthy woman who was granted a place in a life boat. Before she got in, she suddenly rushed back to her stateroom, ignoring her valuable jewelry sitting on the dresser, and instead grabbing three oranges as she rushed back to the boat.

You see, in times of crises we need to know what is truly important. We need to be able to SURVIVE. And this book will instruct you in just how to survive and place the eternal significance where it belongs: on deepening your intimate relationship with the Father, through His Son and Spirit.

To the Pre-Believer: Some of you are reading this book without ever having fully surrendered your heart and life to Jesus Christ. Or, perhaps you follow Him occasionally, attending church a few times a year, but are not fully committed to Him with every area of your heart and life. May this book awaken you to this truth: Revelation teaches that on the coming final *Day of the LORD,* it will be too late for you to follow Him. When Jesus returns, He is bringing both Divine judgment to all who have chosen not to believe, and Divine salvation and mercy to all Believers.

It's time for you to make a decision today to follow Him more fully.

13 Jessie Penn-Lewis, "War on the Saints" An excerpt from Chapter One.

Today, the door of mercy still stands open for you! But remember, the moment that God Himself shut the door of Noah's ark (which was also a "Day of the LORD" that was a worldwide judgment), it was too late for repentance. The hammer of His justice fell (Genesis 7:16). *All those outside of the ark perished on that day.* The good news of mercy in that Day of the LORD? Salvation came to Noah and his family: only.

And on the final DAY, as Jesus returns on His white horse, He *judges and makes war* and the hammer of His justice will fall again, this time for all eternity (Revelation 19:11-19 & 20:11-15).

The time is now for salvation and to *"escape from the wrath to come"*(Matthew 3:7). On the DAY that Jesus returns, that door of mercy is closed... for eternity. But for today, *the Spirit and the Bride say, "Come!"* (Revelation 22:17).

> *Behold, He is coming with the clouds, and every eye will see Him, even those who pierced Him; and all the tribes of the earth will mourn over Him. Even so, Amen* (Revelation 1:7).

The Titanic is going to sink. The world as we know it is going to be judged and all the works of man and of the pride of life will be burned away. Your only hope: allow Jesus to equip you and dress you with an **eternal life jacket and place you in an eternal life boat,** so you will be saved from the waters of judgment as the ship sinks! Keep oil in your lamp!

If you are ready to follow Jesus Christ more fully, turn now to the Prayer of Salvation and Consecration at the end of this book. Pray it in faith, then return here to read on.

To all: the Last Battle is almost here. As Henry V declared to his troops just before a great battle, "The signs of war...advance!"[14]

Let your battle cry become CHRISTUS VICTOR!

Oh, and CHECKMATE. Jesus Wins!

— Rev. Carl Wesley Anderson, Jr.

---

14 William Shakespeare, Henry V, Act 2, Scene 2.

SECTION I

ARE WE THERE YET?

ARE WE THERE
ARE WE THERE
ARE WE THERE
ARE WE THERE
ARE WE THERE
ARE WE THERE
ARE WE THERE
ARE WE THERE

ARE WE THERE YET?

The Times of the Signs & the Signs of the Times

"Now when these things begin to occur, stand tall and lift up your heads [in joy], because [suffering ends as] your redemption is drawing near" (Luke 21:28, Amplified Bible).

"And they overcame him because of the blood of the Lamb and the word of His testimony, and they did not love their life even when faced with death" (Revelation 12:11).

"The power of the gospel," writes N.T. Wright, "is the powerful announcement that God is God, that Jesus is LORD, that the powers of evil have been defeated, that God's new world has begun. It means instantly that all people everywhere are gladly invited to come to it, to join the party, to discover forgiveness for the past, an astonishing destiny in God's future, and a vocation in the present."[15]

Did you know that I, Carl, am also a documentary filmmaker and have created a film series based on this book? Go to this website to watch some stories from the next section. **https://revelationsbattleplans.com/**

15 N.T. Wright, Surprised By Hope, pg. 227. HarperCollins Publishing, 2008.

CHAPTER 1

The Greatest Sign of the Times

Advancing the Witness to the Ends of the Earth

"Rejoice greatly, O daughter of Zion! Shout in triumph, O daughter of Jerusalem! Behold, your king is coming to you; He is just and endowed with salvation, humble, and mounted on a donkey. And He will speak peace to the nations; and His dominion will be from sea to sea, and from the River to the ends of the earth" (Zechariah 9: 9-10).

"And this gospel of the Kingdom shall be preached in the whole world for a witness to all the nations, and then the end shall come" (Matthew 24:14).

So just when shall the End come? How close are we? These next 2 chapters will seek an answer.

While I was researching and reading through some historical biographies of humble men and women that have lived through challenging times of spiritual warfare, remained faithful under trial, and been used mightily by God to help advance the Gospel, I stumbled upon what I believe is an amazing key to back up the proposal of this book. Indeed, the Spirit of God has been on the move in recent decades, and He has a timetable and a plan to bring forth the Second Coming of Christ in our very own generation!

What I am about to share has not been known or understood by very many. In fact, as I was praying over this, I felt that some of this "intel" from the Spirit has been sealed until recently. Now it is being unsealed in this time for Believers to hear about it and enter into new realms of faith and intimacy with the Holy Spirit.

This story comes from the extraordinary life of a young man from a poor district in Wales. He gave his heart to Jesus and surrendered his whole life to the presence of the Spirit in the early 20th century, and then was called by the Father into a life of secret intercession.

Rees Howells was born on October 10th, 1879, the 6th of a family of 11. He grew up poor, but with an amazing, loving mother and father who witnessed Christ to him at a young age.[16]

In 1906, and at the age of 26, he was attending a convention in Keswick, England and was challenged by the preacher from themes from Ephesians 2:1-6: *You hath He quickened...and hath raised us up...and made us sit together in heavenly places in Christ Jesus.*

He asked the question, "Have you been quickened by Christ? Have you been raised up to sit with Him in heavenly places?"

In his heart Rees answered, "Yes, I know I have been quickened, but I have not been raised up with Christ to that place of power." The moment he said that, he saw the Glorified LORD. "As really as I had seen the Crucified Christ and the Risen Christ, I saw the Glorified Christ, and the Spirit's voice spoke, 'Would you like to sit there with Him? There is a place for you.'

"I saw myself raised up with Him. I saw Him as John did at Patmos. When he reveals a thing, it is exactly as it is; it is not imagination. All that night I was in the presence of God and my glorified Savior."[17]

---

16 Norman Grubb, "Rees Howells, Intercessor." Christian Literature Crusade, 1952, pg. 11.
17 Ibid., Grubb, page 34.

So just like John the Revelator on the Isle of Patmos, others in Salvation-History have had similar moments of deep experiences of the presence of God and seeing Him as He is.

We'll return in a few pages to the extraordinary story of Rees Howells, for what soon took place in his journey has implications for the timing of the Second Coming relevant to our very own day and generation!

Let's turn our focus now on the first of two of the greatest signs of the times of our own day.

Recently, I happened to catch a "Billy Graham Classic" broadcast on television. It was a full sermon that the evangelist preached to a crowd of nearly 40,000 in the city of Chicago, Illinois in 1962. He chose as his text a parable from Jesus in Luke 17, on the "days of Noah and Lot".

He preached a bold and uncompromising message on the Second Coming and reminded that audience in Chicago of the atmosphere of sin in America as a similar atmosphere to the evil days of both Noah and Lot (see the next chapter in this book for a closer examination of those days in relation to ours).

He challenged all present to their deep need of a personal relationship with Christ, and to always keep the actual Second Coming of Christ as a living reality before their hearts.

What better theme to help center our focus upon both a holy lifestyle and intimate friendship with Jesus than His soon and coming return?

What a message Graham preached!

What a wake-up call. And that same wake-up call is applicable today. In fact, recently two of Graham's children, Anne Graham Lotz and Franklin Graham, have written articles and books which issue the same challenges that their father issued in his sermons of the 1960s.[18]

18 I have gleaned some wonderful insights through reading the book, "Expecting to See Jesus: A Wake Up Call For God's People" by Anne Graham Lotz, and, "Are We In The Last Hours Before Christ's Return?" by Franklin Graham, published on the web.

Two of his points really reminded me of the importance of a book like this one. First, he shared how overemphasis on end-times teaching can bring imbalance to the lives of Believers. He cited an example of how too much teaching brought interpretations that Mussolini was the actual Anti-Christ in the 1930s.

One only needs to turn on certain cable TV networks today, and see how the Christian market is saturated with teachings on specific interpretations of difficult texts, and then trying to squeeze actual events in the newspaper and media into these texts. This results in sensationalized teaching that never challenges the audience to a deeper personal commitment to Christ.

On the other hand, preached Graham, the opposite is also true. Underemphasis from the pulpits in the land (of the truths of the Second Coming) can lead to a worldly perspective and a lack of true and solid biblical teaching.

In light of the Church not teaching enough on the hope of the return of Jesus, the world steps in and fills the void, resulting in imbalance of understanding.

Here are a few examples of this void and imbalance.

Less Than 90 Seconds to Midnight

Scientists and Hollywood are spending thousands of dollars on studies of the end times and blockbuster movies, and the resulting conclusions can make your head spin (when compared with the truth found only in Scripture).

As far as scientists go, take, for example, a recent study from Oxford University in England and completed in early 2015 (five years before COVID-19). A think-tank of scientific minds set out to determine, from a rational point of view in our post-modern and technologically advanced cultures, "Twelve Ways the World Could End." Among the 12 we find,

— Artificial Intelligence

— Eruption of a Super Volcano

— International Nuclear War

— Global Pandemic

— "Unknown Consequences"

The most amusing to me is, "Unknown Consequences," a category that included the remote possibility of a Zombie Apocalypse by alien invasion. Their reasoning? "Because of earth's isolation, we might be sending signals to extraterrestrial civilizations that attract deadly alien intention."[19]

And the threat of international nuclear war cannot be overlooked from a scientific perspective.

Seth Borenstein recently shared that the Bulletin of Atomic Scientists has declared that "Earth is now closer to human-caused doomsday than it has been in more than 30 years because of global warming and nuclear weaponry." The advocacy group founded by the creators of the atomic bomb moved their famed "Doomsday Clock" ahead two minutes in January of 2015 (that's when I finished writing this original manuscript). It said the world is now three minutes from a catastrophic midnight, instead of five minutes. This was the second closest the world has been to midnight.

I did another search while editing this manuscript in 2024, and now they have moved the clock to *less than* 90 seconds to midnight, which is the closest ever to midnight since its creation in 1947.[20]

Even Hollywood has truly made an entertaining mess of the subject of Armageddon! Could blockbuster examples like World War Z, with Brad Pitt fighting Zombies, be the real coming Apocalypse? Might a Terminator with the body of Arnold Schwarzenegger really be seeking to annihilate you next week? Will an asteroid strike our planet and end all human life? Hollywood has created whole big-budget films that visually excite their audiences with the possibilities of these anti-Christian, apocalyptic scenarios.

And they show no signs of stopping. Americans and Westerners in particular seem to have a curious and insatiable hunger for entertainment that depicts the end of the world (as we know it).

19 Quoted from, "12 Ways the World Could End" as published by Oxford University, 2015.

20 Author, Seth Borenstein, Washington D.C. (AP), "Atomic Scientists: We're Getting Even Closer to Doomsday" January, 2015 & another check on their website in 2024.

So, take away the eternal Word of God, and the truth brought to us through the battle plans found in the Book of Revelation, as well as all that God has revealed to His servants the prophets, and you are left with an age of post-modern realism and atheism that removes the sovereignty of God and replaces it with the glorification of man.

Since God (they believe) is not in the picture somewhere, mankind can choose to destroy itself and the world. Since God is not creator or protector or ultimate redeemer of the world, the world itself carries the possibility of self-destruction or disaster-from-forces-unknown.

How challenging to live in this post-modern culture, surrounded by satanically-energized world systems of political, media-frenzied, technological, social and religious people who leave God the Father, God the Son, and God the Holy Spirit out of their existence!

And yet, this challenging culture surrounding the true people of God who are forced to live among its daily temptations, is exactly the beautiful realm of God's created order that He loves and wishes to redeem through His Son.

Don't Look for Literal Events or Dates, Look for "Conditions"

Out of a fresh, wholehearted devotion to the LORD, He is calling you to know the CONDITIONS that will be present on the earth before the last day of recorded history.

This book does not look at literal events or try to discern specific dates on a calendar as "indicators." There are a number of books published over the last few decades which offer potential events or actual dates to try to focus your attention on specific areas of possible prophetic fulfillment.

This book is written to help you discover your true marching orders to prepare for the final battle and to endure it when it comes. And to endure it, you will need to walk in victory over daily sin and in the holiness that Christ imparts by His Holy Spirit.

"Tragically, multitudes of Christians within the past two thousand years have done a lot of thinking and teaching about the great battle of Armageddon only to lose the daily battle with sin," wrote David Wilkerson. "What good is it to accumulate an entire storehouse of prophetic knowledge, if you drift away from intimacy with Christ? Puritan theologians depicted Armageddon as a symbolic battle—one that's being waged for the soul of the bride of Christ. It's a battle that began at Calvary and will end only with the second coming of our LORD. Satan is waging war on Christ's bride, attempting to turn her into a doubting, dysfunctional harlot before her wedding day. Therefore, all our war efforts should be concentrated on these daily battles."[21]

What CONDITIONS Will I Highlight in this Book?

I believe there are three real signs of the times, all from the words of Jesus. They come to Believers through His Gospels and through His Revelation (it IS called The Revelation of Jesus Christ). They tell us what is here now, and what is coming in stronger waves of reality.

These signs are indicators of the ATMOSPHERE of the End. In other words, the spiritual climate, or CONDITIONS on the earth at the time of the Last of the Last Days, and His soon appearing.

1. **The Complete Harvest of the Nations (the Advancing Army):** God's hope for His Church — Replacing inactivity with fresh laborers in the mission fields.
2. **The Days of Noah and Lot:** God's hope for His Church — Replacing spiritual complacency with spiritual intimacy.
3. **A Coming Worldwide Spiritual Conflict // The Last Battle // Armageddon:** God's hope for His Church — Replacing "falling away" with "holding fast."

So we get to begin with the Good News in this chapter! The army is advancing in the harvest fields! Let's start with this startling thought: ours (or

21 David Wilkerson, God's Plan to Protect His People in the Coming Depression, pg. 96, Wilkerson Trust Publications, 1998.

"I will also make you a

light

to the Gentiles,
so that My salvation may reach

TO THE END

of the earth." (Isaiah 49:6)

the next) could be the final generation. The greatest sign of them all is happening now!

The next chapter will instruct you with 8 ways that our own generation emulates the conditions on the earth just prior to the direct judgment of God in the days of both Noah and Lot.

And the rest of the book gives you information and inspiration to endure in the Last Battle just prior to the Second Coming.

Let's begin in this chapter to look at perhaps the greatest sign of the times that indicates the nearness of the Second Coming: the peaceful and love-filled overtaking of the earth that is currently in motion as our own King Jesus continually conquers sin, defeats evil, and transforms hearts through His Body on earth.

The Greatest Sign of the Times (of Them All)!

Every follower of Jesus who carries the good news of the Gospel is called upon to reproduce their witness and grow in their faith in the earth until the very Day (Second Coming) of Jesus Christ.

It is still very much true that, *The LORD is not slow about His promise, as some count slowness, but is patient toward you, not wishing for any to perish but for all to come to repentance* (2 Peter 3:9).

Does He really have a heart for ALL? Yes!

Isaiah first prophesied about the soon-appearing Servant of the LORD who was to step into world history upon His own Divine initiative and become the light to the Gentiles.

> *"I will also make you* **a light to the Gentiles,** *so that My salvation may reach* **to the end of the earth"** (Isaiah 49:6).

Later, Zechariah saw the ministry of the coming Messiah, the world's true King, as beginning with Jesus entering Jerusalem on a donkey as a humble representative, and His witness spreading around the world and reaching out *"to the ends of the earth"* (Zechariah 9:9-10).

Jesus began His fulfillment of both Isaiah's prophecy and Zechariah's prophecy as He entered Jerusalem on what we now call, Palm Sunday. Read the story of His triumphal entry in Matthew 21:1-11.

He then defeated Satan and his minions through His sacrificial death upon the Cross (John 19:16-37).

He then descended into Hell and rose from the grave on the third day (John 20:1-31).

He then ascended on high, *and when He had disarmed the rulers and authorities, He made a public display of them, having triumphed over them through the cross* (Colossians 2:15).

Then, on the Day of Pentecost, He launched His disciples to continue to carry on His mission and His message to all the nations through the power of the Holy Spirit (Acts 1 and 2).

Enter the DAY. Morning dawns. A rooster crows in the distance. The sun arises. The 120 awaken and gather for prayer in obedience and anticipation.

SUDDENLY...Lightning strikes!

Heaven is joined with earth. A noise *like a violent, rushing wind,* comes, and it *fills the whole house where they were sitting*. And if that isn't enough drama, wait, there's more.

> *And there appeared to them tongues as of fire distributing themselves, and they rested on each one of them* (Acts 2:3).

120 tongues of fire appear and rest on 120 people of all diverse backgrounds.

> *And they were all filled with the Holy Spirit and began to speak with other tongues, as the Spirit was giving them utterance* (Acts 2:4).

Heavenly wind. Heavenly firepower. God creates something completely unique in the earth. A day like no other. A day that has never been repeated in history.

The Promise of the Father (as said by Jesus Himself and recorded in Acts 1:4) is that all followers of the Son would be empowered with the same Holy Spirit dynamite that He had been empowered with. His followers will share in His ministry as ones who bring burning torches of light into the Satanic darkness and begin to light the world on fire for His glory.

... be empowered with the same Holy Spirit dynamite...

So the Mission of the Servant (Isaiah 49) began here as Jesus launches the mission upon His Body, now His representatives, with the power of the Spirit and the authority of His Name to introduce His Kingdom to all!

"The gift of tongues," writes Dr. Lance Wonders, "functioned on the Day of Pentecost as a public "sign" of the start of the Mission to the Gentiles, when via the Servant of the LORD (Jesus), His light would begin to penetrate the spiritual darkness of the Nations. The Great Commission (Matthew 28) was thereby being launched in power, with the promise and prospect that every tongue, tribe, and Nation was being targeted by God's love through the Gospel, and He was about to seal for Himself a "remnant" down through the ages from every portion of mankind/the entire human race (see also Revelation 7).

"In that sense, Pentecost was somewhat unique and unrepeatable—though Acts 8 (mission to the Samaritans), Acts 10 (mission to the Gentiles within the circles of Jewish influence), and Acts 19 (mission to Europe by way of Ephesus) show that even Pentecost more or less opens out in "stages" within salvation-history, as each new generation and each new people-group are first confronted with God's presence, power, and saving Good News found in Christ."[22]

22 Dr. Lance Wonders, Dean of ACTS Bible College, where the author received his Master of Divinity degree. This is an email excerpt which helped me frame my understanding of the power of the gift of tongues as it came forth on the Day of Pentecost.

And He began accomplishing it on that beautiful day, when the disciples stumbled out of the Upper Room and spoke in tongues, and all the nations of the surrounding world were there to hear it. They thought them drunk, or mad. God has a way of adding such drama when He is binding the strong man and spoiling his house (Mark 3:27 and Matthew 12:29) and unleashing His Divine Son, Jesus, to all nations!

They were all there! Acts 2 lists people from all over the known world.

> *"Parthians and Medes and Elamites, and residents of Mesopotamia, Judea and Cappadocia, Pontus and Asia, Phrygia and Pamphylia, Egypt and the districts of Libya around Cyrene, and visitors from Rome, both Jews and Gentile converts, Cretans and Arabs—we hear them in our own tongues speaking of the mighty deeds of God"* (Acts 2:9-12).

I'll bet they all went home after that feast and wondered at these things, and later multitudes of people in all these nations came to faith in Jesus Messiah and were welcomed into His family. Satan couldn't stop it!

"The power of the gospel," writes N.T. Wright, "is the powerful announcement that God is God, that Jesus is LORD, that the powers of evil have been defeated, that God's new world has begun. It means instantly that all people everywhere are gladly invited to come to it, to join the party, to discover forgiveness for the past, an astonishing destiny in God's future, and a vocation in the present."[23]

"The resurrection," writes Canon J. John, "shows that God has accepted Jesus' payment for our sin on the cross, that the power of evil has been decisively broken, that our own personal resurrection from the dead is assured. In the dark days of 1940, Winston Churchill promised his people in their battle against a powerful enemy 'nothing but blood, toil, tears and sweat'. Jesus' promise to his followers in their battle against a greater darkness is similar. The great difference is that, unlike Churchill, Jesus can guarantee his followers an ultimate victory and an ultimate reward."[24]

---

23 N.T. Wright, Surprised By Hope, pg. 227. HarperCollins Publishing, 2008.
24 J.John and Chris Walley, op. cit., pgs. 247 and 252.

The Time of the End: A Marker for Our Attention

Jesus shared in Matthew 24, Acts 1 and Revelation 11:3 (listed below) about His intention that before His final return to earth, that in a sense, "every creature" (or at minimum, every people-group) would have an opportunity to respond positively or negatively to His commission. This can be a real marker of significance for our own day and generation.

Notice especially the usage of the word "witness" in all three of these passages.

> *"And this gospel of the Kingdom shall be preached in the whole world for a* **witness** *to all the nations, and then the end shall come"* (Matthew 24:14).

> *"You shall receive power when the Holy Spirit has come upon you; and you shall be My* **witnesses** *both in Jerusalem, and in all Judea and Samaria, and even* **to the remotest part of the earth"** (Acts 1:8).

> *"And I will grant authority to* **My two witnesses***"* (Revelation 11:3).

For a fuller understanding of the meaning of the two witnesses, read my chapter on the Two Witnesses.

Let's pause for a moment to consider more deeply the words of Jesus in Matthew 24:14. I believe this passage (when aligned with many others) points to the atmosphere of the Last of the Last Days of a strong witness of Christ in all the nations, along with persecutions and many trials to prove our witness is true (Revelation 12:11).

"The disciples asked for the signs of the end of the age," writes author Perry Stone. "This word in Greek means "the completion, or the consummation of a thing." *W.E. Vine's Expository Dictionary of Old and New Testament Words* says the word *end* "does not denote a termination, but the heading up of events to the appointed climax."

"The disciples were requesting certain indicators of the completion and consummation of the age. The word *end* is used in Matthew 24:13 when

Jesus said, "...endure unto the end" (KJV), and in Matthew 24:14, which says that after the gospel is preached around the world, "then shall the end come."

"Notice this word indicates the termination of something but not the end of a time period. In other words, Christ is revealing that certain signs will indicate the termination of one age and the beginning of another.

"It does not refer to "the end of time," a term that some use but that is not found in Scripture. The concept of *the end of time* possibly comes from Revelation 10:6, in which during the future Tribulation an angel states, "There should be time no longer" (KJV). A clearer translation is, *"Time will no longer be delayed."*

"This verse in Revelation alludes to how the prophetic events surrounding the Great Tribulation, which occurs at the time of the end, will suddenly accelerate like an eighteen-wheeler going downhill without any brakes. Once the final time is set in motion, the prophecies will come to pass faster than one can keep up with! There will be no restraining of events, as the restraining power will be removed (See 2 Thessalonians 2:1-8).

"The actual meaning of "the time of the End" refers to when certain prophetic signs related to the return of Christ begin to merge one season and during one generation."[25]

Are we living in the final generation?

Perry Stone really helps us understand something powerful here, especially in reference to Matthew 24:14.

I believe one could say that as we get closer to the time of the end, that there also seems to be an acceleration of the witness of Christ to the nations. There seems to be a fresh urgency in hearts to carry the Good News and advance the Kingdom in greater measure to reach the unreached.

25 Perry Stone, Unleashing the Beast, Charisma House, 2009; see pages 8-11 for a fuller understanding of these wonderful truths.

This is exciting! We are possibly right now living in the final generation!

Let's look at some incredible evidence of the spread of the Gospel of the Kingdom in just the past 90 years to inspire us.

The following is one of the most startling stories of recent Salvation-History to show us just how close we are coming to the Last Battle, and just how powerful the Holy Spirit is in filling His servants to witness the reality of Jesus Christ, *so that none should perish.*

The "Every Creature" Commission Begins

As I shared in my Introduction, the Captain of our salvation is calling to His troops with one word, Advance! (the "standing orders" of God's army of the Last Days).

And as I shared in the very beginning of this chapter with my opening story of Rees Howells in Wales in the early part of the 20th century, I stumbled upon what I believe is an amazing key: that indeed the Spirit of God has been on the move and He has a timetable and a plan to bring forth the Second Coming of Christ in either our own generation, or the next one (which is rising now)!

I highly recommend the book where I read this story, entitled, Rees Howells: Intercessor.[26]

Let's continue now to look more deeply into an incident in Rees' life that led him to a most amazing assignment of intercession from the LORD.

In the very early hours of the morning on December 26, 1934, the Holy Spirit began dialoguing with Rees.[27] He was in bed and mumbling the words, "every creature" and finally awoke, got dressed, and went down to his prayer room at 3 a.m. sensing the Spirit wanted to talk to him.

He asked Rees the question in prayer.

26 Norman Grubb, "Rees Howells, Intercessor." Christian Literature Crusade, 1952.

27 *Note: yes, it is possible to develop your prayer life into an ongoing dialogue with God; and learn more, read Chapter 4 of my book, "Love Speaks: 21 Ways to Recognize God's Multi-Faceted Voice" on the theme of the Inner Voice of the Spirit. https://www.lovespeaks.today

"Do you believe the Savior meant His last command to be obeyed?"

"Yes," answered Rees, "I do!"

"Then," continued the Spirit, "Do you believe that I can give the gospel to every creature?"

"I believe you can. You are God."

"I am dwelling in you. Can I be responsible for this *through you?"*[28]

For years, Rees Howells had been praying for the gospel to go throughout the whole world, and the Spirit had brought before him many times God's promise to His Son in Psalm 2:8. He had prayed every single day that the Savior should have "the heathen for His inheritance and the uttermost parts of the earth for His possession."

He had also served as a missionary in Africa and had a conversation with Andrew Murray, who challenged him with the verse of the "laborers sent out into the harvest." Murray had shared that "the number of missionaries on the field depends entirely on the extent to which someone obeys that command and prays out the laborers."

So this new word from the LORD laid special responsibility on Rees himself. The way this "commission" was interpreted in concrete terms was that in the next thirty years the Holy Spirit would find 10,000 channels from all over the world—men and women whom He would enter and who would allow Him to take complete possession of them for this task (that would date this particular assignment of prayer and outreach for the approximate years 1935 to 1965).

On New Year's Day, 1935, Mr. Howells brought forth this "commission" to his small Bible school near the seaside town of Swansea, in Wales, and students and staff alike resounded with a "yes" in their hearts and began to set aside in separation a unique season of prayer in Wales for this "every creature commission" to come to pass.

28 Grubb's account of Rees Howells, Ibid., pg. 205.

"It was a strong conviction that as really as the Savior came down to the world to make an atonement for every creature, so the Holy Spirit had come down to make that atonement known to every creature, and that He would complete it *in their generation.* This prayer mission meant, if accepted, that Howells himself and all who took it with him would be bond-servants for the rest of their days to this one task—to intercede, to go, to serve others who go—to be responsible for seeing that every creature hears the Gospel."[29]

You might say, "that sounds like, Mission Impossible!" but they didn't say that...they said YES and saw it as, "Mission Possible!"

We can draw some remarkable conclusions from this story.

Is it possible that every generation has the possibility of becoming the final generation to fight in the LORD's final battle? Is it possible that if there are enough laborers in the harvest fields that the LORD can give exposure of the Gospel in a single generation, so all people groups have an opportunity to accept or reject it? It seems, from His perspective, that the answer is, YES.

Jesus spoke these words as the key standing orders of His army in the nations:

> *"All authority has been given to Me in heaven and on earth. Go therefore and make disciples of all the nations, baptizing them in the name of the Father and the Son and the Holy Spirit, teaching them to observe all that I commanded you; and lo, I am with you always, even to the end of the age"* (Matthew 28:18-20).

Note the following four key words as being represented in the story of "The Every Creature Commission" as it relates to Jesus' words in His own standing orders of the mission to all His followers.

1. SOVEREIGNTY: The LORD Himself was the source of this commission so it was His will to see it accomplished.

29 Ibid., pg. 206-207.

2. URGENCY: He established the initial timetable of 1935 to 1965. They began to pray immediately. But as we will soon see, the timetable extended far into our own generation, and the effects of this prayer assignment are still bearing fruit every single day.

3. EXPECTATION: Both Rees and the students and staff of the Bible college firmly believed in the commission and were drawn to those words of Andrew Murray, that the harvest depends on the personal commitment of the workers to expect results and pray them in.

4. HUNGER: The Spirit Himself had deposited the desire for the commission to be fulfilled, and all alike shared an inner witness to the possibility of it happening.[30]

I made a special visit to the actual site of this commission on a recent ministry trip to Wales, to film the story of the "Every Creature Commission" for one of my TV episodes.

I walked the grounds of the estate and sat among the giant oak trees, still standing some 80-plus years since the Spirit spoke there, and this stalwart band of brothers and sisters secretly, and with great emotion, prayed for hours, days, months and even decades to see the "every creature commission" fulfilled in their own lifetime.

I stopped and worshipped the LORD on one of the prayer benches that Rees himself had occupied while praying for the nations to hear of the Savior.

Suddenly, as I prayed, the Spirit of God came upon me with His presence there, and I trembled and shook for several minutes. The power of the Spirit was so strong upon me.

"I heard all their prayers," He seemed to whisper to my heart, "and I have answered, and will continue to answer, all of them."

---

30 For a further challenge to apply these 4 Key Words to our very own decades in which we live today, please read my final chapter in this book, "Hasten the Day."

So what of the "Commission"? They believed truly that the Holy Spirit would answer their prayers to see this vision accomplished in their own generation.

We are all still here.

The gospel has not yet reached every creature.

So what happened?

Well, in a word, WAR.

World War 2.

That's right. One of Satan's dirty tricks (and you will learn many of his own battle plans in Section 3 of this book) is to both BLOCK the plans of the LORD or DELAY those plans and purposes by his own demonic powers.

Howells wrote in 1936, "We knew that France would be on fire in a day, and it meant nothing less than a European war, and the consequent hindrance to the spread of the Gospel."

The following year, Hitler rose to stronger power and began his diabolical invasions of Europe. Rees Howells sensed it was going to be a battle between the Third Person of the Trinity and Satan through Hitler himself.

"It was in March of 1936 that Mr. Howells began to see clearly that Hitler was Satan's agent for preventing the Gospel going to every creature. As he said later, 'In fighting Hitler we have always said that we were not up against a man but the Devil. Mussolini is a man, but Hitler is different. He can tell the day this "spirit" came into him."

For several years of ensuing prayer battles through the major events of the war, Mr. Howells stressed the fact that God must destroy him if the vision of the Gospel to every creature was to be fulfilled."[31]

"Rees Howells had been taught by the Holy Spirit that any person, government, or international situation that hindered the spread of the Gospel

31 Ibid, Grubb, page 241.

would become a legitimate target to be challenged and defeated through intercession."[32]

So, in the Sovereignty, Timing, Expectation and Hunger of God, it is right to ask yourself, "Was it on the LORD's heart to see this "Commission" fulfilled in the previous generation?"

It seems as though the answer to that was a resounding, "Yes!"

Thus, I believe that Satan's tactics to delay, block or even stop the "Commission" led directly to him personally influencing Hitler throughout the war.

Howells and the intercessors actually applied the image of the Beast in Revelation 12, to Hitler and his evil Nazi regime. (You will discover much more about spiritual warfare, the meaning of the Beast in Revelation, and how to become an intercessor yourself as you read through this book.)

Here's what we do know happened as a result of those prayers and intercessions for the harvest. Howells faithfully set at least four times of corporate intercession per day, every day, for six years!

He and his stalwart band of intercessors were led by the Spirit to pray through the campaigns of WWII. These included: Dunkirk, the Battle for Britain, Russia, North Africa, Italy, D-Day, and the end of the war, including the establishment of the United Nations.

In Russia, one very unique prayer assignment was given. Even as the Nazi armies were sure to capture Moscow in 1941, the Spirit spoke to Rees and challenged him.

"Why does Moscow have to fall? Why don't you pray and believe Me, that I will give a setback to the Nazis?"

As a result of that particular prayer assignment that came from the Spirit Himself (intercession to stop the Nazi armies so that Moscow would not fall), Moscow never fell. God called upon nature itself to give a setback anground the Blitzkrieg to a halt![33]

32 Richard Maton, "Samuel Rees Howells: A Life of Intercession", ByFaith Media, Nov. 2012, pg. 35.

33 Search my YouTube Channel (Carl Wesley Anderson / Born to Blaze Ministries) for my 14-minute short film streaming there about this unique moment in WWII of the LORD challenging Howells for Moscow not to fall into the hands of the Nazis. It's entitled, "INTERCESSION Changes History!"

After WWII ended, they kept faithfully praying that the Gospel would go forward.

And what about God's heart to give the Jewish people their own homeland? Few people know that a very special burden of secret intercession came upon Rees Howells for the weeks surrounding the establishment of Israel as a nation and a homeland for the Jews in 1948.

They prayed through to victory and Israel was established!

That Was Then...This Is Now!

Rees Howells' own son, Samuel, took up the charge to continue "The Every Creature Commission," and prayed faithfully (along with intercessors at the Bible College of Wales) until his own death in 2004.

Yes, that was 54 more years of intercession over world events, in order to see Satan's influence hindered and the Gospel go forth! He prayed through every major war and international conflict as led by the Spirit.

What else happened in the years following the demise of Hitler to begin setting in motion a potential timetable for the end?

Satan entered another region with Communism, and the Berlin Wall and Cold War came to stop the spread of the Good News in Russia and Eastern Europe.

One of my favorite stories of Samuel Howells was his personal assignment to pray continuously for decades for the Berlin Wall to crash down, and against the throttling of life in Eastern Europe and the domination of Russia with Communism. The Divine purpose was that the Gospel could be proclaimed without hindrance from evil in those nations behind the Iron Curtain.

And in the year 1987, after 26 years of concentrated intercession, Samuel was given the sense from the Holy Spirit that his prayers had prevailed. The Berlin Wall would come tumbling down! It was only a matter of time before the world would see the victory that had been won in the realm of the Spirit.

On November 9th, 1989, he saw victory for the Kingdom of Jesus Christ when the Wall fell. Many new laborers were sent into the harvest fields of Eastern Europe and Russia, and the army of God advanced. Speaking in November 1989 Samuel said, "The Wall is down! This is the ministry of the Holy Spirit Himself. When you think of what is happening in the countries of Eastern Europe and Eastern Germany just a few months ago, no one would have dreamt such a thing. These people are on the march towards freedom! This is God's day!"[34]

We learn from this story and the stories of the Howells, something of the truths of the Book of Revelation. That is, natural wars, and barriers like the Berlin Wall, are reflections of battles that are taking place in real time in the realms of the Spirit. God's enemies must be opposed. Sometimes He gives special prayer assignments to those who are fully engaged with Him in prayer.

More on these themes is coming to you in Sections II, III, and IV.

The Commission: 1935 to 1965

Let's rewind for a moment to look at the advance of the witness during those first 30 years (1935 to 1965) of "The Every Creature Commission" and the ensuing years after.

What happened after WWII?

In part, because of the stark horrors of the Holocaust and the evil regime of Hitler, people were made aware of the reality of evil and of their need for the light of Christ.

People were shaken to their core. It was the perfect atmosphere for new laborers to be sent out into the vineyard for harvest. Voices of missionaries and evangelists arose in the nations to call them to repentance, even as Howells and his prayer warriors prayed on!

34 Ibid, Maton on Howells, pg. 161.

One of those voices was that of Rev. Billy Graham. He was raised up in obscurity and came thundering upon the scene, preaching Christ and leading countless people to repentance and salvation.

His sermon in Chicago that I opened the chapter with, was just one of many thousands he preached during an awakening to the truth from 1949 onwards (the year of his very first crusade, in Los Angeles).

In 1949, Howells himself was still praying for those 10,000 new laborers, and Graham was one of them!

Graham went on from Los Angeles to preach to more people than any other evangelist in history—nearly 215 million people in person in 99 countries, and perhaps as many as 2 billion in live, closed-circuit broadcasts.[35]

The "Latter Rain Movement" started and with it, over 500 evangelists (both men and women) were raised up by the Spirit, and were holding tent crusades all over America during the decade of the 1950s and beyond.

And just toward the end of that period of time, the Jesus People and Charismatic Movements were birthed, which eventually led to an expression of God's power filling all kinds of people, from hippies and the unchurched, to the Roman Catholic and Protestant Church expressions all over the world. These movements and more brought the Gospel message in fresh power and witness to countless new nations.

Being from Minnesota, I have to also mention the tremendous influence of evangelist Lowell Lundstrom. He was born and ministered during "The Every Creature Commission" (born in 1939 and died in 2012), as another answer to the prayers of Rees Howells. He began his mission for the Gospel in 1957, and is said to have personally led over 1 million people to faith during his 57-year ministry, as well as writing 600 gospel songs!

Another evangelist, Reinhard Bonnke, was trained at the actual Bible College of Wales (under the leadership of Rees' son, Samuel), and began his evangelistic ministry in Africa in 1967. As of his passing in 2019, had seen an estimated 79+ million people turn their hearts to Christ in the continent of Africa.

---

35 Quote from the University of Miami news, Feb. 21, 2018.

Interestingly, Loren Cunningham, the founder of Youth With A Mission (YWAM), had his initial vision of "waves of young people crashing upon the shores in mighty missions endeavors" (my paraphrase) in June of 1956. (Yes, during the first 30 years of "The Every Creature Commission.")[36] From 1956 onwards into the 21st century, over 5 million young people would respond to short-term missions in every nation on earth, through YWAM!

Following the actual answers to this prayer mission during the years 1935 to 1965, I personally believe that besides these examples like Graham, Bonnke and Cunningham, thousands of other evangelists, missionaries, prayer warriors and laborers of all kinds came forth in fresh waves of service in the harvest fields.

And all as a result of one man, Rees Howells, who took seriously the call to pray secretly for "The Every Creature Commission" way back in 1934 to 1935.

The Commission Continues: 1965 to Present Day

Speaking of Loren Cunningham, I had the honor of being invited by Loren himself to conduct two private film interviews with him for my TV series. One in 2019 and another one just before his death in 2023. Many of his stories I have included in my documentary film episodes.

Cunningham was animated during the interviews, full of the Holy Spirit, and enthusiastically shared story after story for two hours for each interview (which felt like two minutes each). He shared how YWAM is working with the Holy Spirit in helping facilitate many movements around the world that are taking seriously the Great Commission.

He hinted (with a glimmer in his eye) that he felt "every nation" could have exposure to the Gospel sometime in the next decade or so!

For example, YWAM is partnering with multiple groups as of this writing, including the "Call2All" Movement, which is currently endeavoring

36 Loren Cunningham, Is That Really You, God? Pg. 28.YWAM Publishing, 1984.

to spread the gospel with seven parts to its mission: eradicating poverty, mobilizing prayer, accelerating evangelism, demonstrating powerful compassion, transforming unengaged unreached people groups (UUPU), reaching and equipping oral learners, and establishing and growing church presence in all seven spheres of the Earth.[37]

Another fine example of the gospel of the kingdom in full acceleration is from the organization, Faith Comes By Hearing, whose vision is to reach the millions of people who learn only through auditory recording. Their cultures teach them to learn by oral storytelling. They also don't have access to print media. They currently have Bible recordings in 2,204 languages—spoken by over 5.7 billion people.[38]

Wycliffe is another amazing missions-oriented organization that has thousands of missionaries in places all over the world, working tirelessly to finish the spread of the Gospel.[39]

According to Wycliffe, there are 6,800 languages spoken in the earth today. Less than 1,300 are without a Bible translation, and Wycliffe International is currently working on those with active missionaries in the world.

God also raised up so many others, like Dr. Ed Silvoso (I believe as another answer to Howell's prayers), an Argentine minister with a heart for cultural transformation. He was a part of many revivals in Argentina and also with evangelist Luis Palau.

He founded the organization, Transform Our World, which is currently active to see whole cities and regions of the earth reached for the Gospel. He advocates that every single Believer can help bring the Good News through the marketplace. Here is one of my favorite quotes from Dr. Ed.

"The most common self-inflicted put-down is, 'I am not a pastor—I am just a layperson.' This is all part of a clever satanic scheme to neutralize

37 For more information about these exciting missions endeavors, please visit www.ywam.org or www.call2all.org

38 For more info please visit: www.FaithComesByHearing.com

39 Please visit their website in the years to come for updates on their statistics: http://www.wycliffe.org/About/Statistics.aspx

apostles, prophets, evangelists, pastors and teachers along with the entire army of disciples, already positioned in the marketplace."[40]

God can use *you*—today—in whatever marketplace you are in!

And time would fail me to tell of all the countless men and women who are giving their lives for the Gospel in so many nations of the earth.

We are getting closer to the Last of the Last Days!

God can use *you*—today—wherever you are!

China: The Greatest Revival of Modern Salvation-History

Another fascinating case study is China! This nation was certainly a prayer target for "The Every Creature Commission," and in 1949, Communism swept this huge territory and overshadowed the Believers there. The Enemy probably thought he had won. The government began persecution of Believers, but the tables were turned as hearts surrendered en masse to Jesus Christ!

It was estimated that there were about four million Christians (three million Catholics and one million Protestants) at the time of the new Regime in 1949.

Although real persecution has since occurred, today there are estimated to be somewhere between 100 million and 130+ million Believers in the underground Church (house churches which are non-registered with the government and therefore, under persecution).

"The revival in China has undergone a dramatic transformation since new draconian laws were implemented last year," writes Paul Hattaway in an article from 2019. "And almost overnight, thousands of churches stopped meeting together in large congregations, and have broken down into tiny home groups of no more than four or five Believers. Most underground Bible schools have been discontinued for now. Just in the past few weeks,

40 Dr. Ed Silvoso, Anointed for Business, pp. 18, 2010.

however, reports have reached our ministry that the dramatic changes in China are causing the churches to grow in many areas, as the light of the gospel attracts new people to the faith in a confused and unstable society." [41]

What hope there is for this flourishing group of Believers amidst Satanic assault! Multiplication of Christianity is happening every day in these house churches, with signs and wonders following.

The Man in White

What of the Islamic Nations and the intensifying spiritual battles they are bringing to the West? 9/11 (the attacks with airplanes in New York and Washington D.C. in September 2001) was a wake-up call to America. Today, there are reportedly Islamic extremist terror cells hiding in secret in many states of America and many countries of Europe. Many Islamic Nations look upon the West as their enemy, not their friend.

Yet, even at the same time as many extremists are targeting Christians, killing them, or trying to destroy Christian values, I pose this question: Does the LORD have a heart to see the descendants of Ishmael brought to the love of the Father and the Son?

The answer is an unequivocal, Yes!

Countless Muslims around the world are reporting unique visitations in the night seasons (in dreams and visions) of "The Man in White." Jesus is currently appearing constantly, somewhere on earth, in one of the Nine Rooms (Regions) of Islam, and personally introducing His love to Muslims. As a result, they are turning their hearts to Him.

"While Christians have a variety of approaches to dreams, Muslims—particularly Shia Muslims—are open to dreams being revelatory," writes Darren Carlson from The Gospel Coalition, "due to both cultural (general acceptance) and religious (precedent in the Qur'an) factors. Dreams of Jesus, then, are taken seriously. In recent field work where I interviewed Christian migrants who'd converted from Islam, many reported a dream that led to their conversion.

41 "Inside the Biggest Revival in History" by Paul Hattaway, Premiere Christianity, U.K.

"Their experiences of dreams and visions fit into the following categories:

— Jesus speaking Scripture to them, even Scripture they had never heard before.

— Jesus telling people to do something (often it's to go and find a particular Christian who can tell them more about Him).

— A dream or vision that led to a feeling of being clean or at peace.

— A "Man in White" physically appearing.

"A friend of mine had heard the gospel in Athens, but she struggled to believe. One day she went home despondent and hid behind the couch in her family's apartment. She began to pray:

> *'You know what, God? Since I have absolutely no excuse, absolutely none, I have run out of excuses. I don't know what to do, but following you means I have to deny everything I have believed and everything all of my family, generation after generation, believed. I can't be in the middle. I have to either follow you or not. I can't do it myself. It's just hard to make that step. I need you to help me.'*

"After she prayed, she did not know whether she was awake or asleep, but A MAN IN WHITE walked into the room. Her reaction was to blurt out, 'Don't come close to me. You are holy, and I am a sinner. Do not get close to me.' The man replied, '[Girl's First Name], I told you, and I tell you again, I am the way and the truth. No one comes to the Father except through me.' That day she believed the gospel and was saved."[42]

"More than 86 percent of all the Muslim movements to Christ in the 1,381 year-history of Islam," writes David Garrison, "have occurred in the last 12 years. A wind is blowing through the House of Islam and God is doing something historic!"[43]

---

42 Darren Carlson, www.thegospelcoalition.org/article/muslims-dream-jesus/

43 David Garrison, "A Wind is Blowing in the House of Islam: How God is Drawing Muslims Around the World to Faith in Jesus", WIGTake Publishers, 2014.

Did you know, Iran itself is one of the nations currently with the fastest growing church, and God is using women there (men too, but predominantly women) to introduce His love to people?

And all of this amazing fruit of the battles to bring the Gospel to the ends of the earth, sprang forth from the heart of the Father, to Rees Howells in 1934!

"This is a staggering fact," writes Jonathan Lewis. "God has entrusted to people, like us, redeemed sinners, the responsibility of carrying out the divine purpose in history. Why has God done it this way? Is He not taking a great risk that His purpose will fail in accomplishment? We do not try to answer the question except to say that such is God's will. Here are the facts: God has entrusted to us this mission; and unless we do it, it will not get done."[44]

Remember this truth, that though we are approaching the End, you can continue to follow the Lamb wherever He leads you, and Jesus Himself will be with you EVEN TO THE END OF THE AGE (see Matthew 28:20).

As we approach that end, we are faced with the challenge of working alongside the Holy Spirit. I believe there is a clear acceleration of His desire to keep spreading the Gospel message far and wide into cultures and atmospheres of spiritual complacency. Put another way, the darkness is getting darker while the light upon the Church is getting brighter and more intense in certain places.

> *Arise, shine; for your light has come,*
> *And the glory of the Lord has risen upon you.*
> *For behold, darkness will cover the earth*
> *And deep darkness the peoples;*
> *But the Lord will rise upon you*
> *And His glory will appear upon you.*
> *Nations will come to your light,*
> *And kings to the brightness of your rising*
> (Isaiah 60:1-3).

---

44 World Mission, Jonathan Lewis, editor, a quote from George Elden Ladd, page 3-29.

Our Heavenly Father is on a Divine mission, through the army of the Son (His Church). That is, to finish the witness of Jesus and His resurrection and to complete what Jesus called, "the fullness of the Gentiles" right to the end. What Jesus promised would happen in Matthew 24 and Luke 21 is being fulfilled in our very own generation.

There's a mission field waiting for you. It's right outside your door. Go forth and make disciples! Share your Testimony of faith in Jesus Christ with everyone you befriend, and *endure hardships and trials as a good soldier of Jesus Christ* (2 Timothy 2:3), remembering the eternal truth of Revelation 12:11,

> *"And they overcame him because of the blood of the Lamb and because of the word of His testimony, and they did not love their life even when faced with death."*

Remember too, on whatever particular day you happen to be reading this, we are officially one day closer to the Second Coming.

He is coming, sooner than He was yesterday!

"He has truly been on the move," writes Jonathan Lewis, quoting from George Elden Ladd, "and is actively working with leaders in the current generation to burden them to continue to take the gospel forward until every nation has been reached, and Jesus can return."[45]

An African Tale: Morning Stars Shining in the Dark

Let me close this chapter with an inspiring story from Salvation-History.[46]

One of the greatest pioneer missionaries to ever have lived was a man named David Livingstone. His story has personally inspired me to give my whole life as an equipping evangelist and media missionary. Let me summarize his extraordinary life of both suffering and witness.

At a young age, David Livingstone had memorized the entire hundred

45 Just one more example from www.missionfrontiers.org

46 I have filmed this story as an illustration of God's direction and it can be watched on my YouTube Channel. Just search, "Carl Wesley Anderson" and watch, "Dr. Livingstone, I Presume?"

and nineteenth Psalm, all 176 verses of it, to recognize the primacy of God's word and set it as a fire in his own heart. As a young man, he stood outside a cluster of African villages, where he saw the smoke spiraling upwards, and in his journal he entered these words:

> *"The haunting specter of the smoke of a thousand tribal villages has burned itself within my heart."*

Then he got on his knees and wrote the following:

> *"Send me anywhere,*
> *Only go with me;*
> *Lay any burden on me,*
> *Only sustain me;*
> *Sever any ties,*
> *But the ties that bind me*
> *To Your service and to Your heart."*

He married Mary Moffat, of the famed missionary family. This poor woman was to suffer want and deprivation for many years because of the torrid conditions under which David and she lived. They lost some of their children. She lost her health completely. In fact, on their second journey to Africa, Livingstone buried her in African soil. Eyewitnesses said that as he lowered her body into the ground, they saw him kneel and heard him utter these words:

> *"My Jesus, my King, I shall place no value on anything I possess,*
> *Or in anything I do,*
> *Except in relation to Thy Kingdom and to Thy service."*

Livingstone said, "The words of Christ came to me, *'Lo, I am with you always, even unto the end of the world"* (Matthew 28:20, KJV).

He went back to his home in Ujiji, where someone had broken into his hut and stolen the medication he needed daily for a body wracked with pain, as he had at one time been viciously attacked by a lion. He went to his knees to pray. "You promised that you would be with me till the end of the age. I need that medicine!"

Almost immediately, he heard footsteps and looked up to see the first white face he had seen in years.

The visitor said, "Dr. Livingstone, I presume?"

Henry M. Stanley, American journalist, introduced himself, and later added, "Let me tell you two things about me. One, I'm the biggest swaggering atheist on the face of the earth, so please don't try to convert me. Newspapers in America have sent me to find you and do a story on your life. Number two, I have some medication here that someone has sent to you."

Are we there yet? Not Yet! But Close!

Talk about an answer to prayer! Before he called, God sent the answer.

About five months later, the "biggest swaggering atheist on the face of the earth" bent his knees on African soil and gave his life to Christ.

The whole dark continent of Africa was filled with multitudes of people in spiritual darkness, and Livingstone would give his life to pave the way for exploring and opening up roadways and water passages so future missionaries could carry the gospel of the Kingdom there. The faster these tribes were allowed access to Christ, the faster the process of the Kingdom Age could come to a glorious end as *every tribe and nation under heaven* would contain some Believers.

He was found dead upon his knees in a final act of full devotion to Christ. His servants cut out his heart and buried it in African soil.

His heart is still there.

Today, millions and millions of Believers fill Africa with songs of praise to God as a result of the sacrifices of men and women like Livingstone.

He once wrote in his journal:

> *"Missionaries in the midst of masses of heathenism seem like voices crying in the wilderness—Reformers before the Reformation;*

future missionaries will see conversions follow every sermon. We prepare the way for them. May they not forget the pioneers who worked in the thick gloom with few rays to cheer, except as flow from God's promises! We work for a glorious future which we are not destined to see. We are only morning stars shining in the dark, but the glorious morn will break..." [47]

I have in my library a book written by a modern-day Livingstone, an evangelist named Reinhard Bonnke, whose famous line, "Africa for JESUS!" has resounded far and wide. His crusades on African soil brought countless millions of people into the Kingdom over the past three decades, before his untimely death at the age of 79.

And as I shared earlier, Bonnke actually attended the Bible College of Wales led by Rees' son, Samuel Howells, and **was trained there**. Talk about a literal answer to the prayers of the "Every Creature Commission"!

Bonnke writes of his first large faith mission in Africa where he booked a 10,000 seat stadium with a church of 40 members. "10,000 came!" he writes. "The first ripe wheat. For the first time I witnessed thousands running forward to respond to the call of salvation. God opened my eyes and I actually saw an invisible, mighty wave of Holy Spirit-power arrive in the stadium. A mass baptism in the Holy Spirit, accompanied by many healing miracles, took place. David Livingstone prophesied that where he hardly saw a convert, later there would be multitudes. And so it was."[48]

So, "Are we there YET?" Not Yet! But Close!

In conclusion, let me share a memory from my childhood. I can remember vividly being an excited child in the backseat of our car on vacation. We took a yearly road trip and my parents brought us to nearly every state in America to see historic sights and awesome landmarks. I would constantly be yearning to arrive at our destination with the phrase, "ARE WE THERE, YET?"

---

47 W.G. Blaikie. The Personal Life of David Livingstone, pg. 162, 1880.

48 Reinhard Bonnke, Evangelism By Fire: Igniting Your Passion for the Lost. Christ For All Nations Publishing, 2002.

The greatest sign of the times of them all is what Jesus said would be present at His Second Coming, and is happening *right now!* The Gospel has almost reached every creature (at least, through technology and new laborers, the advancing army is moving towards every people group).

According to Wikipedia, "Christianity is the world's largest and most widespread religion with over 2.6 billion followers, comprising around 32% of the world's population. Its adherents are estimated to make up a majority of the population in 157 countries and territories."[49]

Begin to pray for the laborers, or better yet, become one of them.

So, as you look at the signs of the times and discern the times of the signs, look more closely at the *conditions* on the earth right now. As Believers, through the Holy Spirit, and because of the words of Jesus and the Book of Revelation, WE CAN KNOW the nearness of His coming. The next chapter will reveal even more of those conditions, and you will feel the time is near.

I am praying continuously (and you can join me in praying), "Come, King Jesus, to my heart, even stronger by your Spirit, and personally return to this earthly realm, as your eternal destination! I long for you to arrive."

In closing, we now remember the words of Jesus that the timing of His coming is related directly to the spread of the Gospel in the Nations.

> *"And this gospel of the Kingdom shall be preached in the whole world for a witness to all the nations, and* **then** *the end shall come"* (Matthew 24:14).

The next chapter will share in-depth on the conditions present in the earth right now that parallel 2 other periods of history that preceded direct interventions of Divine judgment: the days of both Noah and Lot.

Let's dive into this next unique *time of the signs.*

49 Search, "Christianity" on Wikipedia for updated statistics.

Going Deeper Still:

— As we saw, the Holy Spirit initiated a secret prayer mission to pray for the accelerated advance of the gospel in the nations from 1935 to 1965 (and beyond). Thousands of new evangelists and missionaries were sent forth into an atmosphere of spiritual hunger after WWII ended, and revivals broke out in many nations. The "Every Creature Commission" boldly went forth! Are you personally open to the Holy Spirit's invitation to indwell you and help reach the world for Christ?

— Loren Cunningham stated in my interview with him in 2022, that he believed the gospel could reach "every nation" (because of the use of the Internet and the power of media) within the next decade. What are you personally doing or praying to see this happen?

— There is an acceleration in the Spirit to finish the witness of the gospel within our own generation. Great signs and wonders are taking place every day in every nation in fulfillment of Jesus' promise from Matthew 24 and Acts 1. Offer to pray for others' needs, and watch the Holy Spirit bring answers. Who can you ask to pray for today?

— What do these four key words, found in the story of the "Every Creature Commission," mean to you after reading this chapter: **Sovereignty, Urgency, Expectation and Hunger?**

— According to the illustrations in this chapter, what are the "Standing Orders" of God's Last Days army? Study and memorize Matthew 28:18-20. How can you personally obey those orders?

The Days of Noah and Lot

The Atmosphere of Spiritual Complacency in the Last Days

"And just as it happened in the days of Noah, so it shall be also in the days of the Son of Man; they were eating, they were drinking, they were marrying, they were being given in marriage, until the day that Noah entered the ark, and the flood came and destroyed them all. It was the same as happened in the days of Lot: they were eating, they were drinking, they were buying, they were selling, they were planting, they were building; but on the day that Lot went out from Sodom it rained fire and brimstone from heaven and destroyed them all. It will be just the same on the day that the Son of Man is revealed. Remember Lot's wife" (Luke 17:26-30, 32).

Following on from the sign from Jesus that we are to look for the Gospel of the Kingdom reaching all people groups, He offered a fascinating parable and one of the most interesting word-pictures about the key signs to look for in the "atmosphere of the Last Days." It is the sign of Noah and Lot; the sign of absolute spiritual complacency.

In other words, it's the lack of hunger for God and the seeking of God. There will be a kind of coalition of nations who are all ignorant of spiritual truth, and the people are content in living lives fully without the fear of God before their eyes.

Those were the days of Noah.

Those were the days of Lot.

And those are the days we are currently inhabiting.

Jesus is trying to teach that indeed, unlike the "signs of the times" that accompanied His first appearance, and His declaration of judgment upon Jerusalem and the Temple (which would come to pass in just under one generation from then), there would be no major signs in the earth to trumpet His Second Coming, at least that the world would recognize. Only the Church will know the true season of signs.

In fact, the people of the world will sleep on, unaware of the impending Final Judgment that will happen upon His return. They will be caught fully off guard, as did the generations surrounding both Noah and Lot.

As you continue to share the gospel in the nations, remember Jesus' parable! Show mercy and compassion on those who are blinded to the truth and do not yet have eyes to see, as you do, what is really coming. Let's read how Jesus establishes this as a sign of His soon return.

As Jesus shared, there was coming a time of rare complacency when the world systems would sleep on in complete disregard to Him and His sovereign purposes. I have identified eight characteristics of a closer study of Noah and Lot, and all of these are on the increase exponentially in our age.

1. **Preoccupation with physical appetites** (Luke 17:27).
   They were eating, they were drinking, they were marrying, they were being given in marriage, until the day that Noah entered the ark, and the flood came and destroyed them all.

   In our day: The rapid expansion of fast food and ultra-processed foods worldwide reflects an increasing societal fixation on convenience and taste over nutrition.

On the other side of this coin, the global rise of ultra-luxury dining experiences, such as $500 wagyu beef steaks in Japan, gold-covered burgers in Dubai, and Michelin-starred tasting menus, demonstrates society's obsession with indulgence.

2. **Rapid advances in technology** (Genesis 4:22).
As for Zillah, she also gave birth to Tubal-cain, the forger of all implements of bronze and iron; and the sister of Tubal-cain was Naamah.

In our day: A.I. (Artificial Intelligence) and automation are transforming industries worldwide, from self-driving cars, like Tesla, to A.I.-powered chatbots and creative tools, like ChatGPT and Midjourney. China and the U.S. lead in A.I. research, implementing facial recognition for security, and even creating nano-technology that can be injected into humans to track their movements.

And, dare I mention it, scientists are now attempting to clone actual humans. This kind of sinful and anti-biblical technology is increasing. I personally don't believe the Father will allow humans the ability to clone other humans. He will send Jesus back to bring justice. Only HE can create a human spirit!

3. **Grossly materialistic attitudes and interests** (Luke 17:28).
"It was the same as happened in the days of Lot: they were eating, they were drinking, they were buying, they were selling, they were planting, they were building."

In our day: The obsession with high-end luxury brands like Gucci, Louis Vuitton, Rolex, and Hermès reflects a growing culture of materialism.

And one only has to think of the explosion of cryptocurrencies that has created a speculative culture where digital assets are valued more for hype and status than practical use.

4. **Inordinate devotion to pleasure and comfort** (Genesis 4:21).
His brother's name was Jubal; he was the father of all those who play the lyre and pipe.

   In our day: The "Soft Life" movement, popularized on social media, promotes a lifestyle centered on luxury, ease and avoiding struggle.

   Originating in African and Western influencer culture, it encourages people to prioritize pleasure. It glorifies lavish vacations, designer shopping, self-care rituals, and financial independence without hard work.

5. **No concern for God in either belief or conduct** (2 Peter 2:5).
And did not spare the ancient world, but preserved Noah, a preacher of righteousness, with seven others, when He brought a flood upon the world of the ungodly.

   In our day: There has been a sharp rise in people identifying as religiously unaffiliated, often called "nones" (those who claim no religious affiliation). In countries like Sweden, the UK, Canada and the U.S., younger generations are abandoning organized religion in favor of secular or atheist worldviews.

   Many prioritize science, personal ethics, and self-determined spirituality over traditional religious beliefs.

6. **Widespread violence** (Genesis 6:11).
Now the earth was corrupt in the sight of God, and the earth was filled with violence.

   In our day: There are certain violent moments in time that somehow burn themselves into one's memory. September 11th, 2001, 9/11, with the incredible destruction of the Twin Towers, is one of those.

   Another was the martyrdom of 21 Christian Egyptians in the horrible act of beheading at the hands of ISIS terrorists in Libya on the 15th of February, 2015.

   And everyone in this generation will remember the horrible atrocities that occurred in Israel on October 7, 2024, in the attack upon the Jewish people by Hamas and its allies. It was a single day of unprecedented violence and the most horrific attack on Jews since the Holocaust. There are numerous accounts of deliberate killings, hostage abuse, sexual violence, and desecration of both the living and the dead.

7. **Corruption throughout society (including inside the four walls of the Church)** (Genesis 6:12).
   God looked on the earth, and behold, it was corrupt; for all flesh had corrupted their way upon the earth.

   In our day: In many nations around the world, corruption has infiltrated government, business, law enforcement and social institutions, leading to bribery, embezzlement and abuse of power.

   Examples include: Russia's oligarchy (government officials and business elites amass extreme wealth while suppressing dissent).

   Latin American corruption scandals (across Brazil, Peru, and Mexico, with U.S. corporate/political ties, lobbying and "dark money" influencing policy-making, often favoring corporate interests over public good).

   And just like five of the seven churches mentioned in the Book of Revelation with sins being exposed inside the four walls of the Church, so it is in our own day in all three major streams of the Church Universal: Roman Catholic, Protestant and Orthodox churches. Horrible sex abuse scandals involving children, with cover-ups at the highest levels, have increased exponentially in recent decades.

   This leads us to the broader picture of massive sexual sins outside the four walls of the Church.

8. **Preoccupation with illicit sexual activity** (Genesis 19:5).
   And they called to Lot and said to him, "Where are the men who came to you tonight? Bring them out to us that we may have relations with them."

In our day: Just like the dark angels who created the Nephilim in Noah's day through forbidden sexual contact, and the Sodomites of Lot's day, it seems sexual sins are everywhere, on every street corner.

With just two clicks on any cell phone, the user can be exposed to the most graphic sexual content through pornography. The explosion of online pornography has made explicit content widely accessible, fueling addiction, changing sexual norms, and even contributing to relationship dysfunction and unrealistic expectations.

Human Trafficking & Exploitation is a multibillion-dollar industry, with criminal networks exploiting vulnerable people for profit. And the ongoing enslavement of children and young people is part of the global abomination in this category.

When you look closer at the war on terror in the nations, at the increase of abortion, child sex enslavement, killer storms, and governments simply unable to handle the pressures of degradation surrounding them, you can see all eight of these common signs on the increase.

Interestingly, I believe Jesus brings us back to the Genesis accounts of Noah's story and Lot's story, as the three major characters He Himself references have relevant character studies attached to them. Here are three players in the drama that Jesus brings our attention to for a reason:

1. **NOAH**
2. **LOT**
3. **LOT'S WIFE**

Noah, like the later character of Abraham in the story of Lot, was a righteous man. He walked in close relationship with the LORD. He enjoyed a kind of dialogue with God, and he prayed and listened and heard the LORD speak. His very life was a positive witness to godliness and strong faith and highly developed character. Besides his faithfulness in building the Ark, we find in some further details in both First and Second Peter, that he was also a "preacher of righteousness" during the period of years leading up to the flood.

Lot was a religious man, also called righteous by Peter's epistle. Yes, a Believer to be sure, but he represents all those masses of Believers whose faith is shallow and are poor witnesses to the world around them. Lot sat too much at the gates of Sodom, flirting with the world's allurements, and lacked true conviction of the truth. His own children could see through his religious ways, and did not respect him when the command came to leave Sodom.

Lot's wife was a nominal Believer who eventually was living too much on "both sides of the fence." She mixed too much of the world with her faith. She represents that large group of people who, at the End, will be asleep. And as Paul says, will "fall away into apostasy" and end up worse because of it.

Note: she is the only character that Jesus pointed out to every generation as a warning!

> *"Remember Lot's wife"* (Luke 17:32).

Many people who are church-goers and profess religious ways, ought to take special note of Jesus' words. It's a warning to be sure. Do not compromise in your lifestyle and by your daily choices! Do not compromise the truth! Something inside of Lot's wife caused her to "look back" and disobey the LORD. Too much mixture in her motives and character was pulling her back to sinful patterns. So she was turned into a pillar of salt to stand as a frozen monument for many generations, pointing to her compromise and defilement.

Jonathan Edwards, in his now-famous sermon, "Sinners in the Hands of an Angry God," refers to these somber words of Jesus in relating the judgment to come to the days of Lot. His sermon, preached in the days of the Great Awakening that swept New England in the 1730s and caused many people to come to salvation, ends with these themes.

"Therefore, let everyone that is out of Christ," preached Edwards on July 8, 1741, in his church at Enfield, Connecticut, "now awake and fly from the wrath to come. The wrath of Almighty God is now undoubtedly hanging over a great part of this congregation. Let everyone fly out of Sodom. Haste and escape for your lives, look not behind you, escape to the mountain, lest you be consumed."[50]

That Was Then, This Is Now

Here is another scripture, which I quoted partially above, that gives an even more detailed account of the kind of days we are facing now. Paul shares this to Timothy.

> *But the Spirit explicitly says that in later times some will fall away from the faith, paying attention to deceitful spirits and doctrines of demons"* (1 Timothy 4:1). *But realize this, that in the last days difficult times will come, for men will be lovers of self, lovers of money, boastful, arrogant, revilers, disobedient to parents, ungrateful, unholy, unloving, irreconcilable, malicious gossips, without self-control, brutal, haters of good, treacherous, reckless, conceited, lovers of pleasure rather than lovers of God; holding to a form of godliness, although they have denied its power* (2 Timothy 3:1-5).

Note especially the object of the "love" Timothy describes. Instead of people loving one another, they are lovers of themselves and of selfishness on a massive scale.

You might also take special note of Matthew 24. Study it carefully alongside Luke, chapters 16 and 21. In this powerful passage, Jesus answers two questions for His people, in the immediate context of the years 30 A.D. to 70 A.D. (a full generation, about 40 years) and shares the answers to two questions that were posed to Him after He prophesied that the Temple would be destroyed.

The two questions were: "when will this happen?" and "what will be the sign of Your coming, and of the consummation of the age?"

50 Jonathan Edwards, Sinners in the Hands of an Angry God, the final words of the sermon he preached. Quoted from The Works of Jonathan Edwards, Vol. 2, pg. 12. The Banner of Truth Trust, 1974.

I've already written in Chapter 1 my thoughts on the ideas represented by Jesus in this passage. You'll note that many of the verses refer to the actual destruction of the Temple in 70 A.D., and the actual days of horror in Jerusalem, when it was besieged by the Roman army and the Temple was utterly destroyed. There are also special verses towards the end of Matthew 24, and leading directly into Matthew 25, which I believe are relevant for us today about the coming consummation of the age.

I believe that, just because many of these verses have already been literally fulfilled in history, it does not mean that they have lost their potency for our day. They still contain possible hints as to the final days on earth, and a picture of what the very end of history may look like just before Christ appears in the sky and returns to wrap up all redemption and bring full wrath and judgment against sin and iniquity.

In prophetic writings, we call this the possibility of "double fulfillment," meaning the prophetic word had absolute relevance to the time in which it was proclaimed; and yet, it holds a second relevance for the time of the Last Battle at the very close of this Age.

...when will this happen, and what is the sign?

It is very possible, therefore, that the picture that Jesus paints for us of the intensity of the years leading up to 70 A.D., may in reality become a mirror for the very years leading up to the last day upon earth.

So when He says, *"This is going to be trouble on a scale beyond what the world has ever seen, or will see again. If these days of trouble were left to run their course, nobody would make it. But on account of God's chosen people, the trouble will be cut short"* (Matthew 24:22, The Message Bible).

Modern day scholars whom I greatly respect, will look at those words and claim they were absolutely fulfilled in 69-70 A.D. This was when the Roman general surrounded Jerusalem, created a long siege, and then finally entered a city of starving Jews and murdered whole families before finally desecrating the Temple and burning it to the ground. And they would be correct. I do believe these verses were fulfilled then.[51]

That being said, is there any reason we shouldn't also believe that be-

51 N.T. (Tom) Wright, Mark For Everyone, SPCK, London, England, 2001, page 182.

cause Jesus was speaking prophetically here (just as Isaiah or Jeremiah spoke in their own day), that these verses contain power to come to life again at the end of the age in which we live, and give us a mirror of what is coming?

Isaiah prophesied many verses that contained "double fulfillment." They were fulfilled already within 100 years after they were first prophesied, but contained the hope of the approaching Messiah and were fulfilled again at the first coming of Christ.

This time, the "Jerusalem" that will be surrounded and besieged will not necessarily be the literal Jerusalem in the nation of Israel (though it certainly will include it). It will be the "spiritual Jerusalem," or as I will point out, a symbol of the Church, representing the chosen people who are now found, not just in one region of the world like the Middle East, but in every tribe and tongue and people group.

We will suffer briefly and simultaneously by an all-out spiritual war of deception.

Jeremiah also prophesied of this coming time and called it, "the time of Jacob's trouble,"

> *"Alas! for that Day is great, there is none like it; and it is the time of Jacob's distress, but he will be saved from it"* (Jeremiah 30:7).

Some scholars hold this verse to be relating to Israel, but I believe this is what John the Revelator also saw as the Last Battle, and it relates the "one new man" of Ephesians 2 as the Believers of all Jews and Gentiles around the world. At the end of the time of Jacob's distress, Christ Himself will come as a result of the prayers of the afflicted, to cut short that time and usher in Eternity.

So here are some of the scriptural indicators of what we can absolutely expect in the days to come: widespread and deep demonic deception; many nominal Believers falling away and believing doctrines of demons; society crumbling and turning upon itself with hostility, coldness, the love of money and pleasure rather than loving the things of God; persecution and distress for even true Believers who hold fast to the LORD; violence and apostasy like in the days of Noah and Lot; and finally, the Holy Army under a worldwide attack, as the likes of which have never has been seen in the history of the world.

Imagine something like an international coalition of governments with Nazi-type powers, ruling briefly, and causing destruction and death against not just the Jewish people, but mainly focused in extreme hatred against those who are now called Christians.

"That's nothing new," you say, as this has been happening in little pockets of time throughout history. Even John the Revelator could confess the same, even as he wrote the Book of Revelation in pain from the chains around his feet on the prison island of Patmos. Yes, it's true. But according to all the Prophets, Jesus Himself, Paul, Peter, and John, at the culmination of history we can expect much, much worse.

Will You Be a "Noah," a "Lot," or a "Lot's Wife" in the Last Days?

The atmosphere of the first century is not too far off from the atmosphere of the twenty-first century in which we live. Jesus spoke words of challenge and encouragement to two separate groups of His followers in Luke's gospel. I believe that these words were addressed specifically to that generation who would experience His judgment in the destruction of the Temple and the razing of Jerusalem, which occurred in the First Century. I likewise hold that these words are applicable in every generation, and especially to our own generation.

1. **There are those who will be tempted to abandon their faith amidst persecution. To these He shared,** *"But before all these things, they will lay their hands on you and will persecute you, delivering you to the synagogues and prisons, bringing you before kings and governors for My name's sake.* **It will lead to an opportunity for your testimony.** *So make up your minds not to prepare beforehand to defend yourselves; for I will give you utterance and wisdom which none of your opponents will be able to resist or refute. But you will be betrayed*

even by parents and brothers and relatives and friends, and they will put some of you to death, and you will be hated by all because of My name. Yet not a hair of your head will perish. By your endurance you will gain your lives" (Luke 21:12-19).

2. **There are those who will be tempted to abandon their faith amidst the intense seduction of the culture around them.** To these He shared, *"Be on guard, that your hearts may not be weighted down with dissipation and drunkenness and the worries of life, and that day come on you suddenly like a trap; for it will come upon all those who dwell on the face of all the earth. But* **keep on the alert** *at all times,* **praying** *in order that you may have strength to escape all these things that are about to take place and to stand before the Son of Man"* (Luke 21:34-36).

Are you personally in one of those groups? Then it's time to wake up! Today, Jesus is calling His people to a spiritual alertness.

When you are trained in the military, you are taught to live in a "state of alertness" at all times. This means that your disposition is altered to be watchful in every place you go and with every person you meet. You are alert and ready should a crises occur and you be called upon to respond. Military or special ops/special forces or even off-duty police are trained in this way to never relax, but to be watchful in every place they go, looking for potential threats/weapons/recon tactics.

The LORD's army is filled with soldiers who need training in practical matters of daily faith, and who need the vision of the greater picture of the truth of the Last Days in order to prepare and become alert and effective in their warfare.

As in the days of Noah and Lot, the unrighteous did not suspect their own Judgment Day. We, as Believers, are different. We are to be trained and live lives of heightened awareness of the crumbling spiritual atmosphere of our own day, and be watchful for the Second Coming that will likewise bring Judgment Day.

We do not know the day or the hour, but we can know when the Bridegroom is close and He is about to give us the midnight shout!

Think of the acceleration of world wars and events of just in the past 50 years.

How close are we?

ARE YOU READY?

Are your children ready?

There is an urgent calling from the Holy Spirit to raise awareness of the scriptures that deal with the End Times, in order to teach and impart wisdom to the rising generation of warriors all around us.

I challenge each of you to lay aside your worldliness and "remember Lot's wife." I challenge you to become like the Noah of his day, or the Abraham of Lot's day. And in spite of an atmosphere of spiritual complacency in whatever nation you find yourself, go deeper in relationship with the Father, for the glory of the returning Son.

Going Deeper Still:

— In this parable of the Days of Noah and Lot, Jesus was teaching that the culture around you will remain asleep and spiritually unaware and indifferent, almost lethargic. They will not repent and seek the LORD and will not recognize any signs of His coming before Judgment Day.

— I listed eight elements of the spiritual atmosphere that pervaded the Days of Noah and Lot, and now pervades our own generation. Think about those eight points in relation to the breaking news of this very day. Can you see any or all of them happening now?

— I challenged you to learn about the two groups of Believers that Jesus taught would be existing in the days leading up to the destruction of Jerusalem, and that likewise existed later in the days of the writing of

Revelation. First, those undergoing real persecution for their faith. Second, those tempted by the seduction of the culture to "look back" to Sodom like Lot's wife did. Are you in either of those groups?

— The prophecies of Jesus in both Matthew 24 and Luke 21 contain the possibility of "double fulfillment," like many prophetic words. For example, look at Isaiah's prophecy. Can you think of any key passages in Isaiah that had a fulfillment in or just after his own day, and also contain a fulfillment in Jesus as Messiah and are in the process of fulfillment down to our own day? Hint: many of them are found in Isaiah chapters 40 to 66!

— Like Noah and Lot, you need to be alert to the atmosphere of the end. You need to be ready at all times for the Second Coming of Christ, who will bring eternal salvation to you, and Judgment Day to the culture around you. What do you observe in the culture or the news, this very day, that points to the Days of Noah, Lot, or Lot's wife?

— Memorize this verse and live it out.

Forgetting what lies behind, and reaching forward to what lies ahead, I press on toward the goal for the prize of the upward call of God in Christ Jesus (Philippians 3:13-14).

SECTION II

REVELATION REVOLUTION

REVELATION
REVELATION
REVELATION
REVELATION
REVELATION

REVELATION REVOLUTION

A Revolutionary Approach to the Study of the Book of Revelation & a Study of the Coming Last Battle: The Theology of the Last Days

"*Blessed is he who reads and those who hear the words of the prophecy, and heed the things which are written in it; for the time is near*" (Revelation 1:3).

"Can the Book of Revelation be understood? Yes, it can. Its message can be summarized in one sentence: God rules history and will bring it to its consummation in Christ. All Scripture, including Revelation, has practical value for exhortation, comfort, and training in righteousness. Paul underlines this point in 2 Timothy 4:1-5 by drawing a contrast between the solid teaching of the gospel and people's desire to have teachers who "say what their itching ears want to hear" (4:3). God gave us Revelation not to tickle our fancy, but to strengthen our hearts."[52]

Did you know that I, Carl, am also a documentary filmmaker and have created a film series based on this book? Go to this website to watch some stories from the next section. **https://revelationsbattleplans.com/**

52 Vern S. Poythress, The Returning King: A Guide to the Book of Revelation (P & R Publishing, Phillipsburg, New Jersey) 11.

TRUTH IS STRANGER THAN FICTION

A Practical Approach to Understanding Revelation

> "*The Revelation of Jesus Christ, which God gave Him to show to His bond-servants, the things which must shortly take place; and He sent and communicated (or, signified/symbolized) it by His angel to His bond-servant John*" (Revelation 1:1).
>
> "*Blessed is he who reads and those who hear the words of the prophecy, and heed the things which are written in it; for the time is near*" (Revelation 1:3).

Now that we have a Proposal on the table that we, as the Church around the world, are being called into the times of the Last Battle, and into the paths of most resistance in the days ahead, I know many of you reading this will be intrigued and are maybe asking the question: just where in Scripture do we find the details of the coming Last Battle?

Now that we have some indicators to watch for to know when the End is coming, let's answer the *how* question, both with hints in this chapter and in all of the remaining chapters of this book.

The answers and the unveiling of the Battle Plans to help you prepare for both the current world-wide spiritual war and the Last Battle are found in only one place in Scripture: the Book of Revelation.

Have you ever wanted to read the Book of Revelation and actually *understand and apply* more of its teaching? If you can answer, "yes!" to this question, then these chapters are for you.

And did you know: the Book of Revelation contains a very special blessing (not found in any other book of the Bible) for you *to read and heed (follow and obey) the exhortations written in it.* Wow! So let's read it with zeal and live it out! (See both Rev. 1:3 and 22:7, the parallel "bookends" with the blessing.)

Only the Book of Revelation reveals the Battle Plans of the LORD through the Ages to help prepare you for what is soon to come. And only the Book of Revelation also reveals the Enemy's own Battle Plans (so that you know how to counter him in spiritual warfare).

Personally, I have always enjoyed certain verses of Revelation that are scattered about its pages, though for years I simply couldn't grasp it as a whole. As you probably read in my Introduction to this book, part of my task in writing this is to help many people understand the Book of Revelation (which is why we are launching with this here; for those of you saying, "show me this in Scripture").

It is my prayer that the following chapters will be filled with something useful for you; a useful set of tools-of-interpretation perhaps, so you can read and study and seek to understand this "fringe book" and make it one of your "key books," especially in light of the need to build your faith as we all approach the Last of the Last Days together.

Please note that if you have been exposed to a different way of reading the Book (and believe me, there are many different ways that authors and Theologians approach it), you and I can still be friends and fellowship together. Like I shared in my Introduction, the study of Last Days theology is not a prerequisite to our stronger doctrines.

The doctrines that most people formulate for the potential fulfillment of biblical prophecy must be rooted in the love of Christ and allow for the flexibility for various interpretations.

I am very much still learning. And I hope to continue learning. To quote again from Meldenius, "In essentials, unity. In non-essentials, liberty. In all things, charity."

I would like to borrow the following "disclaimer" from Vern Poythress, professor at Westminster Theological Seminary in Philadelphia, who gave me permission to quote from his notes, and in several places I quote his material in this book. He shares, "Let me remind you that these course materials are very much works in progress. They are tentative in nature, and subject to repeated alteration and improvement. Not everything in them represents settled views on my part."[53]

I pray that even if you have a different background in theology than what I am about to represent, you will prayerfully continue to appreciate the truths taught in this Chapter, and see the value of a potentially fresh approach about Revelation.

What Will You Learn in This Chapter?

I will share first, in Revelation Theology 101, a brief explanation of the foundational way that I approach the study of all Scripture. That is, with appreciation for the original context of the text with the question in study, "what DID it mean?" Then, for the purpose of devotional inquiry, "what DOES it mean, to me, personally?"

Next, I will outline some foundational understandings for a fresh way to interpret Revelation, including a brief explanation of the four main schools of interpretation, and my own view of the one I feel is the most helpful.

Finally, I will share in-depth the "what, why, when, how, where, who" of the Book, so you can grasp the context of the text.

53 Vern Poythress quoted from his notes on course NT 311, on the Book of Revelation.

Revelation Theology 101

Our Bible school was very unique in that many of the subjects related to study of the Word of God included a balanced "scholarship" approach and a "prayerful" approach. We learned that there are essentially three simple steps in any study of the Word of God, and these especially apply to a book like Revelation. They are: Observation, Interpretation and Application.

Observation asks, "What does it say?"

Interpretation asks, "What does it mean?"

Application asks, "What does it mean for me, personally?"

This whole section of the book will help you along greatly to answer the first two questions, and the coming three Sections will help you with possible answers to the third.

Among my courses during my ministry training and later my Master of Divinity program, was a course we were required to take called, Hermeneutics 101.

Excuse me, Sir, Herm-a-WHAT?

Exactly.

For those readers who have never encountered this term, allow me to explain. It is the study of the Scriptures to wholly bring forth the meaning that was first intended for the audience that received it. It is called, in the German language, *"Sitz in Leben"* or, *"Settings in Life."* It seeks to understand more fully the "context" of the text, and primarily asks this question,

"What **DOES** it say, and what **DID** it mean, to them?"

Our Hermeneutics class was extra colorful, as it was taught by Dr. Helmar Heckel, a German theologian and Bible teacher who was himself a German immigrant. He taught the course with his thick German accent. We affectionately called him on campus, "Our German Shepherd," because he was also one of our pastors.

Dr. Heckel taught us the context of the passage, and instilled a passion to learn the Word of God in a whole new light.

What did the original audience look like?

What was the history of the author and his own background?

What are the *"Settings in Life"* we can learn from a careful study of a passage?

He also encouraged us to learn Scripture with a unique balance of both the theological *"Sitz in Leben"* and the practical "this text can relate to you today" approach.

In other words, when studying Scripture, take time to pray as you go, and ask the Holy Spirit in your heart, "What **DOES** this mean to me today?" (Learning to read it as devotional inquiry.) So, I have learned to appreciate both of these Bible study tactics, and will seek to share some of the strengths of both as we consider the Book of Revelation.

On the one hand, what did it mean to its original intended audience?

On the other hand, what does it mean for me, today?

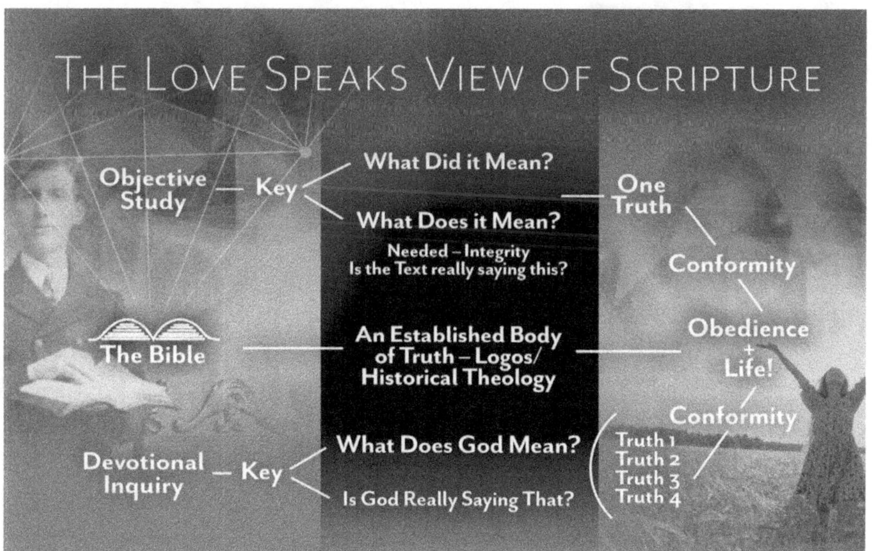

—Diagram above is from "Love Speaks: 21 Ways to Recognize God's Multi-Faceted Voice" available wherever books are sold, and at, https://www.LoveSpeaks.Today

The Kingdom of God: "Now" & "Not Yet"

Also during this time, we had a course that taught us the "inaugurated view" of the Kingdom of God. This was defined as, the Kingdom came (Jesus inaugurated it in His First Coming), the Kingdom is coming now progressively, and the Kingdom will come fully in the future (Jesus will consummate it at His Second Coming).

So, it began with Jesus Christ Himself and the announcement that the Kingdom had arrived. It has continued to arrive fresh in every subsequent generation since the death, burial, resurrection and ascension of Jesus, and it will not finally reach its fullness until the consummation of all things in heaven and earth at the Second Coming of Jesus.

This ongoing view of the Kingdom of God allows for mystery. We are placed in a struggle with Jesus against His enemies the moment we become followers of His, and there is mystery in the struggle.

To put it bluntly, the Kingdom is now! It has been inaugurated in the 1st century, and then freshly proclaimed by the faithful of every generation. And, at the same time, the Kingdom is not yet! That is, it is not yet here in its fullness.

To put it another way, there are two overlapping "Ages" taught in the New Testament by Paul, and also understood by the other Apostles. The first is, this "present, evil age" as Paul calls it in Galatians chapter 1, *and the LORD Jesus Christ, who gave Himself for our sins, that He might deliver us out of* ***this present evil age****"* (Galatians 1:3b,4a).

The other is the "ages to come," as he shares in Ephesians chapter 2, In order that in **the ages to come** *He might show the surpassing riches of His grace in kindness toward us in Christ Jesus* (Ephesians 2:7).

These two ages overlap and progressively move towards each other.

THE NEW TESTAMENT VIEW OF THE AGES

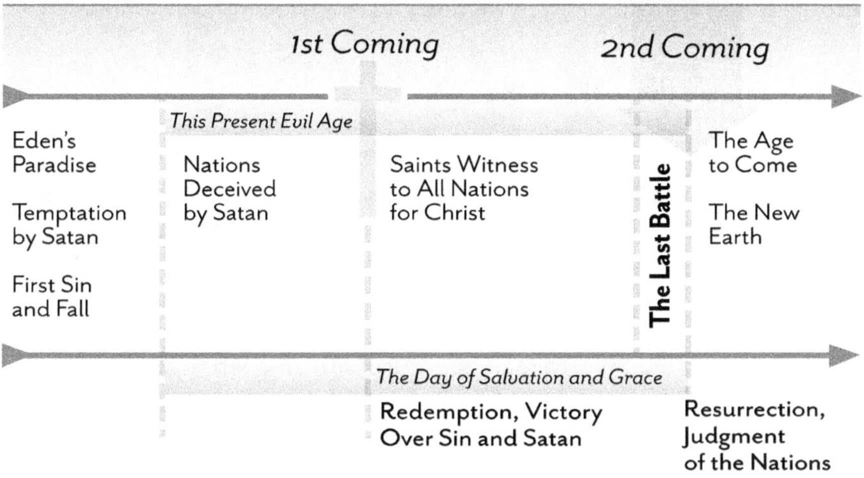

1st Coming 2nd Coming

This Present Evil Age

Eden's Paradise

Temptation by Satan

First Sin and Fall

Nations Deceived by Satan

Saints Witness to All Nations for Christ

The Last Battle

The Age to Come

The New Earth

The Day of Salvation and Grace

Redemption, Victory Over Sin and Satan

Resurrection, Judgment of the Nations

"Christ invaded this present evil age and began His defeat of all His enemies," shared my friend and ministry colleague Scott Kilbur one day. "And Scripture seems to indicate that as we follow Christ and pull the Kingdom into this present evil age, by faith, we encounter battle!"

To put it bluntly, you and I are in a daily battle of the ages. (For Paul's teaching on the daily battle and how we can fight with our own armor, see Ephesians 6:10-20).

The 1st century Believers lived in the same struggle as we are still undergoing today, except for the fact that we are now 20 centuries closer to the finality of the soon-and-coming King and Kingdom!

The Apostle John in his first epistle proclaimed, *The darkness is passing away, and the true light is already shining* (I John 2:8). In essence and in accordance with the proclamations of Jesus and the teachings of all the Apostles, the Kingdom of God has come; and yet, not in its fullness. The "true light" shines in the darkness, and as John's gospel, so beautifully depicts, *the darkness has not overcome it* (John 1:5b).

Since 1950, many leaders have arisen who have written books, proclaimed this truth, and sometime established whole movements of Christianity based upon this truth of the Kingdom. Among them are George Elden Ladd, John Wimber, C. Peter Wagner, and more recently Bill Johnson.[54]

To summarize these three thoughts:

1. I learned early in my walk with the LORD to appreciate the "settings in life" of all Scripture and the context of it, and to attempt proper interpretation by comparison of scriptures and appreciating them in original context, asking myself as I study, "What does it say and what did it mean—to them?"

2. I II learned, likewise, to read Scripture with an open heart in devotional inquiry, asking the Holy Spirit, who originally wrote it, to apply it to my life and understanding that I might obey better.

3. I lFinally, I learned that there is still a "mystery" in my faith as it develops; a mystery of on-going fulfillment of Scripture like Revelation as it relates in time. So, it "has been" fulfilled (it had relevance to the 1st century Christians, and Christians of every epoch of Salvation-History since). It is "being fulfilled" today, and it "will be fulfilled" in the Last of the Last Days, too.

So, just exactly what is my approach in study and interpretation of the visions of John in Revelation? Here is my brief, cumulative case for interpreting the Revelation of Jesus Christ in a way that, through the approach of looking for a series of repeated patterns, it:

1. honors the 1st Century audience to which it was originally written,

2. includes imagery that has spoken and encouraged audiences in every succeeding generation,

3. can offer insights into what is coming in the future, and

4. provides wisdom for our very own current generation.

Thus, we can know how to prepare today for what is surely coming tomorrow.

---

54 For more in-depth study, please see, "On Earth as it is in Heaven" by Bill Johnson.

The Four Main Approaches to Interpreting Revelation

Let me quote here again from Professor Vern Poythress. As a teacher, I really appreciate his straightforward way of explaining the four approaches.

"**Interpreters** disagree concerning the period of time and the manner in which the visions of Revelation are fulfilled.

Preterists think that fulfillment occurred at the fall of Jerusalem (if Revelation was written in A.D. 67 to 68) and/or the Fall of the Roman Empire (A.D. 476).

Futurists think that fulfillment will occur in a period of final crises just before the Second Coming.

Historicists think that Revelation offers a basically chronological outline of the course of church history from the 1st century (Revelation 6:1) until the Second Coming (Revelation 19:11).

Idealists think that the scenes of Revelation depict principles of spiritual war, not specific events. These principles are operative throughout the church age and may have repeated embodiments."[55]

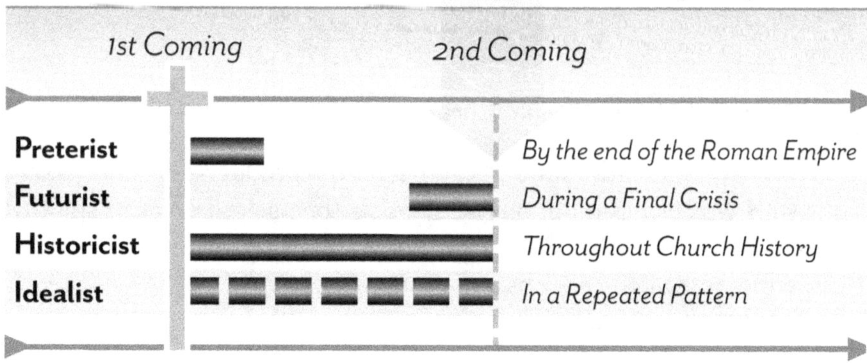

55 Ibid, pg.27.

As you'll learn throughout these pages, I personally hold strongest to the **IDEALIST** approach. This is the lens from which I read/view the Book of Revelation. At the same time, I can appreciate some positive aspects of the other three approaches.

To the Preterists who hold that there was a very real typological fulfillment in the 1st to 5th centuries (especially with God's hand of judgment in the Fall of Rome), I agree. The "what did it mean to the original audience" question would fit here.

To the Futurists, I would agree with them that there are very specific portions of Revelation that will happen in the days to come. I specifically believe that whole portions of Revelation are depicting various aspects of the incredible, earth-shattering and eternity-welcoming events surrounding the Second Coming of Christ as our victorious warrior!

To the Historicists, I would agree that throughout Salvation-History, many events and worldwide embodiments have taken place as John was shown in his visions, because the visions can have multiple embodiments in every generation of the Church Age. The Holy Spirit has been gradually speaking to many people across the ages and bringing hope and discernment of their own world events which the visions in Revelation also have pointed to as applicable.

I believe the visions in Revelation are:

SYMBOLIC in nature (and not to be interpreted literally). They are visions with symbols-in-motion. The symbols themselves point to spiritual truths and supernatural realities. Some of them may have multiple possible embodiments in all the epochs of Salvation-History.[56]

56 For a complete understanding of "Symbolic Speech" which is the LORD's "love language" of both visions and dreams, read Chapter 12 in my book, watch Lesson 12 in the MASTERCLASS or watch Episode 12 of corresponding documentary film Series, "LOVE SPEAKS" available at www.lovespeaks.today

BROAD/HISTORICAL in scope (and not narrow/already fulfilled in history). They are to be studied with a background knowledge of some Old Testament apocalyptic writings and imagery. Think in terms of a broad, spiritual war that Believers have faced since Christ's First Coming and the ongoing war we face all the way through His Second Coming. Think in terms of many generations with their own unique fulfillments, and with certain passages, unique fulfillments still on the horizon for the Last of the Last Days.

PRACTICAL (not theoretical). Can you seek to understand and apply the symbols and the truth they represent and interpret them in light of your daily walk with God now? Yes! As you read and study, be always in prayer and asking the Holy Spirit, "What does this mean to me, personally?"

"We can sum up these insights in a single combined picture," writes Vern Poythress. "The major symbols of Revelation represent a repeated pattern. This pattern has a realization in the 1st century situation of the seven churches. It also has an embodiment in the final crises. And it has an embodiment now. We pay special attention to the embodiment now, because we must apply the lessons of Revelation to where we are."[57]

"The symbols have a parabolic function and are intended to encourage and exhort the audience," writes G.K. Beale. "They portray a transcendent new creation that has penetrated the present old world through the death and resurrection of Christ and the sending of the Spirit at Pentecost.

"John's vision communicates values that run counter to the values of the old world and provide a structure of meaning that grounds the lives of Christians in the new world. He spells out the eternal significance and consequences of Christ's life, death, and resurrection and of the readers' present choices and behavior.

"John thus seeks to motivate the readers not to compromise with the world but to align their thoughts and behavior with the God-centered standards of the new creation. They are to see their own situation in this world in the light of the new world, which is now their true home."[58]

57 Returning King, by Vern Poythress, ISBN 978-0-87552-462-7, published by P&R Publishing Co, P.O. Box 817, Phillipsburg, N.J., 08865, page 37. www.prpbooks.com.

58 The Book of Revelation by G.K. Beale, William B. Eerdmans Publishing Company, 1999. Pg. 69.

The Context of Revelation: To quote Kipling,

"I KEEP six honest serving-men
(They taught me all I knew);
Their names are **What** and **Why** and **When**
And **How** and **Where** and **Who**." – Rudyard Kipling

So, first we will seek to employ these six honest serving-men and gain a bit of the background information on the context of the Book, and of its author, purpose, style, and original intended audience.

The What: It is called the Revelation of Jesus Christ. Some people isolate the word "revelation," which can be translated "apocalypse," which means simply, "unveiling." It is applied to these writings because they contain alleged revelation of the secret purposes of God, the end of the world, and the establishment of God's kingdom on earth. [59] That which had been hidden is now freely revealed and can be understood.

The challenge of course to a modern audience in a post-modern culture like the West, is that this type of literature has disappeared from the earth and it stands as unique!

Most apocalyptic literature occurred during the period leading up to the first Advent of Christ, and for the Christian, ended with the Revelation being placed in the canon of the New Testament.

Here are a few characteristics of the apocalyptic literature of the 1st century (which Revelation likewise carries):

1. The secrets of the universe and of the last days are revealed to the author or chief character of the book in a series of visions, often through angelic mediation.

59 Adapted from a teaching on a website called, https://www.biblicaltraining.org/library/apocalyptic-literature

2. Great use is made of symbols and symmetrical patterns. Numbers play an important part in the unfolding of world history. The time periods themselves are often not taken literally but symbolicly.

3. The genre contains both a historical relevance (spanning many years and including many historical fulfillments), and a focus on the end of the age. This is frequently preceded by the most dreadful persecution of the faithful, and a period of conflict between the forces of good and evil.[60]

Let me also encourage you. As you learn how to read Revelation and interpret the repeated embodiments of the symbols in the visions, you will be able to apply the question, "What does this mean?" by opening the daily newspaper or prayerfully discerning on the evening news the actual spiritual conflicts that fill the news every day. The relevance of these scriptures to our current day and generation will bless you and open your spiritual eyes in new ways.

The Why: As to the "why," John was writing to an audience of at least two groups of Christians within the Imperial Roman Empire.

1. To those Christians undergoing persecution, or about to undergo persecution for their faith, Revelation encourages, *"And they overcame him (Satan) because of the blood of the Lamb and because of the word of His (Christ's) testimony, and they did not love their life even to death." and, Here is the perseverance and the faith of the saints* (Revelation 12:11 & 13:10b).

2. To those Christians within the Church who were being tempted to compromise by the seduction of the culture (the Imperial Greco-Roman culture of the day) around them, Revelation cries, *"Come out of her, My people!" and, "Behold, I am coming like a thief. Blessed is the one who stays awake and keeps his garments, lest he walk about naked and men see his shame"* (Revelation 18:4 & 16:15).

"One thing that can probably be agreed upon by the majority of commentators," writes G. K. Beale, "is that a contributing reason for John's

60 Ibid., adapted from the same website page called, 'biblcialtraining.org'.

motive in writing is the perceived discrepancy in the Christian audience between, on the one hand, belief that the Kingdom had been inaugurated, that God was sovereign over history, and that Christ would soon return to conclude history.

"And on the other hand, the reality that forces of evil continued to exist, to dominate culture and even flourish, while oppressing Believers to varying degrees. How did the truths of the gospel relate practically to the difficult reality of their lives?

"Therefore, the focus of the Book of Revelation is exhortation to the church community to witness to Christ in the midst of a compromising, idolatrous church and world."[61]

The truths of Revelation belong to us today.

Let me thus pose the question: was the situation of the seven churches in Asia Minor really any different than the situation of the Church Universal of all the ages? If you can answer "no" to that question, I believe you would be correct. We are connected, in the Spirit, to every single one of those Christians and their respective lives, and we can relate in the 21st century to the challenge of maintaining scriptural "positional" truth (who we are in Christ as a result of His sacrificial life, death, resurrection and ascension) in the midst of a culture with so much evil and potential for idolatry and compromise.

The **blessings** of Revelation belong to us today.

The **warnings** of Revelation belong to us today.

The **truths** of Revelation, relevant to that original audience and the persecutions they endured, maintain their relevance to us today, no matter what country you are reading this book from.

Allow me to relate some of the visions of John to you in very practical ways from this point forward in the next chapters, while also challenging you to continue to boldly witness for Christ in the midst of the compromising and idolatrous church and culture around you.

61 Ibid, pgs. 28, 33.

The When: As to the date of authorship, there are convincing arguments on both sides of 70 A.D., when Jerusalem and the Temple were destroyed by the Roman army. The Book of Acts records that persecutions had arisen far and wide, including with the Emperor Nero, who killed many Believers in Rome.

I was personally taught that Revelation was probably given to John during the persecutions of the Emperor Domitian, so that would put the date range more around 90 to 96 A.D. That is the date range which I personally favor.[62]

What is vitally important to me is that Revelation made it into the canon of New Testament scripture. It was the final book to make it, and was quoted by the early church fathers extensively and canonized in the 5th century. It spoke to all the early Christians for hundreds of years, and it speaks to us today. In summary, a canonical work has to contain adaptable wisdom on how to live at any time.

However, three other factors come into play. The book must

1. come from the Apostolic circle in the 1st century;

2. contain only orthodox teachings; and

3. show inspiration.[63]

So for me, the actual date of the visions is not as important as these factors. I stand behind the authenticity of Revelation as relevant for me today!

The How: I was in the Spirit on the LORD's day, (Revelation 1:10). I love that! John was in worship and an intimate posture of communication and love before the LORD Himself on the LORD's day as the visions came! He shares that it is the Revelation of Jesus Christ, which God (the Father)

62 "As to its authenticity; Polycarp was a disciple of John and attested to its veracity; both Irenaeus and Hippolytus have written and exegeted it. Justin Martyr, a disciple of Polycarp quotes it and Jerome states it authorship and included it in the Vulgate. Modern criticism in its desire to affirm it's date before 70AD has attempted to challenge it's canonicity, but further evidence has established its composition between 92-95AD." Quoted from Wikipedia and http://hermeneutics.stackexchange.com/questions/13997

63 Ibid., author Frank Luke (from same website).

"Grace to you and peace, from Him

who is

and was,

and who is

TO COME!"

(Revelation 1:4)

gave His Son to show His bondservants; and He sent and communicated it by His angel to His bondservant John" (Revelation 1:1).

So "how" did it come? From the heart of our Heavenly Father, through the Son and the Spirit, via an actual angel from the eternal realms!

The Revelation of Jesus Christ, which God (the Father) gave Him to show to His bond-servants the things which must shortly take place; and He sent and communicated it by His angel to His bond-servant John (Revelation 1:1).

And here's the best part of the "how." It came as a series of visions! It was *communicated*, or another meaning is, *signified* or *symbolized* in the process.

John has a series of visions containing symbols which, when interpreted, contain truth and spiritual realities.

"A number of authors of both popular and scholarly commentaries contend that one should interpret literally except where one is forced to interpret symbolically by clear indications of context. But Revelation 1:1 indicates that *this rule should be turned on its head;* we are told in the book's introduction that the majority of the material in it is revelatory symbolism. Hence, the predominant manner by which to approach the material will be according to a nonliteral interpretative method."[64]

"Some people today come to Revelation with the recipe, 'Interpret everything literally, if possible' writes Poythress. "That recipe misunderstands what kind of book Revelation is. People living in John's own time understood this matter instinctively, because they recognized that John was writing in an "apocalyptic" manner, *a manner already as familiar to them as a political cartoon is to us today.* It would not have seemed as strange then as it does now. The uniqueness of Revelation arises from one central point: it is a Christ-centered vision. Christ is the way to God; He is the mediator of God's plan for history."[65]

And let's look closer at verse 2 of Revelation 1. It says, *"who bore witness to the word of God and to the testimony of Jesus Christ, EVEN TO ALL THAT HE SAW"* (Revelation 1:2).

---

64 Ibid, Beale, pg. 52.
65 Ibid, Poythress, pg. 47.

"This opening statement indicates the book's genre," writes Dennis E. Johnson, "and is therefore a guide to the reading strategy we must use if we are to see its message. The visible, visionary mode of the message is reemphasized in the prophetic commission given to John by the voice of the One like a son of man: *"Write in a book what you SEE, and send it to the seven churches"* (Revelation 1:11). Revelation is a book of symbols in motion. What John has seen in prophetic vision is the true character of events, individuals, forces and trends, the appearance of which is quite different on the physical, sociocultural, observable plane. One of the key themes of the book is things are not what they seem.

"For example, what appear to the naked eye, on the plane of human history, to be weak, helpless, hunted, poor, defeated congregations of Jesus' faithful servants *prove to be the true overcomers who participate in the triumph of the Lion who conquered as a slain Lamb."*[66]

Finally on this point, here is my own definition of symbolic speech, which is the Apocalyptic way of communicating through visions. This is from chapter 12 of my book, "Love Speaks: 21 Ways to Recognize God's Multi-Faceted Voice."

> *"The most indirect and symbolic way of the Holy Spirit speaking. In this particular form, He utilizes common, everyday objects or visual images to teach us lessons. These objects or visual images need interpretation and point to deeper, spiritual realities. The "abstract" becomes "clear and real" as He brings the interpretation."* [67]

The Where: Escape From Alcatraz!

John was himself, a convict when he wrote it. His sentence in the courts of law? Probably bowing his knee to a LORD other than Caesar. He was banished to an island prison cell. This was not a Hawaiian all-inclusive resort, with a pool and a wet bar. This was Alcatraz, and he was an enemy

66 Dennis E. Johnson, Triumph of the Lamb, P & R Publishing, 2001, pgs. 8-9.

67 Carl Wesley Anderson, Love Speaks: 21 Ways to Recognize God's Multi-Faceted Voice, Born to Blaze Ministries Publishing, updated Edition 2024, pg. 167. Available worldwide at https://www.lovespeaks.today

of the State, and he was writing to other enemies of the State who were needing a little encouragement (to say the least).

And so, for the time it took Jesus to communicate through an angel the various visions in Revelation, John was able to "escape from Alcatraz" and visit the Heavenly realms, and experience the presence of the Holy Spirit in freedom and liberty.

Also for "the where," you'll want to know that the original audience, the seven churches, were scattered about an area of Asia Minor (present-day Turkey). I learned recently from a friend of mine, Michael, (who is also a pastor and has taught on the Book of Revelation) that the seven churches were in a royal mail route and popular trading route in Roman times.

For the purposes of this book, I consider these churches as representative of the Church Universal, and so it is helpful to pay close attention to the details that Jesus gives us in their hopes and dreams, struggles and spiritual warfare, rebukes and encouragements. They can apply to any culture and both individual lives and corporate lives of Christians today.

The Who: Revelation is written by a follower of Jesus Christ who identifies himself only as, "John." Most historians attribute John to be the well-known Apostle John. We simply do not know for certain whether it was John the Beloved Disciple or an early follower of Jesus.

When I call him "John the Revelator" in this book, I am fine with an interpretation of either the Apostle John or an early disciple named John. He is certainly, John of Patmos.

What we do know is that he was well-versed in both the ancient Old Testament revelatory visions of the time following the exile: Daniel, Ezekiel, and Zechariah. These three books, along with imagery borrowed from the Exodus of Moses' day and the giving of the law at Mt. Sinai, are the foundation of many of the passages of Revelation. For example, material from most of Ezekiel's chapters is quoted or alluded to in all but one chapter in Revelation.[68]

68 Spiros Zodhiates, The Hebrew-Greek Key Study Bible, pg. 1082. Chattanooga, Tennessee, AMG Publishers, 1984.

AND FINALLY...From the Heart of the Father

Have you ever considered the Source of Revelation as coming from the Father Himself? This incredible insight is worth the price of admission, LOL. Here is how the Book opens.

> *"Grace to you and peace, from Him who is and who was and who is to come (that's the Father); and from the seven Spirits who are before the His throne (that's the Holy Spirit); and from Jesus Christ, the faithful witness, the firstborn of the dead, and the ruler of the kings of the earth (that's the Son, Jesus)" (Revelation 1:4-5).*

GRACE and PEACE are flowing to you personally, right now, directly from the Father, called here amazingly, *"Him who is and who was and who is to come."* In verse 8, Jesus is referred to by this same name. But we must remember the words of Jesus in John's gospel to grasp the meaning here. *"I and My Father are One"* (John 10:30). So, verses 4 and 5 give us the origin of Revelation as coming from the fullness of the Trinity, but STARTING WITH the Father!

Reread that passage (Revelation 1:4-5) in your own Bible this week in your times of devotional inquiry, and let those words speak directly to you. You can receive the Father's grace and peace flowing personally to you, every day!

And you are a son or a daughter of the Father, and as such, remember your identity in His eternal family. It will help you to endure the hardships that are surely to come your way. You can endure trials exactly because you know the character and heart of your Heavenly Father who saw ahead the trials you would be faced with, and knew you would endure to the end.

If you enjoyed this chapter, you'll love the next one. We'll continue to learn some of the most amazing facets of the unique structure, poetic style, and parallel nature of the visions that John sees.

Going Deeper Still

A balanced study of Scripture includes the tools of:

1. Observation,

2. Interpretation, and

3. Application.

Seek to find a balance between objective hermeneutics, and devotional inquiry. Objective hermeneutics studies carefully the context of the text and asks, "What does this say/what did this mean?" Devotional inquiry approaches the text with prayer and meditation and asks, "What does this mean to me?"

The broadest way to read Revelation is to take the inaugurated view of the Kingdom of God. In other words, the Kingdom is "Now" and "Not Yet" here in its fullness, and we are living in a clash of worlds which causes spiritual conflict. The 1st century Believers lived in the same struggle, except for the fact that we are now 20 centuries closer to the finality of the soon-and-coming King and Kingdom!

I believe this book to be SYMBOLIC in nature (and not literal), BROAD/HISTORICAL in scope (and not narrow/already fulfilled in history), and PRACTICAL (not theoretical). What do those words mean to you?

Utilizing these tools, please read Revelation 5:5-6, and attempt a fresh interpretation. Who is the "Lion" of verse 5 and the "Lamb" of verse 6, based on Old Testament background scriptures and other New Testament scriptures? What did that mean to the original audience? How should you respond today to this interpretation?

Remember the same two groups exist today that Revelation was originally written to: Christians undergoing persecution for their faith and tempted to give up, and Christians being tempted to compromise by the seductive culture around them. What are some ways you can think of to combat these temptations?

Have you ever had a vision or a dream that showed you something in the Holy Spirit? Were you able to pray over the symbolism and receive a possible interpretation? If so, how does that encourage you today?

Vantage Point

The Seven Parallel Visionary Cycles of Revelation

"*Blessed is he who reads and those who hear the words of the prophecy, and heed the things which are written in it;* **for the time is near"** (Revelation 1:3).

And he said to me, "Do not seal up the words of the prophecy of this book, **for the time is near"** (Revelation 22:10).

The following chapter is for deeper study of the Book of Revelation, and is helpful for the remainder of this book, as I will provide tools to help you mine the depths of some of the visions and how to interpret them in Revelation. I will cover three main areas:

1. **The Poetic Style and Idea of Parallel Visions.** By understanding Revelation more as a poem with parallel passages that mirror one another, you can search and find clues to lead you to approximate places where the Seven Visionary Cycles begin and end.

2. **Vantage Point: The Big Picture.** Revelation is a series of (at least) seven primary visions, or cycles. These cycles repeat throughout the entire scope of the Church Age and run parallel to one another. Each one contains beautiful, and sometimes startling symbolic images. Many of these visions thus carry with them multiple embodiments,

depending on how and when in Salvation-History you are seeking their potential applications to actual events.

3. **A Brief Outline of All Seven Visionary Cycles with Chapters from Revelation.** As a tool for deeper devotional study, I finish this chapter with a broad outline and suggested chapters within the Book of Revelation for where the Seven Visionary Cycles begin and end. This simply gives interpretations for some of the main points in the visions, and provides you with the themes in each cycle so you can study more closely on your own and build your own faith stronger as you read this wonderful Book of Revelation.

   Note: As you personally study Revelation, you may come to different conclusions about the structure of the content. You will also find that commentators often have differences of opinions as to the number of visions/cycles, and as to their starting and stopping points. I simply ask that you consider prayerfully my suggested vantage points and the wonderful truths they each contain to build faith, hope and love.

The Structure of the Book: Poetic & Synonymous Parallelism

Let's begin now to journey together and learn what I consider are perhaps the most exciting elements of the structure of Revelation; the idea of its poetic style, which is expressed in progressive visions that run parallel to one another.

"The Bible ends with a flourish: vision and song, doom and deliverance, terror and triumph. The rush of color and sound, image and energy, leaves us reeling," writes Eugene H. Peterson, "John's Revelation is not easy reading. Besides being a pastor, John is a poet, fond of metaphor and symbol, image and allusion, passionate in his desire to bring us into the presence of Jesus believing and adoring. But the demands He makes on our intelligence and imagination are well rewarded, for in keeping with John, our worship of God will almost certainly deepen in urgency and joy."[69]

69 Eugene H. Peterson, The Message Bible Translation (already footnoted), 514.

As you make a prayerful decision to really dig in and understand Revelation, you will find it is a challenging task. The writer of Revelation was very familiar with the ancient Hebraic form of writing known widely then as **Poetic Parallelism.**

For example, King David wrote many of the Psalms in various poetic and lyrical forms, utilizing this technique of parallelism. Many chapters of the prophetic books of Isaiah, Joel, Ezekiel & Daniel, and many of the other prophets wrote their books with poetic parallel form, lyrical and symbolic language. John the Revelator also followed this form when he composed his visions together into a single masterpiece.

Thus, to really understand the structure of the Book of Revelation, you'll need to take off your western, Greek methodical "Sherlock Holmes" hat and don a new cap, or maybe get rid of that cap altogether and put a Hebrew prayer shawl over your head!

"In the entire Book of Revelation John records Seven Visionary Cycles dealing with the entire inter-advent period and closes out, in chapters 21 and 22, with the eternal state."[70]

I define the inter-advent period as the time between Christ's First Coming and His Second Coming.

By the way, you will note as you study Revelation, the number 7 is very significant!

"The number 7," writes Troy Brewer, "is the number that marks where God is doing something by His Spirit apart from any other source. It is the number that marks His rest and where He rules over all things created. Seven is perfection of Spirit."[71]

Have you ever learned to read and write Hebrew? If so, you'll understand a little better that approaching Revelation requires a little work. If not, you might be surprised to find out that Hebrew is read and understood from right-to-left, bottom-to-top, and back-to-front!

---

70 Cox, op. cit., pg.4.
71 Troy A. Brewer, Numbers That Preach, Aventine Press, ©2017, page 86.

It is a challenging task to scale the cliffs of the Seven Cycles in Revelation, as we'll soon see. They're like seven mountain peaks overlooking a valley, but the view from the top of each mountain-peak is both reachable and majestic.

So, before we go forward to Revelation, we must first journey back a few thousand years. Many of the Prophets are written in one of 3 types of Hebrew Poetic Parallelism, with one of the most common being **Synonymous Parallelism**, where the second line of the scripture repeats or reinforces the meaning of the first.

Definition of **Synonymous Parallelism:** the second line repeats or reinforces the first line.

Example: Joel 2:1

Blow a trumpet in Zion,
and sound an alarm on My holy mountain!

There's even a famous song that's been sung in many church services the past 30 years or so with these verses as the verses of the song.

Here's how it breaks down in synonymous parallel form.

Synonymous Parallel Form		
Blow	a trumpet	in Zion
Sound	an alarm	on My holy mountain

Do you see how the second line is parallel to the first? It is a wonderful technique that sets the ancient visionary writings in a whole new light, right? In this case, the prophet prophesies with the same thought, but shared in parallel form, and thus two different pictures are presented which paint the whole picture better.

Example: Isaiah 53:5.

But He was pierced through for our transgressions, He was crushed for our iniquities.

Synonymous Parallel Form		
He	was pierced	for our transgressions
He	was crushed	for our iniquities

Example: Isaiah 55:12.

"For you shall go out with joy, and be led forth with peace; the mountains and the hills will break forth into shouts of joy before you, and all the trees of the field will clap their hands."

Synonymous Parallel Form		
Go out with joy	Mountains & hills	Shouts of joy
Be led forth with peace	Trees of the field	Clap their hands

Do trees literally clap their hands, or do you suppose you might want to take this a bit more symbolically? Can you really interpret that literally? Only if you are J.R.R. Tolkien, creating a most wonderful character of a talking tree in the famous *Lord of the Rings* series, the now famous "Treebeard."

If you ever meet Treebeard in person and see him clap his hands, please write to me and I'll change my views immediately on the ancient Hebraic poetic writing we are looking at here!

In Revelation, whole sections of chapters run in **Poetic & Synonymous Parallelism**, and the visions are saying the same thing (conveying the same spiritual realities) but *in their own unique ways.*

For example, here's the **Poetic & Synonymous Parallelism** of the Church (symbolic for the faithful people of God, encompassing both the Old and New Testaments).

Poetic & Synonymous Parallelism	
"And a great sign appeared in heaven; a woman clothed with the sun, and the moon under her feet, and on her head a crown of twelve stars." (Rev.12:1, from Cycle of chapters 12, 13 & 14)	*"Come here, I will show you the Bride, the wife of the Lamb." And he showed me the Holy City, Jerusalem, coming down out of Heaven from God, having the glory of God,"* (Rev.21:9-11, from Cycle of chapters 20, 21 & 22)

"Revelation can be interpreted as a series of repeated and parallel symbolic pictures of the church's struggle from John's day until the Second Coming, the last judgment, and the eternal state. Thus Revelation offers multiple images that provide **different perspectives on the same great warfare**, sometimes in terms of its behind-the-scenes heavenly sources and at other times of their visible, earthly outworking in the experience of churches, countries, and cultures."[72]

Finally, let's see how John creatively calls our LORD and Master, Jesus Christ, various names. Each one describes Him using a unique facet of His character, and each one using a different and creative word picture. He is describing in poetic parallelism the One and Only, **JESUS**. There are, in fact, 25 unique names for Christ in Revelation! Here are just seven of the 25. Notice how each one gives us another unique and poetic expression of the beauty of King Jesus.

72 Triumph of the Lamb by Dennis E Johnson, ISBN 978-0-87552-200-5, published by P&R Publishing Co., P O Box 817, Phillipsburg, N.J., 08865, pg. 360. www.prpbooks.com

1. **The Lamb:** Mentioned about 30 times, the Son of God slain for us-the perfect, unblemished sacrifice = The Redeemer.
2. **The Alpha & Omega:** All things are from Him and for Him, the beginning and the end, the starter and finisher.
3. **The Son of God:** Christ stands as the only mediator between God & man.
4. **The Faithful Witness:** The witness to all the counsels of God from eternity. He can also be known as the Faithful Martyr.
5. **He Who holds the Keys of David:** He has the key of government and authority in and over the Church. Only He can open and shut special doors in the spiritual realms.
6. **Faithful & True:** He will never forsake us. With justice He judges.
7. **The Bright Morningstar:** The morning light of all true prophecy, to assure us of the light of the perfect Day soon approaching!

Vantage Point

Revelation is a series of at least Seven Primary Cycles. These cycles repeat each other in the entire scope of the Church Age and run parallel to one another. I believe that each of them runs FROM the approximate time of the cross/resurrection/ascension of Jesus TO His Second Coming at the end of the Age, OR they zoom in on the events of the Second Coming at times and give us new details.

Note: These cycles are also **PROGRESSIVE PARALLELISM**, which means that they begin to provide progressively more details and information about the Second Coming. They build upon each other until we reach the climax of all recorded history on the final day of our own history to experience the *Parousia*. (*Parousia* is a Greek word meaning, "coming" or "royal presence"; it's another word for the Second Coming.)

Some years ago, on the day that I was up in my study preparing to write this section of chapters, I was meditating on the ancient structure of the

Book of Revelation and praying about how to take the structure and unpack it to a modern audience.

As I was praying about it, my family went to town to rent some movies from the store. Yes, in the old days they had Video Stores and you could rent these things they called, DVDs. (LOL.)

I sat in front of a blank sheet of paper, knowing that there are seven visionary cycles in the Revelation. They are like seven vantage points of seven mountain peaks, each one looking over the same story again and again (in a vast valley below), but from unique perspectives.

I wrote down on this paper a diagram with seven timelines, running parallel and one on top of each other. I wrote to myself this note:

"What I need is an example of a movie that has seven vantage points of the same story that I can use to illustrate how Revelation is constructed, and make it fairly simple for simple people like me to understand."

I went to take a nap to try and rest my mind, as I was coming up blank. I awoke from my nap and came back into my study and sat down, looking at my blank paper. Just then my door opened, and my wonderful 13 year-old son Ethan (he is much older now, but he was 13 when I first wrote this manuscript) enthusiastically handed me this rental DVD (rated PG-13), and asked my permission to watch it.

In my hand was a film produced in 2008 called, "Vantage Point." The front cover shows the actors, Matthew Fox, Dennis Quaid, Forest Whitaker, Sigourney Weaver and William Hurt in this octagon shape with photos. The bottom reads, "8 Strangers. 8 Points of View. 1 Truth." Ethan had hit a goldmine!

That night we all hunkered down for the movie.

Scene 1. Fade in from black. We see a clock with the numbers progressing, 11:57...11:58...11:59...Noon.

As the clock strikes Noon the story begins. It opens in Spain with the public appearance of the President of the United States (played by William Hurt) who is making a public speech. The whole opening takes place from the vantage point of the Media room, where Sigourney Weaver is leading the CNN-type broadcast. As the president takes the platform to speak, two shots ring out from a sniper rifle and strike him down. There is mass mayhem in the public square where the main action is taking place. Suddenly a bomb explodes.

Then, in front of your eyes, the movie-hits-the-**rewind**-button. You see playing in reverse, in fast motion, scenes from that scene until the screen goes black.

Then we see a clock with the same number sequence, 11:57...11:58...11:59... Noon. The clock strikes Noon, and now the fade-in is of a different character and the film follows his unique vantage point.

What makes this intriguing, is that the story unfolds exactly as it did before, but now with completely new information and different characters. The timeline of the story is progressive; that is, it takes us a little further past the bomb exploding and gives us a bit more in the storyline, and then, **REWIND** again and it starts all over. It does this a full 8 cycles, and at the end of the 8th vantage point comes the end of the movie.

That, in a nutshell, is the Book of Revelation!

While there are seven, not eight, visionary cycles in Revelation, the principal of this movie stands true.

First of all (and I will cover this more in detail in the ensuing chapters of the book) Revelation is filled with visionary cycles that contain all sorts of symbolic images, characters, numbers and time periods. These are to be understood as symbolic in nature, and symbols-in-motion.

Reading Revelation is like watching an epic film...

Reading Revelation is kind of like watching an epic film unfold before your eyes. And the key to understanding it is simply to know where to hit the **REWIND** button. As it plays the story forward again and again, each time it gives us fresh insights into the war of the worlds of spiritual light and spiritual darkness, that was happening and has been happening the past 2,000 or so years. It is still happening now, and will continue until the Second Coming.

It's a bit like watching the LORD OF THE RINGS TRILOGY but with this idea: we begin following Frodo's quest to bring the ring to Mordor. The scene opens and we see him begin his journey, and it ends just before he reaches the volcanic Mount Doom. We only are following Frodo and Sam first.

Then, **REWIND**, and now we begin at the start of the journey, but we are travelling with Gandalf, Aragorn, Gimli and Legolas. We watch with excitement all the battles they have to fight and the story takes us to the moment of Frodo casting the ring into Mount Doom.

Then, **REWIND**, and we are back again at the start of the journey, and we follow Merry and Pippin, and all of their eating and drinking and smoking exploits, and their long, drawn-out time with Treebeard. We then see the ultimate destruction of the ring and the reuniting with their companions back at the Shire.

That is how the Book of Revelation is structured! There is no cross-cutting, so-to-speak, or editing the scenes to follow the story all the way through. You just need to know where to hit **REWIND**.

"Suppose you are watching a documentary movie of some significant event in history," wrote R. Loren Sandford, "and imagine that four different reporters filmed it from the perspectives of four eyewitnesses to the event.

"Suppose, for instance, that the subject is the Civil War in the United States, and specifically the turning point Battle of Gettysburg in Pennsylvania, July 1-3, 1863. One eyewitness might be a private in the infantry. Another might be one of the generals, while a third could be a doctor in the medical tent. A fourth could be a reporter for a newspaper surveying the battlefield from a safe vantage point.

"Each of these would give an account of the same battle, each account accurate and true, but each would significantly differ from the others, depending on the perspective from which each person experienced and observed it. Reports on the depth and severity of events witnessed would vary from person to person.

"Told as a documentary film, the story would rewind to the beginning of the timeline after each sequence. The account would be presented again, beginning to end, but from a different angle, based on the vantage point and experience of the subject of that segment.

"The same is true of the end-time accounts given in the Revelation to John. The core of it presents the same sequence of events, reported from different perspectives, each leading up to the return of Jesus. Each successive perspective presents it perhaps more deeply than the one before but remains, nevertheless, the same story with the same ending. Seven is the number for completion, so each sequence presents the completion of the end-time sequence of events, the LORD's return, and the end of the age."[73]

So, the principle here that Loren Sandford taught in his book is identical to the idea of Poetic Parallelism. What you'll find as you begin to study for yourself and pray over the Book of Revelation, is a stunning treasure trove of imagery that teaches you the meaning of many symbols. You can apply the same meaning in looking at the current and future events of the world and the Church to build your faith and hope in the Second Coming.

Reading Revelation is a bit like trying to describe the battle of the ages, light vs. darkness, happening far below us in a valley as we assume a high-up vantage point on top of a kind of circular mountain range, described poetically as Mount Zion, which the ancient prophets called "the people of God."

---

73 R. Loren Sandford, A Vision of Hope for the End Times: Why I Want To Be Left Behind, Destiny Image, Destiny Image Publishers, 2018, pgs. 95-96. I was a personal friend of Loren and interviewed him during COVID for my Documentary TV Series. Tragically he died toward the end of COVID. I highly recommend his book.

The fullness of Mount Zion, at least from Revelation's perspective, is a huge circular mountain with seven distinct peaks, and in the very center of the range, completely enclosed, is this massive valley with a river running through the center. A battle being fought in stages, with advances and retreats through the centuries, right in the center of all these mountain peaks.

When you are on one peak, in a lookout tower, you get to watch the battle from that unique perspective. Then John the Revelator translates you instantly to a whole different peak and you are suddenly watching the same battle and seeing the details of it from that perspective.

What follows below is our artist's creation of what I sensed from the LORD to bring to you as a visual representation of the Book of Revelation. Imagine that John the Revelator is taken up and beholding Mount Zion, from 7 unique lookout towers. You will notice that a river runs through it! Ezekiel 47:1-12 & also Revelation 22 gives us a symbolic picture of the River of LIFE.

It actually began flowing in the Church Age from the moment of the cross/resurrection. It begins as a small stream (the first Believers in Acts) and increases throughout the entire time of Salvation-History from the First Advent to the Second Advent ("coming" or "arrival" of Jesus).

So each Vantage Point gives a new dimension into the realms of the Spirit, and the spiritual warfare that has been raging since the Devil was "thrown down out of heaven forever" (Revelation 12:7-10).

Thus, all of John's visions run parallel to each other and provide multiple embodiments as the generations of new Believers advance the Gospel to all the Nations!

1
2
3
4
5
6
7

The Big Picture: Seven Visionary Cycles of Revelation

Prologue: Chapter 1:1-3

Cycle 1: Chapter 1:4 to Chapter 3:22, The Seven Golden Lampstands *(Details of the Church Age w/Glimpses of the Second Coming)*

Cycle 2: Chapter 4:1 to Chapter 8:1, The Seven Seals *(Details of the Church Age w/Glimpses of the Second Coming)*

Cycle 3: Chapter 8:2 to Chapter 11:19, The Seven Trumpets *(Details of the Church Age w/Glimpses of the Second Coming)*

Cycle 4: Chapter 12:1 to Chapter 14:20, The Seven Symbolic Histories *(Details of the Church Age w/Glimpses of the Second Coming)*

CYCLES NOW SHIFT ANGLES WITH FOCUS ON THE SECOND COMING.

Cycle 5: Chapter 15:1 to Chapter 16:21, The Seven Bowls of Wrath *(Details of the Second Coming w/Relevance of Church Age)*

Cycle 6: Chapter 17:1 to Chapter 19:21, The Judgment of Babylon & The Beasts *(Details of the Second Coming w/Relevance of Church Age)*

Cycle 7: Chapter 20:1 to Chapter 22:5, The Judgment of the Dragon & Eternity *(Details of the Second Coming & Eternity w/Relevance of Church Age)*

Epilogue: Chapter 22:6-21 relevant throughout Church Age

KEY: The first four parallel sections begin at the victory moment of the Cross and the Ascension of Christ, and each gives us more progressive details of the Second Coming. The last three parallel sections contain unique vantage points of the Second Coming and how it affects the earth in God's judgment through bowls of wrath, judgment of the Harlot Babylon, judgment of the Beasts and the Dragon. And each one has embodiments in every generation of the Church Age. Very unique!

We also discover in each parallel cycle some amazing mysteries which reveal that the conflict between the Church and the world, in her sojourn in the wilderness of this world, is in reality the conflict between Christ (the Lamb) and Satan (the Dragon/Beasts/Harlot).

Summary of the Parallel Cycles

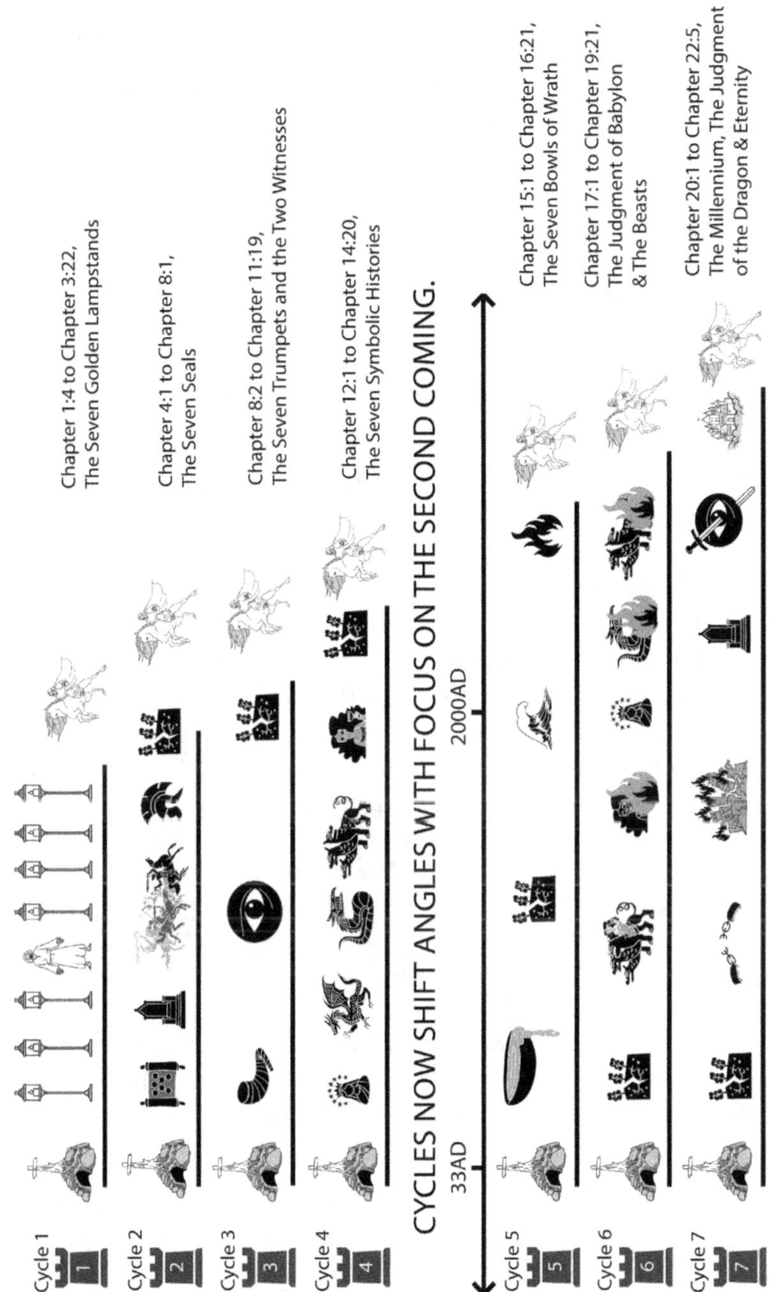

And to make things even more amazing, we see moments of being drawn up to Heaven and worship along with the entire company of the redeemed. These unique moments are called "Interludes" in the text. Hallelujah!

That's because these Visionary Cycles contain two primary elements: **judgment and mercy/salvation**. These two elements are also found in the Bible and known as the "Day of the LORD Scenarios."

Here are just three examples of "Day of the LORD Scenarios" from Genesis. Notice both elements of God's judgment and mercy/salvation in each when you study them.

— God visits Adam & Eve in the Garden after the Fall; they are banished from the Garden but provided for (Gen. 2-3).

— God sends the flood but saves Noah & his family (Gen. 6-8).

— God sends fire and brimstone on Sodom and Gomorrah but saves Lot and his sons (Gen. 19).

I like to draw and make notes right in my Bible. It's filled with highlighter pens of various colors and lots of writing from things I've learned from pastors and teachers. So in my Bible, I have drawn a line between certain chapters to remind myself in my brain that now I'm hitting the **REWIND** button, going back to the historical event of the ascension of Christ and moving forward through my present time and then ahead of me into the future to the Second Coming/Judgment Day.

For example, in my Bible I have a line drawn at the end of each progressive parallel section. I have a line drawn after verses 3:22, 8:1, 11:19, 14:20, 16:21, 19:21, which leads us to 20:1 and the beginning of the Seventh Visionary Cycle.

The end of chapter 19, for example, ends with the most information we have ever been given in a visionary cycle of the Return of the King (Jesus on His white horse, executing Judgment Day). This moment I also featured in my Appendix 1 about the timing of the Rapture, as I believe it happens here during this moment of Christ's return!

Then chapter 20, verse 1, starts over again back at the Cross (the binding of Satan with a great chain) and moves us forward, progressively showing us the ultimate defeat of Satan just after his final persecution of the Church at the very end of this current Church Age. Then comes Judgment Day, the final fate of the wicked and the righteous, and the greatest glimpse of Eternity, the Holy City, that anyone has ever seen in all of Salvation-History.

If Revelation was the movie "Vantage Point," you could draw your line between the sections and then write, "11:57...11:58...11:59....Noon!" to remind yourself.

But in our case, you could write, "**Rewind**."

Or just place a Cross at the beginning of each section.

Be creative if you dare!

I believe with all my heart that these distinctive Seven Visionary Cycles are both thrilling to read and very instructive. Each time I read them and strive to understand them better and pray for more insight, I see more and more of the Father's wisdom in giving us a book like this to build our faith and help prepare us with His Battle Plans for the Last of the Last Days.

So without spending 100 pages of this book going over every transition and trying to explain all the symbols in every verse, let me share a (very) brief outline of each of the main sections, as they pertain to their focus of being Revelation's Battle Plans (both the Plans of the LORD and the Plans of the Enemy).[74]

Let's remember, we serve the victorious King Jesus! He is leading His Church amidst persecution, opposition, progressive judgments, the tactics of Satan through world governments, world religions, seduction and ultimately He's returning with His Eternal Kingdom.

He is 12 moves ahead on that Chess Board, and we will soon see the ultimate demise of the imposter king by the victorious King Jesus!

74 For some INCREDIBLE verse-by-verse Commentaries, which help you discern the deeper spiritual realities and other scriptures from the Old Testament that form the basis of many of John's visions, please see my list of helpful Commentaries at the end of this book.

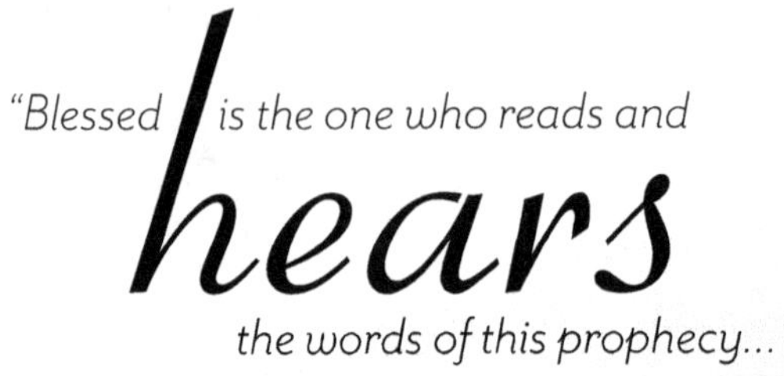

for

THE TIME
IS NEAR.

(Revelation 1:3)

As you prayerfully read through these summaries of some very challenging passages, I have pointed out in each **IN BOLD** where you see the Second Coming. This is an important clue to tell us that these all run parallel to each other and all depict the Second Coming in Poetic and Progressive Parallel language. When you see **REWIND**, go back in time to the Cross and Resurrection (first four cycles), or imagine the first moment of the actual Second Coming (final three cycles).

A Brief Outline of All Seven Visionary Cycles of Judgment/Salvation for a Deeper Study

Prologue: Chapter 1:1-3. *Note: the Revelation is "communicated" or "signified" or another word, "symbolized" by His angel to His bond-servant John, verse 1.* This gives us our way of interpreting the book as visionary and, by prayerfully considering the Old Testament imagery throughout every chapter, we get clues to the deeper spiritual realities behind the symbols themselves. Many visions of what John sees are found in the Old Testament to help us understand their meaning and fulfillment on this side of the Cross and Resurrection!

> *"The Revelation of Jesus Christ, which God gave Him to show to His bond-servants, the things which must soon take place; and He sent and communicated it by His angel to His bond-servant John, who testified to the word of God and to the testimony of Jesus Christ, even to all that he saw. Blessed is he who reads and those who hear the words of the prophecy, and heed the things which are written in it; for the time is near"*
> (Revelation 1:1-3).

Cycle 1: Chapters 1 to 3, The Seven Golden Lampstands. After a Prologue in the opening three verses of chapter 1, which gives us the origin of the epistle as coming from the Father Himself, John introduces the Book and then writes the Letters to the seven churches (chapters 2-3). Chapter 1 starts with the Risen Christ and His ultimate Battle Plan. HE has defeated death, so HE WINS! AND WE WIN! CHECKMATE!

He has ascended on high and is victorious over the regions of death and Hades. He is pictured as moving among the seven golden candlesticks, symbolic of the seven churches of John's day (and our day).

This cycle of three chapters introduces us to the broad themes of the whole epistle by the unveiling of Jesus Christ, who is transforming the kingdoms of this world through his own Sovereign acts. His army of Kings and Priests live a daily lifestyle of warfare by conquering sin on the basis of the Cross, until the climax of all of Salvation-History.

The letters reveal the Battle Plans of the LORD in exhortations to repent, endure and stay faithful and pure. It also shows us the Battle Plans of the Enemy, who is afflicting the various churches with persecutions from without (the ruling governments and the culture itself) and temptations from within (inside the four walls of every church). The **Salvation emphasis** is found in the letters to the churches with the words, *"he who overcomes,"* and judgments are given as warnings to repent.

The letters also depict Christ's personal presence moving among His people, and a visible unity among churches of diversity. *These seven churches represent the Church Universal of all of Salvation-History, and the letters are just as relevant to you and me today as they have been since John first wrote them.* **The Second Coming is depicted briefly in 1:7.**

> *"Behold, He is coming with the clouds, and every eye will see him, even those who pierced Him; and all the tribes of the earth will mourn over Him. Even so. Amen"* (Revelation 1:7).

Cycle 1

Tower
1

The Cross and Tomb
Jesus returns
7 Golden Lampstands
1
CYCLE 1
Jesus

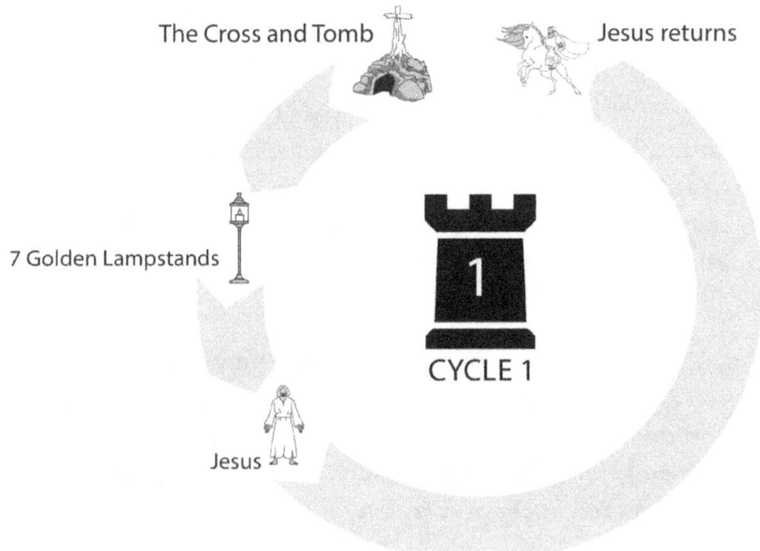

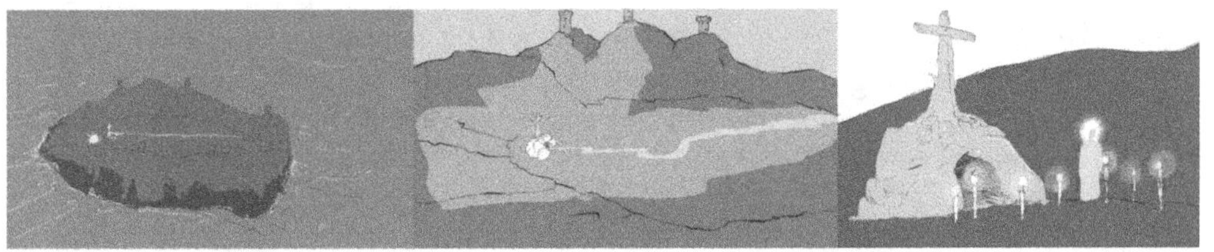

Cycle 2: Chapters 4:1-8:1, REWIND! The Seals. Judgments on earth for persecuting the Church throughout the Church Age. The Cycle opens with heavenly worship of the risen and conquering Lion and Lamb at the ascension of Christ to the eternal Throne of David. This encompasses all Believers of all time, both those who are in heaven and those on earth (symbolized by the 24 elders and the four living creatures). 12 Old Testament Tribes + 12 New Testament Apostles equal = 24; the Church Universal!

We see seven seals being opened; history unfolds as a series of judgments, leading up to the appearing of Christ in the Second Coming.

We first see the Four Horsemen of the Apocalypse galloping, representing conquest, warfare, famine/pestilence and death itself. These calamities (and the other seals) characterize an indefinite period before the Second Coming. Such judgments represent the chastening hand of God on a rebellious world, but the saints are cared for in the midst of such trials by being "sealed" by the Father Himself (chapter 7:15-17).

When you read the details of the seals, try to understand them like the 1st century church did. They contain the perspective of judgments falling on the people and demonic spirits of the world who are persecuting the Church. The seven judgments (seals) move forward toward **the Second Coming, which is depicted in chapter 6:12-17.**[75]

Note: A very amazing symbolic vision of **the Salvation emphasis** found in chapter 7:1-8 includes the numbered Army of the LORD (symbolized by 144,000). This can be interpreted to be the entire number of God's soldiers of His New Covenant Army (billions of people on the earth right now and through all the centuries, encompassing all Jewish Believers and Gentile Believers of all time).

The point of seeing them? They are sealed by the Father and have His Name (representing identity and ownership) unto the Second Coming. We, as God's Army, are spiritually and eternally invincible!

---

75 Ibid, Poythress. I am indebted to his various understandings for several explanations of these cycles.

Cycle 2

Tower
2
The Cross and Tomb
Jesus returns
7 Seals
2
CYCLE 2
Earthquake
The Horsemen of the Apocalypse
The numbered Army

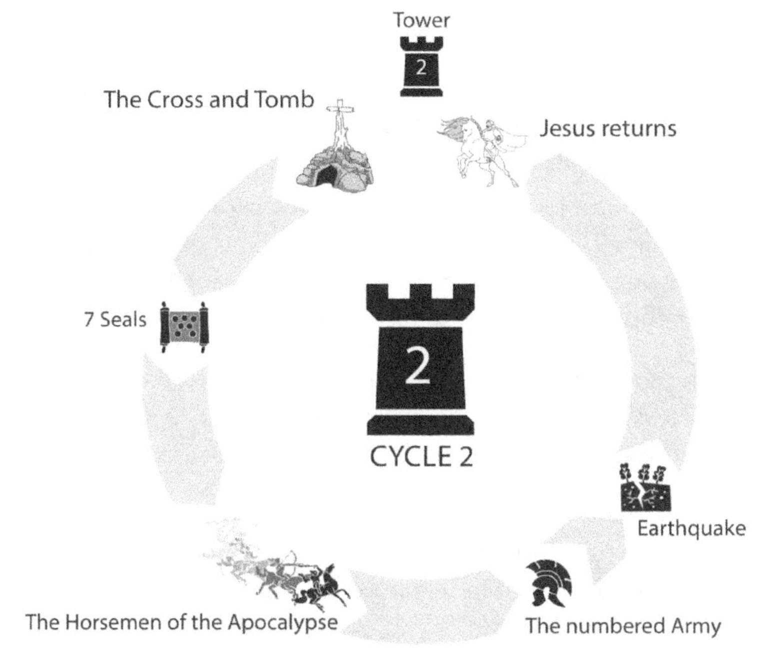

Cycle 3: Chapters 8:2-11:19, REWIND! The Trumpets. They symbolize judgments affecting the Earth itself for persecuting the Church ("creation suffering birth pangs" in Romans 8:22). Trumpets blast, signifying judgments that fall on the Earth (as natural disasters) and affect people in every generation. The Trumpets form another cycle that depict, from various angles, God's rule over history. The Trumpet plagues are reminiscent of the plagues on Egypt (see Exodus as your foundation to understand them), signifying God's judgments on idolatrous power. He pronounces judgments on ruling demonic strongholds, as well as people. Each succeeding catastrophe is a warning that the Final Judgment is coming someday, but most people do not heed the warnings.

The Church (comprised of all Jewish and Gentile Believers) is symbolized by the Two Witnesses who march ahead in advancing the witness of Jesus in the Nations. (We will take our own verse by verse study of them in this book: see Chapter 6).

They exercise His full authority and power of the Spirit. They are not in full defeat until their work is done. That work is the fulfillment of Matthew 24:14:

> *"This Gospel of the Kingdom will be preached to every people group; then the end shall come"* (Matthew 24:14).

At the finishing of the Gospel to the nations, the Enemy (pictured symbolically as this "Beast coming up from the abyss" in 11:7, who is Satan Himself, is allowed to advance his own final assault, a worldwide battle against the Church, such as never has been seen before, or ever will be again.

This will be the time of the LAST BATTLE (and it is also described as the time of "Jacob's Trouble" or "The Greatest Tribulation" or "Armageddon." Thus, just prior to **the Second Coming (which is depicted in chapter 11:19),** we are to expect a violent crisis that will bring intense conflict and brief persecution.

The Salvation emphasis is, of course, that the Church is finally and eternally victorious: the Two Witnesses, (as did Jesus Himself), are resurrected and given eternal life in the greatest moment of triumph in the history of the world!

Cycle 3

Tower
3
The Cross and Tomb
Jesus returns
3
CYCLE 3
7 Shofars
Earthquake
2 Witnesses
The Beast

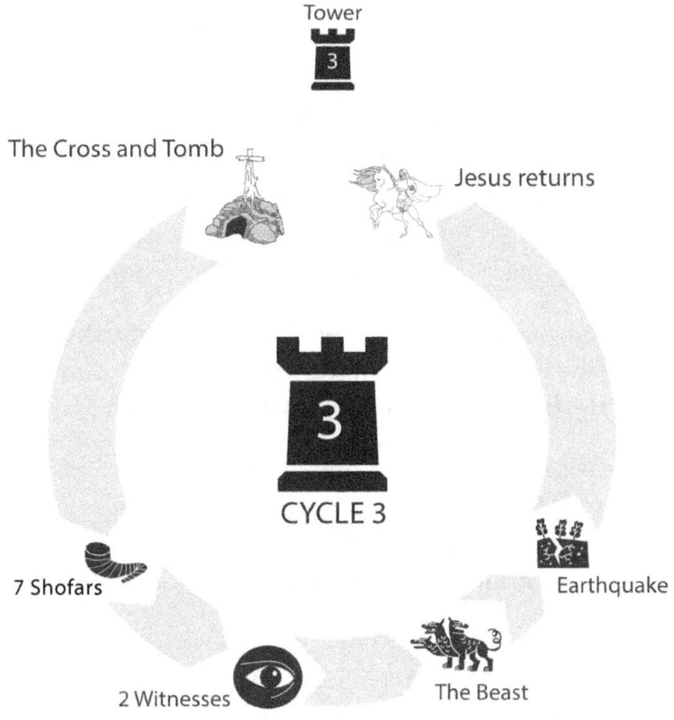

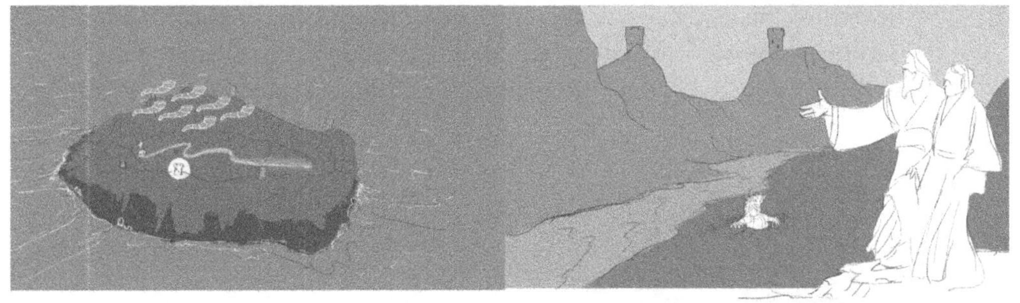

Cycle 4: Chapters 12-14, REWIND! The two preceding cycles focused on the judgments issuing from God's throne. This cycle depicts in-depth the nature of the spiritual conflict of all generations of Salvation-History through seven "symbolic histories" (as Vern Poythress calls them).[76]

Satan (pictured as a great red dragon) attempts to destroy Christ, but He is born from the line of Abraham and then swept away in His ascension to heaven. At the victorious moment of the Cross, Resurrection and Ascension, the dragon is cast down from heaven and goes to make war against the saints in the Church Age, which is spoken of as 42 months, 1260 days and "a short time" (all three symbolizing the entire Church Age).

Satan is here symbolized as counterfeiting the Trinity; **the dragon** is the counterfeit of the Father, **the beast from the sea** is the counterfeit of Jesus the Son, and **the beast from the Earth** is the counterfeit of the Holy Spirit.

The two beasts represent anti-Christian governments and anti-Christian religions. **The harlot** represents anti-Christian seduction with the world (causing Believers to compromise) and the persecution of the Church. She is also the Satanic counterfeit of the true Bride of Christ (the Church of all time).

These weapons are like giant cannons blasting in every generation. God's people, signified by God's seal upon them, are eternally safe, though allowed to be persecuted. Our weapons, based in our relationship with Jesus and the Father, are prayer/intercession, the Armor of God, agape love, light, faith, hope and perseverance (amidst temptations and persecutions), remaining separated from the corruptions of the world. **The Second Coming is depicted in chapter 14:14-20.**

The end of this cycle signals the end of the first half of Revelation. **The Salvation emphasis** is found in chapter 14:1-7 through both the numbered Army who "follow the Lamb wherever he goes" and are sealed with the Father's name, as well as the eternal gospel being preached, which gives mankind an opportunity to repent and follow Christ throughout the Church Age.

76 Ibid., Poythress, pages 133 to 152.

Cycle 4

Tower
4
The Cross and Tomb
Jesus returns
The Beautiful Woman
4
CYCLE 4
The Dragon
The Beast of the Sea
Earthquake
The Beast
The Harlot

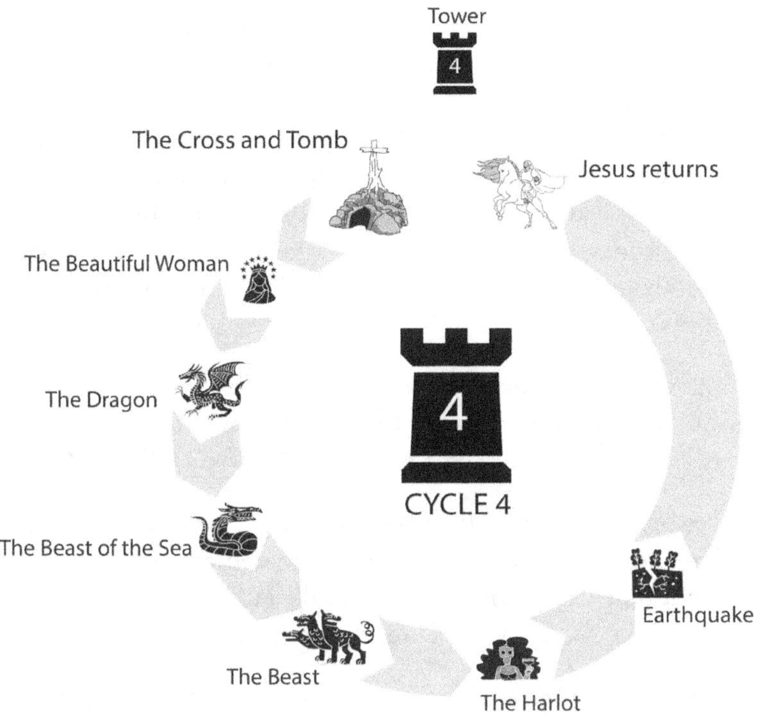

Cycle 5: Chapters 15-16, Bowls of Final Wrath. The judgment on the Earth and demonic realms. Here we see visions of the seven bowls of God's wrath, from both a heavenly and an earthly perspective (foreshadowed throughout history through partial destructions). His wrath is His burning zeal for Divine justice (as HE is holy), coupled with His opposing everything that is evil and opposing Him and His ways. The wrath of God is understood through New Testament theology as the outworking in Salvation-History, our current Church Age, of the natural consequences of the violation of God's moral laws. It's not very often displayed in direct judgments. Please read Romans, chapter 1 for Paul's balanced understanding of God's indirect wrath. John's theology and the other New Testament writers all align themselves with it.

The Bowls follow the same moments in history parallel to the Seals and the Trumpets, but they are also displaying the complete and total judgment of both the earthly and demonic realms **AT THE SECOND COMING.**

God will utilize every portion of the universe to punish the wicked and impenitent persecutors of His people, including the demonic strongholds themselves, at that time (it is pictured symbolically in Cycle 7, Revelation chapter 20:11-15, as the "Great White Throne Judgment").

Believers, who are not subject to the wrath of God, are not affected in any way in this symbol of final judgment. We are safe forever in the presence of the Lamb!

> *"Behold, I am coming like a thief. Blessed is the one who stays awake..."* (Revelation 16:15a).

The Salvation emphasis is seen in chapter 15:3-5, with Believers singing the song of the Lamb. We see Satan's worldwide conspiracy against the Church in the Battle of Armageddon and its ultimate destruction with **the Second Coming (depicted specifically in chapter 16:17-21).**

> *"Great and marvelous are Thy works, O LORD God Almighty; righteous and true are Thy ways, Thou King of the nations! Who will not fear, O LORD, and glorify Thy name? For Thou alone art holy; for all the nations will come and worship before Thee, for Thy righteous acts have been revealed"* (Revelation 15:3-4).

Cycle 5

Tower
5
The Cross and Tomb
Jesus returns
Fire
5
CYCLE 5
Floods
Earthquake
7 Bowls of Wrath

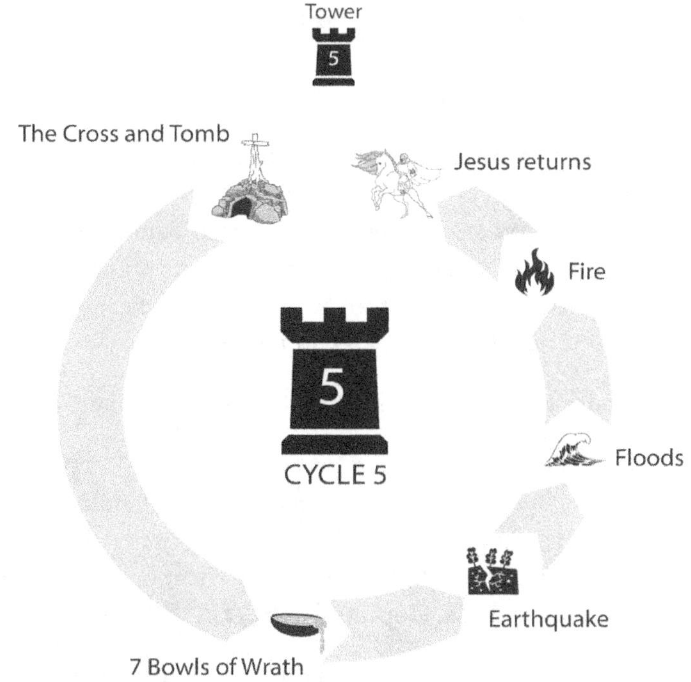

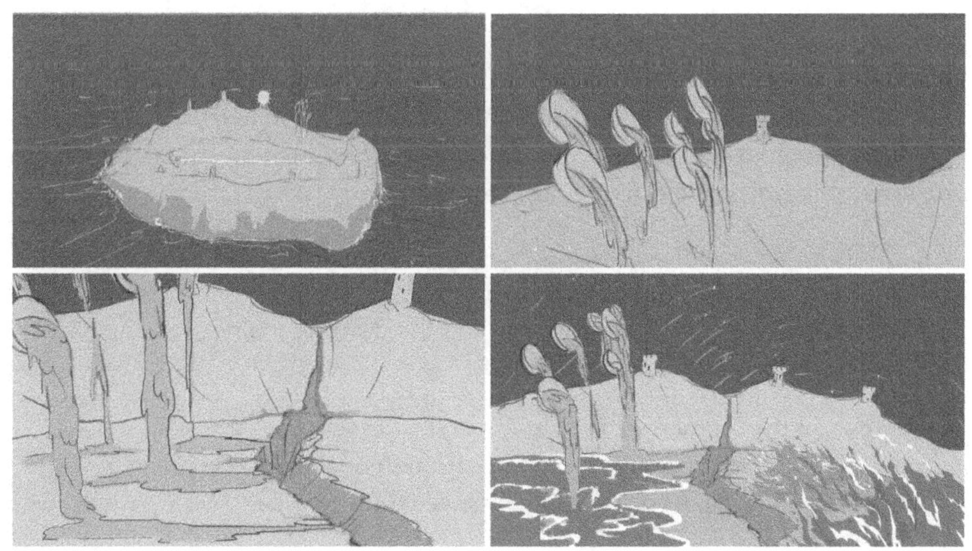

Cycle 6: Chapters 17-19, The Judgment on the harlot Babylon, and Christ conquering in His Second Coming. The allurements and seductions of the harlot are the Satanic, fleshly attacks waging war against the Church during the entire Church Age, which began with the seven churches and continue down to our day.

The corruptions of the counterfeit harlot Babylon contrast with the purity of the Bride of the Lamb. She represents all that is evil in culture: idolatry, greed, materialism and sexual immorality. These Satanic attacks are both inside the Church and outside (in the governments and cultures) and are seeking to make Believers compromise. Our only hope, and the Salvation emphasis: *"Come out of her and be separate!"* (Revelation 18:4).

Believers must maintain a holy lifestyle with the Holy Spirit, and flee temptations at every turn.

These chapters follow the same moments in history parallel to the Seals and the Trumpets; but like the Bowls, they also are mainly displaying the complete and total judgment of both the earthly and demonic realms **AT THE SECOND COMING. Depicted in BOTH 18:1-24, and in 19:11-21.**

The Last Battle brings to a climax all the spiritual battles that God has waged on behalf of His one people of both dispensations, and consummates the triumph achieved by Christ on the cross.

In this cycle, all the events are actually part of the Second Coming, yet the incredible imagery brings full manifestation of the principles of spiritual warfare that have been operative throughout the Church Age. So, in that sense, this runs parallel to the other cycles.

NOTE: I believe this is ALSO the parallel moment of Paul's teaching of the timing of the Rapture in 1 Thessalonians 4, as these events occur simultaneously at the very end of this age and the dawn of the new one. (Read my Appendix 1, "No One Left Behind").

Thus, at the moment of the closing of the Last Battle, the "Rapture" will take place and eternal judgment and salvation begins (see our Diagram at the very end of this book for a fuller visual description).

Cycle 6

Tower
6
The Cross and Tomb
Jesus returns
Beast Destroyed
6
CYCLE 6
Beast Destroyed
Harlot Destroyed
Harlot on the Beast
Earthquake

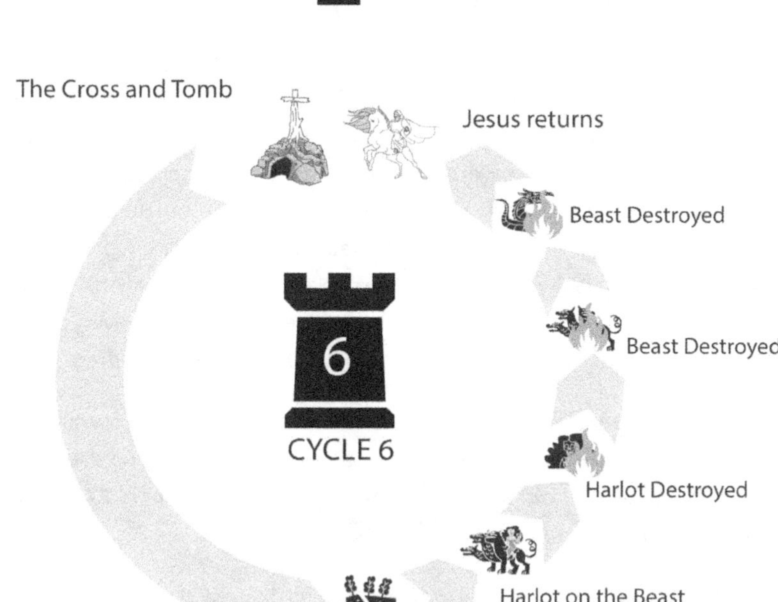

Cycle 7: Chapters 20-22:5, REWIND! The NOW-Millennium, the Judgment of the Dragon, and the Great White Throne Judgment. Beginning at the ascension of Christ and shown in symbolic imagery as the *binding of Satan,* we see that the dragon's active mission against the Church cannot destroy the witness of Christ in the nations. he is bound only in that one single aspect of Salvation-History for "1,000" years, which is symbolic of the Church Age (chapter 20:1-3).

This is the only place in all of Scripture that specifically gives us this unique timeframe of "1,000" years, and is known by many as the Millennium. For a deep dive, verse by verse study, please read my chapter, The NOW-Millennium. Next, we see those who die in battle during the Church Age actually reign with Christ in heaven during this whole dispensation (chapter 20:4-6)! Wow! These verses also seem to be John's main point in this chapter. The Church Triumphant is reigning NOW even as the Church Militant carries out her warfare reign on the earth in the great war.

We then see THE LAST BATTLE as Satan is loosed to wage his last war against the Church in deception of a coalition of nations around the earth simultaneously. **The Second Coming is depicted in 20:9-10 as "fire came down from Heaven." CHECKMATE!**

And finally, we see Satan's ultimate demise, as the imposter king on the chess board receives his own eternal judgment. He is cast into the lake of fire that torments him forever.

We also see the Great White Throne Judgment taking place when the wicked and the righteous are assigned to their eternal homes. And for **the ultimate Salvation emphasis**, we see the children of God depicted as the Holy City, enjoying the Father's personal presence as His TRIUMPHAL BRIDE for all eternity. WE WIN!

NOTE: A very special element is the FATHER HIMSELF coming to dwell on the redeemed earth with His children forever!

See Revelation 21:1-7, which closes with the Father declaring, *"The one who overcomes will inherit these things, and I will be his God, and he shall be My son"* (Revelation 21:7).

Cycle 7

Tower
7

Satan bound
Jesus returns
The New Jerusalem
Satan Destroyed
7
CYCLE 7
Destruction
Satan Unbound
Earthquake
The Death of the Witnesses

Epilogue: Chapter 22:6-22:21. As the Gospel reaches all the Gentiles, it is possible that the LORD Jesus could return at any moment: so the urgency to conform your life in holiness remains. The wicked keep being wicked and finally end up in unrepentant judgment. The righteous become the Holy City. And the invitation to join the crusade and enjoy God's personal presence is available to every generation up until the LAST DAY ON EARTH. *"The Spirit and the Bride continue to say, 'COME!"* (Revelation 22:17). Even so, come LORD Jesus, amen.

The Seven Visionary Cycles in Parallel

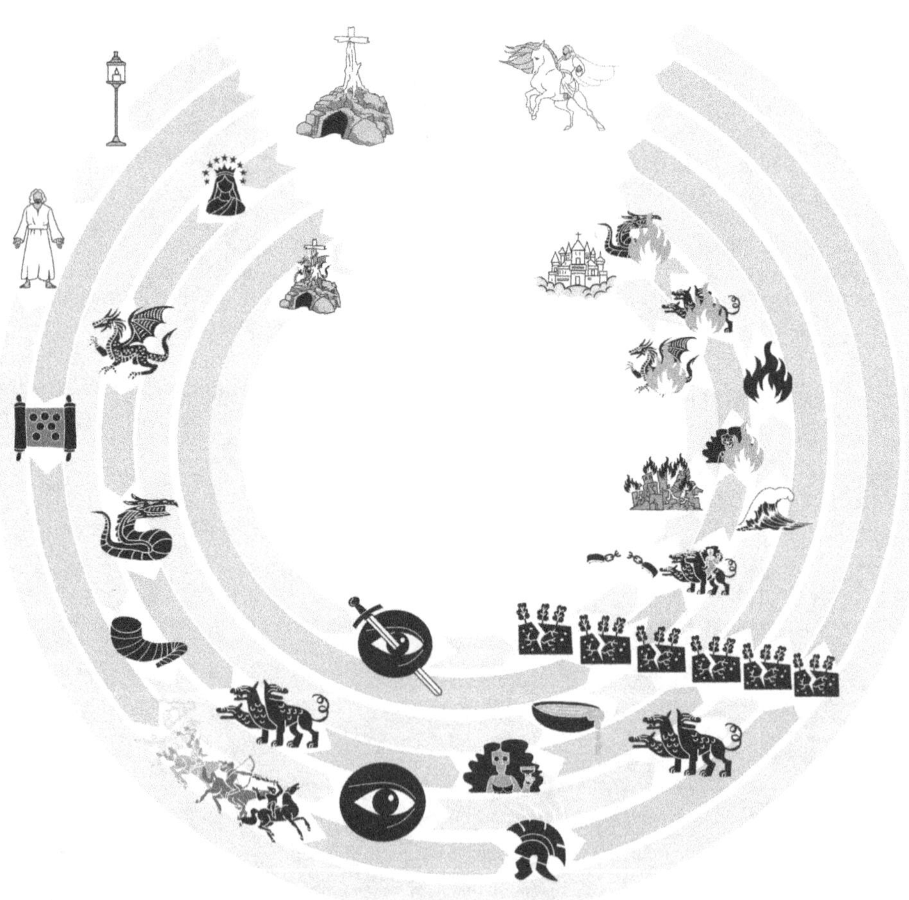

Visual Key for Revelation Diagrams

The Seven Golden Lampstands	The Beautiful Woman	The Harlot Destroyed
Jesus	The Dragon	The Bride
The Seven Seals	The Beast of the Sea	The Beast Destroyed - Sea
Throne	The Beast of the Land	The Beast Destroyed - Land
The Horsemen of the Apocalypse	The Harlot	Satan Unbound
The 144 000 Army	The Seven Bowls of Wrath	The Destruction
The Earthquake	The Floods	The Death of the Witnesses
The Seven Shofars	The Fire	The New Jerusalem
The Two Witnesses	The Harlot on the Beast	

Question: What is the reason that John splits the Cycles 1-4 and 5-7?

Answer: There are many patterns of 4+3 or 3+4 throughout the epistle, which both equal God's perfect number, 7. And as I have deeply studied these cycles, I noticed that John was given such a beautiful "Big Picture" view of the Church in all the cycles, but with a different emphasis on the Second Coming as they begin to come closer to that moment. The "Big Picture" was relevant to the original audience, has been relevant to all generations, is relevant right now, and will also be relevant in the approaching Final Battle.

In Cycles 1-4, the focus appears to be on the Church Age, with glimpses of the Second Coming, with each glimpse progressively giving more details.

In Cycles 5-7, while maintaining my **Idealist** view (which means I believe the principles of spiritual war are relevant to all generations and have repeated embodiments), I see a brilliantly composed and interwoven group of cycles with various "angles" on the Second Coming itself. (They focus on the Second Coming, with glimpses of embodiments throughout the Church Age.)

That is what I feel Cycles 5-7, with the Bowls of Wrath, harlot Babylon, the White Horse Judgment, and the White Throne Judgment, all are depicting: the Second Coming. It's like we're watching an incredible epic film with many unique camera angles upon this scene!

Picture being taken up to each tower...

In speaking of the Bowls of Wrath in Cycle 5 (chapters 15-16), here's what Dennis E. Johnson shares. "This camera angle is the final scene in the bowl sequence (the seventh bowl). Although, in a sense we can view the following visions (the harlot Babylon and her demise, the Last Battle at the end of the thousand years, the last judgment, and presentation of the New Jerusalem as Bride) as contained within the Bowls Cycle, as we see from the role of angels in revealing both the harlot and the Bride (17:1; 21:9)."[77]

77 Ibid, Johnson, pg. 236.

So there you have the Seven Visionary Cycles. Seven unique vantage points, starting in time at roughly the ascension of Christ, finishing progressively further to ultimate judgment. Each vantage point teaches us various truths about the war we are in, and the Final Conflict, the real "war to end all wars" which is, by some accounts, already happening now, and includes the Last Battle which is yet to come.

Take some time in your devotional inquiry this week, and have a read-through of each of those seven Cycles, chapter by chapter in Revelation. Picture yourself being taken up to a round tower on a mountain peak, looking down into the valley of the battle of the ages, which has been waging since the First Coming. In each new cycle, imagine yourself moving to a new vantage point, and see the uniqueness of that view.

Now that you've had two chapters that are filled with methods of interpretation, let's move forward and put those methods to the test and dig deeper to try and understand the Seals, the Trumpets and the Bowls of Wrath. This next chapter has some very practical applications and challenging thoughts for you to consider every time a natural disaster happens. Let's learn of 'Earth's Trauma.'

Going Deeper Still:

- When you read Revelation, it is helpful to take off your methodical "Sherlock Holmes" hat and replace it with your Hebrew prayer shawl. In other words, learn to balance more on the side of your brain that recognizes the pictorial nature of Revelation, rather than the abstract or literal ways to interpret. Interpreting it requires some work.
- By understanding Revelation more as a Poem with parallel passages that mirror one another, you can search and find clues to lead you to approximate places where the visions begin and end. Take some time this week to read the descriptions of a parallel passage and then read the whole passage through (like reading chapters 8-11 together).
- Like the story of the film, *Vantage Point,* the Big Picture of Revelation unfolds in a series of at least seven primary visions, or Cycles. These cycles repeat each other in the entire scope of the Church Age and run parallel to one another. Each one contains beautiful symbolic images. Can you now understand how many of these visions carry with them multiple interpretations and embodiments in Salvation-History?
- I ended this chapter with a brief outline of all seven Visionary Cycles. It may be helpful, if you appreciate this kind of potential structure, to draw a line in your Bible between the chapter breaks, so that as you read the next set of chapters, you realize you are back inside a parallel section that spans many years of time between the Cross and the Second Coming; and then write the word, **REWIND**, or simply draw a Cross to mark each new Cycle.
- Revelation begins and ends with a challenge: the "time" is "near" for the Second Coming. (See the beautiful poetic parallelism of Revelation 1:3 and 22:10.) What does that personally mean to you today?

Earth's Trauma

The Increase of Natural Disasters as Warning Signs of the Coming Final Judgment

"*And there will be great earthquakes, and in various places plagues and famines; and there will be terrors and great signs from heaven; and upon the Earth dismay among nations, in perplexity at the roaring of the sea and of the waves, men fainting from fear and the expectation of the things which are coming upon the world*" (Luke 21:11, 25-26a).

"*Both human beings and the natural world undergo stress until the time of final renewal* (Romans 8:18-25). *The natural world, as well as humanity, is affected by the 2nd Coming* (2 Peter 3:10, 12)." —Vern S. Poythress[78]

78 Vern S. Poythress, The Returning King: A Guide to the Book of Revelation, pg. 122. P and R publishing, 2000.

This chapter will help you discover some incredible truths from the Old Testament, New Testament, and especially from the Book of Revelation, as to the root causes and increase of natural disasters in the earth today.

We are in a kind of a cosmic battle of light against darkness. Have you noticed how natural disasters have been increasing in both size and frequency over these past decades?

Why is this all happening? And what are the possible sources of these natural disasters?

When a natural disaster happens, many people ask, did God do this? The answer can have multiple possibilities.

1. **WE did this.** Meaning mankind, through our generations of accumulated curses in areas of the earth that are being reaped; these natural disasters are expressions of the sphere of God's indirect wrath working itself out in Salvation-History. This is by far the most common answer and events are transpiring with these sowing and reaping effects nearly every day of the year somewhere on earth.

2. **God did this.** Very rarely and only occasionally through direct intervention, God's bowls of wrath fill up and He reaps the sins of mankind in direct judgments.

3. **Satan did this.** The Enemy's evil powers brought this destruction and death to people that he hates and wants to continuously destroy (see Ephesians 6:10-14).

Did you know that according to statistics from the U.S. Geological Survey,[79] approximately 500,000 earthquakes occur and are detectable every year around the earth? About 50 per day, or 18,250, are measurable in size and are above a magnitude of 5.0. About 85 hurricanes occur each year globally,[80] and between 1975 and 2000, about 28 tsunamis caused deaths around the world with the worst tsunami in the Pacific Ocean occurring in December, 2004, when more than 225,000 people lost their

79 https://www.usgs.gov/programs/earthquake-hazards/cool-earthquake-facts
80 http://www.nhm.ac.uk/nature-online/earth/volcanoes-earthquakes/hurricanes/

lives around the Indian Ocean off the coast of Sumatra.[81] Who can forget the horrifying images of absolute destruction as those killer waves struck without warning, wiping away whole villages?

What on earth is going on?

The Earth is the LORD's and HE Wants it Back!

Let's begin by looking at **Answer #1** of the three possible reasons for natural disasters (and especially earthquakes).

The scriptures teach us much about the earth. From the Hebrew writings of Moses and the prophets, we learn that the earth is important to God. In Genesis, He created it as an eternal dwelling. He formed man from the dust of the earth, and woman was taken from his rib to be a perfect complement to man, so she is likewise made of earth. Adam was given a conscience, so the Law of God was written upon his heart and thus, the Law of God is written upon the hearts of all mankind, since we all descended from him.

After the fall of man in the Garden, God cursed the ground and death entered the picture (see Genesis chapter 3). Since that day, the earth has fallen into decay, and mankind has been subject to disease, decay and death itself, which is part of that curse. We are all buried in the earth. We are dust, and unto dust do we return.

In a sense, when anyone dies it is healthy to be reminded of the truth of the Fall, and the truth that death is not the final end (but an abrupt and sometimes shocking change in our existence). The good news: the righteous are instantly transported into the eternal presence of Jesus!

Yet, death should be a wake-up call to the living for repentance and holy living. Believers in Jesus Christ can look forward to the day of His return, as He will then transform our current carnal body, which is still subject to the original curse, into a new, glorious and eternal body, fashioned for us in the heavens. And like His body, it's an eternal combination of the earthly and heavenly.

81 Ibid.

The Jewish concept of Creation filled Paul's mind when he rewrote his theology after becoming a follower of Jesus. Jesus changes everything![82]

Here are a few scriptures about the earth to remember as we place these signs of Earth's decay as signs of the end of history, and why the earth will experience even more trauma as we approach the Second Coming.

> *"The earth is the LORD's, and all it contains, the world, and those who dwell in it. He has founded it upon the seas, and established it upon the rivers"* (Psalm 24:1-2).

> *"Cursed is the ground because of you; in toil you shall eat of it all the days of your life. Both thorns and thistles it shall grow for you; and you shall eat the plants of the field. By the sweat of your face you shall eat bread, till you return to the ground, because from it you were taken; for you are dust, and to dust you shall return"* (Genesis 3:17-18).

So here we have some good news and some bad news. The earth, created by God, is His. Man is a steward over the earth. There is no concept of "Mother Earth" in scripture, or "Mother Nature" for that matter. The bad news is, as a result of our fall in Adam, the earth has been forced to exist under a curse.

The Blood Cries from the Soil

Starting with the first generation after Adam, generational curses came into being, and as a result, there are consequences in the earth itself for sin. A second kind of curse, a very specific kind, came in after that first generation was born: the murder of righteous Able from the cruel hand of his brother Cain.

Here we are examining the effect of sin and unrighteousness as it pertains to the earth, so we can better gain insights into these "killer storms" that are increasing in our generation. The second kind of curse that came forth after the slaying of Able is a blood curse.

82 For further study please read Genesis 3, I Corinthians 15 and II Corinthians 5:1-11.

> *"And He said, 'What have you done? The voice of your brother's blood is crying to Me from the ground. And now, you are cursed from the ground, which has opened its mouth to receive your brother's blood from your hand. When you cultivate the ground, it shall no longer yield its strength to you; you shall be a vagrant and a wanderer on the earth'"* (Genesis 4:10-12).

So, man as a steward has both sinned against God and against his conscience, and added to it, he breaks the law of God daily. It seems in Scripture that the one sin above them all is the sin of murder; of taking another person's life and shedding innocent blood upon the soil. We see then, from the generation of Adam on down through to the generation of Noah (10 generations, which is symbolic language, as we've seen previously with the number 10 as a full cycle), the earth self-destructs even as mankind self-destructs.

> *"Now the earth was corrupt in the sight of God, and the earth was filled with violence. And God looked on the earth, and behold, it was corrupt; for all flesh had corrupted their way upon the earth. Then God said to Noah, 'The end of all flesh has come before Me; for the earth is filled with violence because of them; and behold, I am about to destroy them with the earth'"* (Genesis 6:11-13).

We all know the story. The floods come and destroyed the earth, and with it, His judgment falls and all mankind is destroyed from the face of the earth. A unique detail in the story comes after the waters have receded, as God speaks to Noah again.

> *"And the LORD said to Himself, 'I will never again curse the ground on account of man, for the intent of man's heart is evil from his youth; and I will never again destroy every living thing, as I have done'"* (Genesis 8:21).

Then God creates the rainbow as a sign of what we now call the Noahic Covenant, a covenant of preservation of the earth until the time of the consummation of all things at the close of this Age. Then He leaves us this detail, which is a key to our understanding. He forbids murder and instills capital punishment (an eye for an eye theology).

> *"And surely I will require your lifeblood; from every beast I will require it. And from every man, from every man's brother I will require the life of man. Whoever sheds man's blood, by man his blood shall be shed, for in the image of God He made man."* (Genesis 9:5-6).

The idea of the blood curse upon the ground, and its effect on creation and other human relationships, is given here. Murder is a most serious and grievous crime in God's eyes, as He is the Author of life, the Alpha and Omega as He tells us in Revelation 1:8. Later in Scripture, we find that the consequences of the sins of the ancestors affect later generations (see Exodus 20:5, Joshua 7:24-26).

"Law has its source in the nature of God," wrote John and Paula Sandford, "and whatever a man sows, that shall he also reap (Galatians 6:7). That is the good will of God. He has built the universe to operate upon principles of balance and retribution. For every action there is an equal and opposite reaction.

"When God speaks so often as He does in the Old Testament how He will punish so drastically, He is not speaking of His own first will, which is always to forgive and to heal, but of the way in which His good will, His unbending law, will bring retribution. He says, "I will do this thing," because His law is His law and all things are personal to Him.

"But from our point of view, let us see it as the reaping of what we have sown, not as God's capricious vendetta."[83]

Having established by Scripture the idea that the earth is accumulating the results of the sins of mankind committed upon it, and the idea that the Law is written upon the hearts of all. Yet still all have, for many generations, broken that Law and thus their sin is being reaped upon the ground itself. ("Your brother's blood is crying out to Me from the ground.") Let us turn to one of the most dramatic prophetic scriptures that help us understand how God is sending judgments on the earth as a result of man's disobedience.

83 John and Paula Sandford, The Elijah Task, pg. 111 and 113. Victory House Publishers, 1977.

> *"Behold, the LORD lays the earth waste, devastates it, distorts its surface, and scatters its inhabitants. The earth will be completely laid waste and completely despoiled, for the LORD has spoken this word. The earth mourns and withers, the world fades and withers, the exalted of the people of the earth fade away. The earth is polluted (defiled) by its inhabitants, for they have transgressed laws, violated statutes, broke the everlasting covenant. Therefore, a curse devours the earth, and those who live in it are held guilty. Desolation is left in the city, for thus it will be in the midst of the earth among the peoples"* (Isaiah 24:3-6a, 12-13).

"As a result of the universal transgression, the curse will devour the entire earth," wrote Edward J. Young in his wonderful commentary on Isaiah, "and as a result of this devouring curse, the inhabitants of the earth are reckoned to be guilty, and being reckoned guilty, they must suffer. All nature shares in the sorrow of the land. Through their sins, Earth's inhabitants had introduced desolation and confusion into the world, and so the place of their dwelling becomes a desolation."[84]

Seals, Trumpets and Bowls in the Cycles of Revelation

Time now to focus our attention back to the Book of Revelation to share how John depicts both the Church Age and the Second Coming as they both relate to Earth's Trauma.

I would ask you to reread my descriptions of Cycles 2, 3 & 5, for a better broad understanding of how the earth itself is being (and will be) affected by God's judgments.

Let me summarize a few thoughts here.

The Seals (which Jesus Himself releases in Revelation chapter 6) affect the earth and are pictured by the infamous Four Horseman of the Apocalypse. What you may not realize is that what the Father shows John, through Jesus Himself, echoes the very prophetic declarations made by Jesus in the Gospels about some of the general signs of the times.

84 Edward J. Young's Commentary on Isaiah, Ibid., pg. 164.

He was asked by His disciples what would be the signs of the destruction of Jerusalem, which He prophesied, and the end. Many scholars equate the verses in Matthew 24, Mark 13 and Luke 21 as pertaining to the generation that was to follow Christ's death and resurrection leading up to the actual destruction of Jerusalem in 70 A.D.

While I agree with many of those scholars that the verses have had unique fulfillment in that time (the years leading up to, and including 70 A.D.). I also read them with multiple potential embodiments for the Church Age, BECAUSE of what John sees in Revelation. Thus, here's an example of the Seals of Revelation 6 in parallel to Jesus' teaching,

Seals of Revelation	
Earthquakes, Famines, Pestilence, Persecutions	Famines, Pestilence, Persecutions, Earthquakes
(Luke 21:9-12a, 25-26)	(Revelation 6:2-17, 7:1)

Thus, John shows us in the Seals, that throughout this current dispensation, these kinds of natural disasters (like earthquakes, famines and pestilences, killer viruses) are taking place in every generation. These Seals are opened as responses to those who are persecuting Believers. They happen because God's people are undergoing continuous suffering in various places in the earth and are upholding the witness of Christ alone to godless societies.

The Trumpets, revealed in the next parallel cycle to the Seals, are a call to repentance as these signs (God's judgments) go forth and affect the earth itself, and are ongoing in our current dispensation. Because they are a call to repentance, they can actually be Good News to those who have ears to hear.

"Good News?" writes Darrell W. Johnson. "Yes, it is. For judgment says God cares. Judgment says we and our choices matter to God. Judgment says God takes evil and sin seriously. Judgment says God is not indifferent to, nor tolerant of, evil and sin. Judgment says God moves against evil and sin."[85]

The Trumpets, interestingly, are only partial judgments on the earth. They affect 1/3 only. This too, is a symbolic number. It just means that the natural disasters that are occurring are not going to destroy the whole earth, they are only allowed to affect a portion of it.

(1) A third of the earth (8:7)

(2) A third of the sea (8:8)

(3) A third of the rivers (8:10)

(4) A third of the waters (8:11)

(5) A third of the sun, moon & stars (8:12)

(6) A third of humanity (9:15)

And just who are these Trumpets blasting giving warning to? In Revelation 8:13, John describes them as "those who dwell on the face of the earth." This is a technical, and symbolic, phrase in Revelation. "It refers to those who stand in the way of the coming of God's kingdom. It refers to those in rebellion against God and His ways. Why, then are they (the Trumpets) sounded? They are sounded to warn the world of the pending total judgment."[86]

What Does the Wrath of God Really Look Like?

The Bowls of Wrath (Revelation chapters 15-16) deserve a bit of further explanation, as they are pictured in Cycle 4 as TOTAL destruction. So can we pause a moment and reflect on just what the WRATH of God looks like?

---

85 Darrell W. Johnson, Discipleship on the Edge, 2004 by Regent College Publishing, pg. 193.
86 Ibid, pgs. 194-195.

As John and Paul Sandford reminded us earlier in this chapter, "From our point of view, let us see it as the reaping of what we have sown, not as God's capricious vendetta."

God's character is filled with holiness. And out of His goodness and mercy flows His love. He is always pictured as "slow to anger," and though there are some striking examples in the Old Testament of the wrath of God seemingly flowing from Him, the Apostle Paul, in his epistle to the Romans (as well as John in the Book of Revelation), takes a fresh view of God's wrath. It is known as the wrath of God because God created the universe and the world with His moral law.

These laws are impersonal, just as are His natural laws. If I go up to my roof right now and jump off, I am most likely going to break my legs. This is not a personal judgment of God on me. It is just the impersonal law of gravity that is always in motion, whether I like it or not.

Paul looks at the incredible moment of God's wrath being poured out upon sin on the Cross, as Jesus defeats the powers of evil and lays down His very life in love for us, His enemies. He shares in Romans of the indirect and impartial nature of God's wrath. That is, God longs for people to come to repentance, but if they insist on breaking His moral law, He allows them to experience the reaping of what they have sown.

> *"For the wrath of God is revealed from Heaven against all ungodliness; they exchanged the glory of the incorruptible God for an image; therefore God gave them over in the lusts of their own hearts to impurity, for they exchanged the truth of God for a lie"* (Romans 1: selected verses; please read all of Romans 1 for a complete understanding).

You will note the words, "God gave them over," and this is how Paul, along with all of the New Testament writers including John, define the wrath of God on this side of the Cross. It is an impersonal process. What man has sown in disobeying God, mankind must reap.

God does not very often step into history in a direct measure to bring judgment; that is very rare (though it does happen, as you will see in our Case Study below). One example is that in 70 A.D., the prophetic words of Jesus vindicated Him as the very Son of God, as God stepped into history and judged Israel and fulfilled the words of Jesus exactly, when He said, "not a stone will be left unturned" (Matthew 24:2).

"Wrath means: the working out in history of the consequences of sin. And "the wrath of the Lamb" in Revelation 6:16, is the working out in history of the consequences of the rejection and crucifixion of the Messiah. It is a process, stretching from the Cross to the Second Coming."[87]

"God's wrath arises from His eternal self-consistency. All that opposes Him He resists with a total and final commitment. Without His wrath, God would not be truly holy and His love would degenerate into sentimentality. Nor is His wrath arbitrary, fitful or subject to emotion as in human beings.

"God's wrath is working itself out in history as people reap the moral and spiritual harvest for rejecting God's revelation; this is but a preliminary form of something which is to be revealed at the end of the age and of which the Cross of Christ represents the clearest and most sobering preview (Ps. 78:31: Ho. 5:10: Jn. 3:36; Eph. 2:3; 1 Thess. 1:10; Rev. 6:16).[88]

So, the trumpets sounding are meant to be wake-up calls and alarms to the ungodly. They are actual sign-posts to the coming, worldwide, Final Judgment. With all of the natural disasters occurring almost simultaneously now, people are rightly asking, "What on earth is going on?" And the answer from Believers should be something like, "Wake up! God's final justice on sin is coming. Repent and turn your heart to Him, while you have time."

"The trumpets show the wicked world being offered mercy. The offer is not accepted, and the world will not, in fact, repent (Rev. 9:20). But let it never be said that God has not done all in His power, even to the devastation of His own perfect earth, in order to bring men and women to their senses."[89]

87 Anthony Tyrrell Hanson, The Wrath of the Lamb, William Clowes and Sons, 1957, pg. 170.
88 Bruce Milne, Know the Truth, InterVarsity Press, 1982, 1998, pg. 87.
89 Ibid, Darrell W. Johnson, pg. 200.

Birth Pangs

God has always used illustrations dealing with various aspects of the earth in His dealings with men through prophetic declarations such as these. It was the prophet Jeremiah who first declared, when he was dealing with God's righteous judgment of the sin of idolatry among His own people, that He would send indirect judgments in three forms: the sword, famine and pestilence (Jeremiah 27:8-13). Two of these are actively related to the earth itself: famine, and thus desolation of the ground that should be bearing food (think again of what God told Cain), and pestilence, a part of nature itself turning on the people. We can also include city-wide and world-wide pandemics in this category). These are also echoed in the Four Horsemen of the Apocalypse, as the first four Seals opening in Revelation 6.

Jesus, who was well versed in understanding all that Father was showing Him through the ancient scrolls of both Isaiah and Jeremiah (He quoted from both during His earthly ministry), would have surely read and understood these texts in light of what He openly shared with His disciples. He was warning them of the vast shakings that would be coming upon the earth, including the imminent destruction of the Temple in Jerusalem, and for all of the Ages to come, especially as the end approaches:

> *"And there will be earthquakes in various places; there will also be famines. These things are merely the beginning of birth pangs"* (Mark 13:8).

Jesus seemed to understand, by the Spirit and in line with the Prophets before Him, that the earth was going to start experiencing natural disasters of strong proportions in relation to God's just and indirect judgments as signs in the natural.

Of course, it can be understood that all the signs happened in the generation that followed the crucifixion and resurrection, just prior perhaps to the destruction of the Temple in 70 A.D. Though as we have already noted, Jesus did not return during that generation, and as N.T. Wright puts it,

> "The little church in the first generation cannot afford to settle down and assimilate itself either to the Jewish or the pagan

world. It must certainly remind itself that great events are afoot, that terrifying times are just ahead. The judgment that fell on the Temple is a foretaste, according to other passages in the New Testament, of the judgment that will fall on the whole world."[90]

We, too, as the current generation, need to heed these words of Jesus and remind ourselves that every time a natural disaster occurs, the earth is reaping sin that has been sown upon it, and we are one step closer to the earth "reeling like a drunkard" and reaching a crescendo of natural disasters, just prior to the Second Coming of Christ.

When He returns, He brings with Him the eternal transforming power of both righteous mankind and nature itself, for He brings,

> *"A new Heavens and a new Earth, in which righteousness dwells"* (2 Peter 3:13).

Indeed, for now,

> *"All the foundations of the Earth are shaken,"* as mankind *"walks about in darkness"* (Psalm 82:5).

> "About 4 years ago," wrote John Sandford, "the LORD warned Paula and me that unless the entire Silver Valley (Shoshone County, Idaho) repented of its sins, judgment would come upon it in the form of fire and smoke and cause many deaths (5 open houses of prostitution existed in a town of 3,000 at that time).

> "The Sunshine Mine disaster happened on May 2, about two years later. Carbon monoxide poisoning took the lives of 91 men. Disasters do not necessarily impugn the characters of their victims (Luke 13: 2-5). Our miners were not any more or less sinful than those in any other mine. Men's sins pile up like rocks on a ledge. Eventually that pile will break the ledge and cause a landslide. The man who happens to be walking by at that moment and is crushed is not more or less sinful than

90 Tom Wright, Mark for Everyone, pg. 187. Society For Promoting Christian Knowledge, 2001.

> those who do not. Thus the relation of sin to tragedy is more likely corporate than personal."[91]

The Apostle Paul talks about the effects of grievous sins and sinners on the earth itself, and that all the sufferings that Believers face in the persecutions are not worthy to be compared with the glory that is to be revealed to us.

> *"For the anxious longing of the creation waits eagerly for the revealing of the sons of God. For the creation was subjected to futility, not of its own will, but because of Him who subjected it, in hope that the creation itself also will be set free from its slavery to corruption into the freedom of the glory of the children of God. For we know that the whole creation groans and suffers the pains of childbirth together until now"* (Romans 8:19-22).

Here, Paul is giving us insight on the earth itself, currently in a state of slavery to corruption because of the curse still upon it, a curse upon man and the ground that God put there.

The "birth pangs" here certainly are in line with the same wording that Jesus uses to describe what is taking place on earth in relation to judgment that is falling. Paul also gives us the good news: for Believers, we come to understand that in the Second Coming of Messiah, the creation will be set free! Freedom of the glory of the children of God, rejoicing alongside it. The "renewed earth" with "Heaven joining us" will indeed be amazing. But until then,

"We will see ever-increasing natural disasters," wrote my dear friend and modern prophet, R. Loren Sandford (who tragically died during the COVID-19 pandemic).

> "The recent earthquakes in Haiti, Peru, New Zealand and Japan are mere harbingers of what will yet come. Volcanos will erupt in populated areas as stresses on geological faults increase. Weather disturbances will become more frequent and more violent, leading to flooding and other forms of destruction.

91 John and Paula Sandford, Ibid., pg. 102-103.

> "Earth can no longer bear up under the accumulated sin of mankind, and has begun to react in pain as the whole of creation strains to bring forth the new creation in Jesus our LORD. The whole of Romans 8 speaks to the redemption of all that fell when Adam sinned.
>
> "The whole earth aches and groans for the redemption of mankind because when God redeems mankind, creation itself will be freed from bondage. Our completed salvation will be Earth's redemption."[92]

Remember the beautiful portrait that Isaiah paints us a few chapters before he pronounces the full judgment of the earth. There is coming a brand-new atmosphere, a full renewing of Creation.

> *"And the wolf will dwell with the lamb, and the leopard will lie down with the kid, and the calf and the young lion and the fatling together; and a little boy will lead them. They will not hurt or destroy in all My holy mountain, for the earth will be full of the knowledge of the LORD as the waters cover the sea"* (Isaiah 11:6, 9).

God has an eternal purpose in a full renewal of the earth! And mankind should take warning when natural disasters keep occurring, especially in the magnitude of what is happening more and more as these signs come closer together like Paul wrote, as a *"woman in labor pains."*

> Peter writes, *"Know this first of all, that in the last days mockers will come with their mocking, following after their own lusts, and saying, 'Where is the promise of His coming? For ever since the fathers fell asleep, all continues just as it was from the beginning of creation.' For when they maintain this, it escapes their notice that by the word of God the heavens existed long ago and the earth was formed out of water and by water, through which the world at that time was destroyed, being flooded with water. But the present heavens and earth by His word are being reserved for fire, kept for the Day of Judgment and destruction of ungodly men"* (2 Peter 3:3-7).

92 R. Loren Sandford, Visions of the Coming Days, Ibid., pg. 75, 105.

So, just as the earth suffered and mankind and earth were judged in the flood of Noah, the present Age is coming to a close, and the sovereign LORD is allowing more and more of His judgments to fall on the earth. Yet He is not allowing it to be destroyed in full, until the day of the LORD and Christ Himself returns in retribution.

Every time a disaster happens, we as Believers need to be in prayer. Prayer for the families who are affected; prayers for discernment about the disaster, and prayers for people to respond to God as He still extends mercy.

When these shakings take place, many unbelievers realize that they are alienated from God. In a sense, the earth itself is unstable and offers no security, and God allows this to teach mankind that he or she is indeed in alienation and alone. And if they do not repent of their sins, they will face Judgment Day, and then receive a sentence of eternal insecurity—eternal alienation from His presence.

The blasting Trumpets of Revelation 8 are meant to be a somber warning to the unbelievers: the door of mercy is still open! Repent and return to the LORD with all your heart. The final climax of history is on the horizon. Judgment Day is coming.

"Whenever something catastrophic takes place internationally," writes Anne Graham Lotz, "as occurred when the deadly tsunami struck South Asia, or nationally, when Hurricane Katrina roared ashore in 2005, you and I need to develop the habit of asking God what message there might be in it. This concept of a storm containing a message from God is clearly illustrated in the life of Ezekiel. After being held captive by King Nebuchadnezzar of Babylon, he related that, "I looked, and I saw a windstorm coming out of the north—an immense cloud with flashing lightening and surrounded by brilliant light." His testimony goes on to describe the unique message from God that was brought to him on the wings of that storm. Sometimes we need to be shaken awake."[93]

---

93 Anne Graham Lotz, Expecting to See Jesus, Ibid., pg. 89.

Answer #2: God Did This.

A word about the Bowls of Wrath found in Cycle 5 (Revelation 15-16). If you study them carefully, you will find that they do picture moments in Salvation-History (again, which are very rare) of direct judgments flowing from the Almighty into His creation to judge evil. God may send a cataclysmic event of utmost devastation against idolaters and demonic realms themselves. But their primary focus appears to be the Second Coming.

Therefore, in terms of thinking about the Rapture, the tribulation, and God's wrath being poured out, I get asked this question by people who are of the Dispensational belief.

"Doesn't the "Rapture" have to come BEFORE the final tribulation period, as Christians are not subject to the wrath of God, are they?"

My answer? No and No! The Rapture does not come BEFORE the final tribulation, BECAUSE Christians are not subject to God's wrath and that is poured out AT the Second Coming!

The Rapture (as I have written about in Appendix 1) comes at the very Second Coming of our LORD. The wrath of God as pictured in the Bowls, is a *symbolic view of the Second Coming;* they all happen simultaneously as the earth, the unrepentant, and the demonic realms themselves are all brought to utter and final destruction.

What follows are the Great White Throne Judgment and the Eternal State. Final judgment in the Lake of Fire for the Devil and all his demonic forces, and eternal banishment from the presence of God for unbelievers. And for Believers, the eternal enjoyment of God's presence for all who repented on earth and turned their hearts to a relationship with Jesus Christ before His Second Coming (see Revelation 20:11-15, and chapters 21 & 22).

This coming week in your devotional study time, read chapters 15 and 16 in Revelation with a view that John sees the Second Coming and the finality of all the previous judgments for sin on the earth (the 1/3 in the Trumpets) from a unique angle. He is watching the Final Judgment on the earth at the Second Coming, and Believers are *already* with the LORD forever, not experiencing any of those judgments.

So What About Earthquakes?

The Prophet thunders forth a further declaration.

> *"The Earth is broken asunder, the Earth is split through, and the Earth is shaken violently. The Earth reels to and fro like a drunkard, and it totters like a shack, for its transgression is heavy upon it"* (Isaiah 24:19-20).

"The word, 'shaken,' is suitable for describing an earthquake or some great convulsion that breaks the earth in pieces. Isaiah gives the reason why the earth is so shaken: it is that her transgression now weighs heavily upon her."[94]

From Isaiah's point of view, the LORD announces He is sending judgment to deal with the sin and transgression of mankind in the form of shakings. Though indeed, to put it as clearly as possible, man has transgressed His law, and in so doing, the earth is allowed to feel the weight and reaping of that sin from time to time. Perhaps it waits a generation or two, but surely it comes.

Though God is involved in allowing the earth to undergo a reaping for the sins committed upon it, it is usually connected to the direct or indirect sin, and resulting curses from man himself, that bring it. This is the understanding that the Seals represent in Revelation 6 to 8, with the wrath of God as in indirect wrath.

Yet, once in a while, as I shared earlier through the understanding of the Bowls of Wrath of Revelation 15 and 16, there are moments with earthquakes when they are more than the result of sowing and reaping. God may step into Salvation-History and send a cataclysmic event of utmost devastation against the unrepentant, and even the demonic realms themselves. And those moments truly are a "Day of the LORD" scenario, which means they carry aspects of both judgment and salvation, as His heart is always to see people turn towards Him.

When the next huge earthquake occurs somewhere on earth, many people will ask, *"Did God do that?"*

94 Ibid., pg. 177.

To which you will be able to answer, *"It's possible."*

Here's a rare moment in Salvation-History where God did step in with a Bowl of Judgment being poured out. It was a direct judgment on the sin of a city that had refused to repent.

The year is 1906.

The place: San Francisco, California, USA.

An Earthquake of Judgment that Brought Salvation & Revival

Frank Bartleman was born in 1871 and died in 1936. He was compelled by the Spirit to enter a life of deep prayer and intercession, and the LORD led him to Los Angeles during the time of the Welsh Revival of 1904. He began to be burdened for real revival to break out in California, so he wrote to Evan Roberts, who was leading the revival in Wales, and asked for them to begin to intercede with him. Evan and his team began to pray in agreement. Frank had a walk one day, and the LORD challenged him to "give up all" for this calling.

He said, "Yes, LORD."

He wrote in his journal about his life as a preacher and intercessor,

> "Saying "Yes" means there are hundreds of things people know nothing about in this life of full consecration, such as dangers in traveling, constant change in beds, food, climate, etc. And I have said nothing of the spiritual conflict, the centering of spiritual opposing forces in each battle, and the constant awful pressure of the forces of evil of the highest order."[95]

Sunday, April 15, 1906. Early in the morning, the LORD spoke to Bartleman and said three words, "Tarry ten days." He asked Him why, and no explanation came, but the LORD assured him he would have strength. Bartleman obeyed and began to pray intensely. On Monday and Tuesday, Bartleman tarried alone in prayer. No further directions came.

95 Frank Bartleman, How Pentecost Came to Los Angeles, Christian Life Books, 1925, pg. 130.

Wednesday, April 18, 1906. 5:12 a.m. Suddenly, out of nowhere, San Francisco starts to shake and tremble. The earthquake strikes, and then a devasting fire!

Let me rewind. For the decade preceding this moment, San Francisco was called, "The wickedest city in the world."[96] It had been born in the sins of the time: greed, hedonism, chaos, sexual immorality such as a city had never known, and violence and bloodshed. There was a Red Light District there known as Barbary Coast, which contained evil opium dens, gambling parlors and very wicked and sensual brothels.

Many people don't know that a plague came through Chinatown in 1900. Only 119 people died, but I believe that was an indirect consequence of the accumulating sins of the city (an example of the Seals of Revelation 6 to 8). Even so, people remained hard-hearted and unrepentant.

3,000 people died that day and over 80% of the city was destroyed by either the earthquake or the fire that followed, including all of Chinatown and the wicked Barbary Coast area.

And where was Bartleman on that fateful Wednesday morning? On his knees in prayer, in the midst of his special 10-day assignment from the LORD.

Did the LORD know the day and hour of the earthquake?

Did HE send it as direct judgment?

Let's find out from the words of Bartleman himself from his journal.

> "I discovered on Wednesday that San Francisco was shaken down and burning up. I began to understand. It was in some way a strange answer to our prayers. God would reveal something to me in this connection. It was His hand.
>
> "It was a terrible time. Los Angeles was spell-bound. Nervous tension high. Apprehension filled every breast. Friends, loved

96 The Barbary Coast Historical Essay, online by Foundsf.org.

ones, money were all involved. Business stood still. What would God say to us? I listened for His voice.

"Did God do that?" was the question plainly written over the whole city, expressed or unexpressed. I waited closely on Him. The preachers became a mighty instrument in the hands of Satan to drown His voice, as they labored to convince the people that the quake was not a direct agency of God.

"A brother in the LORD received the following scripture from God a few days before the quake, and escaped the city before the judgment came.

"For this city hath been to Me a provocation of Mine anger and of My fury from the day that they built it even unto this day; that I should remove it from before My face" (Jeremiah 32:31).

"But while Hell itself worked for defeat night and day to blot out the fact of direct agency of God in this, the LORD would offset it by another means. Saturday eve He at last spoke to me. He bade me write. He showed me all Hell was being moved to drown His voice in the earthquake as He sought to awaken the consciences of men.

"I sensed the battle, and it was awful. The armies of Heaven would march forth at the command of the saints, through intercessory prayer, and engage in deadly conflict with the hordes of Hell. The message God was giving me now would be used to beat back the powers of Hell from their purpose and save His voice of warning to the people. They must hear Him. The message must not be lost. He gave me the Word on earthquakes."[97]

Can you feel the intensity of this moment in Frank Bartleman's life? He is in the middle of his 10-day special assignment, which God had initiated three days BEFORE He sent the earthquake.

Think about it!

97 Frank Bartleman, My Story: The Latter Rain, Published in the Way of Faith, Nov., 1907.

What happened next?

The Spirit of the LORD gave Bartleman a most stirring tract of writing on the judgment of God in earthquakes (and he even quoted from the Isaiah passage I utilized earlier). Here are his words,

> "Sunday past. Monday eve He spoke again. The rest was given. It was exhortation, invitation, warning. At 12:30 a.m. it was finished. The Spirit came mightily upon me. From 12:30 to 4 a.m. I was in the presence of God. The Spirit witnessed most powerfully again to the Divine origin of the message. He was making me to realize HIS WRATH for sin. But mercy was remembered. He finally put forth omnipotence of grace on the behalf of souls. Mercy had conquered."

What followed that early morning? He rushed the tract to the printer and the first 75,000 were printed, and he realized this was 10 days exactly after his initial prayer assignment! 50,000 more were soon printed and all of these were distributed by a small army of men in Los Angeles and in Oakland, and distributed in all the areas of the earthquake. Multitudes of people, black and white, young and old, men, women and children, responded to the tract in faith, turned their eyes and hearts to Jesus Christ, and were swept into the Kingdom.

Revival came as a result.

Here are just a few lines of Bartleman's amazing tract from the Spirit of God Himself. For further reading, you can find the whole message online with a simple search, The Earthquake Tract by Frank Bartleman.

> "'*The mountains quake at Him, and the hills melt; and the earth is upheaved at His presence, yea, the world, and all that dwell therein. His fury is poured out like fire, and the rocks are broken asunder by Him*' (Nahum 1:5-6). '*And I will punish the world for their evil. Therefore I will make the heavens to tremble, and the earth shall be shaken out of her place, in the day of His fierce anger*' (Isaiah 13:11, 13).

> *"And the 7th angel (of wrath) poured out his vial into the air and there was a GREAT EARTHQUAKE"* (Rev. 16:17,18). *And will you claim there is no God in earthquakes? John Wesley has said, 'Of all the judgments which the righteous God inflicts on sinners here, the most dreadful and destructive is an earthquake.' Very soon this poor old earth will be struggling in the mighty throes of a final and complete dissolution. "Be ye reconciled to God.""*
>
> – From "Earthquake Tract," by Frank Bartleman, April 1906.[98]

This was a rare moment indeed of "Divine direct agency," as Bartleman put it so truthfully. Let's continue to look now at how Jesus Himself told us that these kinds of signs (both direct and indirect expressions of God's wrath) would be increasing during the times nearing His Second Coming.

Question: What About Satan and His Involvement in the Weather? Can He Also Be Involved?

Answer: Yes! This is Answer #3: Satan Did This.

I know this can be a controversial position and controversial subject, but I am taking it anyway. Just as God is sovereign over His world, He has also allowed evil powers to dominate it for the present time (until the return of the King and eternal justice is finally a reality). These evil powers hate you. They hate your neighbor. They hate your family and friends. Why? Because all of you—Believer or unbeliever—are made in God's image, and the Enemy hates humankind.

The truth is, Scripture reveals that God created everything good, including spiritual beings, who He also gave a free will. Some of them, in time, by free will chose to rebel against God. Satan (known also as Lucifer) was among them as their leader. The problem of evil and the resulting human suffering has plagued theologians down through the Ages.

Let's begin in the Old Testament, where we discover that Satan and his evil forces are known as both, *Leviathan* (evil powers that rule over the seas) and *Behemoth* (evil powers that rule over land). Both of these are terms for

98 Excerpts from, Earthquake Tract by Frank Bartleman, April 1906.

the Enemy's evil strongholds over entire regions of the sea and earth, and are found in the Book of Job, the earliest manuscript we have in the entire Bible. We also discover the free agency of Satan, and how much he hates the righteous who follow after God's ways. In chapter 1 we read,

> *"Now there was a day when the sons of God came to present themselves before the LORD, and Satan also came among them. And the LORD said to Satan, 'From where do you come?' Then Satan answered the LORD and said, 'From roaming about on the earth and walking around on it'"* (Job 1:6-7).

Let's just pause there. We can learn from this passage, written all the way back sometime in the ancient days (many scholars think Job was written around the time of Abraham himself), that Satan was no doubt roaming to and fro, creating evil scenarios and bringing deceit and destruction on mankind. Then the LORD speaks to Satan.

> *"Have you considered my servant Job? For there is no one like him on the earth, a blameless and upright man, revering God and turning away from evil"* (Job 1:8).

So here we have a righteous man! Sounds like a similar description given centuries earlier to Noah. What follows in this discourse, which took place in the Heavenly Courts, is fascinating. (The "sons of God" mentioned in the passage are most likely angelic leaders who were part of the Divine Counsel Chamber of the LORD.) At this time in history, Satan was still, though evil personified, allowed access there. By the way, that all ended on the day of the Cross and resurrection of Jesus Christ. *Christus Victor!*

Most of you probably know the story. Satan challenges the LORD and is allowed to afflict Job in any way he chooses, except he cannot take his life. AND WHAT FOLLOWS: Satan uses *natural disasters* to bring death and destruction to Job's family, including a massive firestorm and a massive hurricane/tornado type of wind, which killed Job's sons and daughters (see Job 1:16-19).

The end of the story? Job endures and is restored by the LORD for his faithfulness.

But the point here is twofold.

1. Satan and his evil forces (the "powers" as the Apostle Paul calls them in Ephesians 6:10-12) have autonomous, free will to attack anywhere and anyone they choose. God is sovereign, yes. But He does not intervene directly with these evil forces very often, as they have free will, just like you and me.

2. Satan, also known as, "the prince of the power of the air" (Ephesians 2:2) has control of the elements of the earth. At times, he utilizes those elements to destroy and wreak havoc on people; both Christians and non-Christians alike.

Leviathan and *Behemoth* are mentioned in Job as spiritually evil forces in Job chapter 40 (Behemoth) and chapter 41 (Leviathan).

Many scholars believe, as do I, that John the Revelator borrows from the imagery of the Beast who comes out of the sea as Leviathan, and the Beast who comes out of the earth as Behemoth. (See Revelation 13:1-10 for a symbolic description of the *Beast from the Sea,* and 13:11-18 for the *Beast from the Earth.*) As I say, I will cover those two Beasts in detail in the next chapter.

For now, know that your adversary has control over many of the elements of the earth.

> "The power of gods (demons) to resist Yahweh in war, to hinder his answers to prayers, to influence "natural" disasters, to inflict diseases on people, to deceive people and the like is assumed throughout the Bible," writes Gregory Boyd, "When humanity rejected Yahweh's lordship, we accepted (by unleashing) a new "god of this world." We compromised our assigned task to have dominion over the world and thus subjected ourselves and all of nature once again to the destructive influence of the forces that oppose God. Through Christ, however, the key has been given back to those originally intended as landlords *(that's the good news for Believers, emphasis mine).*"[99]

99 Gregory A. Boyd, God at War: the Bible and Spiritual Conflict, InterVarsity Press, 1997.

One of my favorite examples of spiritual warfare involving the weather is found in all three Synoptic Gospels, Matthew, Mark and Luke. I'll just choose Mark, chapter 4.

Jesus invites His disciples to join him in the boat and cross over the Sea of Galilee to the other side. It was evening, and they were headed directly to a moment of intense spiritual warfare (though they knew it not) for Jesus was heading for the country of the Gerasenes where a man filled with demons was hiding in a graveyard.

We read how the winds came contrary to the boat:

> *"And there arose a fierce gale of wind, and the waves were breaking over the boat so much that the boat was already filling up"* (Mark 4:37).

I believe Satan and his evil forces (remember, Leviathan, the evil spirit with control of the waters) were trying to kill Jesus and the disciples by capsizing that boat in the middle of the sea. Satan may have somehow known that Jesus was on his way to engage in warfare against him and his evil servant in the tombs.

> *"'Teacher, do you not care that we are perishing?' And being aroused (for He was asleep) He rebuked the wind and said to the sea, 'Hush, be still.' And the wind died down and it became perfectly calm"* (Mark 4:38b-39).

And the result? The next day they arrived at the place of the tombs, and Jesus cast out the demons from that captive of Satan, and he became a servant of God!

Another amazing passage is also found in the Synoptic Gospels. Since we are in Mark, we'll stay there. In chapter 6, we find that directly after the 5,000 are fed (a miracle that involves the earth itself yielding the power to create into the very hands of the One who created it), Jesus departs to seek the LORD, and the disciples again encounter a rough wind.

> *"The wind was against them"* (Mark 6:48).

Here is perhaps the best part of this account. Jesus does NOT "still the sea" but instead, (and I believe just to show Satan a sign of His power and Divinity, though Satan didn't sort out that Jesus was truly Divine at this moment) He comes WALKING ON THE WATER.

> *"He came to them, walking on the sea. He said to them, 'Take courage; it is I, do not be afraid.' And He got into the boat, and the wind stopped; and they were greatly astonished"* (Mark 6:50-51).

For our study here, let me just say this. Over and over, Jesus, as the fulfillment of which Moses was only a type and shadow, does one miracle better than Moses. Just to prove His Divinity!

So instead of "parting" the sea, He comes *walking* on it! No one on earth had ever done that before. This is also a sign of the future Kingdom in its fullness, when nature will be subject to the sons of God, and be in continual obedience under the authority of the LORD and us, His children.

The point here is that in a sense, Jesus as the Warrior King slays Leviathan! He demonstrates His Divine authority over the attacks of the Enemy, who I believe in both of these passages sent the wind and waves to try and destroy or hinder the ministry of Jesus and His disciples.

A Modern Example of Satan's Destruction: COVID-19

As we consider the Pandemic of 2020-2022 (a form of pestilence), and the worldwide fear, the lockdowns, and the incredible deaths in its aftermath, I believe that COVID-19 stands as an instance where Satan utilized "pestilence" as a means to decimate human life and potentially destroy whole cultures. According to statistics, over 700+ million people got the disease, and of those, a staggering 7-plus million died. The coronavirus decimated the earth.

I can vividly remember being in a prayer meeting in the Fall of 2019. I learned that over 20 of the world's largest platform ministries, with influence over millions of people, were planning huge crusades and city-wide evangelistic thrusts for 2020. It was to be a year of huge harvest in the nations. What happened instead? Satan attacked. Every single event was cancelled as a result. I believe that this virus was from the pit of Hell and caused untold damage and spread of fear and uncertainty.

I myself lost several very close friends and former mentors in the pandemic. It's like the Enemy just snuffed out their candle light long before that light would have faded.

The Book of Revelation reveals a most unique vision of the Four Horsemen of the Apocalypse, which are all agents of judgments that befall the world, which is persecuting the Church. (Study carefully the Seals of chapter 6; note the fourth Seal, the ashen-colored horse.)

> *"And I looked, and behold, an ashen horse (sickly pale): and he who sat on it had the name Death; and Hades was following with him. And authority was given to them over a fourth of the earth, to kill with sword and with famine* **and with pestilence...**" (Revelation 6:8).

The AUTHORITY of the BELIEVER: We can Intercede with Power!

Now if Satan is behind some of the disasters and at times, elements of the earth that are attempting to hinder our missions, what can WE do?

We can pray!

Prayer, as shown in the authority of the Two Witnesses, and in the previous example of Rees Howells, can also affect the elements of the earth. They respond to the authority of their Creator, coming through the Body of Christ on earth.

Just one of so many examples in Salvation-History, where Satan was attempting to hinder God's work by controlling nature, is found in the journal of the extraordinary life of J. Hudson Taylor, pioneer missionary to China. You'll discover in this story, it's quite the opposite of when Jesus and the disciples were in their boat. In this case, Satan sent a calm to shipwreck Taylor's boat and kill all the men on it through the savages on the shores! Here's the account in Taylor's own words.

"I was nearly wrecked when I was going out to China the first time. Our vessel was becalmed, and gradually drifting upon the coast of New Guinea. We could see the savages on the shore. They had kindled a fire, and were evidently expecting a good supper that night.

We can pray!

"The captain said to me: 'We can't do anything else but let down the long-boat.' They had tried to turn the head of the vessel around from the shore, but in vain. We had been becalmed for several weeks, with never a breeze, or any sign of one. In a few minutes we would be among the coral reefs. We would be at the mercy of those savages, and they didn't look as if they had much mercy.

"Well," I said, "there is one thing we haven't done yet. Let the Christians on board pray about it." There was a black man on board, a steward, who was a very sweet Christian man, and the captain was a Christian, and myself. I proposed that we should retire to our cabins, and in the name of our Lord Jesus Christ ask our Father, and His Father, for a breeze immediately. They agreed.

"I went to my cabin, and told the Lord that I was just on my way to China; that He had sent me; and that I couldn't get there if I was shipwrecked and killed; and then I was going on to ask Him for a breeze, but I felt so confident about it that I couldn't ask Him.

"So I went up on deck. There was the second officer, the chief mate, a very godless man. I went up to him and said: "If I were you I would let down the mainsail." Said he: "What do you want me to let down the mainsail for?" I said: "We have been praying for a breeze, and it is coming directly, and the sooner we are ready for it the better." With an oath he said he would rather see a breeze than hear of one.

"As he was speaking I instinctively looked up, and noticed that one of the sails was quivering with the coming breeze. Said I: "Don't you see that the corners of the royals are already shaking? My dear fellow, there is a good breeze coming, and we had better be ready for it."

"Of course, the mate went to work, and soon the sailors were tramping over the deck. Before the sails were set the wind was down upon us. The captain came up to see what was the matter. He saw that our prayers had been answered; and we didn't forget to praise God for so signal a deliverance from the perils to which we were exposed."[100]

So, the next time a natural disaster is approaching...PRAY!

You, as a Believer, have been given authority in the name of Jesus over the elements of this world.

I actually believe that Satan's evil servants (witches, warlocks and the like) are praying and fasting to see more and more natural disasters occur, and performing demonic curses to make the storms get worse as they approach land or being stirred up on the land.

Likewise, I believe that many Believers stand up in prayer, and many of the Enemy's plans are thwarted or diminished as a result of the intercession of the people of God here on earth. That's good news!

In Conclusion...

We began this chapter with the quote that 50 measurable earthquakes happen every day in our modern world, and over 20,000 every year above a magnitude of 5.0. We've remembered the truth that God placed His creation under the curse of man, and the earth is reeling like a drunken man, as mankind self-destructs and thus, Earth itself self-destructs, and this reaping of sin gets worse and worse as each generation passes without the return of Christ.

100 J. Hudson Taylor, Hudson Taylor's Spiritual Secret, by Howard and Geraldine Taylor, Hendrickson Publishing, originally published in 1932.

Revelation borrows from the earthquake atop of Mount Sinai imagery of Exodus 19:18, and from Ezekiel 38 (Gog/Magog), with the imagery of an earthquake as marking the final moment of world history and ushering in the great Judgment Day.

> *"And there were flashes of lightning and sounds and peals of thunder; and there was a great earthquake, such as there had not been since man came to be upon the earth, so great an earthquake was it, and so mighty"* (Revelation 16:18).

In our own day, we have not yet reached the last day of history, so the Seals and Trumpets of Revelation chapters 6 to 8 are designed by God to allow a warning to be sounded. Let every reader take notice when another vast natural disaster kills many people. It's a warning. Judgment Day is coming. The final day of reckoning for all the sins of the creation, especially the sin of murder, is fast approaching.

We learned also in this chapter that when a natural disaster happens, and people ask, "Did God do this?" the answer can have multiple possibilities:

1. **WE did this.** Mankind, through our generations of accumulated sins and curses is causing the earth itself to reap what we have sown. These natural disasters are expressions of the sphere of God's indirect wrath working itself out in Salvation-History.

2. **God did this.** Very rarely, and only occasionally through direct intervention, God's bowls of wrath fill up and He reaps the sins of mankind in direct judgments.

3. **Satan did this.** The Enemy's evil "powers" brought this destruction and death to people that he hates and wants to continuously destroy, (see Ephesians 6:10-14).

Yet as of this writing, the Door of Mercy still stands open to all who come to Christ in faith.

> *"The LORD is not slow about His promise as some count slowness, but is patient toward you, not wishing for any to perish but for all to come to repentance"* (2 Peter 3:9).

Let us remember this verse as we await the last day on Earth, a day of a vast earthquake, so strong and mighty, as has never been.

Even so, Come LORD Jesus, Amen.

Going Deeper Still:

— The earth is the LORD's and was originally created as "good" before the fall. As a result of man's sin at the fall, it has been cursed by God. Have you ever thought of the earth as a place that has accumulated curses and responds with a traumatic disaster?

— An accumulation of curses and the sowing of generational sins cause the very ground to shake. Thus, natural disasters can be a sign of judgment on sin, including occasional direct judgments from God, and indirect judgments as a result of the reaping of what has been sown. Both are aspects of His wrath, though in most cases, His wrath is indirect. Read about the Trumpets of Revelation 8 and the Bowls of Revelation 15-16, and pray over those passages. The Bowls happen only at the Second Coming!

— Jesus is coming again and will renew the earth! A golden age of eternity will ensue with all curses broken and the earth itself liberated with the redemption of the sons and daughters of God upon it. Can you imagine what that will be like?

— Study these scriptures in light of this understanding: Luke 21:11, 25-26a, Psalm 24:1-2, Genesis 8:21, Isaiah 24:3-6a, 12-13, and Revelation 16:18.

— Every time a natural disaster shakes people, pray for them to have their spiritual eyes opened to the reality of the coming Judgment Day.

The Two Witnesses as the Saints in the Church Age

A Study on the Advancing Army of the LORD

"**And I will grant authority to my two witnesses,** *and they will prophesy for twelve hundred and sixty days, clothed in sackcloth*" (Revelation 11:3).

"Though parts of the Church's voice throughout history may be temporarily silenced, a universal silence will fall on the Church at the very end of history. And just as small groups of Believers continued to exist throughout earlier temporary silencings, so a small remnant of 'Witnesses' remain in the future scenario of the Final Battle."[101]

Now that you've been exposed to a kind of revolutionary approach to the study of Revelation, I'd like to take 2 whole chapters to zoom in on two particular scriptures, both in two parallel visions with unique sets of symbolism, which point to the reality of the Last Battle itself.

I will share how I posed the question, "What DID it mean?" (explaining the context of the verses and their origins throughout both Old and New

101 Ibid, G.K. Beale, page 590.

Testaments). Along the way, as I expand some thoughts on each verse in this chapter, you can be prayerfully asking yourself,

"What DOES this mean—for me today? AND, for me, TOMORROW?"

As we begin, maybe have a look back at my **Summary of Cycle 3** (encompassing Revelation chapter 8:2 to the end of chapter 11).

If you happened to turn to this chapter out of sheer curiosity (and remember, curiosity killed the cat!), please pause here and **go back** and first read the two previous chapters that lay a solid, theological and strategic foundation for these next two chapters.

For centuries, these two witnesses have fascinated us, and baffled both theologians and students of apocalyptic writing.

And as I shared in my Author's Introduction: Hey, you know what? You may never have read or heard of the fresh perspectives laid out in this book.

Not many people have, especially since during the last 200 years, the Dispensational views have dominated studies of eschatology. Those views tend to interpret these two witnesses in terms of a literal, future-time actual bodily appearance. They believe that perhaps Moses and Elijah are going to appear in person, here on earth, and for a literal and exact 1260 days and fulfill their mission in the nations.

I actually have many good friends, and even dear mentors, who hold to these perspectives.

Here's a very strong, possible interpretation of the symbolism of the two witnesses: They equal the Church and its authority and power in Christ throughout the Church Age.

This was made possible through the victory of Christ on the cross and at the resurrection, when He exercised heavenly authority in "the binding of the strong man" so He could "spoil his goods" (see Matthew 12:29, Mark 3:27, and Luke 11:21-22).

Thus, the Church Age we find ourselves in *right now* gives us hope to continue to be a strong witness in the nations, and keep spreading the Gospel far and wide! Revivals and new moves of God are still upcoming in many nations in our times.

Why is this important? It's not just important: IT'S VITALLY IMPORTANT.

Why? Because this will help inspire you to be a stronger witness in *these* days, and to help *prepare you for what is coming next.*

This chapter is filled with the Battle Plans of the LORD and the Battle Plans of the Enemy! Let's learn about them.

First: Why Not a Literal Moses & Elijah?

> *"And I will grant authority to my two witnesses,"* (Revelation 11:3).

As I shared in the previous chapters, whenever I attempt an interpretation of a symbolic text in Revelation, I first consider the Old Testament as my background for the imagery, and then I look for supplemental texts in the New Testament to compare and contrast.

In the case of the two witnesses, because of the similarities with Moses and Elijah in the passage itself, it becomes paramount to do some digging and see what both Testaments give us as foundational understanding of these two men.

This chapter will surprise all readers who are waiting around for some last-days reappearance of a literal Moses and Elijah. It is quite improbable that the LORD will send them back physically, as even Malachi's prophetic utterance and final admonition had been fulfilled with the coming of John the Baptist. John began heralding the coming of the Kingdom of God, and was followed soon with the ministry of Jesus Christ, who inaugurated it. Then Jesus Himself, after His death, burial, resurrection and ascension, imparted His Holy Spirit and His marching orders to His army, the Church worldwide, to continue His ministry until His personal return.

See how both Moses and Elijah are mentioned in the end of Malachi,

> *"Remember the law of* **Moses My servant;** *Behold, I am going to send you* **Elijah the prophet** *before the coming of the great and terrible day of the LORD. And he will restore the hearts of the fathers to their children, and the hearts of the children to their fathers, lest I come and smite the land with a curse"*
> (Malachi 4:4a, 5-6).

"The rabbis taught that Elijah would return to prepare for and announce the coming of the Messiah (see Matthew 17:10, Mark 9:11). Even in the intertestamental period, Elijah was seen as one of the great O.T. personalities (Sirach 48:1-12a). Jesus publicly identified John the Baptist as the one whom the Jews were expecting to come as Elijah (Matthew 11:11-14). After meeting with Elijah (and Moses) at His transfiguration, Jesus alluded to Malachi 4:5-6 as He explained to Peter, James and John that John the Baptist fulfilled the prophecy about Elijah's return."[102]

At His transfiguration, amazingly *both Moses and Elijah were there.* And just when you thought that their appearance fulfilled everything, here they seem to pop up again right in the middle of a vision in Revelation. But are they two literal figures, brought back seemingly from the dead, and about to literally appear here on the Earth?

As you know it is not my intention to write a verse-by-verse commentary of the Book of Revelation.

However, it is vital for you to have a very clear understanding at a portion of verses in chapter 11 and chapter 20 of Revelation, as they relate directly to the unique idea that the Church is about to undergo a world-wide trial of persecution, just prior to the Second Coming.

So, in the following two chapters, I am going to take a deep dive into a verse-by-verse discussion and the possibly clear, deeper spiritual truths and meanings behind the symbols that John sees in the visions. We'll begin with the symbolic beauty in the two witnesses.

---

102 Spiros Zodhiates, The Hebrew-Greek Key Study Bible, pg. 1255. AMG Publishers, 1990.

We Are His Witnesses

Allow me the privilege of sharing what I believe the proper symbolic definition is of these two. They represent the Church on Earth during her sojourning as the powerful witnesses of the resurrection of Jesus Christ, operating in His love, His authority, His power and His grace.

Firstly, let us remember our structure of the Book of Revelation: seven parallel visions in time. It is seven perfect visions, each one representing a unique vantage point of the Church Age. This particular vision begins in Revelation 8:2, and we see it begin on the morning of Easter (the resurrection). It leads us right through the Church Age and finishes at the very end of chapter 11 with a picture of the Second Coming.

What is interesting about chapter 11 where we find the two witnesses, is the mystery that is being revealed in this incredible symbolism. The vision reveals the following:

One: The Church has incredible authority and power, and is a weapon in the hands of the LORD against the Enemy and Enemy-occupied territory. He is advancing through us, and reconquering the Earth, but not through terrorism, hatred or violence, but through the opposite: agape-love, mercy and grace! And strongholds are tumbling down in various places in all of Salvation-History, based on our unique prayer assignments and the authority of the Name of Jesus.

Two: The public witness of Jesus will finish on a particular day in the future, with a brief attack of Satan upon the Church through demonic deception and power, causing the Church to endure intensified persecution around the world for a short season.

They figuratively represent the ongoing "invincible" message, power and authority of the ministry of the Body of Christ on Earth during the entire Church Age.

Let's have a biblical understanding with three key New Testament verses that speak of the Church Universal as witnesses.

> *"Thus it is written, that the Christ (Messiah) should suffer and rise again from the dead the third day; and that repentance for forgiveness of sins should be proclaimed in His name to all the nations, beginning from Jerusalem. You are* **witnesses** *of these things."*
> —Jesus Himself, The Resurrected Messiah, Luke 24:46-48.

> *"You shall be* **My witnesses**.*"*
> — The Resurrected Messiah, Acts 1:8a.

> *"You put to death the Prince of life, the one whom God raised from the dead, a fact to which* **we are witnesses**.*"*
> — The Apostle Peter, in his second sermon, Acts 3:15.

Beautiful, right? So let's turn to our first portion of this passage where I will give a verse-by-verse interpretation of the symbolism. In the first portion of the passage, we will consider a potential interpretation of the witnesses, and see the power and authority of the advancing Church in the nations. This interpretation is rooted in the Old Testament, and the passage itself gives us the clues to discover the deeper spiritual meanings of the symbols.

> *"And I will grant authority to my two witnesses, and they will prophesy for twelve hundred and sixty days, clothed in sack-cloth." These are the two olive trees and the two lampstands that stand before the Lord of the earth. And if anyone desires to harm them, fire proceeds out of their mouth and devours their enemies; and if anyone would desire to harm them, in this manner he must be killed. These have the power to shut up the sky, in order that rain may not fall during the days of their prophesying; and they have power over the waters to turn them into blood, and to smite the earth with every plague, as often as they desire"*
> (Revelation 11:3-6).

> **"And I will grant authority to my two witnesses, And they will prophesy for 1,260 days, clothed in sackcloth."** (Verse 3)

Interpretation: First off, we note that this is a declarative statement, given in quotations, from the LORD Himself. What follows in the next four verses is the symbolic description of them.

1. He grants them authority. It's helpful here to remember how Jesus, Messiah and King, began His earthly ministry with the casting out of demons, and commanded his followers to utilize His own name as legal grounds for the continuation of His ministry (see Mark 16).

   The word "authority" in the Greek is *exousia*, and it can be defined as, the legal right to act. From the earliest days of His ministry, Jesus gave this legal right to act to His disciples, and then after the resurrection and the Ascension, he left it with them/us to continue to act and continue to rule in His name!

   Part of Jesus' central assignment from the Father was to "bind the strongman and then steal his goods" (Matthew 12:29). The ultimate binding happened at the moment of the death of Jesus upon the cross, followed by the moment of the resurrection of Christ. Jesus' victory is our continued victory!

2. Now why the number two? Firstly, remember that Jesus sent forth His disciples "two by two," meaning that when teamed together, each brings a fullness and what one may lack, the other makes up for and strengthens (Luke 10). Secondly, on the testimony of two witnesses, *"every word shall be established"* (Deuteronomy 19:15).

3. The word "witness" in the Greek is, "martyr." In the opening of Revelation, Jesus Himself is described as, *"the faithful martyr/witness"* (Revelation 1:5). Elsewhere in Revelation, His followers are described with the same word (Revelation 2:13, 17:16). It does not mean that every witness is also an actual martyr, but it signifies this because of the truth that Jesus first laid down His life for us, and many are called to lay down their lives during the battles of this ongoing spiritual war.

4. Next, what are they doing? In this verse, they are described as prophesying. Peter quotes the prophet Joel who saw the Church Age as this unique time where, as he saw it, *"And it shall be in the last days," God says, 'That I will pour out My Spirit upon all mankind, and your sons and your daughters shall prophesy"* (Acts 2:17). In verse 18 of Acts he adds, *"and they shall prophesy."*

5. And what exactly does it mean to prophesy? Joel, Peter and John the Revelator all use this term to symbolically declare that all of God's children in this dispensation are filled with the Spirit. (To what degree you are filled is a whole different matter.)

So, instead of interpreting this to somehow mean that every Christian needs to move in the gift of prophecy as described by Paul in 1 Corinthians 12 and 14, let me instead bring forth this interpretation: *"The testimony of Jesus is the Spirit of prophecy"* (Revelation 19:10).

"To prophesy is to *speak truth into the present,"* shares Dr. Gloria Wiese, one of my mentors and early teachers in Scripture, "calling on people to repent and believe in Christ."[103]

Question: How do we tell time in Revelation?

Answer: In a non-linear fashion.

6. Now to the time: 1,260 days. The way to tell time when it comes to apocalyptic literature is to realize that the numbers and the time measurements in the Book of Revelation are meant to be understood, not as linear measurements, but as symbolic.

Because of the poetic, parallel nature of the seven visions, John comes up with at least three creative ways that all sound the same and all represent the same period of time; the time we are in right now and have been in since the first Easter morning.

Here is my graph to help illustrate this synonymous parallelism.

Synonymous Parallelism		
"42 months" (Revelation 11:2, 13:5)	*"a time, times, and half a time"* (Daniel 7:25, 12:7) (Revelation 12:14)	*"1,260 days"* (Revelation 11:3, 12:6)

103 Blogsite, www.askdrglow.com

Revelation chapter 11 is in one of the seven parallel cycles, while chapter 12 is in a different one. Both are unique vantage points (the round towers on different mountain peaks overlooking the valley of the Church Age), and are describing in their own unique ways the war of the Lamb and the Beast that is ongoing throughout the Church Age. Both utilize time measurement in unique, symbolic language.

"The time period in which the witnesses carry on their proclamation is symbolized in a way that equates it with the whole span of the Dragon's aggressive but frustrated attempts to eradicate the church from the Earth.

"This time is described in three ways: 42 months, 1,260 days and "a time and times and half a time," which is derived from Daniel 7:25, in which it symbolizes one-half of a sabbatical-year cycle: "one year, two years, and half a year" add up to 3 ½ years.

"These three designations all measure the same length of time, for in the ancient world a month was calculated as containing 30 days (42 x 30 = 1,260) and a year as containing 360 (3.5 x 360 = 1,260). The statements that contain these temporal markers provide complimentary perspectives on the same era of history: the Church Age.[104]

"It is in order to ask why the term, 'three years and a half' and the term 'a time, times, and half a time' is used to characterize this long period. To answer this question we must remember that during the old dispensation there was a period of three years and a half that God's people could not forget. It was a period of affliction, yet also a period during which God's Word was exhibited (see I Kings 17; James 5:17).

"When you compare James 5:17 with Revelation 11:6, you immediately see that the apostle was thinking of the days of Ahab and Elijah. The expression 'a time, times, and half a time' occurs first in the Book of Daniel, and is the period of the Antichrist. John emphasizes that the spirit of the Antichrist is in the world already (1 John 4:3). In the Apocalypse, the period of three years and a half refers to the entire gospel age."[105]

104 Johnson, Ibid, pg. 172.
105 William Hendricksen. More than Conquerers. Pg. 143-144. Grand Rapids, MI. Baker Book House, 1940, 1967.

7. And finally, the clothing of the Witnesses: sackcloth?

Interpretation: This suggests mourning over the judgment that their message conveys, possibly with the hope that some may repent. It is a message throughout the Church Age of impending judgment and a call to repentance. Every day they bear witness to the resurrection of Jesus Christ, and every day until the very end of the dispensation, people are invited to repent and receive mercy instead of the judgment to come. "Their witness," writes G.K. Beale, "focuses on the redemptive history of Jesus, especially His death, resurrection, and Lordship."[106]

These are the two olive trees and the two lampstands that stand before the LORD of the Earth (Revelation 11:4).

Interpretation: Before I share some details on verse 4, let's look at some parallel passages from the Old Testament: Zechariah 3:8, 4:2, 3, 6, 7, 12, 13, 14 and 6:12-13.

> *"Now listen, Joshua the high priest, you and your friends who are sitting in front of you—indeed they are men who are a symbol, for behold, I am going to bring in My servant the Branch. And he said to me, 'What do you see?' And I said, 'I see, two olive trees.' 'This is the word of the LORD to Zerubbabel saying, 'Not by might nor by power, but by My Spirit,' says the LORD. The two olive trees are the two anointed ones, who are standing by the LORD of the whole Earth. Behold, a man whose name is Branch, for He will branch out from where He is; and He will build the temple of the LORD, yes, it is He who will bear the honor and sit and rule on His throne."*

So Zechariah sees a vision of the two olive trees which to him were,

One: Joshua

The Priest of the day who is pictured as pointing the way to Messiah, who someday would replace his office with a new Priesthood, and is "The

106 For deeper understandings I am utilizing 3 separate and unique commentators here. (1) William Hendriksen's More Than Conquerors, pgs. 128-130, and (2) Dennis E. Johnson's Triumph of the Lamb, pgs. 168-171, and Ibid, G.K. Beale, The Book of Revelation, pg.576.

Righteous Branch" promised both here and seen symbolically in the olive branch given to Noah, and also found in Isaiah 11:1, 53:2.

Two: Zerubbabel

He was the King of the day who is pictured as pointing the way to Messiah, who would someday replace his office and become the world's true King; and all of this accomplished by "My Spirit" says the LORD (fulfilled in this age and referenced by Joel and Peter in Acts 2). To Zechariah, the olive trees are interpreted as *"the two anointed ones, who are standing by the LORD of the whole Earth"* (Zechariah 4:14).

The context suggests that they are Zerubbabel, the royal figure who was to rebuild God's temple, and Joshua, the priest who is to lead worship in that temple. Both prefigure the coming Servant of God, the Branch who will unite the royal and priestly offices by building the temple, offering atoning sacrifice, and ruling on His throne.

"Thus the two witnesses are explicitly presented as prophets, while the allusion to Zechariah's olive trees implies that they are also kings and priests. Since we have already seen the church portrayed as priests who reign (read Revelation 5:10), we may suspect that these two witnesses symbolize the whole Church in its role as witnesses to God's truth and against the world's lies and wickedness."[107]

"She is to be an olive tree and a lamp before the LORD," wrote Vernard Eller in his excellent Commentary on Revelation, "Olive trees bear fruit, lamps give light; who has ever put the mission of the Church any more succinctly? As lamps, we are so to live and act and speak that the truth of who Jesus is and what He does will be illuminated to the world. As olive trees, we are to engage in the same ministry of service and reconciliation that Jesus Himself pursued."[108]

Interestingly, in the New Covenant, Christ applied this prophesy to Himself in calling Himself "the vine" in John 15, and calling His followers

107 Johnson, Ibid, pg. 170-171.
108 Vernard Eller, "The Most Revealing Book of the Bible: Making Sense out of Revelation." Wm. B. Eerdmans Publishing Co, Grand Rapids, MI, 1974. Page 118.

as "the branches" who receive their spiritual life from Him. It is He who is "the Branch" and He who was both human and Divine, and He who began a spiritual temple/sanctuary for God's presence. Believers are part of the spiritual temple He is building now. (See 1 Corinthians 3:16, 2 Corinthians 6:16, Ephesians 2:21.)

Of course, Christ in His ascension was seen to sit down upon the right hand of the Father, upon the eternal Throne of David, and begin His spiritual reign of all the Earth during this dispensation.

"From Christ, the olive tree, by the Spirit, the olive branch," writes Matthew Henry, "all the golden oil of grace is communicated to Believers, which keeps their lamps burning, and without a constant supply of which would soon go out."[109]

Ah...the "golden oil of grace." One of my most cherished books in my collection in my study is a 1933 illustrated edition of "The Pilgrim's Progress" by John Bunyan. It belonged to my grandparents and was passed down to me after their death. It is the famous story of Christian, who goes upon a journey towards the Celestial City.

During the course of his travels, he meets up with "The Interpreter" and enjoys a rest in a mansion while being shown many interesting scenes.

"Then I saw in my dream," writes Bunyan, "that the Interpreter took Christian by the hand and led him into a place where was a fire burning against a wall, and one standing by it, always casting much water upon it, to quench it; yet did the fire burn higher and hotter. The Interpreter explained its meaning. 'This fire is the work of grace that is wrought in the heart: he that casts water upon it to extinguish and put it out is the devil.'

109 Matthew Henry's Commentary, pg. 1575.

Then he took Christian to the other side of the wall, where he saw a man with a vessel of oil in his hand, of the which he did also continually cast, but secretly, into the fire. 'This is Christ, who continually, with the oil of His grace, maintains the work already begun in the heart."[110]

Can I just pause a moment with a practical application from my own life? As I mentioned in my Introduction, for nearly five years I battled cancer and suffered many setbacks and horrendous side effects from the strong drug treatments. Satan was continually whispering in my ear his lies (just like trying to douse the flames in my heart with water). BUT MY HEAVENLY FATHER was continually allowing me a daily GRACE to endure the trials. My heart was fully His! Christ Wins!

Now back to our actual text and looking deeper into Joshua and Zerubbabel. The Father has always granted His people their true identity! We, as His children, are identified with powerful imagery; no longer are Prophets, Priests and Kings just earthly offices, but their anointing extends in the Church Age to every member of the Body of Christ. So, in Exodus 19:4-6,

> *"You yourselves have seen what I did to the Egyptians, and how I bore you on eagles' wings, and brought you to Myself. Now then, if you will indeed obey My voice and keep My covenant, then you shall be My own possession among all the peoples, for all the Earth is mine; and you shall be to Me a kingdom of priests and a holy nation."*

How wonderful! God's plan is to have one Kingdom among all the Nations. His plan has succeeded and will continue. Revelation 1 opens with this in mind when it declares,

> *"And He (Jesus the Messiah) has made us to be a Kingdom, priests to His God and Father; to Him be the glory and the dominion forever and ever, Amen"* (Revelation 1:6).

And again, John the Revelator emphasizes exactly who we (the Two Witnesses) are in our role with both priestly and kingly (royal) anointing.

110 John Bunyan, The Pilgrim's Progress, pg. 33. The John C. Winston Company, 1933.

> *"And Thou hast made them to be a Kingdom and priests to our God; and they will reign upon the Earth"* (Revelation 5:10).

Any ideas when this kind of prophetic, priestly and royal authority is a reality on Earth? Right now! Until the Age comes to a close, this kind of authority exists upon the Church. So, Paul could also write,

> *"For if by the transgression of the one, death reigned through the one, much more those who receive the abundance of grace and of the gift of righteousness will REIGN IN LIFE through the One, Jesus Christ"* (Romans 5:17).

> **"And if anyone desires to harm them, fire proceeds out of their mouth and devours their enemies; and if anyone would desire to harm them, in this manner he must be killed"** (Revelation 11:5).

Interpretation: Fire! But is this meant to indicate literal fire, or is it symbolic of something else?

Let's turn again to the Old Testament for a great help in interpreting this verse. Here are the words of Jeremiah:

> *"Behold, I am making My words in your mouth FIRE,*
> *And this people wood, and it will consume them.*
> *'Is not My word like FIRE?' declares the LORD"*
> (Jeremiah 5:14, 23:29a).

Likewise, Elijah destroyed his enemies by fire,

> *"Then the fire of God came down and consumed them"*
> (2 Kings 1:10-12).

The preaching of God's word is "like" FIRE. It carries with it an element of judgment for those who refuse to believe. And, in terms of "literal" fire, to stay consistent with our understandings throughout Revelation, this must mean *figurative fire,* or a *symbol* for the deeper spiritual reality: as the Church lives out their witness, unbelievers who refuse to repent and follow Jesus, already begin to be under judgment now, in this dispensation (which will culminate at the Great White Throne Judgement).

A great New Testament comparative moment is found in the life of Jesus. "If we compare this to Luke 9:54-62 and Luke 10:1-16, an allusion to Elijah's ministry of judging by literal fire is followed by a teaching on the difficulty of discipleship, and is applied figuratively to the preaching of judgment by the 70 disciples, as they were commissioned by Christ and sent out two by two. The figurative application in the Revelation text is evident from the fact that no fire ever came from any prophet's mouth in the OT."[111]

Luke 10:1-16 is an amazing passage to read in light of our ongoing fulfillment of the mission of the 70, now revealed in the Two Witnesses. Study there how they went out two by two, and wherever they found the "person of peace" (that is, the person they recognized who was already prepared by God to witness to) they were given a word of wisdom from Jesus. This was a kind of "Divine Blueprint" for being His witnesses, in four phases:

1. Bless them with the peace of Christ.
2. Fellowship with them and build relationship over a meal.
3. Heal them (by the power of the Spirit) if they are sick.
4. Say to them, "The Kingdom of God has come near you" (verses 6-9).

The judgment element is also included. If they were rejected, they were to pronounce judgment (verses 10-14) but with this one powerful truth added:

> *"The one who listens to you listens to me, and the one who rejects you rejects Me; and he who rejects Me rejects the One who sent Me (the Father)" (verse 16).*

So, the Kingdom way to witness in our own time is not to call down literal fire. It's to serve others in Agape Love and pray for them. Seek the people in our lives who are the people of "peace," and if we are rejected for our message of love and forgiveness in Christ, remember: they are not rejecting US, but HIM.

---

111 Ibid, Beale, pg. 584.

These have the power to shut up the sky, in order that rain may not fall during the days of their prophesying; (Revelation 11:6a).

Interpretation: Drought! This is again symbolic, and based in the OT on the drought that God brought through the prophet Elijah. This was a direct judgment of God against the idolatry of the day in Israel, for they were mixing with the world and worshipping Baal, the storm-god. No rain fell according to the ministry of Elijah (see 1 Kings 17:1 and James 5:16-18).

God was also judging the demonic spirits that were causing the idolatry in the people through this drought.

"As they preach, God sends judgments of fire and drought, which earlier in Revelation had been symbolized in the partial plagues of the first four seals and the first four trumpets and which are a foreshadowing within history of the lake of fire that will consume all rebels at history's end."[112]

I love the apostle James and what he shared about Elijah as it relates to a lifestyle of holiness and prayer. *Be patient, therefore, brethren, until the coming of the LORD,* shares James, who finishes his epistle with the example of Elijah as a man with a "nature like ours," who practiced earnest prayer. When the Church is walking in full alignment with the Holy Spirit, she can expect to have the same authority in prayer that Elijah had when he, by faith, "shut up the sky."

"Be patient, therefore, brethern, until the coming of the Lord..."

NOTE! You have dunamis power, and that power has as its source prayer and intimate connection to the LORD! (Dunamis is the same word from which we get the word, dynamite.) This was promised by Jesus, to ALL His witnesses for ALL the Church Age, in Acts 1:8: *"You shall receive POWER when the Holy Spirit has come upon you, and you shall be* ***My witnesses****."* — the Resurrected Messiah, Acts 1:8a.

112 Johnson, Ibid, pg. 172.

And they have power over the waters to turn them to blood, and to smite the Earth with every plague, as often as they desire.
(Revelation 11:6b.)

Interpretation: Here we have the illusion to Moses in the time of Pharaoh, whom I have already talked about as being referenced in Malachi's prophecy about the time of restoration, which includes both blessing and cursing (from God's perspective). Remember that real authority in prayer includes, as Jesus taught us in Matthew 18:18, both binding and loosing. It's important in prayer life to balance one with the other.

You have authority in Jesus' Name to bind and loose in prayer.

How often are you using it?

Moses and Elijah appeared to Jesus toward the end of his First Coming, and thus it can be said that they have appeared in the Church Age. And in that appearance they fulfilled all the OT prophesies about them.

Though now they appear again, figuratively, in the symbolism of the Church itself.

Moses appeared before Pharaoh and performed all the plagues with his staff. His staff was a type or shadow of the New Testament authority that Jesus first gave to his 12, then his 70 disciples (again, sending them out in the harvest fields, two by two) and then to us on the Day of Pentecost as the announcement of the Kingdom gained actual ground and came forcefully (with the anointing of the Spirit's power) into the realms of the Earth.

Did you know that one of Moses' plagues was hail, and it was said, *Moses stretched out his staff* (a type of the authority of Christ in motion) *toward the sky, and the LORD sent thunder and hail, and fire ran down to the earth* (Exodus 9:23).

Just as a side note, during this time of the plagues that Moses was performing with his staff in the sight of Pharaoh, Pharaoh's magicians worked with the demonic realms of darkness that have always existed.

These were especially strong during the days before Christ, when Satan held all the Nations except Israel in full deception and demonic cunning. These demonically-inspired magicians were able to duplicate many of the plagues themselves, but only up to a point.

For example, in Exodus 8 the LORD commands Aaron to strike the dust and it will become gnats. In response to the faith of Aaron, the dust turns into gnats and these nasty gnats swarm over all the land, *and the magicians tried with their secret arts to bring forth gnats, but they could not. Then they said to Pharaoh, "This is the finger of God"* (Exodus 8:18-19).

We can learn a lot in this vision from the reference to the authority that Moses (and Aaron) wielded as he operated in the same kind of faith in God that you and I operate in on the victorious side of the Cross and resurrection!

As mentioned above in reference to Luke 10, when the 70 returned with joy after successfully extending the Kingdom of God, Jesus was delighted and shared this amazing truth with them (they had essentially the same "staff" that Moses used, only theirs was the "staff" of faith in the authority and legal use of the Name of Jesus),

> *"I was watching Satan fall from heaven like lightning. Behold, I have given you authority to tread upon serpents and scorpions, and over all the power of the enemy, and nothing shall injure you"* (Luke 10:18-19).

In proper context, I believe quite literally here that Jesus was telling them that as they went out to proclaim the Kingdom extension over an area of land, Satan's authority plummeted to the Earth and people were set free, brought to salvation, entered the Kingdom by faith, and were healed, too. This all spelled d-e-f-e-a-t to Satan.

He was cast down to earth like lightning in that area, and his influence was smashed to pieces.

A time of salvation and judgment! Salvation for all who believed, and judgment for all who rejected the Good News.

After his resurrection and just prior to His ascension, Jesus tells His disciples,

> *"Go into all the world and preach the gospel to all creation; and these signs will accompany those who have believed..."* (Mark 16:15, 17a).

These "signs" include the authority in His Name to cast out demons and be protected in the midst of spiritual warfare. So, the fact that the Two Witnesses have the same authority that both Elijah and Moses had and the earliest disciples had, indicates that they retain this authority through the entire Church Age. They ought to be about Father's business (their mission) in sharing the Gospel of His Son in ministry in difficult regions of the earth!

"The mighty missionary church," wrote William Hendriksen, "of this present Gospel Age, if its message is rejected, has authority to judge and condemn the world. This power is not imaginary but very real. Not only does the LORD constantly rain woes upon the wicked world in answer to the prayers of the persecuted saints (Rev.8:3-5), but He also assures His Church that, whenever it is engaged in the official ministry of the Word and is true to the Word, its judgments are His judgments (Mt. 16:19, Jn. 20:21-23)."[113]

Remember the words of Jesus Himself,

> *"He who believes in Him is not judged; he who does not believe has been judged already, because he has not believed in the name of the only begotten Son of God. And this is the judgment, that the light is come into the world, and men loved the darkness rather than the light; for their deeds were evil"* (John 3:18-19).

And when they have finished their testimony, the beast that comes up out of the abyss will MAKE WAR with them and kill them (Revelation 11:7).

Interpretation: And finally, we come to the stark end of their mission. Here, as clear as ever, we are given a secret detail as to the reality of the

113 Hendriksen, Ibid, pg. 130.

Church Age: it had a day of beginning. The very day that Jesus vanished into thin air and entered the realm of Heaven as Heaven's champion, and sat down in triumph on the right hand of the Father on the eternal Throne of David to begin his royal reign as King.

And it has a day of ending, when according to this powerful vision, the Enemy of the Church will be able to "make war on the saints and overcome them."

The language that is employed here, the phrase *the beast that comes up out of the abyss,* is borrowed by John from Daniel, who first saw this future-event as the same beast (though he calls Satan a horn). Let it be known; this is the moment of the start of the Final Battle, an epic battle of the Last of the Last Days.

When Jesus the Messiah thundered on the scene and first announced, "the Kingdom of God has come" he startled an entire generation of people. He was, in essence, raising the battle cry and declaring war. He even startled the Enemy, who after tempting him and being defeated, had to leave him alone during much of his ministry.

The demons that He began to cast out, were startled too.

They recognized something that the Jews failed to recognize, that Jesus carried a unique, almost (in their partial understanding) "Divine power" in a human body.

> "The ruler of this world is cast out..."

Of course, WE know that He was divinity and humanity joined forever, and He was starting a campaign of war against their Ruler.

> *"The ruler of this world is cast out," Jesus shared, "and I, when I am lifted up* (literally, lifted up upon the Cross) *shall draw all men unto Me"* (John 12:32).

You know the story by now. Jesus dies upon that Cross, is resurrected the third day, and some days later, He departs from the earthly realm to take His place in the heavenly realm. Luke records the moment,

"And He led them out as far as Bethany, and He lifted up His hands and blessed them. And it came about that while He was blessing them, He parted from them" (Luke 24:50-51).

The prophet Daniel saw in the Spirit what happens next, hundreds of years before the moment. In a vision of the night, long before it all transpired in the natural, he saw the Ancient of Days and the Son of Man.

"I kept looking in the night visions and behold, with the clouds of heaven one like a Son of Man was coming. And He came up to the Ancient of Days and was presented before Him. And to Him was given dominion, glory, and a kingdom, that all the peoples, nations, and men of every language might serve Him. His dominion is an everlasting dominion which will not pass away; and His kingdom is one which will not be destroyed" (Daniel 7:13-14).

Daniel was allowed to see the glorious ascension of our LORD Jesus Christ. (At least that is one strong, possible interpretation of Daniel 7.) And he also sees just after this that a war begins. Jesus has taken His rightful place; He is guaranteed a people who will serve Him from every Nation, and He has declared war on the "horn" representing Satan.

Following this, again in visionary form in the night seasons, Daniel is allowed to see the same spiritual war that existed in his own day and continues to exist today. Here is what Daniel depicts and its counterpart in Revelation:

"I kept looking, and that horn (beast) was waging war with the saints and overpowering them" (Daniel 7:21).

"And when they have finished their testimony, the beast that comes up out of the abyss will make war with them and overcome them and kill them" (Revelation 11:7).

It's time now to prepare for this coming moment!

Let's also consider some interpretation for the remainder of the chapter. I will be very brief here, and am simply providing you with one possible interpretation of the final events of the final days.

Let us bear in mind that this vision employs not just symbolism, but symbolism-on-steroids: a kind of "hyperbole" as a literary technique, employed to over-emphasize the vision. We must NOT think of the phrases as literal, or even as occurring chronologically at times.

I am continuing to apply my three main methods of Symbolic, Broad-Historical and Practical, that I gave you back in chapter 3. Simply put, these following events have not yet happened as of the time of this writing, so in history they are still coming, and practically you can prepare for them by prayer.

The dark days are growing darker.

"Whatever person or system," writes Alan Johnson, "whether political, social, economic, or religious—cooperates with Satan by exalting itself against God's sovereignty and by setting itself up to destroy the followers of Jesus, or entices them to become followers of Satan through deception, idolatry, blasphemy and spiritual adultery, embodies the Beast. John seems to be saying that this blasphemous, blaspheming, and blasphemy-producing reality will have a final, intense, and, for the saints, utterly devastating manifestation."[114]

Here is what follows with the Two Witnesses.

> *"And their dead bodies will lie in the street of the great city which mystically is called Sodom and Egypt, where also their LORD was crucified. And those from the peoples and tribes and tongues and nations will look at their dead bodies for three and a half days, and will not permit their dead bodies to be laid in a tomb.*
>
> *"And those who dwell on the Earth will rejoice over them and make merry; and they will send gifts to one another, because these two prophets tormented those who dwell on the Earth. And after three and a half days the breath of life from God came into them, and they stood on their feet; and great fear fell upon those who were beholding them. And they heard a voice from heaven saying to them, "Come up here." And they went up into heaven in the cloud, and their enemies beheld them. And in that hour there was a great earthquake"* (Revelation 11:8-13a).

114 Ibid, Alan Johnson, page 129.

Interpretations: Very simply and very briefly, here's a summary of what I believe to be the most practical interpretations of the imagery and hyperbole of this passage. [115]

The great city mystically called Sodom and Egypt.

This is symbolic of the whole world, not just literal Jerusalem in modern-day Israel, or literal Sodom (which was destroyed), or literal Egypt. (Egypt represents in itself, that pagan culture which sought to assimilate the Hebrews and their monotheism into its diverse religious culture of many gods. It represents compromise in all its forms.)

Dead bodies not buried.

This is symbolic of indignity in the ancient world (See 1 Samuel 17:44 or 2 Kings 9:10 for examples). It represents not worldwide martyrdom (though it may include martyrs), but "a Church driven underground and seemingly defeated in its role of witness, appearing insignificant to the world."[116]

These are days likened unto the great story of Tolkien, *The Lord of the Rings*, and the battle of Helm's Deep, fought bravely by the surviving remnant of warriors. In the second book of the series called, *The Two Towers*, the remnant, led by Aragorn, is promised by Gandalf that they must hold Helm's deep at all cost, and that on the morning of the 3rd day, he should look to the East, to the rising of the sun, and deliverance would surely come.

In the midst of the battle, Tolkien writes in poetic form of the atmosphere that the soldiers were feeling.

"But late in the night the watchmen cried out, and all awoke. The moon was gone. Stars were shining above; but over the ground there crept a darkness blacker than the night. On both sides of the river it rolled towards them, going northward."[117]

---

115 I refer to the reader several great commentaries at the back of this book for further, deeper discussion of these details. See especially pages 585-608 in Beale, "The New International Greek Testament Commentary," Ibid.

116 G.K. Beale, Ibid., pg. 590.

117 J.R.R. Tolkien, The Two Towers, page 539, Houghton Mifflin Publishers, 1954 edition.

In the ensuing battle, outnumbered and losing hope, Aragorn and the king of Gondor make a bold step and ride out in armor against the enemy. Many of the soldiers fall dead in this final battle, but still the remnant survives and pushes forward. Then, suddenly, just as was prophesied, Gandolf appears in the glory of the morning sun, and along with him an army of reinforcements, and they destroy the enemy and save the day. The evil alliance that was conspiring to destroy men, is itself destroyed.

The entire story can be said to contain wonderful symbolism as to the Final Battle of the ages, where it will be Christ Himself, appearing in glorious procession and mounted on a steed of war, who appears to consume the evil with justice, and pronounce everlasting salvation to all who have called upon His name to be saved, right until the last day (Revelation 19).

So it is with the surviving remnant of God's chosen throughout history, and so it will be for us who are alive and remain until the end. There will be those who misunderstand the times and fall away from the true faith. Those who choose compromise with the world system and fail to grasp the power in suffering and even martyrdom.

But there will also be a surviving remnant, covered by the glory of God as with a canopy, who fight with perseverance right to the end. Then, at the appearing of Christ with angelic reinforcements in the light of a powerful new dawn, receive everlasting glory and eternal reward for their valiant efforts in the conflict.

Three and a half days.

This is symbolic of a very short time (in comparison to the fullness of the Church Age, represented by the previous number of 1260 days). The Final Battle will be brief. This time also echoes the time of the Son of God as He was in the tomb ("I will arise on the third day").

"The heathen were furious," writes William Hendriksen. "They had made war with the Witnesses, conquered them and killed them, and gloated over their misery. Its leaders and voice have been silenced. This condition lasts '3 days and ½, which is a very brief time'. The world has a grand picnic.

Their word will not torment them anymore. The corpse begins to stir, the breath of life enters it! This is no secret Rapture."[118]

Sending gifts/making merry.

This is symbolic of the party that Satan threw for all his minions when Jesus died upon the Cross and was silent and dead for three days. He was absolutely convinced he had won the battle! *"Men hated the light and loved the darkness"* (John 3:20) as John put it. So the cultures of this world will throw a very short-lived party, thinking that they have silenced the witness of the Church, and continue in their sin and hard-hearted idolatry and evil behavior without the witness of the light to convict them openly.

"Revelation gives a clear expectation that Christ's return will be preceded by a period of brief but intense persecution of the Church. Revelation shows in various ways that the Church's present experience of persecution, although genuinely painful, is nevertheless limited by God's powerful restraint of the dragon and his minions.

"The two witnesses' enemies cannot destroy them until their terrifying mission is complete, at which time the beast will conquer and kill them. The evil trio will deceive and gather the kings and nations to wage war against the Lamb and His army, the camp of the saints—but not until the dragon is released to resume the deceptive power he wielded over the Gentiles prior to Christ's death and resurrection.

"History will not go on normally and then Jesus will return. Revelation presents a more complex picture: the kingdom is advancing and gathering in the nations through the Church's witness amid suffering; and then, just before the end, intensified and coordinated hostility of the non-Christian world against the Church, which is rescued by the glorious return of Jesus our Defender."[119]

Apparent resurrection of the Witnesses/ascension/great earthquake.

This is symbolic of the coming Day of the LORD: the final day in history as we know it! The Second Coming of Christ in triumph and judgment!

118 William Hendriksen, Ibid., pg. 130.
119 Ibid, Dennis E. Johnson, pg. 363.

The Church will experience victory at the Second Coming, eternal life will be bestowed upon all who call upon the name of the LORD for salvation, and the same Jesus who returns in victory for the Church, to rescue His Bride, will also bring Judgement Day upon the Nations.

"It seems most consistent to see the witnesses' resurrection as portraying the bodily resurrection of all who belong to Christ's true church by faith at His return, accompanied by the great earthquake of judgment that will compel fear-filled praise even from God's enemies (see Phil. 2:9-11).

"Just as the vision genre sometimes compresses vast historical eons into symbolic images that pass like the twinkling of an eye (see Rev. 12:1-5, which spans redemptive history from Genesis 3 to Acts 1), so also a split-second in time may be expanded in visionary description and simultaneous climactic events presented as successive, in order to help hearers to see different facets of Christ's victory."[120]

The imagery of the earthquake is borrowed by John from the appearance of Yahweh on Mt. Sinai, where it says, *Now Mt. Sinai was all in smoke because the LORD descended upon it in fire; and its smoke ascended like the smoke of a furnace, and the whole mountain quaked violently* (Exodus 19:18).

Found near the end of nearly all of the seven parallel visions in Revelation, you will find an earthquake happening (or, a symbol which clearly speaks of the Second Coming).

The earthquake symbolizes the awesome actual appearance of Jesus Christ on Judgment Day, as He personally appears from heaven, and the world shakes in His presence (as Mt. Sinai once shook at the presence of the Almighty in Exodus 19).

For further study, please consider carefully the following passages in Revelation (which also give us hints as to where the seven visions have an ending point, as they each are pointing to the same coming event of Eternal Judgment & Eternal Salvation).

Let me begin by showing you the first reference to Judgment Day, found all the way back in chapter 4, which opens in the first Heavenly Court vision

---

120 Ibid, Dennis E. Johnson, pg. 176.

and says, *And from the throne proceed flashes of lightning and sounds and peals of thunder* (Revelation 4:5).

You will note that earlier in this book I explained how the parallel visions are progressive in nature. That is, they are moving toward history's end, so each one gives us a little more description and builds upon the last. Revelation 4:5 is the *expectation of and is foreshadowing* the coming Last Judgment, but only from Heaven's perspective, so it begins there and then is actualized in the following four parallel sections shown below.

To add another dimension to this imagery, we turn again to the Old Testament, where John the Revelator had his foundation for the visions that he saw.

We discover that at Mt. Sinai, when the LORD descended upon the mountain, it was also a picture of His coming judgment of all nations. There, we find *flashes of lightning and sounds and peals of thunder...and a great earthquake.*

Parallel Visions			
And I looked when he broke the sixth seal, and there was a great earthquake. (Rev. 6:12)	And there followed peals of thunder and sounds and flashes of lighting and an earthquake. (Rev. 8:5)	And there were flashes of lightning and sounds and peals of thunder and an earthquake and a great hailstorm. (Rev. 11:19)	And there were flashes of lightning and sounds and peals of thunder, and there was a great earthquake and huge hailstones (Rev. 16:21)

"Early Jewish and Christian writings," writes G.K. Beale, "utilized the earthquake imagery associated with the Sinai theophany and the exodus to portray the end of the cosmos. When the Sinai or exodus earthquake is explicitly alluded to as an eschatological event, it is always a sign of the climactic destruction of the world.

"The progressive expansion of the passages noted accords with the increasing severity of each series of judgments, as the visions focus more closely on the End itself."[121]

Going Deeper Still:

1. Moses and Elijah were announced by Malachi that they were coming in Messiah's Age. John the Baptist was said to represent their power and authority, and later Jesus Himself was transfigured on the mount, and both Moses and Elijah appeared to Him. Can you begin to see that the Two Witnesses are not literally Moses & Elijah? And just when, according to this chapter, do the Witnesses prophesy?

2. The Church of this Age symbolically represents the power and authority that Moses and Elijah carried. What is the Standing Order of the last days Army?

3. To prophesy is to speak the truth of the Gospel, and does not always mean to operate in the gift of prophecy, in forth-telling the future. When you speak the truth in love (and share your own testimony of faith), are you prophesying within this definition?

4. Jesus gave His 12 and then His 70 disciples a share of His own Heaven-ordained power and authority. He expects us, as part of His Last Days Army, to operate fully in both, to the very end of the Age. Can you think of an example when you sensed the presence of the LORD and moved out in faith in either power or authority in the name of Jesus?

121 Ibid, G.K. Beale, pgs. 458-459.

5. Part of the Battle Plans of the advancing army, is to continuously bear witness to the truth, and allow that truth to be rejected. As it is, we join with Christ and are representatively called to suffer persecution for the truth. Have you ever been rejected by a friend or family member because of your faith in Jesus? Does it make you feel better now, knowing that this is actually part of bearing His cross?

6. Who/What are the Pharaohs of your own Nation (the Enemy strongholds)? The Pharaohs of our day will not always receive everything we have to say, as in our testimony of Jesus. How can you begin to prepare to suffer for your faith in the coming days?

7. Study the following verses, in fresh context of being the possible ending portions of several of the seven parallel visions contained in Revelation. The Old Testament imagery of **the earthquake** representing the Final Day of Judgement and the awesome presence of God at the end of history, is in Exodus 19:18. Then read Revelation 6:12, 8:5, 11:13/11:19 (same earthquake from two perspectives) and 16:21.

THE NOW-MILLENNIUM: SATAN BOUND AND UNBOUND

An Alternative View of the 1,000-year Reign, how Satan is, (and isn't), Bound Currently, & his Near-Future Unbinding in the Final Battle

"*And I saw an angel coming down from heaven, having the key of the abyss and a great chain in his hand. And he laid hold of the dragon, the serpent of old, who is the devil and Satan, and bound him for a thousand years, and threw him into the abyss, and shut it and sealed it over him, so that he should not deceive the nations any longer, until the thousand years were completed* (Revelation 20:1-3a).

"The Millennium is inaugurated during the Church Age as God limits Satan's deceptive powers, and as deceased Christians are vindicated by reigning in Heaven. The Millennium is concluded by a resurgence of Satan's deceptive assault against the Church and the Final Judgment."[122]

122 Ibid., Beale, page 972.

To begin our journey together in examining what is known as the Millennial Reign, this chapter will define exactly what the binding and unbinding of Satan looks like in context of the NOW-Millennial View.

Understanding this beautiful interpretation gives us hope and the reason why the Two Witnesses can have such a strong ministry as the community of the Saints during this Church Age. It also paints a very clear picture of what's coming at history's End.

Can I please remind you that you and I must remain in liberty in the non-essentials of our faith. That means: please read this chapter prayerfully and carefully, and at the end, feel free to draw your own conclusions (and even totally disagree with mine).

We can still be brothers and sisters in Christ, even if we don't see eye to eye on the Millennial Reign.

Let's begin.

First off, the 1,000 year (in Latin, a millennium) period of time that Satan is said to be bound is *only* found in Revelation 20:1-10.

Now, there *are* other passages in Revelation with numbers that we will consider a bit later, that will help confirm that this number is intended by John the Revelator as a symbolic, NOT a literal, number.

This passage is perhaps the most hotly-debated passage of Scripture in the whole of the New Testament, from the earliest days of the Church until today, within the subject of eschatology.

We are dealing primarily in this chapter with a fresh definition of time, (the time of the Church Age), as well as the intriguing truth of Satan bound and the implications of that (and the scriptural boundaries of it).

The NOW-Millennium

There are three primary views on this mysterious 1000-year number, and what exact period of time in history it represents. The other two are called, Premillennial and Postmillennial. A variety of my friends and ministry colleagues are in these two other camps. We are called to love each other, no matter what perspective we have on the Millennium![123]

Over the course of this book, I am writing from the unique approach known more widely in academic circles as the Amillennial approach (which I am personally renaming the NOW-Millennial approach).

In this chapter I will seek to define, a little more clearly, the uniqueness of this particular approach. The next chapter and whole Section of this book will take a closer look at what happens during the end of this time, and the very Last of the Last Days, and reveal both the Battle Plans of Jesus and the Battle Plans of our Enemy.

Question: What exactly is Amillennialism anyway?

Answer: First of all, the word itself is composed of two meanings. The letter, A means "no," and the word millennial means 1,000. So, by combining the two you get the general meaning, no millennium.

Amillennialists all believe that the 1,000 years are a symbolic time period between the First Coming and Second Coming of Christ. The 1,000 years refers to the Church Age in its fullness of time.

Though I hold the position of Amillennialists, I personally prefer a slightly different (and, I believe, improved) term. I call myself a NOW-millennialist (NOW-mill) or, to simply apply this to the 1,000 year period, NOW-Millennium, as in:

"the-thousand-years-are-happening-right-now-and-is-actually-way-more-than-a thousand-years" sense! [124]

The purpose of this chapter is to more closely examine the idea of the 1,000 years as a *symbolic period of time,* and to clearly show how Satan is, and isn't, currently BOUND, and what will happen soon when he is UNBOUND.

123 In Appendix 3, see the explanation of the other 2 views, (in relation to the view of Amillennialism/ Millennium NOW), if you are curious and want to dig deeper in those understandings.

124 For the remainder of this chapter and throughout various sections of my book, I have transformed the entire school of "Amillennial" eschatological thought and the words *Amillennialist* or *Amilleniarian* into the two simplified words, *Millennium NOW.*

Thus I pose a question:

WHAT IF the number 1,000 is a *symbolic number* and represents *the entire Kingdom age between the first appearance of Jesus Christ and His Second and Final Appearance?*

What if ... ?

In other words, what if the Millennium is actually happening now and is *about to finish?*

Here is a further definition. "Satan is conceived as bound at the First Coming of Christ, shares John F. Walvoord, "and the present age between the First and Second Comings is the fulfillment of the Millennium. It may be summed up in the idea that there will be no more **Millennium** than there is **now** *(my bold emphasis),* and that the eternal state immediately follows the Second Coming of Christ."[125]

Is there a specific relevance to this approach for my own life and current world events and the shakings that are happening and about to happen?

Yes, there is! Because...

WHAT IF there is no secret Rapture coming next on the eschatological timetable (as described in Appendix 1)?

WHAT IF what's actually coming next is the Final Battle, immediately prior to the Second Coming?

If this is really true, then it's vital to understand the Word of God and the Battle Plans that Revelation provides.

It's time to prepare for battle!

Next, I will offer some unique understandings of the concept of actual numbers in the Book of Revelation, and how the numbers utilized are best understood when taken to be *symbolic* rather than *literal*.

John uses different numbers for periods of time, for example, which all echo the same Church Age. Remember, too, as you read the following and

125 John F. Walvoord, *The Millennial Kingdom,* p. 6. Findley, Ohio: Dunham Publishing Company, 1959.

think deeper about the challenging thought that we are in the NOW-Millennium, that Revelation is a book of parallelism, and the seven visions that John saw are parallel periods of time.

In that sense, you could say that all of the visions cover the NOW-Millennium and give us unique insights and details of the story and how the story ends with our Enemy's ultimate demise.

The NOW-Millennium viewpoint places the two passages, Revelation chapters 11 & 20, in parallel visions, encompassing the identical period of time, which has lasted not 1,000 years, but nearly 2,000 years at present time (beginning at the Cross and moving forward to present day).

When 1,000 Does Not Equal 1,000

Remember in chapter 4 where I gave you the word picture of Mount Zion being a circular range with seven mountain peaks, each with a round tower looking into the same valley below?

It's like in Revelation 11. We are on the top of Mount Zion on the north, and then we are suddenly transported in chapter 20 to the mountain peak on the south, seeing what is happening from a different perspective. As we already learned, different visions in Revelation show us Mount Zion from differing vantage points during the same period of time.

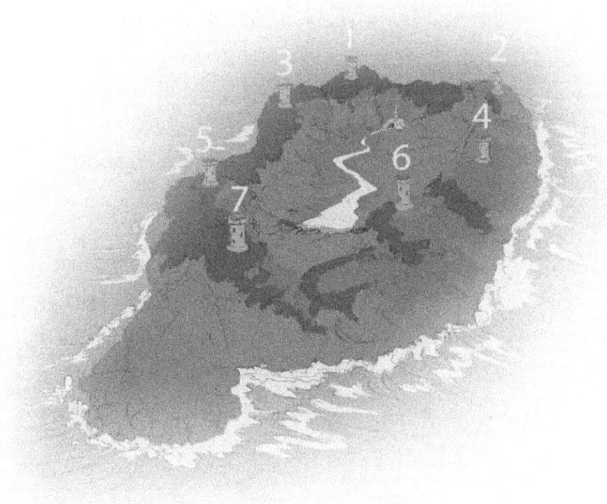

What the summit looks like from a southern vantage point will be a different description than from a northern vantage point. When taken together, both descriptions aid in a fuller picture of the Battle.

Let us place the entire passage of Revelation 20:1-3 in front of us for a full picture, so we can talk specifically about the timeframe, or thousand years, that is symbolically pictured here.

> *"And I saw an angel coming down from heaven, having the key of the abyss and a great chain in his hand. And he laid hold of the dragon, the serpent of old, who is the devil and Satan,* **and bound him for a thousand years,** *and threw him into the abyss, and shut it and sealed it over him, so that he should not deceive the nations any longer, until the thousand years were completed;* **after these things he must be released for a short time***"* (Revelation 20:1-3).

So you read here of two very significant times. First, the 1,000 years that Satan is said to be bound. Second, the short time that Satan is said to be released.

Question: When does 1,000 not truly equal 1,000?

Answer: When you are trying to compare a literal number to a symbolic number.

In other words, Our Father lives outside of linear time, and measures time differently in His prophetic symbols than a mere linear interpretation.

> *"But do not let this one fact escape your notice, beloved, that with the LORD one day is as a thousand years, and a thousand years as one day"* (2 Peter 3:5).

What of the number 1,000 anyway? Since it is only found here, many theologians over the years have debated whether they hold to a literal or symbolic interpretation. As I have labored to show, I hold to the symbolic view.

"When God uses numbers to speak," shares Troy Brewer, "there is incredible power in it. The LORD loves what I call, "inside information." He loves to say things in a way that only those who seek Him and study His ways, know what He is actually saying. God speaks through parable, type and symbol as a way to conceal what He is saying, and as a way to illustrate and reveal what He is saying. When you don't know what God says through the type and symbol of certain numbers, you miss what God is saying altogether."[126]

The number 10 in Scripture is God's number for "perfection of divine order."

TEN: Perfection of divine order

— Noah was the tenth generation from Adam (Genesis 5:1-32).

— Ten plagues on Egypt (Exodus 7:14-12:30).

— Ten Commandments (Exodus 20:1-17; Deuteronomy 5:6-21).

— Ten virgins in Jesus' kingdom parable (Matthew 25:1-13).[127]

"The number 10 has to do with timelines and how God carries out a plan in perfect order. It's the number where God reveals His plan and sets things in order according to that plan. One of the four "perfect" numbers, 10 has to do with God setting things up for His purpose."[128]

Notice, the number 10 cubed = 1,000 (10 times 10 times 10).

Thus, a perfect cube representing a perfect period of time of God's sovereign plan in the Nations is presented. In fact, there are exactly 10 uses of the number 10 in the Book of Revelation, the first being in 2:10 and the last being here in chapter 20.[129]

From this we can deduce that John has cloaked the period of time of the binding of Satan into *an unknown, long time period,* which symbolized *the marking of the entire timeframe of the Church Age in completion.* "Ten im-

126 Ibid, Troy Brewer, pages 5-6.
127 Michal Elizabeth Hunt. *Agape Catholic Bible Study,* online website.
128 Ibid, Troy Brewer, page 116.
129 Ernest Brown. *The Number 10 in Scripture,* online website.

plies that nothing is wanting, that the number and order are perfect; that the whole cycle is complete."[130]

Remember, please, when studying all this to keep your Hebrew prayer shawl on, not your Greek hat, for these four passages that mention "time" are all written in the form of synonymous parallelism to poetically designate the same period of time: the Church Age.

Here is how I believe Revelation borrows from the Prophets' use of synonymous parallelism for the time period of our Church Age as we ADD the "1,000" years from Revelation 20:1-3 to the other time periods as all representing the Church Age:

Synonymous Parallelism			
"42 months" (Revelation 11:2, 13:5)	*"a time, times, and half a time"* (Daniel 7:25, 12:7) (Revelation 12:14)	*"1,260 days"* (Revelation 11:3, 12:6)	*"1,000 years"* (Rev. 20:1-3, Rev. 11:3, 12:6)

"Contrary to assertions otherwise, the number 1,000 can be used figuratively. Indeed, multiples of 1,000 have already been so used. (See Revelation 5:11, 7:4-9, 9:16, 14:1.) The Millennium of Revelation 20 could also be associated broadly with the early rabbinic tradition of a thousand-year reign, and especially the tradition reflected in Jubilees, 2 Enoch, and Barnabus. If so, it would *not* be a *literal* one thousand years, but would represent a long epoch, *the last epoch of world history*."[131]

130 E.W. Bullinger. *Number in Scripture: it's Supernatural Design and Spiritual Significance,* online website Bullinger also notes (1) There are 10 I am's of Jesus in John, (2) Abraham's faith was completed by a cycle of ten trials, and (3) The Tenth Generation completed the whole existence of a family or nation. *Dt. 23:3 and Nehemiah 13:1.*

131 Ibid, Beale, pages 1017 & 1020.

Satan Bound: He Cannot Stop the Advance of the Gospel in the Nations

Let me summarize some thoughts on the approach of NOW-Millennium, based upon some of the conclusions of Sam Storms, who wrote a recent book entitled, "Kingdom Come: The Amillennial Alternative."

In the final chapter of his book, Storms lists 30 points to prove his, "Cumulative Case Argument for Amillennialism." I will share with you just three of his 30 thoughts as a kind of summary for the approach we are outlining in this book.

1. "Amillennialism is better suited to explain the restriction placed on Satan in Revelation 20:1-3. Satan is pictured as being prevented from perpetuating the spiritual blindness of the Nations and keep them in Gospel darkness. He is prevented from provoking a premature global assault on the Church, which we know to be the battle of Armageddon.

2. Amillennialism also makes sense of the structure of the Book of Revelation. There we find the principle of progressive parallelism, in which the same period of time (the Church Age, spanning the two advents of Christ) is described from different but complementary perspectives.

3. Revelation 20:1-10 should be interpreted as a progressive parallelism of the present Church Age, rather than as following in historical sequence upon the Second Coming of Christ as described in Revelation 19. Amillennialism alone affirms the New Testament truth that all hope for salvation terminates with the second coming of Christ. The opportunity for eternal life is now, in the present church age, before Christ comes, not later."[132]

132 Sam Storms, Kingdom Come: The Amillennialist Alternative, Mentor Publications, 2013.

So remember, for me, "A-millennialism" = "NOW-Millennialism:"

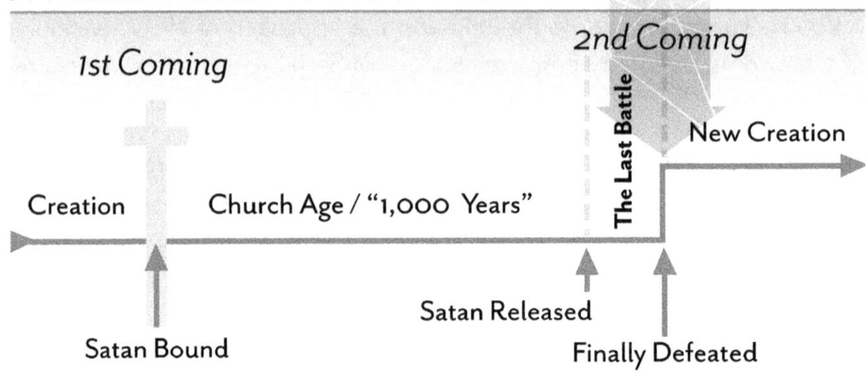

Here again is our key text which describes this amazing vision.

> *And I saw an angel coming down from heaven, having the key of the abyss and a great chain in his hand. And he laid hold of the dragon, the serpent of old, who is the devil and Satan, and bound him for a thousand years, and threw him into the abyss, and shut it and sealed it over him,* **so that he should not deceive the nations any longer,** *until the thousand years were completed; after these things he must be released for a short time* (Revelation 20:1-3).

Fantastic! As they say, "that will preach." The serpent of old has finally been dealt with! Satan, who all scholars emphatically agree is here represented through the symbolic names of serpent, dragon and devil, has been bound, thrown into an abyss, shut away and sealed. And here is both the meaning and the limit of this binding and sealing within the context of the verse: **that he should not deceive the Nations any longer.**

Let us stop for a moment and consider those words, for they are the key to interpreting the full meaning of the text, and they also establish the entire background for the timetable of the present dispensation for the Church.

I believe the full picture of the vision is symbolic.

You will notice that the angel is carrying something. It's a key, and a chain. Is it a *literal key* and a *literal chain*? Of course not. It is symbolic of the idea that Satan has been dealt with at the First Coming of Christ, when Christ met him on his own ground and defeated him and stopped his deception in the nations.

The context: Satan cannot continue to keep the people in the Nations of the world bound in deception as it pertains to the missionary calling of the Church to spread the Gospel (until the Last Battle, when he will be unbound).

In that way, and **only** in that way (though it is a very significant way as this chapter lays out for you to consider) is Satan thought of in Scripture as being bound.

Remember Christ's own words in Matthew 12:29. *"Or else how can one enter into a strong man's house, and spoil his goods, except he first* **bind** *the strong man? And then he will spoil his house."*

And I love the New Living Translation of this verse. *"For who is powerful enough to enter the house of a strong man like Satan and plunder his goods? Only someone even stronger—someone who could* **tie him up** *and then plunder his house."*

You'll remember from my Introduction that I used the wonderful term, CHRISTUS VICTOR! Christ is Victorious! He, as God, was stronger than the fallen angel, the Prince of the power of the air (Satan). Christ opposed him during His ministry on earth and defeated him forever at the Cross.

Note the word, **BIND** in Matthew 12. It's the *same exact word* in the original text as we find in Revelation 20:1! And it's ONLY USED in these two places in the New Testament.

Part of the mission of the Servant of the LORD (which we talked about earlier in my section, The Greatest Sign of the Times of Them All), is to **bind** the strong man. That is, to render him powerless to deceive all the nations anymore.

To "**bind**" means literally, "to forbid." Whereas to "loose" means literally, "to allow." So, literally we are learning that in this dispensation, Jesus has forbidden Satan from keeping all nations in bondage to deception.

He **BOUND** him and has been spoiling his goods ever since, as you see in these passages.

> *"When He had disarmed the rulers and authorities, He made a public display of them, having triumphed over them through Him"* (Colossians 2:15).

> *"When He had disarmed the rulers and authorities [those supernatural forces of evil operating against us], He made a public example of them [exhibiting them as captives in His triumphal procession], having triumphed over them through the Cross"* (Colossians 2:15, Amplified Bible).

And just what are the "key" and the "chain" in the deeper spiritual meanings behind the vision?

The **key** is the *Authority* of Jesus Christ (who is pictured in the most powerful imagery in Revelation 1:18 as, *"holding the keys of Death and Hades")*.

The **chain** is the *Power* of Jesus Christ.

When you put both together, along with the action of throwing down the dragon and binding and sealing, you find a wonderful interpretation: the LORD is absolutely sovereign with both!

Can you also see the amazing correlation of the authority and power He is still displaying through His Two Witnesses (i.e. the Church)?!

Satan has been bound, and someday He will be loosed to wage a final spiritual battle against Believers.

In other words, according to a simple examination of the text itself, Satan is seen here as **limited** in his scope and reach in the **area of deception of the nations.** He cannot hold all the nations of the world in deception and stop the Gospel, God's good news and His glorious Presence, that is overspreading the world, nation by nation. Nor can he destroy the Church completely in her sojourn here on earth.

Here's how a prophet once saw in a vision this glorious timeframe of the Messianic Age (Age of the Messiah reigning) we know as the Church Age. For the earth will be filled with the knowledge of the glory of the LORD, as the waters cover the sea (Habakkuk 2:14).

Have You Read Today's Headline? "Satan is Bound!"

This must have been the war cry across all sorts of different battle lines in the early Church, on the very first day and the first years that the visions of the Revelation of Jesus Christ were read out to His earliest bondservants. This vision put a whole new spin on their situation, and gave them a whole new idea, that for a long period of time (long AFTER their own time), the witness of the Truth was going to continue. Satan was bound (he could no longer deceive the nations), which meant the Gospel could be proclaimed in them.

Though Believers were being persecuted, they could have the understanding that Satan himself could not stop the authority of the name of Jesus Christ and the commission of the Church to shine the Kingdom light. It's true, the darkness did not instantly dissipate on the morning of the Resurrection.

Satan was bound then, but he sure didn't want anyone to know it.

The truth of the early Church was that they were filled with the presence of God and called as witnesses of the Resurrection and the true light which was already shining. (See 1 John 2:8.)

It was also true that it was illegal for them in Roman culture to swear allegiance to a historical figure outside of Caesar. They became sworn enemies of the state because of it. They were still living in what Paul termed, *the present evil age (Galatians 1:4),* but had been transferred to the *kingdom of the Son,* and were now a part of *the age to come by faith.*

"And have tasted the good Word of God and the powers of the age to come" (Hebrews 6:5).

Satan UNBOUND From the Garden of Eden to the Cross

Question: How was Satan doing with his deception in the earth throughout the Old Testament when he was unbound from the moment of the Fall of Man in the Garden of Eden, all the way through the close of Jesus' Ministry and His binding of Satan at the Cross?

Answer: So well that hardly anything is written about him in the Old Testament!

I will allow Thomas Cahill to help summarize the Satanic deception of all peoples in all nations around the time of the calling of Abram, and all the way up to the moment of Christ dying upon the Cross.

"In Africa and Europe," writes Cahill, "prehistoric animism was the norm, and artists were carving and painting on stone the heavenly symbols of the Great Wheel of Life and Death. The Greeks followed Prometheus, whose quest for fire of the gods ended in personal disaster. The people of India believed time is black, irrational, and merciless. In China, they believed there is no purpose in any kind of earthly striving; the great thing is to abolish time by escaping for the law of change. The ancestors of Maya in America believed in their circular calendars, which, like those of the Chinese, repeat the pattern of years in various succession, and explain that each man's fate is fixed.

He is the way, the truth, and the life.

"On every continent, wise men as diverse as Heraclitus, Lao-Tsu, and Siddhartha believed that you should sit by the river and meditate on its ceaseless and meaningless flow—on all that is past or passing or to come—until you have absorbed the pattern and have come to peace with the Great Wheel and with your own death and the death of all things in the corruptible sphere."[133]

133 Thomas Cahill, *The Gifts of the Jews: How a Tribe of Desert Nomads Changed the Way Everyone Thinks and Feels.* Selections from pgs. 63 and 64. Doubleday Publishing Group, 1998.

Isn't that a powerful summary of the nations before the Cross?

Yet, Jesus Christ stepped into the realms of darkness and all this deception, declaring He was *"the way, the truth, and the life"* (John 14:6), in order to invite the deceived to repent and walk with Him and His Father forever.

His announced mission was to BIND THE STRONGMAN.

So, Jesus Christ, CHRISTUS VICTOR, has come forth and sent out His challenge to all the realms of darkness. Heaven's challenge still stands forth! The light will continue to invade and shine forth brightly until the end of the Age, and then endless light will shine abundantly!

Sunshine and shadow will no longer coexist.

Here's the big picture of what this actually looks like, from the Garden of Eden to the approaching Last Battle:

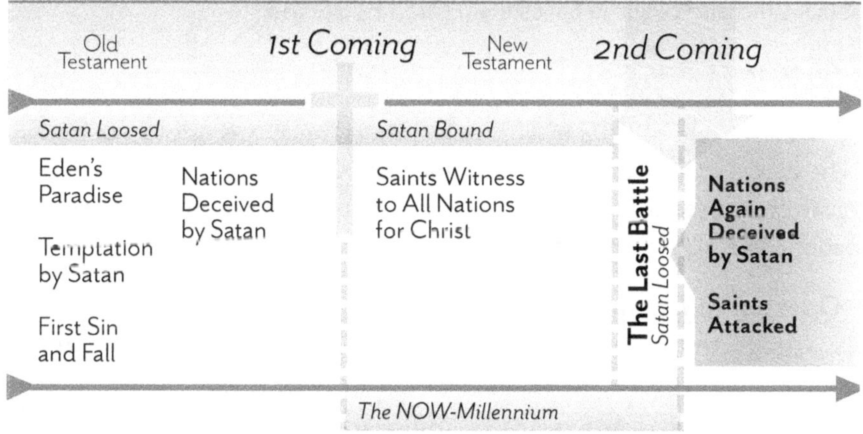

On the NOW-Millennium Road to Kingdom Come

"God has already accomplished the first great stage in His work of redemption. Satan is the 'god of this Age,' yet the power of Satan has been broken that people may know the rule of God in their lives. The evil Age goes on, yet the powers of the Age to Come have been made available to people. To the human eye, the world appears little changed; the Kingdom of Satan is unshaken. Yet the Kingdom of God has come among men; and those who receive it will be prepared to enter the Kingdom of Glory when Christ comes to finish the good work He has already begun."[134]

"When Jesus said that the Kingdom or rulership of God had come in him," wrote John Wimber, "he meant that God had come to claim what was rightfully his. The future age, the Kingdom of God, invaded the present age, the realm of Satan. Jesus did not consign the kingdom of God to a future Millennium. When he said that the kingdom of God had come in Him, he claimed for himself the position of a divine invader, coming to set everything straight: *The reason the Son of God appeared was to destroy the devil's work* (1 John 3:8)."[135]

Satan did not seem to be bound in his granted authority to stir up persecution among the earliest Believers, did he?

Question: Were the thousands of earliest Believers, both Jew and Gentile, (that were swept into the Church in the Book of Acts and beyond), persecuted and in some cases even killed by Satan?

Answer: Yes.

Tertullian, one of the early Church Fathers, once was quoted as saying, "The blood of the martyrs is the seed of the Church." He also proclaimed this truth in directly addressing the Roman Empire: "We are not a new philosophy but a Divine revelation!"[136]

Question: Were the early Believers still able to obey the command of Jesus to "go and make disciples of all nations," even though they were suffering for it?

Answer: Yes!

The proclamation of the gospel was going forth daily, and Acts chapter 2 tells us that numbers were being added daily to the Body of Messiah (Christ).

---

134 George Elden Ladd, The Gospel of the Kingdom, pg. 50-51. Wm. B. Eerdmans Publishing Company, Grand Rapids, MI. 1959.
135 John Wimber and Kevin Springer, Power Evangelism, pg. 33. HarperCollins Publishers, 1985, 1992.
136 Tertullian, 2nd century.

Day after day after day, the world was being transformed one-by-one, as individual people were transferred out of Satan's domain of darkness, and translated into the realm and reality of the Kingdom of God.

The earth is currently and truly being filled with the knowledge of the LORD, even as the waters cover the sea, *as it says in Habakkuk2:14*.

Question: IF Satan is bound (in a symbolic sense) right now, why is there so much evil in the world today?

Answer: He is currently only bound in ONE area of his deception. He cannot stop the spread of the Good News to all people groups and organize a final world-wide assault to deceive the nations and attempt to stop the witness.

That means, evil spirits will continue to ravage humankind in their many other areas of deception. Satan and his demonic hordes were active inside the seven churches of Revelation chapters 2-3, and outside those churches in the culture.

One of the coming sections of this book, in fact, will teach very specifically the various ways in Revelation that our Enemy is following his own battle plans against you and me (and how to combat them).

And...when I sit back and ponder the increase of Satanic deception, both inside and outside the Church, during even the last half of my own lifetime, I am shocked.

Here are just a few phrases to get you thinking.

— Progressive Christianity: (which filters Biblical principles through the world's values).

— Deconstructing Faith: (a critical reevaluating of religious beliefs and practices).

— Sexual abuse and assault of innocent children INSIDE the Church: (both in the Roman Catholic and Protestant churches worldwide).

— Worldwide human sex trafficking OUTSIDE the Church.

— Islamic Jihad and the torture and beheading of Christians.

- — Increased Governmental pressure to stop people from sharing their faith in public.
- — Christian Nationalism in America: (which people call "a threat to democracy").
- — Transgenderism and Gay Pride.

These are just a few of the many examples of Satanically induced deceptions of darkness, both inside and outside the Church.

Thus, God's definition of Satan bound does not necessarily equal ours, especially in these poetic, visionary passages of Revelation 20. If you try to add to what the Scripture actually says, and say that Satan cannot be bound because evil is everywhere, you mistake the text of this chapter.

He obviously still continues to exercise evil. And the demonic forces that are with him, known and declared by the Apostle Paul as the "powers" collectively (see Ephesians 6:12), are active everywhere. This is true! But in context of the text, this is NOT what the binding refers to!

And all of these powers are continuing to plague our days, and so many people are joining in active rebellion against God and His ways. Let's continue in our verse-by-verse analysis of this intriguing passage.

Satan Unbound Again (Satan's own Second Coming & the Final War Against the Saints)

> "*And when the thousand years are completed, Satan will be released from his prison, and will come out to deceive the nations which are in the four corners of the Earth, Gog and Magog, to gather them together for THE WAR; the number of them is like the sand of the seashore. And they came up on the broad plain of the Earth and surrounded the camp of the saints and the beloved city, and fire came down from heaven and devoured them.*"
> (Revelation 20:7-9).

Firstly, you will note my title for this section and be wondering: Satan's own Second Coming? REALLY?

Yes! Everything he does is a counterfeit to the Truth. Jesus had His First Coming. His mission, in part, was to bind the strongman and spoil his goods. He bound Satan at the Cross, and earlier in this chapter, we see the imagery of the binding of Satan (in limiting his ability to destroy the Two Witnesses).

So, the Father shows us here that Satan, indeed, has his very own Second Coming, in a sense, and, it is very short lived.

This **Final WAR** will not last long. Could it be a moment? A day? A month? A year? Longer than a year? The answer to any of these is, YES. It is simply a mystery. We know it will be somewhere from a single moment to years, but it will fall into the Father's definition of SHORT, in terms of time.

You will note that here, too, Christ is sovereign. For it is He who releases Satan from His prison. (He is released, he does not escape!) So the timing of this event in the order of Salvation-Future-History, is completely up to the Sovereign will of God!

> *"...and he will come out to deceive the nations which are in the four corners of the Earth, Gog and Magog, to gather them together for* **THE WAR***; the number of them is like the sand of the seashore"* (verse 8).

This verse represents the final attack and final battle of worldwide, anti-Christian forces against the Church. The reference to Gog and Magog, from Ezekiel 38 and 39, is an event in history (and is also pictured in the Battle of Armageddon in the parallel passage of Revelation 17).

The area of Syria under the strategic forces of Antiochus Epiphanes attacked Israel in one last great oppression that the people of God had to endure in the Old Dispensation. [137]

137 A.H. Sayce, The Races of the Old Testament, pg. 73.

Revelation uses this imagery from Ezekiel directly to illustrate affliction and woe as a *symbol* of Satan and his hordes against the Church, and to illustrate just how victorious the Father and the Warrior Lamb will be in the utter destruction of all of their (and our) enemies at the Second Coming. CHECKMATE!

Here are the other parallel passages in Revelation that all introduced the coming final war but here, since we are at the final reference, we get the most information about it.

Parallel Passages			
"And when they have finished their testimony, the beast that comes up out of the abyss will **MAKE WAR** with them and kill them." (Rev. 11: 7)	"To gather them together for **THE WAR** of the great day of God, the Almighty; and they gathered them together to the place which in Hebrew is called, **Armageddon.**" (Rev. 16:14,16)	"And I saw Heaven opened; and behold, a white horse... and the beast and the kings of the earth, and their armies, assembled to **MAKE WAR** against Him who sat upon the horse, and against His army." (Rev. 19: 11,19)	"And when the thousand years are completed, Satan will be released from his prison and will come out to deceive the nations which are in the four corners of the Earth, Gog and Magog, to gather them together for **THE WAR."** (Rev. 20: 7-8)

Here's what Sam Storms also notes,

"This is all confirmed by reference to "**THE WAR**" (19:19; already noted in 16:14, 16; cross-reference 20:8). The same Greek phrase "**THE WAR**" (*ton polemon*) is used in all three texts (Revelation 16:14, 19:19, 20:8). In fact, in 16:14 and 20:8 the same extended phrase "to gather them together unto **THE WAR**" (*sunagagein autous eis ton polemon*) is used.[138]

> *"And they came up on the broad plain of the earth and surrounded the camp of the saints and the beloved city"* (Revelation 20:9a).

Amazingly, the Church is described only here in Revelation, under a unique, double-symbolism of both a *camp* and a *city*. Some are scattered underground at this point, "the camp of the saints," sojourning in tents (meaning, in secret). Others are established in more fortified community configurations, "the beloved city," pooling their resources together in standing against Satan's attacks.

> *"And fire came down from Heaven and devoured them (the attacking nations)"* (Revelation 20:9b).

This same imagery is brought forth in all seven visions of this moment in different ways. Here, John sees fire as God's destructive force, similar to the judgment He brought on Sodom and Gomorrah by raining fire down from Heaven (see Genesis 19:24).

"This follows the pattern of Ezekiel's prophecy (Gog & Magog), where Israel's enemy is destroyed by fire. The actual wording of the fiery defeat is drawn from 2 Kings 1:1-14, which describes God's deliverance of Elijah from the armies of the ungodly king Ahaziah. The fire probably is not to be taken literally, but regardless, the point is that God will deliver His people by judging their enemies."[139]

> *"And the devil who deceived them was thrown into the lake of fire and brimstone, where the beast and the false prophet are also; and they will be tormented day and night forever and ever"* (verse 10).

Thus comes the eternal judgment for that Dragon! His forces of anti-Christian government and anti-Christian religion have already been judged in chapters 18-19. They are in the lake of fire awaiting him when he

138 Ibid, Storms, pg. 555.
139 Ibid, Beale, pg. 1028.

arrives. And of course, Babylon the Great is not mentioned here, for she, too, with her harlotry and attempts to draw Believers into idolatry, has already been judged and is a distant memory in this moment.

Fire comes down from Heaven and devours Satan, once and for all.

Christ wins! CHECKMATE!

The Church wins the battle and is forever TRIUMPHANT!

She has endured the greatest persecution in all of recorded Salvation-History. She has gained the victory through her perseverance and faith during her sojourn on earth by enduring rejection by the unrepentant, suffering and martyrdom. Exactly as Jesus Himself did in His mission and His final hours on earth in His First Coming.

Christ made it clear, and it is made clear elsewhere, that there will indeed be Christians alive and well here on Earth on the day of the *Return of the King.*

Though He does issue this one great challenge regarding this unique period of time, right at the close of the Age.

> *"However, when the Son of Man comes, will He find faith on the earth?"* (Luke 18:8).

In Summary: a Final Battle of World-wide Deception is on the Horizon.

To sum up, here are two unique perspectives that each and every believer ought to consider, **if we are the generation** enlisted to wage war in this Final Conflict of spiritual light against darkness.

1. **The perspective of Satan:** He thinks he wins in his own Second Coming as the world's great imposter and false King on the chess board. He will be allowed one final battle against the Church, and seek to deceive the nations and overcome all Believers of every nation.

2. **The perspective of the Believer:** You are to bear witness to Christ and suffer in patience. The visions do not literally mean that all members of the Church will die, but that the world will experience a short period of intensified persecution (when it is possible that there will be many martyrs).

   Some will be underground and some in visible communities, but all with the glory of the LORD upon them and His manifest presence to guide and comfort them.

Here, once again, are the two passages we have been learning about, in poetic parallel form, in these two chapters:

Parallel Passages	
"And when they have finished their testimony, the beast that comes up out of the abyss will **MAKE WAR** with them and kill them. "And their dead bodies will lie in the street of the great city which mystically is called Sodom and Egypt, where also their LORD was crucified." (Revelation 11:7-8)	"And when the thousand years are completed, Satan will be released from his prison and will come out to deceive the nations which are in the four corners of the Earth, Gog and Magog, to gather them together for **THE WAR**. The number of them is like the sand of the seashore." (Revelation 20:7-8)

John sees the same coming worldwide event, but from two unique vantage points, with various special symbolism in each vision to share different aspects of the battle with us.

Having finished now a closer look at some of the symbolism and meaning of the Book of Revelation, let's answer the following questions.

How will the End come?

What will the Last Battle look like?

What clues from what Revelation unveils about the ongoing battles of spiritual warfare have been happening in all the eras of Salvation-History revealing the Warrior Lamb conquering the Beasts and Harlot Babylon?

And what relevance is that to me today for what is transpiring in the world?

Read on for answers!

Going Deeper Still

— How has this chapter helped shape, enhance, enlarge, or change your previous view of the Millennial Reign of Christ?

— According to the teachings in this chapter, how was Satan bound by Christ after the Cross until today? How isn't he?

— Define the Kingdom of God as both now/not yet. Can you draw it as a diagram?

— How was Satan unbound in the Old Testament?

— The Final Battle will not simply take place in one geographical location like the Middle East. Instead, look for a brief, worldwide battle which will affect every nation on earth, simultaneously. Have you ever considered this before? What does the thought of "persecution" and "deception" look like in your particular region of the earth right now, as you read this?

— Endurance, trust, faith and personal sacrifice, will help all Believers endure that brief war amidst cataclysmic times and worldwide persecution. What are some spiritual disciplines you can personally grow in to help you prepare?

— Compare Matthew 12:29, 1 John 3:8 and Revelation 20:1-3. What do they mean to you today? How can they give faith and hope in your tomorrow?

SECTION III

APOCALYPSE NOW

APOCALYPSE NOW

Near-Future Scenarios & Offensive and Defensive Spiritual Warfare Tactics.

"Then I heard a TRIUMPHANT voice in heaven proclaiming:
"Now salvation and power are set in place,
and the kingdom reign of our God
and the ruling authority of his Anointed One
are established.
For the accuser of our brothers and sisters,
who relentlessly accused them day and night before our God,
has now been defeated—cast out once and for all!
They conquered him completely through the blood of the Lamb
and the powerful word of His testimony.
They triumphed because they did
not love and cling to their own lives, even when faced with death.
So rejoice, you heavens, and every heavenly being!
But woe to the earth and the sea,
for the devil has come down to you with great fury,
because he knows his time is short."
—John the Revelator's poetic praise from Revelation 12:10-12.[140]

Did you know that I, Carl, am also a documentary filmmaker and have created a film series based on this book? Go to this website to watch some stories from the next section. **https://revelationsbattleplans.com/**

140 From, "The Passion Translation" by Brian Simmons.

Illegal Gospel

Historical Examples & Possible Future Scenarios

"But realize this, that in the last days difficult times will come, for men will be lovers of self, lovers of money, boastful, arrogant, revilers, disobedient to parents, ungrateful, unholy, unloving, irreconcilable, malicious gossips, without self-control, brutal, haters of good, treacherous, reckless, conceited, lovers of pleasure rather than lovers of God; holding to a form of godliness, although they have denied its power" (2 Timothy 3:1-5, NASB).

"You emphatically must know what I am about to tell you! In the very last part of the last days, in the very end of the age, hurtful, harmful, dangerous, unpredictable, uncontrollable, high-risk periods of time will come." (–a summary from 2 Timothy 3)[141]

"When the end comes, the hostility towards Jesus and His disciples will be made manifest the whole world over." — Dietrich Bonhoeffer

141 Translation courtesy of Rick Renner, Sparkling Gems From the Greek (Rick Renner Publishing, 2003) pg. 144.

"The Church reveals the light of heaven to a world that lies in darkness. The Church and the world—a conflict is unavoidable. The darkness hates the light. As a result, persecution is in store for the Church."[142]
—William Hendriksen

I am aiming at very practical applications to some very initially-shocking truths about our Enemy and his tactical warfare and cannons firing against God's people. So, I would like to pause in this chapter as we attempt in this new Section to answer the question, "Just what will the Last Battle look like?

Part of that answer is: it will look like the past periods of persecution and the Enemy's attempts at silencing the true witness of Jesus Christ.

Thus, I will share a few historical examples of how he has waged warfare against us in the past, with a view to look ahead and make our best guesses as to just how he might wage that intensified warfare against us in the future. He certainly is not creative, and he, too, is limited by the sovereignty of the Father regarding his own boundaries in tactical warfare against the Church.

So we'll look backwards here in order to look forward.

A Look at Satan's Big 3 Cannons Aimed at Believers

With Revelation, John's vision of the Great Whore of Babylon is borrowed from Israel's exile in Babylon herself, where the righteous Daniel found himself being tempted by the culture. The idolatrous paganism of the culture was attempting to lure the pureness of the worship of Israel's God to compromise.

This very picture is what is represented in full blossom as perhaps the Church's greatest temptation: allowing whatever culture you are in to impose its negative elements on your life. Indeed, its goal is to change your focus from a pure heart of worship of the Most High God, to a position of unholiness and compromise.

142 Hendriksen, Op.Sit, pgs. 25-26.

Satan seeks to counterfeit all that is true. He even has his own counterfeit trinity, which are described in chapters 12 to 14: the Dragon, the Beast from the Sea, and the Beast from the Earth (the False Prophet). Here his deception is revealed as he counterfeits the work of the Father, Son, and Holy Spirit.

"As the Dragon, he is a *counterfeit* of God the Father. The Beast (coming out of the sea), a kind of pseudo-incarnation of Satan, is a *counterfeit* unholy warrior opposed to Christ the holy warrior (compare 13:1-10 to 19:11-21). The False Prophet (the Beast coming out of the Earth) is a counterfeit of the Holy Spirit. By his deceiving signs the False Prophet promotes worship of the Beast. His actions are analogous to the manner in which the Holy Spirit works miracles in Acts (and the Church Age) to promote allegiance to Christ."[143]

In chapters 12-14, Revelation teaches, among other things, that Satan is aiming and firing three huge cannons at you in warfare. They are pictured symbolically, and here are the deeper spiritual realities behind the imagery.

1. **The Sea Beast:** ANTI-CHRISTIAN PERSECUTION through governments and nations.
2. **The Earth Beast:** (The False Prophet): Persecution and allurements from ANTI-CHRISTIAN RELIGIONS (also coming through governments and nations).
3. **The Harlot Babylon:** ANTI-CHRISTIAN SEDUCTION (worldwide in scope: she surrounds the people of God everywhere).

Satan works in counterfeiting Jesus and truth. In unique imagery we, as the people of Jesus, are called the Bride of Christ. Satan's counterfeit is an opposite female figure: the Great Whore of Babylon.

Satan is pictured as your arch-enemy in Revelation. All three of these figures are further defined, and their mysteries unveiled, in this Section so that you can practically discern how those three weapons, or demonic tactics, are at work in the world today.

143 Vern S. Poythress, "Counterfeiting in the Book of Revelation as a Perspective on Non-Christian Culture." A paper presented at the 1995 annual meeting of the Evangelical Theological Society.

You can see all three of them in the newspaper or televised on the evening news, every day, if you know how and where to look for them. Now that's practical help!

The three Cannons fire upon you daily, and they are causing millions of people in millions of places to focus their worship on ANYTHING but the LORD.

Daniel's own battle tactics against the spiritual Enemy in his surroundings in Babylon, included fasting, disciplined prayer, faith, boldness, determination and intimacy with the LORD. Not a bad place to start!

The Multiple Embodiments in Salvation-History of the Beast

Now let's take a closer look at the symbolism with Satan's first of the "Big 3" cannons he is firing at the Church right now, considering that this weapon will be fully loaded and fully armed during the final conflict. I speak of the Beast from the Sea, or anti-Christian persecution, from Revelation 13.

> *"And I saw a beast coming up out of the sea, having ten horns on seven heads, and on his horns were ten diadems, and on his heads were blasphemous names. And there was given to him a mouth speaking arrogant words and blasphemies; and it was given to him to make war with the saints"* (Revelation 13:1, 5a, 7a).

This hideous beast represents various forms of persecutions against the saints throughout the history of the Church.

The ten horns are a "complete" number, symbolizing all Nations in their entirety; the seven heads represent that the beast takes many forms in its persecuting power.

And we've already seen that the blasphemous names are the *counterfeits* of the *holy* names of the Father and the Son and the Spirit (the *Holy* Spirit).

"The beast then, is a trans-cultural, trans-temporal symbol for all individual and collective, Satanically-inspired, opposition to Jesus and His people," writes Sam Storms, "It is anything and everything (whether a principle, a person, or a power) utilized by the Enemy to deceive and destroy the influence and advance of the kingdom of God.

"Thus, the Beast is, at one time, the Roman Empire; at another, the Arian heresy (4th century). The Beast is, at one time, the Emperor Decius (3rd century persecutor of the church); at another, secular evolutionary Darwinism (21st century).

"The Beast is the late medieval Roman Catholic papacy, modern Protestant Liberalism, Marxism, the radical feminist movement, the Pelagian heresy of the 5th century, communism, Joseph Stalin, the 17th century Enlightenment, 18th century deism, Roe v. Wade (Abortion), the State persecution of Christians in China, radical Islamic fundamentalism, angry 21st century atheism, etc.

"Each of these is, individually and on its own, the Beast. All of these are, collectively and in unity, the Beast."[144]

So his seven heads allow him this kind of variety in his tactics, and depending on the culture in which you live, elements of any of these historical examples may become very intense, and the people surrounding the Church within various cultures will reject you, misunderstand your heart, and seek to destroy your witness and make it illegal for you to keep a life that is consecrated to your Heavenly Father in the nature of the Son.

And throughout Salvation-History this Beast has caused intense, short seasons of legal prosecution and punishment against the Lamb's army.

The Greatest Ambassadors in Chains

From its earliest hours after the Ascension of Christ in victory on the Mount of Olives, the Church militant has been looked at by the governments of the world as a menacing army that needs to be silenced at times, or at times destroyed, or rendered powerless to affect the culture with its revolutionary ideas.

144 Sam Storms, Kingdom Come: the Amillennial Alternative, pg. 488. Christian Focus Publications, Ross-Shire, Scotland, 2013.

We know that Satan is behind the scenes, of course, pulling the strings of the government minions of the world, and causing disruption, delay, and in some cases, destruction against the Lamb's army. The gospel, in many places, has been illegal. And it will be illegal again.

The Book of Acts shows us just how the earliest Church thrived in unity under such conditions of persecutions, as it was made illegal by the Roman government to yield allegiance to any superior Deity other than the Emperor Caesar himself. In the first 40 years of the Church, the prophecy of Jesus about the sufferings of His followers as the gospel expanded was fulfilled. Nearly all of the original apostles were martyred or suffered imprisonment, including the apostle Paul, who historians say was martyred in Rome a few years prior to the destruction of Jerusalem in 70 A.D.

"God dares to put his ambassadors in chains..."

"God dares to put his greatest ambassadors in chains" wrote Watchman Nee, considering the sufferings of the Apostle Paul. Indeed, his greatest ambassadors have spent many hours suffering in horrible conditions in the prisons of their day.

Nero himself, the Emperor-God who lived a life of blasphemy and had an intense hatred for the spreading message of Jesus, was the Hitler or Stalin of the day. But he was far worse than Hitler or Stalin in terms of his persecutions of Christians. John the Revelator poetically records his visions with the backdrop of the cruelty of Nero and his successors, like Domitian, in mind.

In fact, Domitian issued an order against the illegal followers of Christ. "That no Christian, once brought before the tribunal, should be exempted from punishment without renouncing his religion."[145]

Christians were hunted down in their meetings, brought before these tribunals, and ritually killed for their failure to renounce Christ.

Of course, there were no church buildings of any kind either. No state-allowed places of worship where the Church could meet legally. Until Constantine some 300 years later, the government did not legally recognize

145 John Foxe, Foxe's Book of Martyrs, Ibid., pg.10.

the Church and she, like her LORD before her, had nowhere to lay her head. Remember this thought as we look into the "Property Question" of the Church a bit later during the Last Battle.

And so, for the past 2,000 or so years, depending on which nation and historical record you look at, up to present day, the Enemy has made the proclamation of the Gospel and the allegiance to Jesus as LORD illegal.

Tottlebank

Some dear, lifelong friends of mine in the U.K. are Ian and his wife Linda, and they live in a wonderful and very historic area called Ulverston, England. Ian has invited me on several occasions to visit and to preach there. On one of our visits, I had a Saturday morning off and he decided to take me on a local tour and visit three historical churches. The first two were quite dreary, and to both of us, felt very worldly and "religious." I won't mention their names, but both were at one time strong churches. But with the current spiritual dryness and moral license of certain denominations within England, they have fallen into disarray.

"Now we'll visit a secret church," Ian told me, "and see if God is there!" We drove along a winding road, right into the English countryside, and stopped along a steep embankment.

"Here it is!" Ian shared enthusiastically.

"Where?" I remarked, looking around the entire countryside and seeing nothing.

"It's here. I told you it was a secret," shared Ian.

So we got out of the car and stood on the edge of the embankment, overlooking a long and beautiful view of woods, fields and moors. Still, I did not see the building. I was beginning to wonder exactly what was in Ian's coffee that morning, when suddenly he said, "Take a walk with me!" We set off down the steep bank and turned a corner and...there it was!

Back in the 1600s in England, the government (a.k.a. a manifestation of the Beast) made it illegal for people to worship God outside of the state-backed religion.

So there arose a large underground group of Believers that became known as, "dissenters." The laws of the time literally made it illegal for more than two Christians to meet together for worship. Even a group of three, if captured, could be imprisoned or killed. So in this particular region of England, known today as the Lakes District, a group of seven dissenters got together to form their own expression of church.

They built this initial building very strategically and secretly, literally right into the lower end of the steep bank of the main road. So if you were traveling on the main road by horse, and you did not know the exact place to stop, you would pass by this church as it is virtually invisible, even to this day, from the road.

A true underground church: TOTTLEBANK!

There are stories that during those initial decades, the English authorities sent from London to try to arrest these groups, would traverse that road up and down, and they never did find the building.

That day, Ian and I met together and prayed with the pastor, Phil, who was a wonderful and very joyful man, full of depth in the LORD. The Holy Spirit's presence still hovered over this ancient site, built first in the year 1669, during that time of intense persecution in England. There is something sweet about being in places where people have defied the Beast and, armed with prayer and sacrifice, taken a stand against him and built an altar of worship to the Lamb.

George Fox and the Quaking Saints

Those years in the middle of the 17th Century were very turbulent for the Lamb's army. Just a few miles away from Tottlebank lies the town of Ulverston, where Ian & Linda live. Ulverston became the northern headquarters for a rising movement of deeply spiritual Believers named the Quakers.

They were founded by a young man named George Fox.

Fox became convinced after reading John, chapter 1, that since the light of Jesus Christ had gone out to all the world and had enlightened everyone, everyone had an opportunity to find Christ and surrender, obey and serve Him from their heart. They did not need outward religious practices, or an external priesthood, to find and worship Christ daily.

He set off throughout the countryside preaching, and soon many people became convinced of the truth, and began to turn their hearts to Christ.

Fox would preach in the countryside, in the fields, in the pubs and taverns, and even walk into church services that were in session, stand up upon a pew, and start preaching the Word. (Yes, disrupting the service!)

He was many times beaten and imprisoned, but through his ministry, he raised up over 30,000 new converts in two decades. At one time he was leading over 60 preaching men and women who were itinerants all over England. They were called, "The Valiant 60."

He came to Ulverston in 1653, and through his preaching, made a new convert, a woman named Margaret Bell, who lived at Swarthmoor Hall with her husband and eight children. Swarthmoor became the headquarters for the Quaker movement.

Why were they called Quakers? It was a derogatory term at first, given by the heathen crowds, who observed that during Fox's animated preaching, people who were being drawn towards the LORD would begin to shake and quake. God's presence literally caused the quaking, and so they became known as, Quakers!

Just to put into context the kind of suffering that these people were constantly in danger of, here's a quote from Fox's journal from just a decade before Tottlebank was built.

> "At Ulverston I was taken to the common moss and the Constables beat me. Then they gave me over to the rude multitude which then fell upon me with their hedge stakes and clubs, and they beat me as hard as they could, striking my head and arms

> and shoulders. At last I collapsed on the wet common. I lay there a long while, and when I recovered myself, suddenly the power of the LORD sprang through me.
>
> "I stood up, in the eternal power of God, and spread out my hands and with a loud voice said, "Strike again! Here is my arms and my head and my cheeks." Then a rude fellow gave me a strike atop my head with all his might. And the skin was struck off my hand and blood came. And I looked at it in the love of God, and I was in the love of God to them all that had persecuted me."[146]

Isn't that incredible? Can you see that the Beast and the Lamb are at war, and there are sufferings to endure as a result? The most amazing part of that tale is the power of the Spirit which rose up in Fox, and caused him to react to this mob in the very love of Christ Himself.

For in a very real sense, it is Christ's light, within the heart of Fox, that was clashing with the deep spiritual darkness in the hearts of these people.

"The Spirit is the one who conforms the Messiah's people to His suffering and glory," writes N.T. Wright, "and the Spirit is the one who enables God's people to endure suffering without illusion, but also without despair. We may even be right to suggest that, through the Spirit, the Christian engages in the present with the ongoing battle which derives from the victory of the Cross."[147]

Light Shone in the Darkest Days of WWII

Moving down through Salvation-History we come to a few examples of what the Beast has been up to with a more modern twist. Prior to WWII, as you've already read, Rees Howells had gathered his group of intercessors out in the western edge of Wales, and they were praying daily for the events of the day leading up to WWII, with a God-given mandate to pray for the "Every Creature Commission." During that same decade, the LORD raised

146 George Fox, The Journal of George Fox, pg. 128. Philadelphia, The Religious Society of Friends, 1985.
147 N.T.Wright, Paul, Ibid., pg. 149.

up a most unique vessel (I'm sure he was one of the "10,000 vessels to carry the Word" that Howells was responsible for praying into existence)!

This vessel was a young man named J. Edwin Orr. He was originally from Belfast, just a short boat ride across the Irish Sea from where Howells was praying in Wales. Orr had a most remarkable calling from God to absolutely trust God for every need in his life, as he was called to ride his bicycle and preach the gospel everywhere the Spirit led him.

He wrote a most intriguing book about his travels called, "10,000 Miles of Miracles in Britain," which chronicled his faith journeys on his bicycle. He then was led by the Spirit to travel up into Scandinavia, by faith, and then make a loop around Russia, Europe, and then back to the U.K. In his second book, "Prove Me Now!" he shared his stories.

During his mission to Russia, he found the culture there most dark. There was a gathering storm cloud of war coming to the Russian people in the 1930s, and the Christians there were persecuted severely and met only in small groups, hidden and secret, and mostly "underground."

The Beast was rising in that nation and the Lamb's army was hidden. He shares in his own words what happened as he encountered a group of these Christians. They were at first wary of establishing contact with Orr, since he may have been followed by the secret police, and then their group of Believers might be arrested and killed.

Here's what happened after the service and Orr spoke with the pastor.

> "It is dangerous, dear brother," they told young Edwin, "but go and tell all the Believers in the West about us. Tell them, it is very difficult for us to be Christians. We do not know what may happen next. Some have been sent away—and some have not come back. It is so impossible that we almost despair. But we are still holding on.
>
> "We pray continually for revival. Take our love to every congregation of the LORD's people. Ask them to pray for us. Goodbye, dear English brother. We shall meet in Heaven."

Then Orr had to slip out a secret exit and follow a different route from where he came in. On the crowded streets, seeing thousands of soldiers being secretly trained for a possible coming battle (WWII was only a few years away at the time), he felt the intensity of the spiritual war of the Beast versus the Lamb. He prayed out in strong tears, "O God, in Thy love and mercy, remember Russia. Remember the hundred millions who don't have the light and are being prevented from seeing the light."[148]

Another vessel that was a direct answer to the prayers of the, "Every Creature Commission" from Rees Howells and those intercessors, praying fervently from 1935 onward, was a precious woman named Corrie ten Boom. She was one of countless Christians who suffered deeply alongside the Jews. She has become known all over the world for her remarkable testimony in the film and story, "The Hiding Place."

She shared this story from one of her experiences in the concentration camp that gives us hope and courage in the midst of our battle.

> "When I was in a concentration camp during the war—Ravensbruck—the Bible was called there, "das Lugenbuch" (The Book of Lies). It was a miracle that I still had my Bible. The room in which we lived with seven hundred women was so dirty that we were all full of lice. One day we got a new supervisor whose name was Lony. She was a fellow prisoner, a cruel woman; she told the guards everything we did (we were having secret Bible studies).
>
> "One day I opened my Bible. A friend of mine said, 'Don't do it today. Lony is sitting right behind you. If she knows you have a Bible, she will see to it that you will be killed in a cruel way.'
>
> "I prayed, 'God, give me the strength even now to bring your Word.' He answered that prayer.
>
> "I read the Bible, brought the message, prayed, and then we sang a hymn, 'Commit thy ways unto the LORD.' When the

148 J. Edwin Orr, Prove Me Now! Pg. 66. Marshall, Morgan and Scott Publishers, 1935.

song had finished, we heard someone call, "Another song like that!" It was Lony; she had enjoyed the singing.

"Afterwards I got a chance to explain the Gospel to her, to show her the way of salvation. I am not a hero. When you know that what you are saying can mean a cruel death, then every word is as heavy as lead. But I have never had such a joy and peace in my heart as when I gave that message, neither before that time, nor afterwards."[149]

We know the end of that story...

That is so inspiring!

Now, we are approaching the time of the final conflict. All of these historical records seem to indicate that what has happened, is happening right now somewhere in the world, and will happen again, as the Father allows this cosmic struggle between good and evil, or light and darkness, to continue. We know this struggle is the ongoing war that Jesus initiated against Satan at the Cross.

Of course, we also know the end of the story in Revelation. The Beast is forever destroyed! (See Revelation 20:10.)

So for now, borrowing a phrase from N.T. Wright, let's turn our attention for a brief moment to *"signposts in the fog of the future."* We'll attempt to discern just what it will potentially look like as this final conflict begins and we, whoever are still alive and filled with faith and love for our Savior, will be the called and chosen to endure this war.

We will live together in a daily "surrender" to Christ, enjoying His presence, His peace, and His joy, even while we endure suffering, as George Fox did, or those Russian Believers before the war, or Corrie Ten Boom in the concentration camp. Let's pause here and consider the subject of suffering patiently.

149 Corrie Ten Boom, Marching Orders for the End Time Battle, pg.106. CLC Publications, 1969, 2012.

Suffering Patiently amid the Witness

Let's face it, the sermon subjects of suffering patiently, of people rejecting the truth, and even of martyrdom for one's faith, are not preached that often from pulpits anymore. They are not part of the "Top 10" subjects that pastors preach.

Jesus Himself suffered and was rejected, and in Revelation 1:5 is referred to as, *the faithful witness (martyr).* He shared with His disciples that they, too, must suffer patiently as they maintain their witness throughout this Age. The truth is, the darkness hates the light and continues to persecute it. Peter confirms this thought in his first epistle.

> *"If you are reviled for the name of Christ, you are blessed, because the Spirit of glory and of God rests upon you. By no means let any of you suffer as a murderer, or thief, or evildoer, or a troublesome meddler; but if anyone suffers as a Christian, let him not feel ashamed, but in that name let him glorify God. For it is time for judgment to begin at the house of God; and if it begins with us first, what will be the outcome for those who do not obey the gospel of God? And if it is with difficulty that the righteous is saved, what will become of the godless man and the sinner? Therefore, let those also who suffer according to the will of God, entrust their souls to a faithful Creator in doing what is right"* (1 Peter 4:14-19).

Let that Scripture lead you forward, if you are indeed blessed to suffer for Christ's name, both now and perhaps in the war that will soon be declared upon the Church!

For whenever we truly suffer for representing the risen Christ, we are "sharing in His sufferings" and the "suffering Church" is enduring the evil that surrounds her in the righteousness of Christ. And just why else may the LORD allow suffering in these Last of the Last Days?

"The LORD needs to wean us off our love for the world," shared my English evangelist mentor, Eric Delve, one day with me, "and the things of this world, like our contentment of what we currently have. The only way to wean us is by God (in His mercy and grace) allowing us to go through the pains of persecution. A dreadful thought! I myself am not volunteering to be a martyr, but I know this is on Satan's agenda. Suffering, sometimes torture, sometimes death. So we need to go through the tough times, when we only have Jesus, and nothing else. HE is enough."[150]

Suffering is occurring right now in many places in the world. "Over one million Christians were martyred for their faith between the years 2000 and 2010," writes Dr. Gloria Wiese in her blog. "That means that in the 21st century, 270 people lose their life every 24 hours because of their faith in Christ."[151]

"The cross means sharing the suffering of Christ to the last and to the fullest. Only a man or woman thus totally committed in discipleship can experience the meaning of the cross. Each must endure his allotted share of suffering and rejection. But each has a different share: some God deems worthy of the highest form of suffering, and gives them the grace of martyrdom, while others he does not allow to be tempted above which they are able to bear."[152]

Question: What might "the end" look like?

Answer: It will look like it has in glimpses of world history, AND it will look as it has "never looked."

The Seizure of Many Church Properties in Various Cultures

There are massive worldwide shifts of persecution on the rise, and "a change of residence" for the Body of Christ is very possible.

Christians living in the turbulent End will do well to remember that the people of God have always been a nomadic culture! We are called, "pilgrims" and "sojourners" for a real reason.

150 Rev. Eric Delve, from a conversation we had together about the End Times.

151 www.askdrglow.com

152Dietrich Bonhoeffer, Ibid., pg. 89. Incredibly, when Bonhoeffer first wrote those words, little did he know (or did he?) that he himself would be given the "highest form of suffering." Arrested for treason against Hitler (Hitler had a personal hatred for Bonhoeffer and all he stood for) and imprisoned, Bonhoeffer lived the last of his short life in pain. In April of 1945, just a week before the Allies invaded Berlin and the war ended, Hitler ordered the hanging of Bonhoeffer. Stripped naked and alone, he mounted the scaffold in a lonely courtyard and yielded his life to Christ. He is one of those who have received the highest eternal honor in the Court of Heaven, clothed in a white robe and with a crown of glory over his head.

> *"Beloved, I urge you as sojourners and pilgrims on this earth... "* (1 Peter 2:11).

God's chosen have always dwelt in tents, in temporary structures, and in family units. The earliest records in Acts confirm this truth. In an "illegal" culture, church buildings will be taken away, destroyed, seized, or given into the hands of unbelievers.

In America, this will have a dramatic effect. Multi-million dollar facilities with state-of-the-art electronics, gymnasiums, coffee shops and cinemas, Christian day-care facilities, and church buildings of all sizes could all be seized and shut down.

The Church will most likely go nomadic in these days (however long they last) and follow after her LORD, who lived a life of example for those of us at the end of time. He, Himself said He was a nomad.

> *"The Son of Man has nowhere to lay His head"* (Luke 9:58).

Remember His life of faith if you are reading this in the midst of church properties being seized or destroyed. He was born in the lowliest of places, a muddy and smelly stable, as there was no room in the inn. He lived a nomadic life as a Rabbi and lived in His friend's houses, not knowing where He would sleep the next day. He borrowed everything: a boat to preach in, even a donkey to ride on into Jerusalem. And when He died, He did not even own a graveyard plot. Joseph of Arimathea provided a cave for His body to lie in.

Thinking deeply and seriously about this aspect of the Church in her final sojourn, I turned back to the suffering of Dietrich Bonhoeffer, the deep-thinking Lutheran theologian and teacher who was imprisoned and became a martyr during WWII.

"When the end comes, the hostility towards Jesus and His disciples will be made manifest the whole world over," wrote Bonhoeffer, "and only then must the messengers flee from city to city. This assurance that in their suffering they will be as their Master is the greatest consolation the messengers of Jesus have. The older the world grows, the more heated becomes the conflict between Christ and the Antichrist, and the more thorough the efforts of the world to get rid of the Christians.

"Until now the world had always granted them a lodging-place by allowing them to work for their own food and clothing. But a world that has become one hundred percent anti-Christian cannot allow them even this private sphere of work for their daily bread. The Christians are now forced to deny their LORD for every crumb of bread they need. Either they must flee from the world, or go to prison; there is no other alternative. **When the Christian community has been deprived of its last inch of space on the earth, the end will be near.**"[153]

One only has to remember the seasons of time in Salvation-History when the Beast has erupted in fury against the Lamb, and destroyed church properties (both Roman Catholic and Protestant, depending on the decade or century or place) or seized control of them and rendered the people helpless.

Or call to mind the images of church buildings being destroyed in recent government persecution crackdowns of Believers throughout China.

I remember the very real pain that a pastor was feeling, and a huge feeling of uncertainty and fear, as his worldwide denomination was making a decision to allow homosexual priests to be leaders of churches without renouncing their position.

They were being openly homosexual, and this was very cultural-friendly. And this denomination made all the pastors either go along with this position or be fired.

One evening I was visiting friends in Sydney, Australia with one of my mentors, Alan Langstaff. A friend of his, this pastor, was visiting too. That evening, in his conscience, he decided he could not go along with the denomination. What followed in the month after? They seized his church property, shut down the doors of the church, and evicted him, his wife, and children from the parsonage.

153 Dietrich Bonhoeffer, The Cost of Discipleship, Ibid., pgs.216, 266-67.

This Godly man and his family were sent out to become nomads, not knowing where they were going to live or how they were going to survive. And this kind of thing will become the rule, not the exception, in every nation on Earth during this time.

The Body of Christ will have nowhere to lay her head.

"In the Book of Revelation, union with Christ comes to bear in many ways. It is expressed in holding fast to the "testimony of Jesus," in endurance even to the point of martyrdom, in the joy in having access to the presence of God's heavenly throne. In true worship, as mediated through Jesus Christ, we put away idols. And in the satisfaction of fellowship with God we put away the seductions of the world.

"Instead of the Beast's power, we look to the power of God's throne. Instead of the Harlot's luxury, we look to the riches of the New Jerusalem. Instead of the Harlot's sexual enticement, we look to the pleasure of the marriage supper of the Lamb.

"Thus, Revelation empowers our spiritual warfare not only by revealing the devices of Satan, but by providing a continuing remedy in God himself—until we experience consummate triumph over sin and evil in the new Jerusalem."[154]

SWAT Teams and Deportations...Coming to America?!

On July 12, 2012, a SWAT team was sent in and arrested a pastor in his home, outside of Phoenix, Arizona, for holding a Bible study, and sentenced him to 60 days of prison. The local community said that the people coming to the Bible study were breaking the zoning rules for that area with their cars parked around the block.

Uwe and Hannelore Romeike moved their five children to Tennessee (a sixth child has since been born) in 2008 to escape thousands of dollars in fines and increasing pressure from local police and education officials to enroll their children in school. All German parents are required by law to send their children to a state-recognized school, whether public or private.

154 Ibid, Poythress, 1995.

The Romeikes are evangelical Christians and say they should be allowed to keep their children home to teach them Christian values. Before they left Germany, the police forcibly escorted the older Romeike children to school one day. Other German families have lost custody of their children because they persist in home-schooling.[155]

If you research the historical records of the Nazi Regime in WWII, now declassified documents available for public study, you will find something shocking. Their agenda was to completely silence the Christian witness (kill the Two Witnesses, as it were) during the years leading up to the War in Germany.

Nazi Persecution (to hasten the demise of the Christian Witness) in WWII:

Here is a short list of just some of the elements of policies and persecution that they established and carried out in ruthless fashion upon the Church scattered throughout Germany.

— Arrests and incarceration in concentration camps

— Banning of all Christian organizations

— Church publications censored or forbidden

— Surveillance of worship services and church leaders

— Dissolution of all "religious" political parties

— Total submission of the Church to the State

— Prayers forbidden at School assemblies

— Civil Servants required to remove their children from religious youth meetings

— Murders of Christians & Clergy opposed to the regime

Battle Plans: The Now and Future Battle for the Church

To apply these thoughts to your personal life, you have to realize the truth

155 Krista Kapralos, Religion News Service, May 16, 2013.

that your tactics must be individualized depending on which culture in the nations you are reading this material, and even what decade you are reading this in the 21st century, or the particular century you are living in.

"Your entire life has been involved in an unseen cosmic war..."

Why? Because Satan is crafty and he builds his strategies upon the free-will choices of mankind, which man and woman have been making for many generations on specific places on earth.

For example, areas which took a long period of time for the Lamb (through His followers) to penetrate with Truth, conversions, and victories in the Spirit over the Enemy, are more prone to still be strongholds.

A "stronghold" of Enemy spiritual forces can be defined as demonic powers that have never been prayed out of an area or region; they are still existing there. One of the reasons may be that not enough intercessors have stood strong in persistent prayer, or in unity of faith, to resist the Enemy.[156]

"Your entire life has been involved in an unseen cosmic war," writes Joseph Z., "that began before time itself. The conflict is territorial, the stakes are eternal, and all of it involves you more than you might realize. This conflict rages daily and will only increase as we find ourselves closer to the end of the age."[157]

For example, there are "strongholds" of evil spiritual forces over whole nations. If you are reading this in China today and are part of the secret, underground Church, you are already experiencing what the rest of the Church, worldwide, will likely be experiencing on some level (or a variation on the same theme) when it comes to real imprisonment and physical persecution. So, we could say the Beast from the sea is in full force there. Christianity, in many places, is illegal and punishable by imprisonment.

156 For further reading on these particular themes, the Author recommends some of the following books: "The Last of the Giants" by George Otis, Jr., "Engaging the Enemy: How to Fight and Defeat Territorial Spirits" by C. Peter Wagner, "Clash of Worlds" by David Burnett, and, "Impacting the City" by Martin Scott.

157 Josesph Z., Servants of Fire: Secrets of the Unseen War & Angels Fighting For You, Harrison House, 2023, pg. 43.

If you live in Tibet and are reading this, you are surrounded by temples dedicated to the worship of demons. That statement may seem very strong, but the reality of the Beast from the Land, known as the False Prophet, is that his primary force is to draw people away from the pure worship of the LORD through Anti-Christian religions. Tibet is primarily Buddhist. Those Buddhist temples are, at the core, idolatrous and demonically energized, just like the ancient Guild-feasts in Thyatira that were sacrificing food to idols. (See Revelation 2:20.) The False Prophet is Satan's tactic at present time to try and keep Tibetans from the pure worship of Jesus Christ. Whereas if you cross the border, his tactic is different and related to the symbol of the Beast from the Sea.

When it comes to America and the West, the third cannon, or, the Whore of Babylon, is one of the strongest forces at work by Satan, to draw people away. As of this writing, the government of the United States will not imprison you, torture you, or kill you for preaching the gospel.

And though the influence of other world religions is present and a growing threat to Christianity in America and the West, our whole basis of culture is a breeding ground for individualism, materialism, and humanism. All of which equates to Harlot Babylon.

The landscape is changing, of course, at present.

But for the most part, Satan appears to be most actively masquerading himself as the Great Whore in the United States, with rampant sensuality everywhere, and the enticements of the flesh and the worship of "SELF" and comfort in all the cities and even in many churches. You can find self-help materials, some even written by well-known pastors and church leaders, everywhere here.

With the Harlot, Satan is attempting daily to draw Believers away from the pure worship of the Father by offering many alternatives; the focus seems to be on the TEMPORAL instead of the eternal.

So to summarize, your tactics for battle and your Marching Orders will vary, depending on when and where in the world you find yourself reading this, especially as Satan's limited authority is about to be allowed to expand by Jesus in order to see the final war to be waged and the final battle to begin. The spiritual landscape of earth is about to shift in radical proportions.

In the next chapter, we'll have a look at some of the crafty ways Satan impacted individual lives in Scripture, and then compare those tactics to two time-periods: the time of this writing and the time of the Last Battle.

By looking at times when Believers were walking closer to the LORD and relative peace was present (and seeing what tactics the Enemy was using against them in those times), and then comparing those times to later times, (and the tactics Satan was attacking those Believers with), we can begin to hypothesize the same or similar tactics to what Satan may be doing in these latter days.

The pattern throughout much of Scripture was that slowly, many Believers abandoned the worship of the LORD and turned to idols. Whole battles were waged to destroy them or silence their witness to that culture and area and time period.

People of "The Way"

As you consider these days of battle, consider a change in the name of the followers of Jesus. They were never meant to become a worldwide sect or "extra religion" on the platter of so many choices. We have always claimed relationship with Jesus and the Spirit and the Father (talked about in full measure in a following chapter called, The Word, the Voice, and the Love).

That relationship is indeed extraordinary as it sets us apart, as we communicate daily with a personal God in an impersonal world.

In the Book of Acts, the name "Christian" began in chapter 11, where we read, *and the disciples were first called Christians in Antioch* (Acts 11:26b). This name for God's new people only appears once more in the entire Book of Acts! *And Agrippa replied to Paul, "In a short time you will persuade me to become a Christian!"* (Acts 26:28).

But prior to being known as Christians in chapter 11, would it surprise you to know that actually another name for this new group of disciples of the risen Messiah appeared before the name Christian as a means of identification?

> *"Now Saul, still breathing threats and murder against the disciples of the LORD, went to the high priest, and asked for letters from him to the synagogues at Damascus, so that if he found any belonging to the Way, both men and women, he might bring them bound to Jerusalem"* (Acts 9:2).

This same phrase, identifying disciples as belonging to "The Way," is also found in Acts 19:9 and 19:23. Presumably, this term has a kind of direct connection to the beautiful words of Jesus Himself, when He shared with Thomas, "I am the way, and the truth, and the life; no one comes to the Father, but through Me" *(John 14:6)*.

"I Am the Way."

These words set us apart from every other possible connection point of any group on earth, religious or secular! You cannot possibly be content in the Last Battle by calling yourself an exclusive Catholic, Protestant, Orthodox, or any other church group or breakaway denomination that may or may not exist in the end.

You must return to a simpler time, a secret time, where the earliest followers of Jesus were known as belonging to *The Way*, and actually had their own secret symbol to identify one another in a culture where, like Saul (the Apostle Paul prior to his own conversion), leaders were rounding up the Jesus freaks of the culture and imprisoning them.

The earliest followers of Jesus took upon them a secret symbol, and it was imperative that they do so as their faith in Christ alone as LORD caused their very lives to be in danger. They no longer swore allegiance to Caesar as LORD, and thus, their faith was illegal and punishable in some cases by death. They developed the symbol of the fish, and used the Greek letters, "IXOUS."

In Greek, these letters spelled out precisely what they believed in. It is an acrostic, a term given and used quite frequently in the ancient days where each letter represents a word or picture. In this case, the letters were as follows. "I" represents Jesus, "X" represents Christ, "O" represents God, "U" represents Son, and "S" represents Savior. Or, "JESUS CHRIST, GOD'S SON—SAVIOR!"[158]

Consider for a moment that in the end battle, it won't matter if a particular world government is asking you to deny the name Roman Catholic, or Protestant, or Orthodox, or Pentecostal, or even the term, Christian.

It will only matter that you never deny your identity as a follower of Jesus Christ, the Holy Spirit, and being a son or daughter of the Father. You are a follower of The Way, and you follow exclusively, "Jesus Christ, God's Son—Savior!" Remember these words, even as the name "Christian" is spoken in derision all around you,

> *"There is one body and one Spirit, just as also you were called in one hope of your calling; one LORD, one faith, one baptism, one God and Father of all who is over all and through all in in all"* (Ephesians 4:4-6).

"The Highest Christian Persecution Ever"

Would you believe it if I shared that as of the year 2026 with the publication of this First Edition, I just watched a current report that nearly 400 million Christians in over 30 Nations are under threats, imprisonments, martyrdoms, and suffering of various degrees through persecution, and it's getting worse?[159]

This is just one example of Satan's tactics through the Beasts and Harlot to persecute Believers, and I believe tactics like this will be employed internationally at some point in the Last Battle.

A Final Thought: Here are a few questions to ask yourself to determine "what time it is" on the Last of the Last Days timeline in your particular nation.

158 Carl Wesley Anderson, Changing of the Guard: The Rising of Generation Xtreme (Born to Blaze Ministries, copyright 2003). Available for purchase on our ministry website: www.borntoblaze.com
159Quoted from a Report from the U.S. Commission on International Religious Freedom, January, 2026.

— If I go out today from my front door into the city and actively share my faith, what will happen to me? Is it dangerous?

— As a Believer, how am I looked upon by my government, my neighbors, and my family?

— Do I have freedom to meet with other Believers freely and openly, or are there restrictions or consequences? Do I have a place outside my home to worship King Jesus freely?

Let me close with a wonderful and deep quote from a leader within the current underground church in China.

> "Perhaps we're fortunate," shared Chinese house pastor Samuel Lamb, "we suffered so much and have so little. If we were secure and well supplied as we hear of Christians in other places, we might be less sincere on our discipleship. The Christian faith is most precious when we experience it under testing. The primary purpose of prayer is not for gaining wealth or comfort or earthly security. Faith and prayer are to make us true followers of our LORD, who suffered as the greatest example of purpose in life. A Christian who has not suffered is as a child without training. Such Christians cannot receive or understand the fullness of God's blessing."[160]

160 Ken Anderson, quoting Pastor Samuel Lamb from China, in, "Bold As A Lamb." Zondervan Publishing, 1991.

Going Deeper Still:

Satan's Big Three Cannons Aimed at You (his Large-scale and Individual Battle Plans):

1. **The Beast from the Sea:** Governmental Anti-Christian Persecution, Imprisonment, Suffering, Martyrdom.

2. **The Beast from the Earth:** Anti-Christian Religion, Idolatry, Heresy, Occultism, Modern Philosophy, Science and "Reason" above "Perception," Liberal Theology, Secular Humanism, and Financial Pressures and Ruin.

3. **The Great Whore of Babylon:** Anti-Christian Seduction, Allurements of the Flesh, and Modern Materialism of the West (the focus of quality of life in place of eternal perspective).

— How can you personally "come out of Babylon" and separate yourself from the world? Make a list. Pray for daily help from the Holy Spirit.

— In the very Last of the Last Days, it is very possible that Satan will attempt a worldwide seizure of church property and the Church universal will have to meet again in small groups, secret gatherings, and secret locations. The Son of Man may find nowhere to lay His head. How can you begin to prepare for underground scenarios, just like Tottlebank near Ulverston, England? Make a list.

CHAPTER

THE ENEMY'S TACTICS ON THE BATTLEFIELD

Knowing the Enemy's Strategy & Your Counter Attacks

"The LORD will go forth like a warrior, He will arouse His zeal like a man of war, He will utter a shout, yes, He will raise a war cry, He will prevail against His enemies" (Isaiah 42:13).

The Son of God appeared for this purpose, that He might destroy the works of the devil" (1 John 3:8).

"History will not go on normally and then Jesus will return. Revelation presents a more complex picture: the kingdom is advancing and gathering in the nations through the church's witness amid suffering; and then, just before the end, intensified and coordinated hostility of the non-Christian world against the church, which is rescued by the glorious return of Jesus our Defender."[161]

161 Dennis E. Johnson, Ibid, pg. 363.

Once again, let us remember the words of C.S. Lewis and Screwtape's letters I quoted earlier. We are not falling into the ditch here of an "excessive and unhealthy interest in our Enemy."[162]

That being said, you must realize the importance of learning and growing daily (and I do mean daily) in your employment of tactics and strategies from the Word of God to set up BOTH defensive and offensive positions in the battles today, and the final battle to come.

Here is a wonderful truth written by a Roman Catholic Nun in the early 1980s, when she dared to listen to the LORD and write what she felt He might be saying when it comes to warfare.

> "This is Divine warfare you are in
>
> and it requires Divinity to fight it.
>
> You cannot fight it with your natural mind.
>
> You cannot fight it with your natural spirit.
>
> It must be fought in the Spirit
>
> and so I will teach you to fight in the Spirit.
>
> I will teach you to bring down those forces
>
> by the power of My Blood
>
> and by the sword of My Word."[163]

Though it seems we live behind enemy lines each day, remember that we are the *victors*, and not the *victims*. Develop an attitude of just who you are in the Lamb's Army.

General Creighton W. Abrams was a mobile tank commander in WWII, and helped break up the German forces at the now-famous Battle of the Bulge, helping the 101st Airborne Division to move out of their position in the forest. He was noted for his concern for his soldiers, his emphasis on combat readiness, and his insistence on personal integrity.

162 Ibid, C.S. Lewis.
163 Sister Francis Clare, "Your Move, God." New Leaf Press, 1982.

At one point in the campaign against the German army, his company became cut off from his supply lines and the Germans were surrounding them. That evening, Abrams' scout reported to him in his tent, "Sir, we're surrounded." Abrams thought about what he would tell his men, and in the morning he gathered them all together.

> "Gentlemen! We are now faced with the best situation we have had in this war. For today we can attack in any direction we choose!"

That is the reality. All around you there is a war on, and though you are surrounded so-to-speak, you can develop the right understanding of what your Enemy's tactics are, and begin to advance in this spiritual war against his schemes.

You have advanced weapons to help you attack the enemy as well as defend yourself and your family.

Abrams also said, "When eating an elephant, take one bite at a time."

So, even though I've just written about Satan's worldwide conspiracy against Christ, and it may seem like a daunting Enemy to strategize against, just take it easy. Eat this elephant one bite at a time.

Military strategy and tactics are essential to the conduct of warfare. Broadly stated, I agree with the following definition of "strategy:"

"The planning, coordination, and general direction of military operations to meet overall objectives. Tactics themselves implement strategy by short-term decisions on the movement of troops, supplies, and employment of weapons on the field of battle. A newer, strategic form of warfare has been developed, the mobile SPECIAL FORCE, armed with light but sophisticated weapons and trained in guerrilla tactics, they can be rapidly deployed and as rapidly withdrawn from hostile territory."[164]

Since you are probably not called to assault Satanic forces on a global scale, I'd like to focus my attention in this chapter on more specific, prac-

164 Ronald E.M. Goodman, quoted in Grolier Electronic Publishing, 1995.

tical strategies in which you can be trained under the command of your 7-star General, Jesus Christ. He will help you develop offensive and defensive strategies for you and those loved ones in the Church, so you can join forces and attack the enemy in small numbers, just like a special forces team.

Let us place before our minds a few significant facts:

1. The Book of Revelation comes from the heart of the Father Himself, through Jesus Christ, to us, His bondservants. Therefore, we must remember that whatever we learn from its pages, our first encouragement is: The Father, Son and Holy Spirit are sovereign!

Even the Enemy himself, as a created being, is ultimately subject to the LORD, and can only **counterfeit** the reality of the LORD. Remember that word. He even receives his own counterfeit "second coming" as we already have learned.

If we have been shown the Battle Plans of all time and history, there is a reason why God wanted us to know, from His unique and eternal perspective, what is coming, and how.

Satan, although the adversary of God and our greatest foe, is by no means His equal. Jesus opens the seals by His own authority in Revelation 6. He binds the strong man in Revelation 20. He defeats him finally in Revelation 19. And Satan and all his dark minions are forever banished to everlasting torment in the lake of fire in Revelation 20-21.

2. We, as Believers, walk in daily victory over Satan, as we overcome him by the Blood of the Lamb, the Word of His Testimony, and our faithful witness, even unto death if required (Revelation 12:11).

It would serve us well to recount a famous quote from C.S. Lewis.

"Enemy-occupied territory—that is what this world is. Christianity is the story of how the rightful King has landed, you might say landed in disguise, and is calling us to take part in a great campaign of sabotage."[165]

---

165 Ibid, C.S. Lewis, Mere Christianity.

Here are a few scriptures that will lay a foundation in your theology about the fact that God is indeed a Warrior. And through your relationship as part of the Body of Christ on earth, He is actively at war against His Enemy.

> *"Then it came about when the ark set out that Moses said, "Rise up, O LORD! And let Your enemies be scattered, and let those who hate You flee before You"* (Numbers 10:35).

> *And he said, "No rather I indeed come now as Captain of the host of the LORD"* (Joshua 5:14a).

> *"The LORD will go forth like a warrior, He will arouse His zeal like a man of war, He will utter a shout, yes, He will raise a war cry, He will prevail against His enemies"* (Isaiah 42:13).

> *"The Son of God appeared for this purpose, that He might destroy the works of the devil"* (1 John 3:8).

> *"And they overcame him because of the blood of the Lamb and because of the word of His testimony, and they did not love their life even to death"* (Revelation 12:11).

Satan's Various War Tactics and How You Counter Them in the Last Battle

> "The arch-deceiver is not only the deceiver of the whole unregenerate world," wrote Jessie Penn-Lewis, "but of the children of God also; with this difference, that in the deception he seeks to practice upon the saints, he changes his tactics, and works with acutest strategy, in wiles of error, and deception concerning the things of God (Matthew 24: 24; 2 Corinthians 11: 3, 13, 14, 15)."[166]

Remember as you read the following four central tactics to Satan's warfare against you, that the truth is:

> *"The Son of God appeared for this purpose, that He might destroy the works of the devil"* (1 John 3:8).

166 Jessie Penn-Lewis, "War On The Saints" Chapter One. Salty Brine Software, Kindle Edition.

Central Tactic #1

Questioning the truth through "half-truth," and trying to make you believe a lie by forming it in your mind.

O.T. Example: This is his earliest tactic! Read Genesis chapter 3. Satan loves delusion and diluting, like mixing the "pure" water with the "impure" so that the whole stream becomes infected. In the Garden of Eden, he approaches Eve and poses a tantalizing question in her mind. *"Has God said?"* He then proceeds to mix the full truth of what God had said with a lie, making it a half-truth (see Genesis 3:1-6).

N.T. Example: Remember Jesus' example for you of how He successfully fought Satan in the wilderness. Read Luke 4:1-13.

When the whisper of half-truth came to His ears, He countered it by proclaiming the Word (the full truth). He boldly spoke those three incredible words which won Him the battle: **"IT IS WRITTEN."**

He then quoted the living Word of God and overcame the temptation by standing upon it. I will share on each of the three attacks of Satan's lies below, so you can have a better understanding of how to counter him.

Satan's tactic of sowing seeds of unbelief has been successful since Eve in the Garden of Eden. That sneaky little word, "IF," has worked on thousands upon thousands of people for thousands of years. He tried the same tactic with Jesus in Luke 4, but finally, Jesus as our Warrior, shows us how to defend ourselves against this attack.

Now Jesus, full of the Holy Spirit, returned from the Jordan and was led around by the Spirit in the wilderness for forty days, being tempted by the devil. And He ate nothing during those days, and when they had ended, He was hungry. And the devil said to Him, **"If** You are the Son of God, tell this stone to become bread." And Jesus answered him, **"IT IS WRITTEN,** *'Man shall not live on bread alone'"* (Luke 4:1-4).

Here is one of the tactics that Satan still commonly uses to attack you in your mind, causing you to believe half-truths and lies and stopping you from growing in your faith.

1. **He questions God's ability in the area of Provision.**

Jesus was hungry. Satan wants Him to prove His identity by turning the stone into bread. Could Jesus have actually done that? Sure. How do we know? We know He could because a few chapters later, He essentially does the same supernatural creation of provision by turning a few fish and loaves of bread into enough food to feed 5,000.

For you and me, Satan takes a two-prong approach when it comes to supernatural provision. He whispers to your mind, "Is HE faithful? Will He supply for you?"

Jesus exercised self-denial. He was fully consecrated and refused to use His powers for selfish reasons and create provision of the bread. Instead, He would trust Father to provide for His physical needs and bring the food when it had to come.

Many people lose faith and lose heart because they turn to man for answers in place of turning to God alone. Remind yourself every day that HE is faithful and HE is well able and will supply all your needs according to Christ Jesus!

Remember also, the DISCIPLINE OF FASTING, as it breaks your flesh's desires for food, and reminds you of God's way of the power of self-denial.

Your Counterattacks: KNOW THE ESTABLISHED WORD OF GOD AND SPEAK OUT THE RHEMA WORD OF GOD

Be able to quote it out loud, memorize it, pray in the Spirit, stand on it and live it out (in spite of your circumstances).

Know the context of the Word and the power behind it. Make godly choices every day that are in alignment with the Word and the Spirit. When thoughts arise in your mind that are contrary to the truth, cast them out, and replace them with the truth.

> *"So shall My word be which goes forth from My mouth; It shall not return to Me empty without accomplishing what I desire, and without succeeding in the matter for which I sent it"* (Isaiah 55:11).
>
> *"You shall know the truth, and the truth shall make you free"* (John 8:32).

And let's recall the powerful, symbolic imagery of the actual Second Coming in Revelation 19 where we read, *"His name is called The Word of God and from His mouth comes a sharp sword"* (Revelation 19:13, 15).

Five Hills To Die On

To truly follow the Father, Son and Spirit, you must ultimately form your own convictions and adopt the "essentials" that you know to be eternally true. Here are my "five hills to die on" as we approach the Last of the Last Days. These, or truths like these, that you adopt yourself through the Apostle's Creed or Nicene Creed, should become living truths to you. They must be areas where, if confronted, you absolutely will not compromise in your belief or actions. Where, if called upon to die on a hill of conviction, you will remain true to the LORD in these truths, and *"love not your life even unto death."* Here are mine.

1. The Deity of our LORD Jesus Christ (100 percent fully God and fully Man).

2. The Virgin Birth.

3. The Blood Atonement.

4. The Bodily Resurrection, Ascension, and Second Coming of Jesus Christ.

5. The Authority of the Word of God (and absolute confidence in the God of the Word).

All five of these are contained in both the Apostle's Creed and Nicene Creed, and all five are becoming increasingly scarce among the "essential" doctrines of even the most conservative evangelical denominations in the West.

Dietrich Bonhoeffer, the Lutheran theologian (hated by Adolf Hitler and Hitler's evil regime), coined the incredible phrase, "You must develop an exclusive allegiance to Jesus Christ."

Can you develop such an allegiance?

It was a cold morning in April of 1945, just weeks before Berlin was liberated and Hitler committed suicide in cowardice.

Bonhoeffer was hanged. He paid the ultimate price in personal defense of that phrase as he was forced to suffer for it and lay down his life in martyrdom.

As you develop an exclusive allegiance to the living Christ, you will note that the Holy Spirit, as the agent of God's voice and leading on Earth, is the One who spoke through the "law and the prophets" (the Old Testament), through the Gospels and the apostles (the New Testament), and then to this I add my own truthful spin: He is still speaking to us today![167]

Central Tactic #2

The Enemy attacks in multiple waves and techniques.

Over and over again, Satan attacks once, and then he comes again. Many Believers are aware of the first attack, and often times resist properly. But they forget that Satan does not take naps. That is, he never quits. He comes in waves. When one wave is resisted successfully, he will look for another weakness and come again.

O.T. Example: As we learned earlier in the "Earth's Trauma" chapter, in the Book of Job we find an amazing account of Satan asking permission

167 To learn more about the 21 Ways to Recognize God's Multi-Faceted Voice, see my Appendix, "Love Speaks" near the back of this book.

you are

BLESSED

because the Spirit of glory and of God
rests upon you."

(I Peter 4:14)

of God to attack Job. God held Job in high esteem and utilized Job as an example of a man who would remain true to the LORD even if attacked. Satan goes out in "waves" against Job.

Wave 1: He attacked Job's wealth and took it away.

Wave 2: He attacked Job's family and killed his sons and daughters through demonic weather patterns.

Wave 3: He attacked Job's health and put boils on his skin until he was greatly afflicted (see Job 1-2). You will note: he did not stop with one attack!

N.T. Example: Even with Jesus in the wilderness, when Jesus resisted Satan's temptation for turning a stone into bread, Satan did not give up. We have a record of four distinct attacks, each targeting a different area of truth, before he finally gives up and leaves Jesus alone and the Word says he, *"departed from Him until an opportune time"* (Luke 4:13).

In the Book of Acts, he tries over and over again to stop the Apostle Paul from successful ministry. Paul writes about some of these Satanic assaults and waves of attacks.

> *"Five times I received from the Jews thirty-nine lashes. Three times I was beaten with rods, once I was stoned, three times I was shipwrecked, a night and a day I have spent in the deep. I have been on frequent journeys; in dangers from rivers, dangers from robbers, dangers from my countrymen, dangers from the Gentiles, dangers in the city, dangers in the wilderness, dangers on the sea, dangers among false brethren"* (2 Corinthians 11:24-26).

Your Counterattacks: PERSISTANCE and RESISTANCE!

Never give up in your persistence and resistance! Take seriously the parables that Jesus Himself taught about the power of persistence when it comes to resisting the Enemy and prayer power (for example read Luke 18:1-8).

See how Jesus kept proclaiming the Word, and that as He did so, it contained power. See how Paul kept rising every day and no matter what circumstance he faced, he was *"not disobedient to the heavenly vision."*

With Job, Satan used financial hardship, deaths of family members, and sickness and disease to discourage him.

If you hold to the truths of the Kingdom, that God's Kingdom power is available for you today in any of these areas, you will walk in victory.

Take the subject of healing as one example. When you get diagnosed with disease, have people pray for you for healing, and make healing declarations over yourself.

If and when you are healed from an ailment, DO NOT STOP RESISTING. Some of the greatest defeats of God's people through the ages have been that they successfully win a battle against, say, cancer, but then they stop fighting. They stop a daily resistance against it or any form of disease, and as a result, Satan attacks again in another wave and they are defeated and give up.

My Own Battle for My Life with Cancer

In my own life, as I shared with you in my Author's Introduction, I was attacked directly from the pit of Hell with cancer. The LORD spoke to me very early in the battle and gave me the command to fight as aggressively (with the most aggressive medical treatments that were being offered), as the Enemy was in fighting me.

> Never give up in your persistence and resistance!

I remember having to battle through fevers. Immunotherapy, the kind of treatment I was offered, heightens the immune system and you get a fever as a side effect. I had to endure 69 weeks of fevers during my first two years of treatments. With the first round of those treatments, we successfully killed the cancer.

But the Enemy attacked again.

Again, we resisted with another treatment and killed the cancer.

And he attacked yet again.

And we had to resist him with another round of different treatments. Until finally, and it was nearly five years along with two major operations, the cancer was defeated and I lived on. Praise God! It took persistence and resistance, and years of prayer, too. I had to keep fighting!

Whether you want to learn how to defend yourself, and also how to attack the Enemy, is up to you. But know this: if he sees potential in warfare against you or a member of your household, he will not stop attacking you in wave upon wave, using multiple tactics. You must learn to persist in resistance.

The Message Bible translation for Luke 18:1 declares,

> *"Jesus told them a story showing it was necessary for them to pray consistently and never quit."*

There will be more about prayer as a weapon in the following Section, but for now, remember the fact that you can attack the Enemy with multiple prayers, and consistent and persistent prayers that wipe away his authority, and bring change and real transformation to your life.

Central Tactic #3

Satan tries to keep you from prayer and communion with God.

It is hinted at in Ezekiel that Satan (known also as Lucifer) was the worship leader, long ago, in Heaven. If this is true, you can imagine how much he hates it when redeemed people seek the LORD and worship and praise Him, trusting Him in spite of their circumstances, and seeking His fellowship through disciplined prayer and times of worship. Satan seeks to keep people bound on earth by constantly arranging circumstances to discourage Believers and cause them to abandon prayer and communion with God.

O.T. Example: In the time of Daniel, we have a remarkable moment of Satan's tactic of trying to stop Believers from prayer, worship and communion with God alone. Daniel was part of the group of exiled Jews in Babylon. The Jewish people had finally rejected the pure worship of Yahweh through compromise with idolatry, and were sent into exile, away from their own land of Israel.

"Babylonia, the type or symbol of hostile opposition to God's people, finally overthrew Jerusalem," wrote Edward J. Young in his commentary of Isaiah, "The exile seemed to form the climax in human history of the curses that came upon the nation. Actually it was not the climax, for the cursing will reach its most severe point when world judgment shall fall upon all men and the LORD alone will be exalted. Then, at that last day, which belongs to the LORD, it will appear that only the LORD is sovereign."[168]

Daniel's situation can be said to be a mirror of our own, when you interpret it in the light of the understandings of the Book of Revelation with the Beasts and the Harlot Babylon and the eventual destruction of evil at the end of this age.

In Daniel chapter 6, we find a most remarkable story. By this time, Daniel himself has been faithful to the LORD for years in fasting, prayer, communion with God, and in service to the King in remarkable Holy Spirit led manifestations. Satan was furious. He targeted Daniel by stirring up several men of wicked counsels to pass a statute in which any man praying to a "god" other than the king himself, was to be thrown into the lion's den.

> *"When Daniel knew that the document was signed, he entered his house (now in his roof chamber he had windows open to Jerusalem); and he continued kneeling on his knees three times a day, praying and giving thanks before his God, as he had been doing previously"* (Daniel 6:10).

So much can be gleaned from this story when it comes to supernatural tactics and spiritual discipline in thwarting the enemy's plans!

168 Edward J. Young, The Book of Isaiah, Commentary Volume I. William B. Eerdmans Publishing Company, 1965.

As a result of this governmental and cultural attack against Daniel to stop him from the enjoyment of God alone, he was indeed found guilty by that statute and thrown into the lion's den. I'm sure you've heard the end of the story. God Himself delivered him as he trusted in God alone. Later, Daniel would even be given the visions that become the apocryphal backdrop to the Book of Revelation (see Daniel chapter 6).

"There was nothing impersonal about Daniel's praying," wrote E.M. Bounds, "it always had an objective, and was an appeal to a great God, who could do all things. Daniel's praying was an essential factor in defeating the king's decree and in discomfiting the wicked, envious rulers."[169]

N.T. Example: A parallel example to Daniel happens in the Book of Acts, chapter 16. Paul and Silas are on their second missionary journey and having revival in the city of Thyatira. As they are on their way to the place of prayer to commune with God alone, Satan stirs up a slave girl with a spirit of divination to stop them from that prayer and communion. Satan was successful, *"for many days"* (Acts 16:18), but finally Paul, feeling annoyed, casts out that demonic spirit and in so doing, frees the girl. Yet her masters then report Paul and Silas to the authorities, and the government sends the police force to beat them and cast them into prison.

When you read this story in the context of Satan's tactics, you can actually see two of them in motion here. First, his tactic of attacking in multiple waves and techniques (he used the slave girl, then the girl's masters and the city officials and police). Then, his tactic of stopping these men from both prayer, devotion and communion with God.

Once again, we see these two apostles, like Daniel centuries before, deciding in the middle of impossible circumstances to praise God.

> *"But about midnight Paul and Silas were praying and singing hymns of praise to God"* (Acts 16:25).

Cast into deep darkness, their bodies bleeding from the wounds they had received, their feet fastened securely in stocks and probably in severe pain, these two weak men begin to wax strong in faith, giving glory to God,

169 E.M. Bounds, The Weapon of Prayer, pg. 19. Baker Books, 1931.

being fully assured that deliverance would come. Their voices lifted up, not in complaining or doubt, but in songs of praise to God!

Through their praise and prayer and worship, Satan's attack turns into a revival meeting. God Himself shows up with a counterattack of an earthquake in the jail, and all the doors swing open. As a result, the jailor and his whole family become Believers in Jesus Christ!

Your Counterattacks: PRAYER, PRAISE and THANKSGIVING

Yes! Even in spite of any circumstances that might cause you to doubt God's faithfulness or be roadblocks of complaint.

I find in my life that to enter God's presence is as simple as following Psalm 100.

> *"Enter His gates with thanksgiving and His courts with praise"* (Psalm 100:4).

Satan hates the sound of thanksgiving as much as he hates the sound of praise. Both thanksgiving and praise can be forms of tactical counterattack against him. And you can use these two weapons every single hour of every day if you so choose, no matter what circumstances you are going through.

I find that every morning, if I just think back on the previous day or even hour, I can find something, large or small, to be thankful for. If Corrie Ten Boom could be thankful for the lice that were growing in her hair in the concentration camp (as they kept the guards from punishing the women) then I can find something to be thankful for today!

> *"God's mercies are new every morning; He will never leave you or forsake you; He remembers your frame and knows that you are dust, and He created you for His glory"* (Lamentations 3:23, Joshua 1:5, Psalm 103).

Here is another wonderful passage to remember.

> *"My flesh and my heart may fail, But God is the strength of my heart and my portion forever. As for me, the nearness of God is*

my good; I have made the LORD God my refuge that I may tell of all Thy works" (Psalm 73:26, 28).

Note also that Daniel was disciplined. His practice of going upon his knees and verbally praising God three times every day (other people outside the windows could hear him), was a daily lifestyle of tactical advancement in the battle.

Paul and Silas did not sing their praises in silence either. Their voices were heard by all th people in that prison at midnight *(...and the prisoners were listening to them. Acts 16:25b)*. Clearly this was not an isolated incident, as they must have lived a disciplined lifestyle of daily prayer and praise, in order to be able to react in such a splendid and powerful spiritual manner at that hour of midnight. I'm sure they didn't *feel* like praising, but praise they did!

God's mercies are new every morning!

C.S. Lewis once again said it so well.

"Do not be deceived, Wormwood. Our cause is never more in danger than when a human, no longer desiring, but still intending, to do our Enemy's will, looks round upon a universe from which every trace of Him seems to have vanished, and asks why he has been forsaken, and still obeys."[170]

Central Tactic #4

Satan will tempt you to sin through lust of the eyes and lust of the flesh (making you grieve the Holy Spirit) and through the pride of life (causing unforgiveness, bitterness, and disputes with people).

"For all that is in the world, the lust of the flesh and the lust of the eyes and the boastful pride of life, is not from the Father" (1 John 2:16).

These attacks come in various forms as we have seen and they were all happening throughout the Old and New Testaments, and even within each of the seven churches of Revelation.

170 C.S. Lewis, Ibid. The Screwtape Letters.

Satan will increase his tactics as we get closer to the end.

O.T. Examples: Satan utilized all three of these tactics against Eve and Adam in the Garden of Eden. *"When the woman* **saw** *that the tree was good for food* (the lust of the flesh) *and that it was* **a delight** *to the eyes* (the lust of the eyes), *and that the tree was* **desirable to make one wise** (the boastful pride of life), *she took from its fruit and ate, and she gave also to her husband with her, and he ate"* (Genesis 3:6).

King David, worship leader, prayer warrior, deliverer of Israel, encourager, example of strength and fortitude, and follower of God's ways, was also a murderer and adulterer, and filled at times with sin in all three areas!

I could choose a dozen characters of the Old Covenant who fell into temptation with their eyes and their flesh, but David comes as a strong one. His weakness in the area of lust finally caught up with him one night, when he spotted Bathsheba upon a rooftop bathing. His lust then turned to adultery and then to murder, and he grieved the Holy Spirit's anointing.

It took the Prophet Nathan to come and rebuke him to his face before he was able to see his sin for what it was, and then repent. Read Psalm 51 for a record of his transformation. *"Create in me a clean heart, O God, and renew a steadfast spirit within me"* (Psalm 51:10). Everyone needs a new beginning once in a while.

As for the "boastful pride of life," there are likewise many examples to choose from. Consider Nebuchadnezzar in the days of Daniel.

In a dream, God revealed to the king a metaphorical picture of a towering, beautiful tree being cut down. Daniel interprets this for the king as revealing a heart of pride and how God was about to humble him.

"It is you, O king," shares Daniel, *"for you have become great and grown strong, and your majesty has become great and reached to the sky and your dominion to the end of the earth. You will be driven away from mankind—until you recognize that the Most High is ruler over the realm of mankind, and bestows it on whomever he wishes"* (Daniel 4:22, 25).

It is good to remember the powerful prophetic words spoken so long ago by Hannah, who was the mother of the prophet Samuel. In her song of thanksgiving recorded for us in 1 Samuel 2, she sings,

> *"There is no one holy like the LORD, indeed, there is no one besides Thee, nor is there any rock like our God. Boast no more so very proudly, do not let arrogance come out of your mouth; for the LORD is a God of knowledge, and with Him, actions are weighed. The LORD makes poor and rich; He brings low, He also exults. Those who contend with the LORD will be shattered; against them He will thunder in the heavens, the LORD will judge the ends of the earth"* (1 Samuel 1:2-10, selected verses).

N.T. Examples: Jesus hammered the truth about adultery in the Sermon on the Mount by bringing home to every man the idea that *"any man who even looks upon a woman with lust after her has already committed adultery with her in his heart"* (Matthew 5:28).

The way to avoid the Satanic assault of lust begins with disciplining the mind to be pure in the Spirit; to look upon women not as objects of desire and lust, but as creatures of beauty and honor.

> *"Do you not know that you are a temple of God, and that the Spirit of God dwells in you? Or do you not know that your body is a temple of the Holy Spirit who is in you, whom you have from God, and that you are not your own? For you have been bought with a price: therefore, glorify God in your body"* (1 Corinthians 3:16, 6:19-20).

It can also be said that the Harlot Babylon, who seeks to keep the world systems trapped in daily seduction, is akin to cities like modern day Las Vegas in that her seductions are everywhere, in all places, at all times. *"And the woman whom you saw is the great city which reigns over the kings of the earth"* (Revelation 17:18).

In the seven churches to which Jesus specifically speaks in Revelation 2-3, we have warnings and admonitions in phrases like these: *"some who hold the teaching of Balaam, who kept teaching Balak to put a stumbling block before the sons of Israel...and to commit acts of immorality...you tolerate the woman Jezebel...who leads my people astray and commit acts of immorality...*

but you have a few people who have not soiled their garments...that you may clothe yourself, and that the shame of your nakedness may not be revealed..." (Revelation 2 and 3, selected).

The Believers in several of the cities of these churches were mixing and compromising with various sins of the flesh, and needed to receive a rebuke from Jesus.

Paul writes a most interesting admonition to the church at Ephesus.

"And do not grieve the Holy Spirit of God" (Ephesians 4:30).

"The word, *grieve*, was taken from the Greek word *lupete*. This word *lupe* would normally be used to picture a husband or wife who has discovered his or her mate has been unfaithful. As a result of this unfaithfulness, the betrayed spouse is *shocked, devastated, hurt, wounded, and grieved* because of the pain that accompanies unfaithfulness. Just as a husband or wife would feel who has just discovered that his or her spouse has committed adultery, the Holy Spirit is *shocked* when we dishonor His presence in our lives."[171]

As to Satan's tactic of "the boastful pride of life," we find numerous examples in the New Testament. The original disciples themselves were caught red-handed in the sin of pride by having secret discussions among themselves as to *who will be the greatest in the Kingdom*. To answer such a question, Jesus takes a little child and sets him down in their midst and says, *"Whoever then humbles himself as this child is the greatest in the Kingdom of heaven"* (Matthew 18:1-5).

Paul's writing about the humility of Jesus Himself, in Philippians chapter 2, is among some of the most astonishing verses about Christ, who came in the opposite spirit of pride by, *"emptying Himself, taking the form of a bond-servant...He humbled Himself"* (Philippians 2:7-8).

There are two stories of pride in Acts, one in Acts 12 and the other in Acts 15. The incident in Acts 12 is that of the king, Herod, who set himself up as a god and began delivering a prideful speech. *"And the people kept crying out, "The voice of a god and not of a man!" And immediately an angel of the*

171 Rick Renner, "Sparkling Gems from the Greek" Ibid., pgs. 9-10.

LORD struck him because he did not give God the glory, and he was eaten by worms and died" (Acts 12:22-23). This is an example of how Satan's "boastful pride of life" tactic hit an unbeliever and wicked king like Herod. It is likewise a rare example of the wrath of God, through an angel, bringing a direct judgment upon a man. It is rare, but it does happen in Salvation-History. Truly a warning to all.

The Apostle Paul had to fight pride in his development, too. An interesting incident happens with him in Acts 15 at the start of what is called his 2nd Missionary Journey. He refuses his good friend Barnabus' suggestion to take along with them the disciple Mark, whom Paul alleges had abandoned them in a previous point of need. You can see here a root of pride in Paul, who held bitterness and resentment against Mark. It caused a rift even between himself and Barnabus, and the scripture says, *"And there arose such a sharp disagreement that they separated from one another, and Barnabus took Mark with him and sailed away to Cyprus"* (Acts 15:37-41).

One of Satan's tactics related to the arena of pride, is to divide and conquer. Once he has sent division in families, in friendships, in churches, and their pastors and members, he can fragment those relationships.

Even though Paul was reacting in pride, bitterness and unforgiveness at that moment, he would later write to the Believers at Rome some words which he learned the hard way. *"For through the grace given to me I say to every man among you, not to think more highly of himself than he ought to think"* (Romans 12:3a).

The Apostle James reminds us, *"Who among you is wise and understanding? Let him show by his good behavior his deeds in the gentleness of wisdom. But if you have bitter jealousy and selfish ambition in your heart, do not be arrogant and so lie against the truth"* (James 3:13-14).

Your Counterattacks: PERSEVERANCE UNDER TRIAL and TEMPTATION, A HOLY LIFESTYLE, and A DAILY HUMILITY as an HONEST LOOK AT YOURSELF and OTHERS.

So many scriptural examples could be mentioned here under the themes of persevering under trial, walking in holiness (conforming your character to the character of Christ), walking in the fruit of the Holy Spirit, a daily humility, an ability to look at yourself honestly, and to see all people as *God sees them,* and not through your own lens of resentment or bitterness.

"Humility is simply the disposition which prepares the soul for living on trust," wrote Andrew Murray, "and every, even the most secret breathing of pride, in self-seeking, self-will, self-confidence, or self-exaltation, is just the strengthening of that self which cannot enter the kingdom, or possess the things of the kingdom, because it refuses to allow God to be what He is and must be there—the All in All."[172]

Revelation's great counterattack for Believers who are exiled in the worldwide Babylonian-Lustful-Seductive-City-Atmosphere is powerful:

> *"And I heard another voice from heaven, saying, 'Come out of her, my people, that you may not participate in her sins'"*
> (Revelation 18:4).

How do you fight Satan's weapon of harlotry? COME OUT OF HER!

How do you do that?

By clothing yourself with Christ:

His purity,

His chastity,

His holiness.

The armor of God is your best defense when Satan's attacks come (see the list of armor in Ephesians 6:10-18).

Learn the truth that Paul teaches us in Romans chapter 6: we have the power daily to say "NO!" when sinful patterns rise around us. And you can learn to consecrate yourself and humble yourself every day. You can learn to walk in lowliness of mind, true humility, and esteem others as more highly than yourself.

---

172 Andrew Murray, "Humility: The Beauty of Holiness." Pg. 52. Fleming H. Revell Company, 1961.

Like Jesus prayed upon the Cross, *"Father, forgive them, for they know not what they do,"* you and I, as His representatives, have the power of that mindset and prayer in our own arsenal.

The words of Jeremiah also come to mind. *"Thus says the LORD: "Let not a wise man boast of his wisdom, and let not the mighty man boast of his might, let not a rich man boast of his riches, but let him who boasts boast of this, that he understands and knows Me, that I am the LORD who exercises lovingkindness, justice, and righteousness on earth; for I delight in these things," declares the LORD"* (Jeremiah 9:23-24).

A Summary of Satan's Tactics:

Satan's Battle Plans have 4 Central Tactics:

1. **Central Tactic #1:** Questioning the truth through "half-truth" and trying to make you believe a lie by forming it in your mind.
2. **Central Tactic #2:** He attacks in multiple waves and techniques.
3. **Central Tactic #3:** Satan tries to keep you from Prayer and Communion with God.
4. **Central Tactic #4:** Satan will tempt you to sin through the lust of the eyes and lust of the flesh (making you grieve the Holy Spirit), and through the pride of life (causing unforgiveness, bitterness and disputes with people).

The LORD's Battle Plans give you Counterattacks in the Fight:

— Proclaim "It Is Written" with the Word of God

— Fasting (like Jesus in the wilderness)

— Persistence & Resistance

— Prayer, Praise & Thanksgiving

— Perseverance, A Holy Lifestyle, and A Daily Humility

Going Deeper Still:

— A question to honestly answer: Which of these areas of counterattack in developing your Marching Orders can you personally say you need to grow into better? Can you start today? If so, how?

— In chapters 12-14, Revelation teaches, among other things, that Satan is aiming and firing three huge cannons at you in warfare. They are pictured symbolically as follows:

The Sea Beast: ANTI-CHRISTIAN PERSECUTION through governments and nations.

The Earth Beast: (The False Prophet): ANTI-CHRISTIAN RELIGION (also coming through governments and nations).

The Harlot Babylon: ANTI-CHRISTIAN SEDUCTION (worldwide in scope: she surrounds the people of God everywhere).

— Consider your own city and nation for a moment. Can you now discern these cannons? If so, what do they actually look like?

— **Assignment:** When you open your newspaper this week or watch any news broadcast, take special note of the governments and religions of the world and how they represent, in part, the twin cannons firing against Believers and bringing deception to keep people from a pure relationship with God the Father.

— Can you think of examples of the Harlot Babylon cannon, firing her tactical ammunition at you in causing you to be seduced away from the pureness of your thought life? What counter-weaponry do you possess in the Spirit to fight against this seduction, through the word of God?

— When was the last time you held a fast? Pray about the timing of starting one this very week. Dedicate that time to the LORD and remember to pray during your fast.

— How can you develop a humble disposition?

— What are three areas you feel you need to start persevering for in prayer?

SECTION IV

MARCHING ORDERS

MARCHING
MARCHING
MARCHING
MARCHING
MARCHING

MARCHING ORDERS

Practical Applications to Prepare For & Endure the Last Battle

"*And He has made us to be a Kingdom, priests to His God and Father; to Him be the glory and the dominion forever and ever. Amen*" (Revelation 1:6).

"Our LORD Jesus Christ is conquering now; that is, throughout this present dispensation His cause is going forward, for He is exercising both His spiritual and His universal Kingship. By means of the Word (Gospel, Matthew 24:14) and the Spirit, the testimonies and tears of His disciples, His own intercession and their prayers, the angels of heaven and the armies on earth; our LORD is riding forth victoriously, conquering and to conquer."[173]

Did you know that I, Carl, am also a documentary filmmaker and have created a film series based on this book? Go to this website to watch some stories from the next section. **https://revelationsbattleplans.com/**

173 William Hendriksen, More Than Conquerors, ibid, pg. 96.

Persistent Prayer: Your Most Powerful Weapon

Practical Prayer Tactics for the Last Days

"And another angel came and stood at the altar, holding a golden censer; and much incense was given to him, that he might add it to the prayers of all the saints upon the golden altar which was before the throne. And the smoke of the incense, with the prayers of the saints, went up before God out of the angel's hand" (Revelation 8:3-4).

"A breed of Christian is sorely needed who will seek tirelessly after God," wrote E.M. Bounds, "who will give Him no rest, day and night, until He hearkens to their cry. These times demand praying men and praying women who are broad and unselfish in their desires, quenchless for God, who seek His glory to be spread abroad the face of the earth."[174]

174 Here we have a quote on prayer by a prayer warrior himself; he awoke at 4 a.m. each morning and prayed until 7 a.m. What a legacy on the subject he left behind. This is an excerpt from E.M. Bounds, The Weapon of Prayer, pg. 66. First published in 1931 and reprinted by Baker Books, 1973.

With a hope and an expectation in your heart that you indeed might remain alive until the very moment of the last trumpet sound and the ushering in of all redemption, judgment and eternity, you can PREPARE as Jesus calls you to prepare.

One of the greatest needs of this hour and the hour to come is the need to be in persistent prayer. If the Gospel writer, Luke, wove in the parable of persisting prayer within other passages about the End, how vital is it to look afresh at the subject of prayer, as it relates now in preparation, and as it will relate soon in persecuting times?

Let's begin this chapter with the full parable that Jesus taught about this subject. Then we will turn our attention to the Book of Revelation and what it teaches us about prayer, and how the prayers of the saints, mingled with intercession from heaven, bring real and present answers in the midst of trials.

Persistent Prayers Take Practice and Bring Answers

Jesus gives us a remarkable parable on prayer, and an even more remarkable statement about the days which lay ahead. These words give us a clear path of practical preparation for what's coming.

They contain a wonderful truth, a thought-provoking challenge, and align themselves with what Revelation teaches about prayer.

Here is His parable, brought forth in contemporary language.

> *"Jesus told them a story showing that it was necessary for them to pray consistently and never quit. He said, "There was once a judge in some city who never gave God a thought and cared nothing for people. A widow in that city kept after him: 'My rights are being violated. Protect me!'*
>
> *"He never gave her the time of day. But after this went on and on he said to himself, 'I care nothing what God thinks, even less what people think. But because this widow won't quit badgering me, I'd better do something and see that she gets justice—otherwise I'm going to end up beaten black-and-blue by her pounding.'"*

Then the Master said, "Do you hear what that judge, corrupt as he is, is saying? So what makes you think God won't step in and work justice for His chosen people, who continue to cry out for help? Won't He stick up for them? I assure you, He will. He will not drag His feet.

"But how much of that kind of persistent faith will the Son of Man find on the earth when He returns?" (Luke 18:1-8, The Message Translation).

Here are some key points to apply in this passage as you prepare for the final war, as you *"add oil to your lamps and await the shout of the Bridegroom"* (Matthew 25:1-3).

1. Persistent, constant prayer is absolutely necessary to both learn as a discipline and grow into in relationship.

2. The context of the widow is that her rights are being violated. Whenever the people of the LORD are experiencing pressure situations where their very rights are being violated and they are undergoing persecution, the answer is: intercession.

   Constant intercession will bring an answer from heaven and bring justice to the realms of the earth. Protection for God's chosen will be provided as an answer to prayer.

3. Even if the atmosphere of the spiritual realm around you grows dark, and people everywhere seem to be abandoning their relationship with God because of the pressure to conform to that darkness, YOU MUST KEEP PRAYING IN PERSISTENT FAITH.

   The last verse is absolutely a key to these "Last of the Last Days," and it is only found once in the whole of Jesus' ministry.

   He likens the days immediately prior to His coming, as days where many people will abandon their persistent faith. May it not be so with you.

LORD, Teach Us To Pray!

Luke 11:1-13.

> *"And it came about that while He was praying in a certain place, after He had finished, one of His disciples said to Him, "Lord, teach us to pray just as John also taught his disciples"* (verse 1).

Jesus taught us the principles of prayer, and in context of the intensity of the worldwide shakings of these days, it is healthy to pause here and reflect. Remember one of your key tactics in battle is: Persistence. This is what Jesus really wants you to exercise in prayer! This key element is to be found when you study the Greek tense in which the following passage was written. It becomes clearer in the Amplified Bible.

> *"Ask, and keep on asking, and it shall be given to you; seek, and keep on seeking, and you shall find; knock, and keep on knocking, and it shall be opened to you"* (verse 9, The Amplified Bible).

Persistence! Yes, we have a pattern here, both in the parable He taught and in continuous tense of the Greek phrases like, "ask and keep on asking!" One of the disciplines I have added to my daily prayers of petition is the discipline of proclaiming this exact verse, as it pertains to my unique prayer requests at the time.

So try this. After you finish praying a petition, declare Jesus' phrase over that petition, out loud, and personalize it to yourself.

> "LORD, you said I need to 'ask and keep on asking and it shall be given to me; seek and keep on seeking and I shall find; knock and keep on knocking and the doors will be opened to me.' Amen."

And consider a daily proclamation of The Lord's Prayer. Each verse, if prayed methodically and meaningfully from your heart, will yield daily treasure and reminders of truths.

And why not pray the following prayer every day? It's the LORD's Prayer, and it will be just as powerful up to and including the very last day of recorded history, as when it was first taught by Jesus. Pray this right now.

> *"Father,*
> *Reveal who you are.*
> *Set the world right.*
> *Keep us alive with three square meals.*
> *Keep us forgiven with you and forgiving others.*
> *Keep us safe from ourselves and the Devil. Amen."*
> (Luke 11:2-4, The Message Translation).

Jesus combined the idea of the importance of prayer with the atmosphere of the Last of the Last Days when He shared this in Luke.

> *"But keep on the alert at all times, praying in order that you may have strength"* (Luke 22:36).

If you read all of Luke chapter 22, you'll find that prayer is a vital ingredient to survival and hope in the midst of the spiritual battles to come. I believe His point is that through prayer and discernment, you can know that you are sealed in protection by the LORD in the midst of the turbulent and dark spiritual forces that are at work and that will be at work more intensely.

Did you know the early Christians had the instructions of Jesus in places like Matthew 24 and Luke 21 and 22? Many Believers who knew these words escaped the city of Jerusalem in 69 A.D. just prior to its invasion by Titus from Rome. Many Believers were able to escape imprisonment and even death as they kept constant in prayer and understanding of the times in which they were living, as they related to these fulfillments of Jesus' prophecies. Let it be so with you in a time of trial.

A Conquering Army of Priests in Prayer

From the very first chapter of the Revelation of Jesus Christ comes forth a most amazing verse.

> *"To Him who loves us, and released us from our sins by His blood,* **and He has made us to be a kingdom, priests to His God and Father;** *to Him be the glory and the dominion forever and ever. Amen"* (Revelation 1:5b, 6).

John the Revelator is giving us the substance of God's heart for His people, all the way back to the very formation of His people at Mt. Sinai. There, in the Exodus, He revealed these startling words,

> *"Now then, if you will indeed obey My voice and keep My covenant, then you shall be My own possession among all the peoples, for all the earth is Mine; and you shall be to Me a kingdom of priests and a holy nation"* (Exodus 19:5-6).

What an understanding here! In fact, with the original Hebrew the words, *"My own possession"* can be translated, *"My special treasure."*

You and I are His special treasure!

We are one Body now, made up of Jewish Believers and Gentile Believers into One New Man (see Ephesians 2), and scattered abroad over the face of the earth.

John brings back this original intention of the Father and gives us our identity, from the 1st century and marching right on down as a conquering army to the final centuries.

You and I are His special treasure!

By the covering of the blood of the Redeemer, we are now loved and created into a royal priesthood.

The ministry of prayer is not supposed to be for just a small group of elite. It is given freely as a commission to every member of the Body, and Jesus expects *us* to enter into daily intercession *with* Him, as our Royal High Priest, and join in the identity of being a priesthood.

The tragedy of Mt. Sinai will never happen again. There, instead of accepting this high calling and becoming that holy nation of a kingdom of priests, the generation that received the Law rebelled against the Most High, and none of them entered into the Promised Land.

God had to wait until His perfect Son would come and display for all of us a lifestyle of prayer and identification with us. He would then shed His blood out of His love for us, and call us back to this "royal priesthood" to share forever in the ministry of prayer with Him.

The opening 5 chapters of Revelation unveil Jesus Christ as the One who is behind the curtains and the very center of all of Salvation-History!

He is portrayed as *both* a Warrior Lion (from the Tribe of Judah) and a Warrior Lamb (see Revelation 5:5-6), continuously transforming the kingdoms of this world until each one shares in His Father's eternal kingdom (see Revelation 11:15 and 1 Corinthians 15).

He is shown as absolutely Sovereign in His acts. As we've seen, He is the only One in heaven or earth who has the authority to open the final seal and unleash the elements of the final battle (See Revelation 8:1).

This battle could begin any day now as we finish our key assignment in the revealed Battle Plans of reaching the nations of the earth with the Gospel. We must all be ready.

Until the very climax of all history, we worship Him and become an army of priests before the world, praying and exercising authority in His name.

Let me define a true "priest."

A priest is a mediator, in verbal witness and lifestyle (clothed in fine linen, which means purity and holiness), who joins with the Mediator Jesus in praying through daily situations to the Father.

A priest is also a prayer warrior, which means you have actual involvement in the purposes of God in the earth.

As part of being a priest, you also share in the covering of the blood of the Lamb and the sealing by the Father. This sealing issues a mandate of protection around you, your family, and your subjects of prayer.

Here are a few scriptures which illustrate these themes of sealing,

> *"And it was given to her to clothe herself in fine linen, bright and clean; for the fine linen is the righteous acts of the saints"* (Revelation 19:8).

> *"And you were sealed in Him with the Holy Spirit of promise"* (Ephesians 1:13).
>
> *"And they overcame him (Satan himself and his Satanic assaults) because of the blood of the Lamb and because of the word of His (Christ's) testimony, and they did not love their life even to death"* (Revelation 12:11).

We have a great understanding now of just what it means to be a royal priesthood. Please remember the promise that goes along with that and to all eternity: you are a part of God's "special treasure."

Revelation chapter 1 gives you your identity. Now let's turn our focus to a most amazing passage and see just how that identity plays itself out in practical and powerful means.

> *"And another angel came and stood at the altar, holding a golden censer; and much incense was given to him, that he might add it to the prayers of all the saints upon the golden altar which was before the throne.*
>
> *"And the smoke of the incense, with the prayers of the saints, went up before God out of the angel's hand.*
>
> *"And the angel took the censer; and he filled it with the fire of the altar and threw it to the earth"* (Revelation 8:3-5a).

This is one of the most remarkable passages of scripture that has ever been written on the subject of the power of prayer from a Christian perspective.

Allow me to explain by pointing out a few key details.

1. This angel could possibly be the Lord Jesus Himself. It is not known for certain, though several commentators I have read leave that possibility open, based upon other places in Revelation where Jesus is pictured as an angel. Regardless of that detail, it is a heavenly being with heavenly authority; that is the central point.

Note, it mixes the incense from the golden censer, WITH the prayers of the saints. It is in this ACTION of mixing that a heavenly answer comes forth from the throne of God.

2. In an earlier passage in Revelation, we read that the prayers of the saints are like incense. So in this case, the angel appears to be mixing his own incense WITH other incense, and the answer comes in the form of gathering of fire from the altar and casting it to earth. Once cast, the symbolic language tells us of judgments which fall to earth in response.

Do you know that Jesus, your Mediator, presents your prayers to the Father?

Jesus is at the right hand of God, interceding for us (Romans 8:34).

And it is only through the moment-by-moment eternal action of Jesus that your prayers are heard by the Father and answered by Him.

In this vision we have a confirmation: the prayers of the saints, mixed with the incense of the angel, together come before God and bring an answer!

The royal priesthood marches on. E.M. Bounds declares,

"Thus says the LORD, the Holy One of Israel, His Maker: Ask of Me of things to come and concerning my sons, and concerning the work of My hands, command ye me." As though God places Himself in the hands and at the disposal of His people who pray—as indeed He does.[175]

Revelation teaches that whenever God's people are suffering in times of trial and making petitions to God for deliverance, their prayers are heard and God himself sends judgments upon the earth as a direct answer to those prayers. Here are a few encouraging passages about Jesus as our high priest.

175 Here we have a quote on prayer by a prayer warrior himself; he awoke at 4 a.m. each morning and prayed until 7 a.m. What a legacy on the subject he left behind. This is an excerpt from E.M. Bounds, The Weapon of Prayer, pg. 66. First published in 1931 and reprinted by Baker Books, 1973.

JESUS

is at the right hand of God,

interceding

for us.

(Romans 8:34)

> *"Since then we have a great high priest who has passed through the heavens, Jesus the Son of God, let us hold fast our confession. Hence, also, He is able to save forever those who draw near to God through Him, since He always lives to make intercession for them. But now He has obtained a more excellent ministry, by as much as He is also the Mediator of a better covenant, which has been enacted on better promises"* (Hebrews 4:14, 7:25, 8:6).

> *"For there is one God, and one Mediator also between God and men, the man Christ Jesus, who gave Himself as a ransom for all, the testimony borne at the proper time"* (1 Timothy 2:5-6).

In conclusion: you've learned of the truth of persistent prayer as a powerful weapon in your spiritual arsenal. Jesus Himself urges you to it (all the way until the Second Coming), and John the Revelator confirms your identity as a member of the royal priesthood. Revelation's vision in heaven shows you the real power of intercession when an angelic being mixes his incense with your prayers, and answers begin to come.

Going Deeper Still:

- Only Luke's gospel weaves together the parable that Jesus taught on persistent prayer (Luke 18), with the prophecies, instructions and other scriptures about the time of His return. Why did Jesus do this?
- Can you think of your last prayer you prayed faithfully until it was answered? How long did it take to see your answer?
- Persist in your prayers through fervent petition: don't take resistance from the Enemy as an answer from God! His answers are coming. Persevere!
- Revelation teaches that you are part of a "conquering army of priests." Have you ever thought of yourself as a priest before God, having the power of interceding for others in the authority of Jesus' name?

— Never give up in your prayers. "Ask—and keep on asking." Try praying for a person, situation, or request, and add this to the end of your prayer,

"LORD, you said I need to 'ask and keep on asking and it shall be given to me; seek and keep on seeking and I shall find; knock and keep on knocking and the doors will be opened to me. Amen.'"

— Pray the LORD's Prayer, out loud, in faith, today!

CHAPTER

Out of the Limelight & Into the Lamplight

Your Place & His Presence in the Battle

"*Many will be purged, purified and refined; but the wicked will act wickedly, and none of the wicked will understand, but those who have insight will understand*" (Daniel 12:10).

"*And there will be a shelter to give shade from the heat by day, and refuge and protection from the storm and the rain*" (Isaiah 4:6).

"*Blessed are those who are invited to the marriage supper of the Lamb*" (Revelation 19:9).

Time now to consider your personal place in the coming spiritual battle. I do so by looking at two disciples, and remembering each of their unique circumstances as they faced their own battles and encountered real opposition: James and Peter.

Next, we'll look at how God's glory is promised to overshadow His suffering Church in the End, and how "revival" might look when the Church is in various places underground and hidden.

I will also provide you with a few helpful historical examples of the power of persistent prayers that can change hearts and alter the course of Salvation-History (just like we looked at with Rees Howells Intercessor and the "Every Creature Commission" in an earlier chapter).

I will conclude with the striking thought that, perhaps, as Jesus is calling His Bride to holiness, persecution may arise to purify her.

In the Last of the Last Days, His glory will appear as a canopy of grace as the Church endures the persecution, and advances on the battlefield through prayer with, and heartfelt guidance from, Him.

At this point, allow me to pose this question for you to ponder:

"What will be YOUR place in the final battle?"

Some Will Be a "James," Some Will Be a "Peter"

With the atmosphere of a battle of universal proportions on the horizon, a battle of ultimate light vs. ultimate darkness, it's good to pause and return to the days of the earliest witness of Jesus in His Church in the Book of Acts.

There we find the tales of two of the original Apostles who were undergoing tribulation and suffering for their bold witness. These two sons of thunder were advancing the Kingdom in power and both were imprisoned for it: James and Peter.

By comparing the two stories, you can draw your own conclusions as to which of these two you might become in the ensuing final battle. In every culture and in every city around the world, in the time of trial and Armageddon (Revelation 16:16), Believers will share the fates of both James and Peter. That is, some will be martyred, and some will remain in safety with miraculous provision.

We read first of James.

> *"Now about that time Herod the king laid hands on some who belonged to the church, in order to mistreat them. And he had James the brother of John put to death with a sword. And when he saw that it pleased the Jews, he proceeded to arrest Peter also"* (Acts 12:1-2).

So sadly (from our perspective), James the Apostle, one of the most intimate of three (Peter, James and John) who had accompanied Jesus up the Mount of Transfiguration and seen Him in His eternal glory and experienced deep friendship with Him, is here killed for his faith.

He pays the ultimate price for His obedience. It is actually portrayed in the Book of Revelation as Heaven's highest honor: martyrdom.

To this day, we do not have an epistle from James as we do from Peter. Revelation gives us the eternal picture of James and the millions of Believers who gave their lives in witness to Christ in those 50 years following his beheading, and those millions more who have died a martyr's death down through the centuries and will yet die in the coming century (the number is at least 70 million and counting).[176] John describes this picture in Revelation.

> *"These who are clothed in the white robes, who are they, and from where have they come?" And I said to him, "My Lord, you know." And He said to me, "These are the ones who come out of the great tribulation, and they have washed their robes and made them white in the blood of the Lamb.*
>
> *"They shall hunger no more, neither thirst anymore; neither shall the sun beat down on them, nor any heat; for the Lamb in the center of the throne shall be their shepherd, and shall guide them to springs of the water of life; and God shall wipe every tear from their eyes"* (Revelation 7:13-14, 16-17).

176 Statistics compiled by Christianity Today, June 27, 2014. The number is higher now.

From the LORD's perspective, James is beheaded and is instantly in the presence of Jesus, greeted in Heaven with a victor's shout upon arrival. He and all who die in the LORD from now on, are just the opposite to what the evil men like Herod or Nero or any other person who kills a Believer thinks.

The wicked think they have the upper hand in silencing the temporary witness of Jesus, but John turns the picture around and provides us the eternal perspective. All those killed in the LORD are part of the "great tribulation," and receive the white robes of righteousness and victory crowns for all eternity!

In this way, the symbolic statement of the "great tribulation" covers the entire Church Age. The battles have been raging since this time to ours, and will continue to rage; 2,000 years and counting. Though I believe we can also apply this phrase with capitals, "The Greatest Tribulation" to the time of the End.

THE NOW-MILLENNIUM: *Timing of the Rapture*

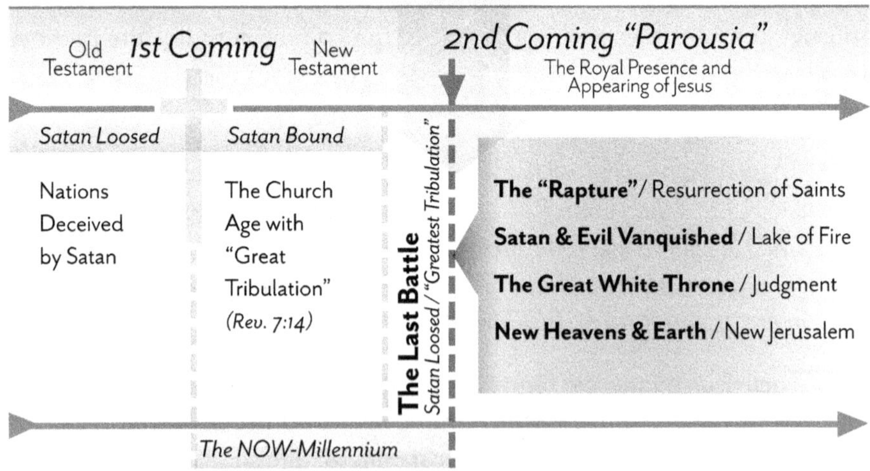

Back to James and all the people that John saw in his visions on Patmos. Did these martyrs sacrifice a few years of temporary life? Yes. But ultimately, that sacrifice of temporal enjoyment yields a harvest of endless years of eternal enjoyment of Christ and His blessings and comforts.

The Enemy, with his persecution, cannot win (as I said earlier, he cannot cast our soul into Hell)! In fact, just the opposite is true. Heaven awaits the Champions who lay down their lives here in sacrifice to the LORD. God has the final authority and those who experience suffering in tribulation are handed a victor's crown and share immortality away from all earthly suffering. Every tear is forever wiped away by the gentle touch of the Lamb.

Peter's Angelic Deliverance Through Prayers of Faith

Let's turn back to our story and look at the tale of Peter. His story does not end the same way as James. We find that, *"So Peter was kept in prison* (he is awaiting his own sentence of beheading) *but PRAYER was being made fervently by the church to God"* (Acts 12:5).

What an interesting detail. We have no record of prayer being made in intercession for James. Probably before the prayer warriors even knew that he was in trouble, Herod had him beheaded, and this must have sent shock waves to the young church at that time.

So here we have a unique element to the sufferings of the Last of the Last Days, and why it is so important that each individual soldier knows his or her own Marching Orders in advance. Each soldier (you and me) must know the power of the armor of God for strong defense (see Ephesians 6:10 12), and the power of unified intercessory prayer on behalf of those who are undergoing persecution. PRAYER was being made on Peter's behalf.

"The Greek word used here for prayer is *proseuche*, or a prayer of gathering," writes my good friend Joseph Z. "It gives the sense of praying together with others anywhere."[177]

The story itself is found in Acts 12:1-17. In essence, on the night before his own potential execution, the LORD answers those intercessors by sending an angel to Peter's prison cell. His chains fall off him, and he is led miraculously out of the prison, passing the guards with invisibility, and with the

177 Joseph Z, Servants of FIRE: Secrets of the Unseen War & Angels Fighting for You, Harrison House, 2023, pg. 30.

iron gate unlocking and opening by itself with the power of God. He then departs in safety to the very house where prayers were being made, and out of sheer joy and astonishment, the girl Rhoda did not even open the door! And nobody in the prayer meeting believed her story that Peter was outside their gate.

"Prayers from a united people caused Peter's miraculous release from prison. I find this story humorous as it speaks to the unexpectedness of answered prayer. The point can be made that when you enact prayers of agreement with others, miraculous things begin to happen, even if you don't believe it when you see it!"[178]

Can you see the amazing elements of supernatural provision? God can deliver you from persecution. When prayers of intercession are going forth, whole areas of Christianity in the world will be safely delivered. God can cloak you with invisibility and cause locked and bolted doors in your way to supernaturally unlock themselves, and then bring you home to your family of brothers and sisters safely!

Peter, as we know from history, eventually paid the ultimate price that James did, by being crucified for his faith in Rome. That being said, remember the understanding that God can seal and protect His children in the midst of times of trial and suffering. He lived many years after this, and left us two amazing epistles of hope for days of suffering.

A friend of mine from Vietnam met with a leader there recently. This man had encouraged thousands of Believers to remain true to the LORD during a time of persecution by the Communists, and during that same time, this man saw true revival take place. He related a few amazing examples of supernatural protection,

"On one occasion, we were warned by the police chief, who was a believer, that a raid was coming to the place where we were gathering. He warned us to leave the premises before the raid party arrived. This policeman accompanied the official raid party, and "found" no one there.

---

178 Ibid, Joseph Z.

"Later, when he met up with me, he asked me where we had moved to. "We hadn't moved!" I shared. He had a surprised look on his face. "We felt we should ignore your advice and keep praying together," I shared, "as the Holy Spirit told us to stay put and not flee in this time.

"There was no "raid" from our perspective and no interruption to our meeting." The police chief shared that they had surrounded the building and searched it and found no one in it at the exact time and place of the gathering!

Another story this revival leader told my friend was quite the opposite. The Christians in a prayer gathering supernaturally heard the sounds of a coming secret raid party, as if they were right outside. The Christians fled the scene and were safe and hidden, and later they found out that indeed this raid party had been sent to that very place, but much later that same night, and had returned empty-handed!

So the Holy Spirit in this case was able to provide warning far in advance and the Believers were quite safe and a long ways away when the danger came.[179]

Will I be on the Front Lines or Supply Lines?

"Though every Christian is called to serve in God's Army," writes Bishop Bill Hamon, "not every saint is called to the same function. Like any army, the Army of the LORD requires a variety of people with different skills to sustain itself. It has three main divisions: preaching, praying and provision. Saints called to preach are the five-fold ministers, missionaries, and those working in full-time ministry (see Ephesians 4:11-13). The praying saints are the faithful Christian soldiers who intercede in prayer for the frontline warriors, and the provision division provide all the natural resources that are needed to accomplish God's purposes."[180]

When you seriously consider the probability in Scripture of the coming

179 Because of security reasons, I am unable to provide the name of this Vietnamese revival leader; but both of these are first-hand accounts from him and he lived through a time of intense persecution and saw true revival break out in the midst of it.

180 Ibid, Bishop Hamon.

world-wide battle against the Lamb, no member of the Church will be spared a fight. The question is simply this.

"Is my individual calling on the Front Lines or the Supply Lines?"

There will be no room in-between. When the war breaks out, the atmosphere will be charged with the grandeur of God upon the Church, as she shines out the light. And the demonic fury of the darkness will grow in intensity, as Satan musters all his might to try and snuff out that light (see Isaiah 60:1-3, Revelation 16:13-18).

Is my calling on the Front or the Supply Lines?

Will you be the Christian who secretly smuggles the Bibles across the borders of harassing territories, risking your life in the process, to get the illegal Word of God through to groups of surviving Believers who desperately need to read it? Or will you be the one secretly financing that mission, or perhaps providing intercessory prayer cover for those Bible-smugglers and their families?

Perhaps you will be called to lead a "spiritual sabotage" mission into enemy-held territory, much like the "resistance" movements of the French or Dutch underground during WWII. They did reconnaissance for the allies and helped the allies know when, where, and how many of the enemy was all around them.

It will be important to know who you can trust, and who you cannot trust. Some front-line leaders will be called to be vocal about their faith, and stand up strong in the face of opposition, and not stop publicly proclaiming their absolute faith in Jesus Christ alone.

Others will remain as hidden Believers in the midst of certain cultures, hidden in their verbal witness, but of course never in their lifestyle of mirroring Christ's character by their love for one another, and the fruit of the Spirit displayed in their lives.

In the example above, Peter was on the front lines and the group of intercessors was on the supply lines. No matter which of the two you are called to serve in, prayer will continue to be your most powerful weapon and your most intimate deepening of your relationship with God.

The Heavenly Man

During a wave of terrible persecution in China, a young man named Brother Yun was arrested. Because of his living faith and deep prayer life, the guards in the prison had a nickname for him: they called him, *"The Heavenly Man."* I found great inspiration in reading his life story in an auto-biographical book by the same name. Its pages are filled with deeply distressing details of his persecution and what he endured.

It is necessary at this point to pause and consider just one story from his testimony. As he suffered in prison, he never knew from day to day whether he would end up as a "James" or somehow escape and be a "Peter."

As you will soon see, the best way to prepare yourself for these kinds of potential scenarios is to pray and seek the LORD, and know that He will be faithful to give you your personal Marching Orders in the midst of the trial. Father, Son and Spirit will speak through circumstances, dreams, visions, and the Word, and the lines of communication will be opened for you as they were for him. Here is a story in his own words.

> "I was taken to a torture room. They handcuffed me and used electric batons, whips and sticks to beat and torture me. My flesh was ripped open and wounds covered my body. Before I lapsed into unconsciousness, the word of the LORD came to me,
>
> *"This is your calling. You should patiently endure because of the Word of God and the testimony of Jesus."*
>
> "After I regained consciousness, I lay still on the ground like a dead man. The guards took me and threw me back into the tiny cell. My hands and my feet were manacled with chains.
>
> "That same night the LORD gave me a vivid dream. In it, my handcuffs suddenly snapped and I was free! In the dream I

> was reading a study Bible. The Catholic Father Yu came to me joyfully and repeated, "Jesus is victorious over all!" I told him, "When I was first locked in this tiny dark cell I prayed God would give me a Bible to study." Then in my dream we both gave thanks to the LORD in Heaven.
>
> "When I awoke from my dream I found that the handcuffs were still on my hands, but the Holy Spirit told me, "Relax your hands." As soon as I did, the handcuffs fell off! I prayed to the LORD according to what I'd seen in the dream. I said, "LORD Jesus, I love you. Thank you for allowing me to sing. Please give me a Bible."
>
> "At around 8 a.m. the next morning a remarkable thing happened. The prison director opened the iron gate and came to my cell. He called out my name, "Yun, although you've committed many crimes, we still respect your faith. Yesterday we had a meeting and decided to give you a Bible. Come, take it!"
>
> "I knelt down and wept, thanking the LORD for this great gift. I could scarcely believe my dream had come true! Through this incident the LORD showed me that regardless of men's evil plans for me, he had not forgotten me and was in control of my life. There is no government of human power that can prevent the Almighty God from carrying out His will!"[181]

Isn't that powerful?!

Sometimes the very scriptures will come alive for you in the midst of your suffering! Here, too, are some scriptures for you to memorize. Please discipline yourself to memorize them in the next few days, as they will bring you endless strength in the Spirit if you are ever called to suffer to the extent of "The Heavenly Man" in a prison cell somewhere in the coming final battle.

181 Brother Yun with Paul Hattaway, "The Heavenly Man: the remarkable true story of Chinese Christian Brother Yun." Piquant Editions, 2003, excerpt from pages 178-179.

Isaiah 51:11
1 Peter 1:6-9
Philippians 4:6-8
Psalm 138:7
John 14:1, 27
2 Corinthians 4:8-9
Hebrews 10:35-36
Galatians 6:9
Psalm 31:24
Joshua 1:5-9
ALL OF PSALM 91 & PSALM 27.

So, as you personally hear his Marching Orders and discover your place in the battle, you will sense His presence and glory in the midst of any trial, or even prison cell, you are called upon to endure.

Days of Fire, Days of Glory Lay Ahead

I love the promises of the Father in Scripture. He always promises that He will be with us as we enter, endure, and emerge from trials of fire (see James 1:2-4, 12). And if we KNOW our identity as a son or daughter of the Father, then when He allows these kinds of trials to happen to us, we know His character and faithfulness will never change. He loves us every moment as we walk through the fire.

He is preparing the Bride for His Son! Thus, it is simply no longer a question of, "will the fiery trials affect me?" But, "when the fiery trials affect me, how will I respond?"

By learning to cultivate a life of prayer now, you will be adequately prepared when fire comes. God promises to protect us (that's His part) and we in turn learn to seek Him during the fire (that's our part) and trust Him in the midst of any daily trials that occur.

Let's look first at three passages in Isaiah that talk about God's promises (His part) to be with us and provide protection and His presence in the closing days of this glorious age. Isaiah wrote these three wonderful truths prophetically looking ahead at what Messiah will accomplish in the whole of the Church Age. I believe they have particular potency as we approach the ends of this Age.

> *"Then the LORD will create over the whole area of Mount Zion and over her assemblies a cloud by day, even smoke, and the brightness of a flaming fire by night; for over all the glory will be a canopy. And there will be a shelter to give shade from the heat by day, and refuge and protection from the storm and the rain"* (Isaiah 4:5-6).

Isn't that a beautiful picture painted for us by the prophet? Let's remember first his usage of terms that apply meaning to broader understandings. His use of the term, "Mount Zion," is a symbolic picture of the whole of the Mountain of God's people, scattered over the face of the whole earth, filling the whole earth, as it were.

It is a reference point to the then-standing temple in Jerusalem, but he speaks here in symbolic speech of all of God's people, in any generation, of the Age of Messiah (the Church Age). John the Revelator uses the same symbols to point to the Church (all Jewish and Gentile Believers).

He speaks of her "assemblies," which are the small, clustered groups of faithful Disciples of Christ in every culture, be they in a church meeting or a home prayer gathering.

He then gives us the remembrance of that wonderful substance of God's presence, the "cloud" that He provided as His children wandered in the desert (the whole story of that cloud is found in Numbers chapter 11). It wasn't a real cloud, but it had the appearance of one. What do you need in the cold desert at evening time? A fire in the cloud above for warmth, of course! And what do you need to block the heat of the day in the desert wandering? That same "cloud." It will give shade, or even smoke to block the sun's rays and provide coolness and comfort (see Deuteronomy 1:33).

He calls His presence, right over your own home or dwelling place right now as you read these words, a canopy and His glory. His glory is a canopy over you to be with you through the days of fire.

Finally, He promises a "booth" for protection from stormy days. This is reminiscent of the booths that were located in the fields, and shepherds could go into them for protection and covering. These are not literal, this is poetic language like Revelation. These "booths" can also represent the idea that Jesus Himself, with the Spirit's direction, will offer you protection from many Satanic strategies that he is trying to implement in the areas around which you live.

Now to another two passages about His promise to be with you.

> *"When you pass through the waters, I will be with you; and through the rivers, they will not overflow you. When you walk through the fire, you will not be scorched, nor will the flame burn you"* (Isaiah 43:2).
>
> *"A bruised reed He will not break, and a dimly burning wick He will not extinguish"* (Isaiah 42:3).

When I ponder the truths of these verses, I think of John the Baptist, called the greatest prophet whoever was (by Jesus). He was known as the transitional prophet who stood between the promises of the coming Messiah from the old prophets, like Isaiah, to the fulfillment of those very promises as Messiah came and began to establish His Kingdom.

Did John live to old age in comfort, with no trial by fire? No. We know of the records of the gospels that he met a tragic end. Again, tragic from our perspective, not God's. Revelation promises that his robe was washed in the blood of the Lamb and he now wears an eternal victor's crown.

He gets arrested for obeying the Spirit, and he gets imprisoned. While suffering in prison, we find him having to fight discouragement.

Even John the Baptist, mighty prophet of the LORD, who was clothed in discernment and power and lived a sacrificial life, got very discouraged while in prison. He even began to wonder if the very Jesus of Nazareth he had baptized truly was the Messiah. In those dark hours in his prison cell, he was in the middle of *"the waters,"* and in the midst of *"the fire,"* and he felt it.

He was, in Isaiah's language, feeling like a bruised reed or a dimly burning wick. It was a low point for him, having second thoughts about who Jesus was, based upon what he was hearing. He became offended.

John Bevere writes of this moment, putting us in John's shoes for a minute. "The temptation to become offended grows greater the longer you're in prison. 'This Man for whom I have spent my life preparing the way, has not even come and visited me in jail! How can this be? If He is the Messiah, why doesn't He get me out of this prison? I've done no wrong.'"[182]

If you have ever had second thoughts about the faithfulness of Jesus, like John was having, be encouraged by Jesus and His reply to John's questioning,

> *"John the Baptist has sent us to You, saying, 'Are You the Expected One, or do we look for someone else?'" At that very time He cured many people of diseases and afflictions and evil spirits; and He granted sight to many who were blind. And He answered and said to them, "Go and report to John what you have seen and heard; the blind receive sight, the lame walk, the lepers are cleansed, and the deaf hear, the dead are raised up, the poor have the gospel preached to them, and blessed is he who keeps from stumbling over Me"* (Luke 7:20-23).

Here Jesus marvelously displays the power of the Kingdom in front of John's disciples, and then He quotes directly from Isaiah the prophet who prophesied that those very works would be the proven works of the Coming One.

I imagine that those disciples went back and reported exactly what they saw Jesus do, as eyewitnesses, and what Jesus said. John knew all too well the words of the prophet Isaiah.

Deep in that prison cell, in the midst of his suffering, a light began to shine again like the brightness of the glory of God. John let go of any discouragement and offense, and was at peace in the midst of his storm. Even as John was soon led away to be beheaded, he had the glowing fire of the Spirit in His heart as he laid his head down on the chopping block.

182 John Bevere, "The Bait of Satan" Charisma House Publishing, 2004.

And once again, just like the Apostle James who was one of the three closest to Jesus Himself, and the first Apostle martyred for his faith (all of them eventually were martyred), God does not deliver John from that prison and his death.

He lets him go through it.

Yet, He warmed his heart with the fire of truth in the midst of it.

As you ponder these truths, know that these are God's promises (His part) in the days of trial which lay ahead. But you still have your responsibility to seek Him and trust Him (your part), both before the fire gets turned up, and even when you can feel the heat.

Underground Revival

In these days of persecution, it will be vital to remain in connection with fellow Believers, even as the Enemy seeks to destroy churches, both large and small. He thinks he is succeeding in causing Christians to depart from the faith. The writer of Hebrews declared otherwise.

> *"Let us hold fast the confession of our hope without wavering, for He who promised is faithful; and let us consider how to stimulate one another to love and good deeds, not forsaking our own assembling together, as is the habit of some, but encouraging one another, and all the more, as you see THE DAY drawing near"* (Hebrews 10:23-25).

As of this writing, we are now some time since COVID-19 struck the world and assaulted the Church in the process. As I shared at the end of "Earth's Trauma" to give a modern example, I believe that viruses like that are not from God: they are from our Enemy. And as I also shared earlier, he hates us. I lost many, many dear friends to that disease. And one of the outcomes was, many churches simply had to close their doors. Thousands of Christians-in-name-only around the world simply walked away from the faith and didn't stay connected in online communities.

But there is power in obedience to this verse in Hebrews.

It's vital to stay in community and continual fellowship with your brothers and sisters in the Last Battle!

I would like to illustrate this truth of the coming "Underground Revival" with an idea that I heard taught by a close friend and ministry colleague of mine, Jeff Orluck. He was sharing about the power of community and being in strong relationship with one another, even in an atmosphere or culture that is opposite of this.

He shared with me the concept of the *mycelium* growth of mushrooms. This is unique in that it forms in underground fashion and can spread in strength over large areas, seemingly invisible to the naked eye above the surface. But even though it remains underground, it can spread and bring change to that actual surface.

For example, *mycelium* can act as a binder, holding new soil into place and preventing washouts above it. It can form a massive colony and provide a food source for the soil around it. And once in a while, while this network is silently growing, the right atmosphere above, like a rain shower, can turn a seemingly empty forest bed into a vibrant array of mushrooms, almost overnight![183]

You see, even as the Enemy seeks to destroy the outward witness of Christianity and its outward forms of worship, as Believers choose to go underground and collectively and deliberately seek out fellowship with one another, true underground revival can spread in secret. And as it spreads, new Believers add to the "nutrients of the soil."

To put it another way, the spiritual atmosphere they are in can actually grow in God's glory, bringing growth and true Christian community in places all over the world, seemingly invisible from the Enemy.

"The final form of the Enemy's attempted deception, as predicted in Scripture," writes my colleague Dr. Lance Wonders, "will be his attempt to impose a supernatural control over all of the existing (or at least primary) structures of human survival and activity (religious, economic, political) under a human leadership and "worldview" that tacitly abandons the true

183 From Wikipedia on the subject of Mycelium.

("old") God and His ways, and which put in their place the new "man-is-God-hood" that is culturally on the Devil's own terms, instead.

"When this final alternative approaches in world history, then it will be virtually impossible for "mere human resistance" to stand up to the anti-truth world culture of the day.

"Only hinterlands less networked into the nexuses of power at that time, like smaller, "pockets of refuge" (like ancient Goshen was in Egypt at the time of the divine punishment of Pharaoh) will keep the Faith during this time of tribulation. Meanwhile, a sort of underground revival will continue among the Nations, claiming a "remnant" from every tongue, tribe and nation."[184]

One Degree More!
(Example #1)

And now to a few examples of "our part," or how we can choose to respond in the midst of the fiery trials that are around us. Let me share the stories of three men, mostly forgotten in history, but true Generals in heaven who have gone before us to receive their crowns. Their names were Teddy Hodgson, Blaise Pascal and Paul Munson. First to Teddy.

One of the strongest missionaries during a move of the Spirit in the Congo (Zaire) Evangelistic Mission back in the 1920s and '30s was a man named Teddy Hodgson.

Teddy was described as a man full of laughter, love, strength and faith, and a strong man when facing evil or pain. In Africa, he fearlessly faced lions and elephants to protect frightened villagers from death or starvation.

He also faced the most desperate of men in his missionary endeavors—members of vile secret societies—in order to save girls sold into slavery or boys being tortured. He was also a man mighty in the word and in prayer. He met a violent martyr's death in 1960 while on a mercy mission.

184 Dr. Lance Wonders, my dear mentor, friend, and ministry colleague, in a paper he wrote called, "A Three-fold, Biblical Platform for a One New Man Approach to Church-Life During the Coming "Final Conflict" (June, 2012).

In a sermon preached at the revival in Sunderland in England in 1931, he shared,

> "There are degrees in knowing God. There is a place where we stand as ordinary people, but there is a bigger place just beyond where God has placed His extraordinary blessing and power.
>
> "I read just the other day of something which describes God's people.
>
> "There were three boilers, each full of pure water, and all exactly the same. In the first one the water was beautifully clear but icy cold; in the second one the water was again beautifully clear but hot; while the third boiler contained water *just one extra degree more,* and was boiling and moving machinery and bringing something to pass.
>
> "Let us be the people who are taken hold of and used by God. Hot water is no good as a moving force at all.
>
> "Only one degree more brings it to boiling point, and out of it comes steam that can move wheels and bring power.
>
> "Let us reign as kings and priests to God—reigning in life through Jesus Christ. God wants us to go that greater degree where signs and wonders are wrought in His name.
>
> "Let us move out until it costs us something."[185]

Just one degree more! If you've been praying and seeking God, do not give up until His blessing comes! Think of this in relation to the words of Jesus to the church of Laodicea in Revelation chapter 3,

> *"I know your deeds, that you are neither cold nor hot; I would that you were cold or hot. So because you are lukewarm, and neither hot nor cold, I will spit you (vomit you) out of my mouth"* (Revelation 3:15-16).

185 Adapted from an Article in New Life Publishing Company of "Joy" Magazine, Nottingham, England.

Jesus is looking for burning hearts, hearts ablaze with His passion and glory for serving this fallen world until the end. *One degree more* and your faith will begin to move the mountains in front of you. *One degree more* will light your soul on fire, so that the fire in you is greater than any fire of trial that may come to you.

Think for a moment of those three brave men in Daniel's day who did not bow their knee to cultural idolatry and as a result were cast into a furnace of fire.

> "The fire of the Holy Spirit in the lives of Shadrach, Meshach and Abednego, preserved them from the fire in the fiery furnace," wrote Sister Gwen Shaw. "You and I, as we watch the furnace of persecution begin to be heated seven times hotter, are going to have to be heated seven times hotter through the Holy Spirit than what we have been before.
>
> "Every mortal will be wrapped in the conflict at the end of this age. There will be no neutrals in this end-time army. He that is holy will become even more holy and he that's defiled will become more defiled.
>
> **"Let the fire within you always be greater than the fire you are in.**
>
> "And you and I have been born for such a time as this."[186]

Let us remember too, John's powerful admonition to Believers to help them overcome the spirit of Antichrist, which, he adds, is already at work in this world.

> *"Greater is He who is in you than he who is in the world"* (1 John 4: 4b).

Let the fire of God grow greater inside of you by seeking a deeper experience of the Holy Spirit in your spirit.

186 Sister Gwen Shaw, The Revival Call, page 19. Published in the official magazine of the End Time Handmaidens, Jasper, Arkansas, November 2008.

The "Night of Fire." (Example #2)

I've always been inspired by the story of Blaise Pascal, mathematician, physicist, and inventor, who had a deep experience with God's presence and the reality of the Holy Spirit in 1654. He called it his "night of fire." He wrote a short reminder to himself and sowed it inside his coat, and secretly transferred it to new coats as they came, so that the reality of the Spirit and the Spirit's experience in deepening the fire of God was always with him. Here is a portion of that poetic testament, discovered by a servant only after his death at the age of 39.

"The year of grace 1654.
Fire.
'God of Abraham, God of Isaac, God of Jacob,' not of philosophers and scholars.
Certainty, certainty, heartfelt, joy, peace.
God of Jesus Christ.
God of Jesus Christ.

The world forgotten, and everything except God.
He can only be found by the ways taught in the Gospels.
Greatness of the human soul.

Joy, joy, joy, tears of joy!
Sweet and total renunciation.
Total submission to Jesus Christ and my director.

Everlasting joy in return for a day of hard training in this world.
I will not forget thy word. Amen."[187]

Beautiful, isn't it? He kept that small scrap of paper, to remind him of his experience of the fire of God and his covenant and commitment to Christ. It was kept near his heart every remaining day of his life.

---

187 From an English translation given in Marvin O'Connell's book "Blaise Pascal, Reasons of the Heart."

Let's learn from that "night of fire" that we, too, can share his perspective. What seems like a "day of hard training" in the trials of this life, is nothing in comparison to the eternal bliss of knowing Christ Jesus our LORD.[188]

Out of the Limelight, Into the Lamplight You Go... (Example #3)

For a final example I turn to a man who had such a genuine and unique quality, that I simply must include his own experience of his consecration to God to inspire you that truly anything is possible.

The man whom I will close this chapter with was a common prayer warrior, hidden away in a basement of a small house in Bloomington, Minnesota, by the name of Paul Munson. The following testimony of his life was told to me first-hand by one of 12 disciples that Paul had.

Paul was a simple shoe salesman in the 1940s following WWII. He had a desire to be used mightily by God in the work of the gospel after his conversion.

One night in 1949, Munson was in prayer about his own calling. It was the same year of the breakthrough crusade of Rev. Billy Graham in Los Angeles that set Graham's ministry in full motion, Munson was asking God, would he be an evangelist like Graham? The LORD spoke to his heart,

"I am calling you out of the LIMELIGHT and INTO THE LAMPLIGHT."

For Billy Graham and many others, limelight awaited, and that was their calling. Evangelicalism in America began to flourish in the 1950s and beyond.

I believe this was a direct result from the intercessors like Rees Howells, who had begun the "Every Creature Commission" prayer burden. Howells died in February of 1950, and I believe Munson was one of God's secret intercessors who were raised up to carry on the prayer ministry for the Gospel and the Commission to be widespread.

188 In Episode 20 of my documentary film Series, "Love Speaks" I filmed Pascal's amazing story. Visit our Ministry website to learn how you can stream or download it today. https://www.lovespeaks.today

Paul Munson consecrated himself to the calling of God in 1949, and began a hidden ministry of intimacy and intercession before the LORD. This ministry lasted faithfully, every single day, from that day in 1949 for exactly 39 years. He decided to engage the LORD in relationship in four areas every day.

1. Confession of his sins before the Father in Jesus' name
2. Study of the Word of God
3. Prayer and Intercession
4. Worshipping and Praising the LORD in song

Those were the four daily pillars of spiritual discipline that Munson had practiced. They are simple and yet still excellent reminders of a strong and intimate relationship with God that each soldier of the Cross needs to practice.

Munson was encouraged by the LORD to balance his time between reading his Bible, being in prayer, and lifting up praise. So if he chose on a particular day to read the word for three hours, he was also encouraged to pray for three hours and worship and praise for three more. Next to his piano in the little basement where he sought the LORD, was a stack of hymnals that he had literally worn out over the years of praising and singing. The papers hardly stayed in the bindings.

He was also told to assemble 12 disciples and teach them these simple and powerful principles, which he did. And over many years, he saw personal revivals and the birth of powerful prayer ministries in the lives of each of these 12.

Let me share just one story with you about Paul's experiences, though I'm sure if he had written his memoir, he could fill the pages of this book with many more.

On one occasion, Paul was spending about eight hours of his day in the Word, prayer, worship and waiting on the LORD. His house was a typical 1940s rambler, with a kitchen door adjacent to a door with stairs leading down to the basement. There was a knock on his kitchen door, and his wife, Martha, answered the door. Paul heard some talking, and then this man came down the stairs to the basement prayer room. He was dressed in a fine suit with expensive shoes, Paul remembered.

He identified himself as Satan!

After a few brief words of discouragement towards Paul, Jesus Himself suddenly walked through the wall of the basement, proceeded to rebuke Satan on behalf of Paul, and instantly Satan disappeared. Then Jesus walked on through the room and disappeared, but His glory remained for days in the room!

So this simple shoe salesman maintained this season of the glory of the LORD, out of the limelight of public ministry and platforms, shining in the lamplight for 39 years. In 1988, the year of his passing the LORD spoke to Paul and said that He had heard every prayer and that He knew that never a day had passed where Paul had not exercised the four spiritual disciplines of confession of his sins, study of the Bible, prayer and worship, and that he always kept them in balance.

Paul asked the LORD if there were more people, like him, that had secretly been called and chosen to not be on the "front lines" as it were, but to remain on the "supply lines" and help pray for the witness of the Gospel in the nations.

The LORD told Paul to go find his phone book. Paul did so. The Minneapolis phone book was filled with hundreds of thousands of names and phone numbers. As he opened the phone book, the LORD highlighted three different names of people Paul had never met and knew nothing of.[189] He said, "Call them, Paul."

In blind obedience and simple faith, Paul Munson picked up his phone and called one by one the three random names that Jesus had told him to call. Upon talking with each one, he discovered an amazing and stunning truth: all three had secretly been called to a life of prayer and intimacy, in the "lamplight," in the same year of 1949!

189 This was by operation of the Gift of the Word of Knowledge, by the Holy Spirit.

All four of these prayer warriors died that same year after 39 years of faithful intercession!

Thus, we see that God is always at work, through many of His servants in many diverse places, even when we don't know there are others just like us living out lives of faithful service.

So, from Teddy Hodgson we are reminded to go *"one degree more"* in our seeking of the LORD. Blaise Pascal inspires us that, as we seek the LORD in going *"one degree more"* like he did when he received his unique *"night of fire,"* we can deepen our relationship with the LORD. And Paul Munson reminds us that walking in those four spiritual disciplines is a powerful way to live daily, even as we remain *"in the lamplight."*

A hidden, secret and very deep life of prayer, worship and intimacy is something you can begin *today*. His glory will be a canopy over you as you consecrate your heart, and the fire of God will glow brighter as you make sacrifices daily to seek His presence in the secret places of the earth.

In Conclusion: Those Who Have Insight Will Understand

> *"Many will be purged, purified and refined; but the wicked will act wickedly, and none of the wicked will understand, but those who have insight will understand"* (Daniel 12:10).

Let us remember the great truths written about in this chapter.

Some people will be called to be martyrs, like James and John the Baptist were, and will witness the faithfulness and truth of the LORD as they face wicked rulers like Herod (a type of the coming Antichrist).

Others will be protected in the Battle like Peter was, and continue to proclaim the truth until the end. Others will be the prayer warriors praying for miraculous signs of deliverance.

Some will be active and vocal on the front lines of battle and be in the limelight, while multitudes will be hidden away as supply lines in the lamplight.

Those in each group will be waiting upon the LORD and crying out for His Second Coming to finish His fullness of redemption on the last day of Salvation-History.

To all Believers in the Last of the Last Days, the glory of the LORD is promised like a canopy (Isaiah 4), and it will offer protection and comfort. His presence will grow like a deep fire inside your heart, and you will experience Him in *"nights of fire"* like Pascal, or in days of intimacy with Jesus like Paul Munson. Many people in many places will need to survive the onslaught of Satanic darkness by assuming a position on the battlefield on either the front lines or the supply lines in prayer, finances, or encouragement.

And through fires of persecution, when the Spirit turns up the heat and the Church is *"one degree more"* in wholehearted devotion, the Father will surely purge and purify the Bride for His Son and present her as,

> *"Having no spot or wrinkle or any such thing; but that she should be holy and blameless"* (Ephesians 5:27).

Therefore...

> *"Let us rejoice and be glad and give the glory to Him, for the marriage of the Lamb has come and His bride has made herself ready." And it was given to her to clothe herself in fine linen, bright and clean; for the fine linen is the righteous acts of the saints. "Blessed are those who are invited to the marriage supper of the Lamb"* (Revelation 19:7-9).

Going Deeper Still

- James and Peter represent Last Days character studies, and many people will share their sacrifice. James became a martyr, and Peter was rescued by prayer warriors and endured suffering while experiencing God's miraculous presence. The front lines of battle and the supply lines of prayer will be filled soon. Which would you rather be on?
- What did you learn from the stories of Brother Yun ("The Heavenly Man"), John the Baptist, Teddy Hodgson, Blaise Pascal and Paul Munson?
- One of the characteristics of the Last of the Last Days Army will be in its hiddenness, and underground revivals will spread like wildfire. Whenever you pray, the place where you are will become a place of refuge, and the presence and glory of the LORD will be over all. Invite His presence to be with you, right now, wherever you are reading this.
- Ask the Holy Spirit to reveal your own particular and unique role as the Final Battle commences. What do you sense are your personal Marching Orders after reading this chapter?

CHAPTER

The Word, the Voice, and the Love

21 Ways to Hear God's Voice to Discern Your Personal Marching Orders from the Father

"*The LORD appeared to me from afar, saying, "I have loved you with an everlasting love; therefore I have drawn you with lovingkindness"* (Jeremiah 31:3).

"Call to Me, and I will answer you, and I will tell you great and mighty things which you do not know" (Jeremiah 33:3).

In my many years of research (I started writing this book, in a sense, about 30+ years ago during my days at Bible School), I would often take some of my mentors out to lunch to seek their help in better understanding some of the subjects I was writing about. On one particular day I was joined by Chuck Porta, who is a very inspirational Bible teacher. Another story he told me caught my attention.

In the late 1970s, everyone around us was expecting the Second Coming any day. We had all read Hal Lindsey's book, "The Late Great Planet Earth," and thought that the signs of the times pointed to the End. My wife

Kitty was in deep prayer and intercession one day, and asking the LORD, "LORD, what do I need to make it to the End, to the very Last Day?"

The LORD replied, *"Only three things: the Word, the Voice, and the Love."*

After that lunch, I went home and prayed, and the next morning I got up early and the Holy Spirit gave me a kind of download (known as a Word of Wisdom) as to how to help equip the Church to hear God's voice and "make it to the End."

So literally in one day, I wrote an entire 100-page document called provisionally, "The Word, the Voice, and the Love" and it helped people hear the voice of the members of the Trinity.

Jesus Christ: "The Word" in His Established Word, Living Word, and in the Preaching of His Word.

The Holy Spirit: "The Voice" in His Inner Witness, Inner Voice, Desires of the Heart, Visions, Dreams, the Revelatory Gifts of the Spirit, and so forth.

The Father: "The Love" in His indirect and outward leadings like Nature/Creation, Providence, Divine Appointments, Media, External Voice, and so forth.

On another day, the LORD instructed me to expand and re-write "The Word, the Voice, and the Love" and re-name it to: "Love Speaks." That became my first book that the LORD told me to publish (I shared this briefly in my Introduction). I developed a worldwide media platform (as a Media Missionary) to share these truths with the world and help equip the Church to hear the voice of God more clearly and more often.

Here, in "Revelation's Battle Plans," I want to give each of you a brief summary of all 21 ways to hear God's voice, along with a scripture, so you can begin to develop your faith and expectation in all of them. In so doing, you can discover from the Father himself, speaking through His Agent on earth, the Holy Spirit, what your individual Marching Orders are. This chapter is based in full on my book, documentary film Series, and MASTERCLASS titled, "LOVE SPEAKS: 21 Ways to Recognize God's Multi-Faceted Voice."

Here we go!

Note: these are in order from the "Most Common" (the Bible) to the "Least Common" (the Audible Voice).

LOVE SPEAKS™

by Carl Wesley Anderson
©2024. All Rights Reserved.

QUICK REFERENCE CARD:

21 ways to recognize God's multi-faceted voice

Very Common Ways	Common Ways	Uncommon Ways
1 The Established Word of Jesus *(John 1:1).*	8 The Preaching of the Word of Jesus *(2 Thess. 2:13).*	15 The Revelatory Gifts: The Gift of Prophecy *(I Cor. 14:1).*
2 The Living Word of Jesus *(Romans 10:17).*	9 Other Believers Speaking Confirmation *(Matthew 18:16).*	16 The Revelatory Gifts: The Word of Wisdom *(I Cor. 12:4-11).*
3 The Inner Witness of the Holy Spirit *(Acts 9:31).*	10 Visions: Conscious Pictures from the Holy Spirit *(Acts 2:17-21).*	17 The Revelatory Gifts: The Word of Knowledge *(I Cor. 12:4-11).*
4 The Inner Voice of the Holy Spirit *(Acts 8:29).*	11 Dreams: Sub-conscious Pictures from the Holy Spirit *(Acts 2:17-21).*	18 The Revelatory Gifts: The Discerning of Spirits *(I Cor. 12:4-11).*
5 Holy Spirit Inception: The Desires of your Heart *(Psalm 37:4).*	12 Symbolic Speech: Metaphors from the Holy Spirit *(Numbers 12:8).*	19 Angels (by Dreams or in Reality) *(Acts 12:7-10).*
6 Father Speaks Through All of Creation & Nature *(Romans 1:19).*	13 Divine Appointments from the Father, "Holy Coincidences" *(Acts 8:27).*	20 Jesus Himself Speaks (by Dreams or in Reality) *(John 20:19).*
7 Providential Outward Signs & Circumstances *(Romans 8:28).*	14 Father Speaks Through All Forms of Media & Culture *(Nehemiah 9:6).*	21 The Audible Voice of the Father *(Matthew 17:5).*

What if you could recognize God's voice everywhere?

You can!

In the midst of the uncertainty in this impersonal world, you can discern the personal voice of the Father, flowing through His Son, Jesus Christ, and the Holy Spirit.

All 3 Persons are One God, yet they all have their own unique ways that they communicate with you every week.

The more ways you recognize, the more faith you can apply to be in continual contact with God, feel & know His love for you, and share His love with others.

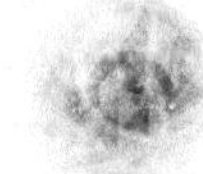

Keep listening!

Carl Wesley Anderson
Email:
carl@BornToBlaze.com

Subscribe to our monthly eLetter & YouTube Channel for free resources:

www.LoveSpeaks.Today

www.youtube.com/
Search: Carl Wesley Anderson

"I pray that the God of our Lord Jesus Christ, the Father of glory, may give to you a spirit of wisdom and of revelation in the knowledge of Him" (Ephesians 1:17).

Way #1: The Established Word of Jesus. *Logos, Greek.* This word can ord of Jesus. Logos, Greek. This word can be best defined as, "the established body of Truth" in the whole of Scripture. Expect that Jesus will guide you every time you study the Word in its original context. The *Logos* is important for doctrine, correction, training in righteousness, and truly understanding how the God of both Testaments has chosen to lead, train, and speak to His people in all generations. Whenever you sit down to a Bible study and learn about the time the original passage was written, and try to understand the exact context of what the writer was trying to communicate, you are studying the *Logos*.

Way #2: The Living Word of Jesus. *Rhema, Greek.* This is the other word in the Greek that is translated "word of God." This word can best be defined as the living, breathing, personal and fully applicable Word of God. It's whenever you personally recognize that God may be speaking a "word from the Word" to you. It breathes new life into your spirit, opens your spiritual eyes, and adds fresh illumination from the Word into your spirit.

Way #3: The Inner Witness of the Holy Spirit. A spiritual "sense" of PEACE and JOY in your inner spirit (like a green light or YES! in particular guidance, and originating from your inner spirit) OR a spiritual sense of "tightness" inside (a "yellow" light or a "red" light) witnessing, "CAUTION" or "NO!" to particular guidance.

Way #4: The Inner Voice of the Holy Spirit. An inaudible voice, originating in your sanctified inner spirit. It flows out through your mind simultaneously as a "thought" or even a flood of thoughts. **Note:** It is usually short, to the point, powerful, and sometimes comes as a question, which God expects you to ponder and answer Him.

Way #5: The Desires of the Heart. It is the activity of the Holy Spirit inside your heart, first planting seeds of destiny in you, then watering those same seeds and helping you fulfill the plans and purposes He has first placed there. He brings those seeds to full-grown maturity as you joyfully walk out your paths and follow your desires.

Way #6: Nature/Creation. God our Father speaks in many outward ways every day, indirectly, through all of His creation and nature. These "outward signs" are confirmed inwardly by both the Word and the Spirit. Take a walk with your Heavenly Father today. Leave your cell phone behind. Allow Him to speak to you through His wonderful creation!

Way #7: Providence. Your Father is speaking through His direct and indirect leadings of circumstances and outward signs. Often, you will not notice His guidance through these outward circumstances, but later, when you look back, you recognize how everything worked itself out for your good, and it was He that was taking the initiative to bring His will to pass for you.

Way #8: The Preaching of the Word. It is the Established Word *(Logos)* and the Living Word *(Rhema)* coming forth from an anointed servant in preaching and teaching. The Holy Spirit is active, and a community of Believers is present in which to apply that Word, in love, to one another, and then to the unredeemed world around us.

Way #9: Other Believers Speaking Confirmation. Jesus affirming and confirming words of encouragement and direction, directly to us, through other members of His Body on earth. This happens by the inspiration of the Holy Spirit in a very "naturally supernatural" way. This includes through the living, breathing members of His Body now, and through the departed saints who left behind their writings (both biographies and journals) as records of God's dealings with them. The living and those who went before us in Christ, thus speak every day if we are listening.

Way #10: Visions. The Holy Spirit originating a picture that flows from your inner spirit and out through your mind. They can be either literal or symbolic in nature, and either given to oneself for your own direction, or given for the edification of others. They can be "objective" or "subjective" in nature. Ask the Spirit for a vision while you are praying today, and then wait upon Him to receive it.

Way #11: Dreams. The Holy Spirit originating a picture or a "movie" that flows through your subconscious mind while you are asleep. They can be either literal or symbolic in nature, and either given to oneself for their own direction, or given for the edification of others, or even as warnings from God, or information about the future. They can be "objective" or "subjective" in nature. Before you go to sleep tonight, pray and ask the LORD to encounter you in a special dream, and when He does, make sure to write down all that you can remember and pray over it!

Way #12: Symbolic Speech. The "Love Language" of both Visions and Dreams. It is the most indirect and symbolic way of the Holy Spirit speaking. In this particular form, He utilizes common, everyday objects to teach us deeper lessons. These ob¬jects are like the symbols in an abstract painting, symbols which need interpretation and point to something real. The "abstract" becomes "clear and real" as He brings the interpretation. They also serve to paint words of knowledge for direction and encouragement. NOTE: this "Way" is exactly how John the Revelator wrote the Book of Revelation!

Way #13: Divine Appointments. The idea that your Heav¬enly Father has gone before you on your journey and prepared a sur¬prise person, people, or even objects in the normal circumstances of life to encounter unexpectedly.

Way #14: All Forms of Media. The Father reaching outwardly in all areas of media and cul¬ture is an extension of His love and grace. This literally includes all modern mass-media within nine forms: books, blogs/blogging, the Internet, magazines, movies, newspapers, radio, music recordings, and television. Added to this are all advertising, like billboards for example, and all areas of a particular culture that are unique to that culture.

Way #15: The Revelatory Gifts: Prophecy. These next 4 are known as 'The Revelatory Gifts' of the Holy Spirit and all of them are related to His voice. Prophecy is an inspi¬rational gift, and is speaking to another as the Spirit gives utterance. It is an inspired utterance, often with a beauty of expression. It is also a gift which Paul encourages us to earnestly seek for the edification of Believers.

Way #16: The Revelatory Gifts: The Word of Wisdom. A supernatural revelation of the mind and purpose of God communicated by the Holy Spirit. When the Lord specifically reveals His purpose to an individual, that person receives it through a word of God's wisdom. It is His wisdom flowing to you. These are beautiful, "Divine Blueprints from Heaven." They can also come through dreams and reveal new inventions and ideas!

Way #17: The Revelatory Gifts: The Word of Knowledge. A supernatural revelation of the existence, or nature, of a person or a thing; or the knowledge of some event, given to us by the Holy Spirit for a specific purpose. I personally define words of knowledge as "isolated pieces of God's Omniscience" and they are powerful. When you follow the LORD, it's like He drops a breadcrumb trail in front of you via a word of knowledge, and as you keep following Him by faith, you'll find the next breadcrumb and know that you are flowing in His will for you!

Way #18: The Revelatory Gifts: The Discerning of Spirits/Discernment. A supernatural enable¬ment to see or sense spiritually into the spirit world. By this insight, you can discern the glory of God, or of the risen Christ, or the Holy Spirit, or cherubim, or seraphim, archangels or the hosts of angels, or Satan and his legions. By the Discerning of Spirits we see and sense beyond the sphere for which we have been created, since we are natural beings. It is only by the revelation of the Holy Spirit that we can perceive the beings that live in the spirit world.

Way #19: Angels. Through the operation of the gift of discerning of spirits, and possibly in tandem with other means of God's communication, like visions and dreams, actual angels can and do appear to people. They sometimes speak and carry on dialogue with people, or open a person's spiritual eyes to behold new dimensions of God's love and the spiritual battle that is all around us. They also appear in visions and dreams.

Way #20: Jesus Himself Appearing. Jesus Christ, risen and anointed Son of God, can appear to you in a vision, in a dream, or in reality. He is Lord of all. He can choose to appear directly and speak with you, or share insights into the Bible, or speak to you about your calling. Sometimes He just visits in His awesome presence of eternal love, speaking no words, but holding our hand.

Way #21: The Audible Voice of the Father. This is the rarest and least common of all! God the Father, in all His majesty and glory, may choose the most direct means of communication by speaking with His voice. If and when He does, it is usually short, sweet, and to the point. I believe He would rather be communicating most often in the previous 20 ways, as He doesn't often risk direct contact with us through an external voice, as we might misinterpret it.

So that is the list of the 21 Ways! In the diagram you will note they are organized in, Very Common, Common, and Uncommon Ways. And a special note: if you were thinking that receiving a Word of Prophecy was one of the most common ways to hear God's voice for yourself, you will be surprised to learn there are 14 other "Ways" to hear His voice before you arrive at the wonderful Gift of Prophecy.

As you walk confidently through the coming days of both Judgment and Salvation, know that learning to hear the Father's voice (spoken through the Holy Spirit inside of you) on a regular basis, is part of His "preparing the Bride" to meet Him. And it takes continuous effort to engage with the Holy Spirit on a continual basis.

Also note: many people think of "hearing God's voice" as an audible or external voice, like Jesus heard twice. The truth is, that is the most rare (and thus, Way #21). The Very Common Way is, and has always been, to hear God's voice through His Word! The Bible itself is, and always will be, the #1 Way.

The Inner Voice is also very common and can be a daily experience for you, once you learn how He is speaking from within and yearning to carry out an ongoing dialogue with you.

Keep Oil in Your Lamp

As I shared briefly in my Introduction, in Matthew 25 Jesus tells the parable of the ten virgins, urging His people to be different from the world: to keep oil in their lamps (stay on the alert), and to stay awake and watch and prepare themselves, with urgency, for Him to come at any moment. Here is a portion of that parable.

> *"But at midnight there was a shout, 'Behold, the bridegroom! Come out to meet him.' The* **bridegroom came,** *and* **those who were ready** *went in with him to the wedding feast; and the door was shut.* **BE ON THE ALERT** *then, for you do not know the day nor the hour"* (Matthew 25:1-13, selected).

He metaphorically calls us, His people, "virgins," and we are His pure, spotless Bride that is making herself ready (Revelation 19:7).

To *"keep oil in your lamp"* means you have a personal responsibility to be wise and prudent with your spiritual resources, and to fall in love more and more with Him every day, choosing to remain uncompromising and faithful. **And LIVE IN EXPECTATION EVERY DAY to hear His voice!**

In the case of our current day, the Bridegroom has indeed been tarrying now, for approximately 2,000 years. He may continue to tarry, or perhaps this very year the final battle will commence, and sometime during that battle, Scripture says a war trumpet will sound (like a shout) and He will come for His Church who is ready to meet Him! Do you long to see Him?

Here, I think, in the greater context then of Matthew's weaving together of these parables of Jesus, is the point:

Stay alert, watchful and ready for His return! Be wise and prudent and put the fresh oil of deepening, persistent prayer and intimacy of worship to Jesus in your lamp! Know your personal Marching Orders!

Thus, follow the Word of the LORD given to Kitty Porta, and you shall endure until the very Last Day. Practice continually hearing God's voice through, *"The Word, the Voice, and the Love."*

We do not know the day or the hour, but we can know when the Bridegroom is close and He is about to give us the midnight shout!

Think of the acceleration of world events of the past 90 years since the Rees Howells *"Every Creature Commission"* began!

ARE YOU READY?

Are you staying alert?

Are your children ready?

You have the full armor of God (listed in Ephesians 6) with defensive resources. And you have His offensive resources and weapons like the power of His Living Word and intercessory prayer to utilize every day.

And just to remind you how powerful the Book of Revelation truly is, always remember, it came directly from the heart of Our Father through Jesus His Son, to us.

When you truly know your identity as a son or daughter of the Father, on the basis of that, you receive His Marching Orders and follow them fully into hardships, trials, and victories! All the while experiencing His comfort, love, and joy (because you know of His faithfulness, and that He put you in that season and foreknew you would make it)!

My dear friend and mentor of many years, Kermit Fox, once shared with me, "The Father is calling His cadre of Troops from every tribe, tongue and people group in these days, to readiness and preparation for the Last Battle."

We've had 2,000 years of emphasis on teaching about the Son, and the last 100 or so with an emphasis on the Holy Spirit. Now in this new season, we are experiencing more understanding on the Father Himself. His direct influence is coming forth!

And his General, standing Marching Orders for His cadre of troops are strong and direct,

"The Army Will Advance!"

From His gift to you, His very personal Holy Spirit (and through the commands of your 7-Star General, Jesus), you can receive your very own, personal, Marching Orders for the coming Battle!

Let's also call to mind that the storms of life are growing more intense as the battles rage on. Also, remember my opening story in the Introduction of the day that a battle was declared by the Enemy against me personally, and he fought against me in that cancer battle.

It was very difficult, and I suffered greatly. But I always kept my eyes upon the Father and Jesus, and kept worshipping them through the power of the Holy Spirit.

I knew who I was in Christ, and that I was personally loved by Him and my Father. And I heard His voice every single week and knew my own personal Marching Orders.

"In Revelation chapters 1 to 5, we can be encouraged that, Christ's role as judge and sovereign king is the model for true Believers who will overcome. Christians who suffer can be comforted that the Father and Christ are sovereign over all things, and will bring salvation and good out of their suffering. The conclusions of chapters 4 and 5 climax respectively with the glory of God and the glory of both the Father and the Lamb because of their sovereign rule."[190]

So, Soli Deo Gloria, even in your days of shadow. The eternal sunshine is coming soon as Christ Himself breaks through the Eastern sky and, *"every eye will see Him!"*

Thus, let "Love Speak" in every day of your life, and, "Keep Listening!" Amen.

---

190 Greg Beale from his commentary on Chapters 1 to 5, ibid., page 146.

Hasten the Day

Could Your Prayers Help Accelerate the Second Coming?

"*What sort of people ought you to be in holy conduct and godliness, looking for and HASTENING the coming Day of God* (2 Peter 3:11-12).

"BE ON THE ALERT then, for you do not know the day nor the hour" (Matthew 25:13).

You were born to run to the battle. And since, in the battle, your greatest weapon is the weapon of prayer (remember that Revelation 1:6 calls you part of God's Royal Army of Priests), perhaps part of your own Marching Orders are to place a whole new emphasis on prayer.

Prayer changes history!

Prayer, spiritual hunger and thirst, and faith and intimacy—all part of your Marching Orders!

In this closing chapter of the book, I would simply like to challenge you with this question:

Is it possible our prevailing prayers—yours and mine—as well as an ongoing, continuous, bold outreach around the world—could bring Jesus back?

It is my sincere prayer that each of you reading this book will honestly consider the scriptures, the approach I am taking to understanding apocalyptic literature, the visions and prophesies that pertain to the End within the Book of Revelation, and the heart of the LORD in preparing His Bride, and create your own plan of action for the days ahead.

I know this is a challenging question, especially in light of thinking through the idea of God's sovereignty vs. man's and woman's choices as they relate to the timing of the Second Coming.

It is my prayer that after reading (and rereading Sections of this book as the Holy Spirit prompts you), and praying over the themes contained in it, you would form your own convictions and apply the truths to yourself and your family. Fit them to your own walk of faith, and if you have children or any influence in the next generation, share your convictions to help prepare the young for the battle which lies ahead.

HASTENING THE DAY

Peter wrote that scoffers would come in the last days, mockers he called them.

> *"Know this first of all, that in the last days mockers will come with their mocking, following after their own lusts, and saying, "Where is the promise of His coming? For ever since the fathers fell asleep, all continues just as it was from the beginning of creation."*
>
> *"But the day of the LORD will come like a thief, in which the heavens will pass away with a roar and the elements will be destroyed with intense heat, and the earth and its works will be burned up. Since all these things are to be destroyed in this way,*

> *what sort of people ought you to be in holy conduct and godliness,* **looking for and hastening the coming day of God,** *on account of which the heavens will be destroyed by burning, and the elements will melt with intense heat! But according to His promise we are looking for new heavens and a new earth, in which righteousness dwells. Therefore, beloved, since you look for these things, be diligent to be found by Him in peace, spotless and blameless* (2 Peter 3:3-4, 10-14).

I want to bring these verses to your mind, and especially emphasize Peter's words, as he was a passionate preacher and brings out a vividness that sometimes is lacking in Paul's writings.

He shares, LOOKING FOR AND HASTENING the coming Day of God. Here we have the idea of "looking for" brought forth.

Looking for and hastening...

In my Introduction of this book, I quoted the parable of the foolish and wise virgins. Since Jesus is coming like a thief in the night, the unbelievers will all be caught unaware. They will all be like the foolish virgins who were not granted access to the Bridegroom. They will not recognize the times of the signs and they will experience destruction. They did not have *"oil in their lamps"* of true relationship with Jesus Christ.

The Titanic sank with very few life boats...

But the wise, the prudent, the true children of the King, will be daily watching for Him, and daily desiring His appearing, and thus *"keep oil in their lamps."* They will be ready for Him with eternal life jackets and seated inside eternal life boats.

Peter brings out the truth that everything that mankind is striving in the flesh to bring about: natural security, natural blessings, pride and lust and greed and avarice; all of it is going to self-destruct, just as it did in the days of Noah.

In the very end, when Jesus Messiah comes to finish what He started, part of the blessing of the fullness of redemption is a destruction of the natural works of man that have been built. This is depicted in symbolic imagery as both "the Fall of Mystery Babylon" and the "Bowls of Wrath" in Revelation chapters 15 to 19.

And at the Second Coming, there will be a renewal by fire of the earth, and the joining of the eternal Heavens with the eternal Earth in a newness of all Creation!

Because of this, we, as followers of Jesus, ought to put our hope upon His coming and expect Him to come in our generation, to make right all that is wrong around us, to execute true judgment and justice for all mankind, and to bring about His plan to "make all things new."

In so doing, turn your attention to that word, HASTENING.

Perhaps if you will fervently pray for and tirelessly work for the Gospel of the Kingdom to continue to permeate every culture (as when we finish the work of the witness), and if enough of us in every Nation are laboring in prayer and fasting and asking Him to come and complete His redemption...

PERHAPS YOU AND I CAN BRING HIM BACK!

HASTEN the coming day of God by your action, by your heart, by your prayers, and by your witness in times of suffering.

Seek first His Kingdom (Matthew 6:33) every day above all the cares of this life. Know this: the earth will someday be transformed by fire, and all the works of God which have been accomplished for His glory, will pass through those fires of judgment and be a permanent and eternal part of His New Creation. While at the same time, all the evil works of mankind and the demonic realms will be burned away and have no part in the New Creation.

So the Apostle Peter shares a word about HASTENING the return. Thus, a worldwide hunger for the physical return of Jesus Christ will be present, and prayer movements will direct their focus on His return as the greatest need of the hour.

Is it possible that you and I can actually participate in the timing of the sovereign plan of the LORD? The timing of the End will coincide with an intense desire in the hearts of many of His people for that very End to come.

As I shared in Section II of this book, I truly believe that the return of King Jesus will be based on a set of conditions that exist on the earth at that time, rather than on a specific date in the future. The conditions themselves are dependent upon the free will choices of men, women and children in the Kingdom in every new generation.

Our involvement is important! Hence, Peter carefully and forcefully uses this word, HASTENING.

Rick Joyner had a visionary dream and heard these words spoken about the days in which we live.

> "Go and call My captains to the last battle. Go and defend the poor and the oppressed, the widows and the orphans. This is the commission of My captains, and it is where you will find them. My children are worth more to Me than the stars in the heavens. Feed my lambs. Watch over My little ones. Give the word of God to them that they may live. Go to the battle. Go and do not retreat. Go quickly for I will come quickly. Obey Me and hasten the day of My coming."[191]

This thought brings us all the way back to one of the earliest benedictions of our family of Believers in the days of Corinth, who spurred each other onwards with that ancient Aramaic word, *Maranatha: O LORD, Come (1 Corinthians 16:22)!*

There is an element of the real possibility of hastening His return through prevailing prayer and continuous bold outreach around the world.

There is also another adaptation to the Aramaic phrase which gives it this potential meaning, "Our LORD is coming, and He will judge those who have set him at nought."[192]

---

191 Rick Joyner, an excerpt from, "The Hordes of Hell are Marching III" printed in The Morningstar Journal, pg. 90, 1996.

192 Bible Study Tools, meaning of, "Maranatha."

That must become also our prayer. LORD come, and bring eternal justice to all who have oppressed your people and all the demonic forces behind that oppression! *"Will not the Judge of all the earth do right?"* (Genesis 18:25).

On a positive note for your own heart's desire to see Him, let me ask you this question.

Do you yearn to see Christ, experience Him personally, and delight yourself in His presence for all eternity?

The Bridegroom yearns for the presence of the Bride, and the Bride is making Herself ready (Revelation 19:7).

Begin to pray earnestly, daily, and yearn for Him to COME.

"Be strong against a world of unbelief," wrote Corrie Ten Boom, "without being ashamed for your King. We must be Spirit-filled soldiers and must fight to gain the victory, until Jesus comes. He is our strength now, and also in the Last Battle. When you kneel before Him, will He be your Judge or your Savior?"[193]

Run To The Battle

Finally, be inspired by the faith of young David, who valiantly charged the enemy, Goliath, in the face of all danger, and did not count his life to be his, but in the LORD's hands in the battle. The following was said of David.

> *"Then it happened when the Philistine rose and came and drew near to meet David, that DAVID RAN QUICKLY TOWARD THE BATTLE LINE to meet the Philistine"* (1 Samuel 17:48).

And we all know the end of that story. The battle belonged to the LORD. He used David's sling and cunning and faith to win it, but it was still His battle.

193 Corrie Ten Boom, Marching Orders For The End Battle, (CLC Publications, Fort Washington, PA, 1969), pg. 115.

As you and I approach the Last Battle, Armageddon (as it is called by one of its symbolical names in Revelation chapter 16), know that it is His battle. He alone is fighting it as the Warrior Lamb alongside, and in the presence of His followers. He is going to cause all His enemies to be eternally destroyed, and "Goliath" and all pride and evil will crumble forever. The demonic strongholds that influenced Goliath were routed in the days of David. They will be eternally judged and tormented in the Second Coming.

> Let us, *"lift up your heads, for your redemption is drawing near"* (Luke 21:28).

"My foes are many, they rise against me,
But I will hold my ground.
I will not fear the war, I will not fear the storm.
My help is on the way, my help is on the way.

Oh, my God, He will not delay!
My refuge and strength always.
I will not fear, His promise is true,
My God will come through always, always."[194]

—A selection from the worship song, "Always" by One Sonic Society.

"This is my prayer in the battle,
When triumph is still on its way.
I am a conqueror and co-heir with Christ,
So firm on His promise I'll stand."[195]

—A selection from the worship song, "The Desert Song" by Brooke Frasier.

Always remember, you are a conquer and co-heir with Christ!

As the day of the Final Battle approaches and we are experiencing it, in the twinkling of an eye, right in the midst of the Final Conflict, you will hear

194 One Sonic Society, Provident Music, 2012.
195 Brooke Frasier, musician, from her song, "The Desert Song" on Hillsong United's album.

a valiant war trumpet blow, and then you will receive your reward and forever be with King Jesus. (See 1 Corinthians 15:50-58.)

So follow His Marching Orders for your own life with courage! To quote from Mickey Robinson, "Spiritual bravery is activated as our will aligns with God's will for His purposes."[196]

I will see you at the Wedding Feast of the Lamb, soon.

Come and find me at the Feast if you read this book and received encouragement from it!

> *"These will wage war against the Lamb, and the Lamb will overcome them, because He is Lord of Lords and King of Kings, and those who are with Him are the called and chosen and faithful"* (Revelation 17:14).

---

196 Mickey Robinson, Supernatural Courage: Activating Spiritual Bravery to Win Today's Battle, Chosen Books, 2020.

EPILOGUE

The Five Most Dangerous Words in Scripture

For centuries now, one simple prayer of five words has been prayed in thousands of settings with thousands of different Believers. It's time our own generation joined with theirs to pray these "dangerous" words. They are dangerous because they set in motion the desire for the Second Coming. And when enough people here on earth as part of the Body of Christ align their hearts with Christ in Heaven, then together we can turn to the Father and Jesus Himself can say, "It's time Father! Send me now!"

When He returns, He brings eternal transformation. He ushers in the Eternal State; new resurrection life in new Eternal Vessels. Evil, sin, and death itself are destroyed. There will be a combining of Heaven with Earth and a re-creation of all things. The earth's curses will be broken, and the earth's blessings will be bountiful. His Kingdom will reign here forever. He makes all things NEW.

The greatest love story in the world opens near a river flowing with water, and man, created in the image of God and known as the "First Adam," chooses to reject the presence of his Maker and exercise his own will. God's enemy of the war, Satan, slithers in near the river and tempts both woman and man. Sin enters, and death because of sin, and the earth is cursed (Genesis 1-3).

But that same love story ends near another river, but this time it is the River of life. The "Last Adam" is there, along with His Bride, and the curse has been broken and removed forever, and the Father enjoys the presence of His sons and daughters.

There is no more death. There is no more Enemy: the slithering snake is remembered no more. The war has finally ended and Jesus Christ is the Conqueror (Revelation 21-22).

And so Jesus Christ, the Son of God, is the real focus of all of history. And it takes faith to see that.

"The whole basis of the creation is the setting for a Heavenly romance!" shared my friend, Rev. Eric Delve of London. St. John of the Cross, in one of his poems, confirmed this when he wrote, "From the beginning, the whole purpose of creation was to bring forth a Bride for the Son of God." So that's the purpose of the entire created order! We are that Bride!

"What Jesus does not want is a reluctant Bride, who says, 'Well, if you must come, you can come now...!' Make it possible for our generation to have the return, LORD! Come! I want to see the clouds tear back and the Son coming and all Heaven pouring into the presence of our fallen world! Even So, Come LORD JESUS!"[197]

Can I dare you to pray the following five words every day for the rest of your life? Let the thought of them take root deeply. Desire the return of Christ from your heart more than anything this world offers. For when HE comes, He will transform you to be able to see Him as He is! His love will fill you—eternally!

"MARANATHA: EVEN SO, COME, LORD JESUS!"
(1 Corinthians 16:22 and Revelation 22:20)
Amen.

197 Rev. Eric Delve is a well-known English evangelist, father of the faith, and a mentor to many younger evangelists. This quote came from a conversation we had about the Second Coming of Christ.

Recommended Reading for Further Study

I thought it would be helpful to list just a few of the resources I have found helpful in formulating some of the material in this book. Note: I do not necessarily agree with all of the diverse theological viewpoints in these books. I encourage you to pray and seek the LORD for understanding and deeper study. And as always, listen wholly to the Holy Spirit and draw your own conclusions and personal Marching Orders!

Devotional:

Norman Grubb, Rees Howells: Intercessor (Christian Literature Crusade, 1952).

Corrie ten Boom, Marching Orders for the End Battle (CLC Publications, 1969).

Brother Yun with Paul Hattaway, The Heavenly Man: the remarkable true story of Chinese Christian Brother Yun (Piquant Editions, 2003).

R. Loren Sandford, Visions of the Coming Days: What to Look For and How to Prepare (Chosen Books, Baker Book Group, Minneapolis, Minnesota, 2012).

Anne Graham Lotz, Expecting to See Jesus (Zondervan, 2011).

Loren Cunningham, Is That Really You, God? (YWAM Publishing, 1984).

Reinhard Bonnke, Evangelism By Fire: Igniting Your Passion for the Lost (Christ For All Nations Publishing, 2002).

Troy A. Brewer, Numbers That Preach: Understanding God's Mathematical Lingo (Aventine Press, 2016).

Joseph Z., Servants of Fire: Secrets of the Unseen War & Angels Fighting For You (Harrison House Publishers, 2023).

R. Loren Sandford, A Vision of Hope for the End Times: Why I Want To Be Left Behind (Destiny Image Publishers, 2018).

Dr. Bill "Bishop" Hamon, God's Weapons of War: Arming the Church to Destroy the Kingdom of Darkness (Chosen Books, 2018).

Jennifer Weiss, Holy Spirit Adventures (Dove Publishing House, LLC, 2021).

Commentaries on the Book of Revelation:

Verne Poythress, Returning King (ISBN 978-0-87552-462-7, published by P&R Publishing Co., P.O. Box 817, Phillipsburg, N.J., 08865), www.prpbooks.com

Dennis E. Johnson, Triumph of the Lamb (ISBN 978-0-87552-200-5, published by P&R Publishing Co., P O Box 817, Phillipsburg, N.J., 08865), www.prpbooks.com

G.K. Beal, The New International Greek Testament Commentary: The Book of Revelation (William B. Eerdmans Publishing, Grand Rapids, MI).

William Hendriksen, More than Conquerors (Baker Book House, Grand Rapids, Michigan, 1940).

George Elden Ladd, A Commentary on the Revelation of John (Wm. B. Eerdmans Publishing, Grand Rapids, Michigan, 1972).

Darrell W. Johnson, Discipleship on the Edge: An Expository Journey Through the Book of Revelation (Regent College Publishing, 2004).

Vernard Eller, The Most Revealing Book of the Bible: Making Sense out of Revelation (Wm. B. Eerdmans Publishing Co, 1974).

Nancy Guthrie, BLESSED: Experiencing the Promise of the Book of Revelation (Crossway Publishing, 2022).

Theological:

N.T Wright, Paul in Fresh Perspective (Fortress Press, Minneapolis, 2005).

Sam Storms, Kingdom Come: the Amillennial Alternative (Christian Focus Publications, Ross-Shire, Scotland, 2013).

AUTHOR'S CONCLUSION:

From the Church Militant to the Church Triumphant

What did you discover in this book?

Let's Review Section I:
What did you find in this book?

Chapter 1: The Greatest Sign of the Times.

Just WHEN will the End come? To answer this question and realize just how close we are coming to the End, I turned to a wonderful scripture from Matthew 24, where Jesus gives us some positive news: the Gospel of the Kingdom will advance to the very ends of the earth before His return.

Revivals should still be prayed in and believed for. Missions will continue to be effective, even more so as we are called as missionaries and warriors into territories of spiritual complacency, and "people groups" that have not yet heard the Good News. The light and glory on the Church grows brighter as the darkness increases.

You'll remember that I also shared about a stirring message that Rev. Billy Graham preached in Chicago some years ago. Two of his points really reminded me of the importance of a book like this one. First, he shared of how over-emphasis on end-times teaching can bring imbalance to the lives of Believers. He cited an example of how too much teaching brought interpretations such as Mussolini being the actual Antichrist in the 1930s.

One only needs to turn on certain television networks today and see the Christian market is saturated with whole teachings on specific interpretations of difficult texts, trying to squeeze actual events in the newspaper and media into these texts. This results in sensationalized teaching that never challenges the audience to a deeper, personal commitment to Christ.

On the other hand, preached Graham, the opposite is also true. Under-emphasis from the pulpits in the land (of the truths of the Second Coming) can lead to a worldly perspective and a lack of true and solid Biblical teaching. In light of the Church not teaching enough on the hope of the return of Jesus, the world steps in and fills the void, resulting in an imbalance of understanding.

Could our own generation finish the witness of the gospel in the nations?

How close are we to this? Where we are on the apocalyptic end-times timetable of the Last of the Last Days?

To answer this, I shared the incredible story of the hidden intercessor, Rees Howells, and his prayer team in Wales, who were given a special prayer Assignment in 1935, "The Every Creature Commission," which is bearing fruit to this very day in the spirit realms!

Their intercession was taught to them by the Holy Spirit, who showed them that every government or entity that attempts to block the Gospel going forth is a legitimate target to pray against in the spiritual realms!

All of our current and vast missions movements in the earth are the fruit of those strong prayers, tears, fasting and travails that went forth for the first 30 years (1935 to 1965) and the subsequent years of Rees' son, Samuel, after his death (1950 to 2003). They have continued in order to see the Gospel offered to every "creature" (every tribe and tongue) so that Jesus could return: perhaps even in our own Generation.

And I shared some amazing testimonies of people like my dear friend, the late Loren Cunningham, who shared with me before his death that he sensed we could be about 10 years away from the Bible being translated and distributed to all people groups, with the missions endeavors finishing in the nations.

What part will you personally take in this Army? Continue to pray and ask the Holy Spirit for His guidance for you personally. And pray for Laborers! (see the words of Jesus in Luke 10 for further inspiration).

For now, His key "standing order" to His Army is this: **advance** in the witness of the truth! We are truly "morning stars, shining in the night."[198]

Chapter 2: The Days of Noah and Lot. What is one massive indicator of the coming of the LORD? Spiritual complacency in the earth.

Here you learned of 8 striking similarities to the days of Noah and Lot that Jesus taught us in His parable. Both of those times were just preceding a direct judgement of God; in the one case, He flooded the entire earth; in the other He rained down fire and brimstone and destroyed Sodom and Gomorrah. But this time around, we are facing His ultimate Day of the LORD; a day of salvation for the righteous and of destruction for evil. You also were challenged to become like a "Noah" or "Abraham" instead of many people around you who are more like "Lot" or "Lot's wife." We must follow the Apostle Paul who said,

> *"Forgetting what lies behind, and reaching forward to what lies ahead, I press on toward the goal for the prize of the upward call of God in Christ Jesus"* (Philippians 3:13-14).

Let's Review Section II:

Fresh Tools of Interpretation for the Book of Revelation (including an overview of Revelation and the Seven Visionary Cycles), Earth's Trauma, the Two Witnesses, & the Approaching Last Battle at the end of the Millennial Reign.

Part of my original intention in writing this book was to help you apply faith in the "big picture" of the timing of the Last Battle and understand the battle plans of the Last of the Last Days as discovered in the Book of Revelation.

198 A quote from the end of Chapter 1 from the story of David Livingstone who gave his entire life as a pioneer missionary to Africa.

And finally, for you to find your specific applications—your own Marching Orders—so you can know how you personally fit into those plans.

In Section II we turned fully to the Book of Revelation to answer the questions, "HOW will the End come?" and "Where is this Last Battle described in Scripture?"

I utilized the Book of Revelation as more of a topical study than a verse-by-verse commentary. You first learned the "What and Why and When and How and Where and Who" of the Book to grasp its' historical context.

As apocalyptic literature and also based on the Prophets themselves, Revelation is best understood as containing seven parallel visions, each one beginning at the First Coming of Christ and ending at His Second Coming.

It progressively reveals various creative aspects of the battle of the whole Church Age, while also giving you hope in the Second Coming and the events that quickly unfold.

It is also structured uniquely. I believe it isn't meant to be taken in chronological order of the chapters, nor in a literal interpretation of the visions.

Thus, I wrote two chapters to help with a "big picture" of Revelation itself; a broad, wide-angle lens view, and an eye-opening, fresh approach to how to read it. because **"Chapter 3: Truth Is Stranger Than Fiction."** Revelation can be read and understood and you will discover a whole new appreciation for its beauty. You can learn the original context of the text while also continually asking yourself, as you read it and study, "What does this mean to me, personally?"

You learned in **"Chapter 4: The Seven Parallel Visionary Cycles"** just how unique the book is structured (also with unique ancient prophetic tools known as "Chiasms").

I offered the idea of seven unique Cycles, or "vantage points" on Mount Zion (seven round towers where you catch glimpses of unique details of the warfare in all Ages of Salvation-History). You learned of its poetic parallel structure, which is how John composed it, basing his structure on the O.T. Prophets themselves, namely Isaiah, Daniel, Ezekiel, Joel, Zechariah and others.

BONUS: Turn to Appendix 2 to study deeper and more in-depth the "CHIASTIC Structure" or the Book with multiple "CHIASMS" to add depth and beauty. This form of poetic writing is lost to us today, but it was well-known and understood to the 1st century seven Churches and audiences. They recognized the structure immediately, just like you and I recognize a Political Cartoon today.

Chapter 5: Earth's Trauma. In chapter 5, I took a deep-dive study of the symbolism in the Book of Revelation of the Seals, Trumpets and Bowls of Wrath. You learned how natural disasters are on the increase as the "Birth Pangs" of all Creation nearing the Second Coming of the Creator: Jesus Christ! I posed the question and offered potential wisdom and insights to the following:

"When natural disasters (especially earthquakes) happen, are they a result of mankind's sins being reaped (the indirect wrath of God in His moral universe of His laws being transgressed); OR are they a direct judgment from God as reaping of sins, OR are they the result of Satan himself bringing destruction to this world that he hates?"

You learned some very sobering scriptural truth about all three of these possibilities, and some amazing examples from Salvation-History about them.

Finally, you learned that every single time a natural disaster takes place, it is a trumpet blast: a warning sign from the LORD of His coming Final Judgment. That gives us all pause: Judgment Day is coming.

Next, I devoted two more chapters to zooming in for a close-up view and a handy verse-by-verse deeper study into the parallel visions in Revelation chapters 11 & 20. There, I give a detailed description of two of the main visions of the Book: the tale of the Two Witnesses (chapter 11) and the vision of the Binding and Loosing of Satan himself (chapter 20).

Chapter 6: The "Two Witnesses" as the Saints in the Church Age. These Two Witnesses and their potential meaning has both fascinated common people like me, and baffled theologians alike for the past two thousand years. In this section, I suggested a symbolic approach that the

Two Witnesses actually represent the story of the advancing Church in the nations during the entire historical time-period of the Church Age: the time between the First Coming of Christ and His Second Coming.

It is not an easy passage to interpret, nor does it focus on making you feel comfortable. Its meaning and its understanding serves more as a wake-up call to sleeping soldiers in the Army. We also learned of the coming Final Battle and how the Enemy will attempt to silence the Witness of Jesus in the earth, and how, in many nations, the Church will go "underground," and in doing so will thrive in revival and under God's glory.

Chapter 7: The NOW-Millennium: Satan Bound and Unbound. This chapter gave you a deep-dive and verse by verse study of one of the most misunderstood symbolic visions in all of Scripture. It gave you a glimpse into an alternative view of the 1,000-year Millennial Reign, how Satan is, (and isn't), bound currently, and his near-future "unbinding" in the Final Battle.

If the "NOW-Millennium" is true, it has deep and urgent implications in our current events and the cataclysmic times that are soon to follow.

What did you find in this book?

Let's Review Section III:
Apocalypse Now: the Spiritual Warfare of the Last of the Last Days

Section III of this book helped you get ready for the End. As you learned, you can start today!

Next was **Chapter 8: Illegal Gospel.** Looking at some amazing examples in Salvation-History, we saw just what it may be like when Satan is allowed, briefly, his Final Battle just prior to the Second Coming. Sometimes you have to look backwards in order to look forwards.

Satan seeks to *counterfeit* all that is true; he even has his own *counterfeit Trinity*. They are described in chapters 12 to 14: the Dragon, the Beast from the Sea, and the Beast from the Earth. Here his deception is revealed, as he counterfeits the work of the Father, Son, and Holy Spirit.

"As the Dragon, he is a *counterfeit* of God the Father. The Beast (coming out of the sea), a kind of pseudo-incarnation of Satan, is a *counterfeit* unholy warrior opposed to Christ the holy warrior (compare 13:1-10 to 19:11-21). The False Prophet (the Beast coming out of the Earth) is a *counterfeit* of the Holy Spirit. By his deceiving signs the False Prophet promotes worship of the Beast. His actions are analogous to the manner in which the Holy Spirit works miracles in Acts (and the Church Age) to promote allegiance to Christ."[199]

Satan works in *counterfeiting* Jesus and truth. In unique imagery we, as the people of Jesus, are called the Bride of Christ. Satan's counterfeit is an opposite female figure: the Great Whore of Babylon.

Satan is pictured as your arch-enemy in Revelation. All three of these figures are further defined and their mysteries unveiled in this Section so that you can practically discern how those three "weapons" or "demonic tactics" are at work in the world today.

You can see all three of them in the newspaper or televised on the evening news, every day, if you know how and where to look for them. Read and watch the news with your glasses of a spiritual warfare worldview on and you can discern the times in which you live accurately and with faith in a Sovereign LORD.

We learned of Tottlebank and George Fox, of J. Edwin Orr and Corrie ten Boom in WWII, of the future of most church buildings being destroyed as the Church goes underground in many areas, of Nazi Persecution against Believers in WWII, and of coming conflicts as the two Beasts and the Harlot try to tighten their hold on Christian freedoms and liberty.

Then we turned to **Chapter 9: The Enemy's Tactics on the Battlefield.** Utilizing the Book of Revelation once again for our Battle Plans, I revealed just what it teaches, and offered a relevant look at our current times and the battle of spiritual light and darkness for the times ahead.

C.S. Lewis called our world system, *enemy occupied territory,* and this

199 Vern S. Poythress, "Counterfeiting in the Book of Revelation as a Perspective on Non-Christian Culture." A paper presented at the 1995 annual meeting of the Evangelical Theological Society.

Section is a refreshing look at the subject of *spiritual warfare*. I believe we never graduate from the basics, but we benefit from fresh teaching to gain further insights into the basics of the faith, such as warfare.

Now that's practical help!

Question: How can you know if the final battle is nearing completion?

Answer: Ask yourself the following questions in whatever nation you are in.

- *If I go out today from my front door into the city and actively share my faith, what will happen to me? Is it dangerous?*
- *As a Believer, how am I looked upon by my government, my neighbors, and my family?*
- *Do I have freedom to meet with other Believers freely and openly, or are there restrictions or consequences? Do I have a place outside my home to worship King Jesus freely?*

We closed this practical Section with a look at Satan's tactics and dirty tricks to keep you in a sinful lifestyle, or from knowing how to battle him and defeat him on a regular basis.

- You learned how to fight him with your RHEMA Sword, by knowing the Word and receiving fresh, heavenly Scriptures tailored just for you.
- You learned to develop your very own "Hills To Die On" and resist "the lust of the flesh, the lust of the eyes, and the boastful pride of life" through a holy lifestyle (which also is a strong witness to unbelievers around you at all times).

What did you find in this book?

Let's Review Section IV: Marching Orders: Practical Applications to Prepare For & Endure the Final Battle

In divine preparation for the approaching brief war, the Father is issuing fresh Marching Orders to the Army of the Son. He wants to train you to listen to Him and grow deeper in relationship to Him through prayer. Jesus, as the Captain of the Hosts (our very own 7-Star General), has promised never to leave you nor forsake you, and so His presence is upon you during every moment of both these times of preparation and in the actual battle itself, yet to come.

As you read Section IV, you developed a new hunger and thirst for Jesus and for His coming.

Why do you desire the "end" to come? Is it not so that you will be changed into His likeness and be able to be with Him...forever? The early disciples all experienced His love and longed to see Him again.

In Chapter 10: Persistent Prayer: Your Most Powerful Weapon, you were challenged to think about your life in these terms, even as you ask:

— How do persistent prayer and learning to listen to God help me endure the trials of these days of preparation and the coming Last Battle?

— What is my personal part in the coming Last Battle?

— What can I do to deepen my relationship with the Father, Son and Spirit, to increase His presence and glory amidst the shakings in the world around me?"

I hope you can boldly answer these questions and proclaim a resounding YES to His presence being with you personally all the way to the Last Day on Earth.

In Chapter 11: Out of the Limelight & Into the Lamplight, you have learned the importance of persistence in prayer; finding your place in the Army; experiencing his daily presence and power on the battlefield; and finally to come *"out of the limelight"* (if you are not one of the Leaders in the Battle who are part of the five-fold Ministry and are preaching and witnessing on the Front Lines) and *"into the lamplight"* to be part of the key Supply Lines (for those on the Front Lines) in the Army.

You were also inspired by three people from Salvation-History who lived in similar times as ours. With the Enemy raging in the cultures around them to try to influence them to compromise or give up, they stayed faithful: Teddy Hodges, Blaise Pascal, and Paul Munson.

The truth is, Jesus is making His Bride ready (through our suffering times)!

> *"That He might present to Himself the church in all her glory, having no spot or wrinkle or any such thing; but that she should be holy and blameless"* (Ephesians 5:27).

Chapter 12: The Word, the Voice and the Love was a special compilation of a summary of 21 Ways to Recognize God's Multi-Faceted voice from my book, "Love Speaks," and you learned all 21! Now you can begin to EXPECT to hear the voice of the LORD and develop your own, Marching Orders for the Final Battle! And you were challenged to the meaning of, "keep oil in your lamp" through intimacy in prayer with Jesus every day. You only need 3 things to endure until the last Day of recorded history!

The final chapter, **Chapter 13: Hasten the Day,** challenged you with the phrase, HASTEN THE DAY, and brought us all the way back to one of the earliest benedictions of our family of Believers in the days of Corinth who spurred each other onwards with that ancient Aramaic word, *"Maranatha": O LORD, Come!*

There is an element of the real possibility of hastening His return through prevailing prayer and continuous bold outreach around the world.

My Hope For The Reader

My hope was that you gained a clearer understanding of the times in which we live, and that knowing these times requires you to exercise patience and, of course, faith.

When it comes to studying text that is apocalyptic in nature, you need to allow for the fact that you are "seeing through a glass, darkly," as Paul put it. You see in part, and others are likewise seeing in part. Somehow, what the LORD reveals to each of His servants at a particular time of understanding, can bring a fuller recognition of each piece of the puzzle. Together, we can try to fit them into the puzzle by applying our faith to what we are seeing.

I hope that you have seen how Revelation can be widely read and easily understood no matter what school of interpretation you have personally focused your study on or come to know through others.

It is my hope for you that at various times and in various places, as you read and reread and seek to understand key thoughts in the approach of this book, you have had an "epiphany" and perhaps proclaimed,

"Wow! I never thought of that before!"

The word, *epiphany*, comes from Matthew 2, and the story of the Magi. They had a *fresh, new understanding* of Christ being sent to the Gentiles, and were among some of the earliest witnesses of His divine manifestation to the Gentiles.

This brings me to another of my hopes for you as the reader. It's the hope that you have discovered truths and developed firmer convictions as to what you believe about the End.

This includes convictions related to preparing for cataclysmic world events leading up to the End, convictions about *how to make it through and endure* those events, and convictions about how to be a firm witness to the truth of Jesus *in the midst* of those events.

The Father is on the march with the Son, and the Spirit is empowering His Army with fresh, individual Marching Orders that will lead you to victory and your eternal reward.

As these convictions draw you closer to the Father, the Son and the Spirit, I hope you have developed, or are now in the process of developing, a strong devotional and persistent prayer life containing a daily, listening posture before the LORD.

The Revelation of Jesus Christ

Have you also learned how to discover your own personal Marching Orders in facing your own areas of the battle to come? If not yet, that's okay. This discipline can take time.

Go back and reread chapter 12, "The Word, the Voice, and the Love" to learn and grow in expecting all of the 21 Ways to Recognize God's Multi-Faceted Voice to be activated in your life.

And since you have new convictions and a lifestyle of hope, you can pass along that hope to a world of people who are fearful of what may lie ahead. Fill the world with faith, hope and love!

Only the follower of Jesus can redefine the landscape of the End of Days and see, not *doomsday, fear-filled scenarios,* like Hollywood and pop-culture sees, but just the opposite. Believers can expect **glorious, hope-filled scenarios.**

We alone, as the CHURCH MILITANT, understand that our Father has a divine purpose behind the scenes of the world events of the End. He always has! He showed the ancient prophets such wonderful imagery of the light dispelling the darkness and the knowledge of the glory of the LORD filling the earth, even as the waters fill the sea!

That's why I opened this book with hope, and an emphasis on the Person of Jesus Christ as its focus. I also challenged you with what Scripture shows us is a ferocious Enemy in a worldwide battle on the near horizon, that will quite literally affect every single Believer in every culture for a brief time. No member of the Body of Christ will be exempt from this battle.

All of history revolves around the Person of Jesus Christ. And really, all prophecy, especially the subject of the Last Days, revolves around Him. Thus, the Book of Revelation is rightly called, "The Revelation of Jesus Christ."

Can you see Jesus in Revelation? If you are looking for Him, you will see Him in every Section. He is truly the Alpha and Omega of all true writings about the last days or end times.

God revealed to His Prophets, unique glimpses of His own attributes throughout history. Let's consider just three of His Prophets: Ezekiel, Daniel, and John the Revelator. They all beheld Him by faith and passed along beautiful visions and pictures of who He is. They also saw the spiritual battle and the Enemy facing the people of God around the world.

Note my emphasis on the importance of a revelation of how *awesome* God is. That sets the stage for understanding the battle He is placing His people into, and allowing the attacks from the Enemy himself.

Ezekiel saw the holiness of the LORD as a blazing fire, with four distinct living creatures being catapulted throughout the earth by Wheels. And wherever the Wheels moved, the living creatures moved (see Ezekiel 1). What a wonderful word-picture to illustrate to us that the Sovereign purposes of God are going forth as the backdrop of all international events!

He is seeking to redeem mankind (all who will receive Him) and all of His creation itself, in the spreading Kingdom of His Messiah! Later, Ezekiel saw the Enemy as a vast army who would surround God's people and attempt to destroy them from the earth (Ezekiel 38-39).

Note that these verses were literally fulfilled in the time before Christ came, but they have a symbolic meaning also in the visions of John in Revelation chapter 20. We, as Believers, are not looking for a literal war in the Middle East to be fulfilling Scripture. Instead, we are looking for a worldwide war (as Bishop Hamon calls it, WWIII)[200] that will encompass all nations at the same time (see again Revelation 20:7-9).

Daniel was allowed to see into the spirit realm through His night visions, and beheld a picture of the Son of Man ascending up to the Ancient of Days (see Daniel 7:13-14), which was fulfilled after the Cross and resurrection in the glorious Ascension of Jesus to the right hand of the Father! Later, he would see the Enemy as a Beast with horns attempting to destroy God's people through world domination (see Daniel 7:19-27).

And of course the author John, in Revelation, saw first the image of the resurrected Christ in the midst of the candlesticks (chapter 1), followed by

200 Ibid, Bishop Bill Hamon.

an incredible vision of the Father and the Son and the people of God and all of nature and creation at the very center of the universe (chapter 4)!

Each of these prophets *saw the LORD first, before they saw the Enemy*. We could say they each saw Jesus Himself. The Old Covenant Believers saw Him as the coming suffering Messiah Prince, looking ahead to the Cross. The New Covenant Believers look back to the Cross and the empty grave, and see Him as the conquering Messiah Prince. Both saw the mission of the Servant of the LORD as prophesied in Isaiah 49 as being continuously fulfilled even to the Last Day on Earth.

Always remember that in the Book of Revelation, before you start reading of the visions of Satan and His helpers as hideous, evil Beasts, and a Harlot influencing the world for selfish sinful degradation, you saw the visions of the glorious Father, Son, Holy Spirit, angels, redeemed creation and the victorious Army of God at the center of time and space and history! In other words, focus on JESUS in every circumstance of every day of Battle!

And this much we know. In terms of timing, on whatever day you are reading this book, we are one day closer to the Second Coming of Christ.

I am praying that you will learn to appreciate the fresh approach to the Book of Revelation contained here, and see Jesus revealed in the interpretations of texts given long ago. They had relevance to their particular audience then, and still have relevance to us as the audience today.

To summarize my hope for you as you finish this book:

Glorify Jesus every day!

Thank God for moments you read and felt, "I never thought of it this way before!"

Pray through those moments and develop fresh convictions!

Let convictions lead to repentance, faith and fresh preparation!

Tune your ears to God's personal Marching Orders to prepare!

And finally, pass along to others the hope of the Second Coming. Share your testimony with everyone you can in faith, all the way up to the Last Day!

"So this time has now come upon all of you: a time of judgment and of purification" wrote Father Michael Scanlan. "Sin will be called sin. Satan will be unmasked. Fidelity will be held up for what it is and should be. My faithful servants will be seen and will come together. They will not be many in number. It will be a difficult and a necessary time. There will be collapse and difficulties throughout the world. But more to the issue, there will be purification and persecution among My people. You will have to stand for what you believe."[201]

Marching Orders

The very subtitle of the book includes the words, Marching Orders. This is borrowed from the life of Major Robert Rogers, who is the father of modern-day covert warfare.

His marching orders were first published and issued to his band-of-brother warriors who fought in the early conflicts of the states. Rogers is considered the father of American Special Operations (which include Delta Force, Army Rangers, Navy Seals, Covert Ops, Green Berets, and all the areas of the Army, Navy, Air Force and Marines who carry out special operations, either in advance of a battle or in the midst of one).

Rogers honed his unconventional combat skills and tactics behind enemy lines in the French and Indian War leading up to the Revolutionary War. These orders were issued in the year 1759.

*When you're on the march, act the way you would if you were sneaking up on a deer. See the enemy first.

*Tell the truth about what you see and what you do. There is an army depending on us for correct information.

*If somebody's trailing you, make a circle, come back onto your own tracks, and ambush the folks that aim to ambush you.

*Let the enemy come till he's almost close enough to touch and then let him have it and jump out and finish him.[202]

201 Fr. Michael Scanlan, prophetic declaration given at the National Service Committee of the Catholic Charismatic Renewal. Quoted from "God's Warning, God's Remedy" by Kevin and Dorothy Ranaghan, published in New Covenant, 1980.

202 Special Forces: America's Elite, page 26. Published by the Media Source, 2012.

Of course, you understand the context of what Rogers was facing in 1759, along with his weaponry and tactics of the day. But there is so much good spiritual and Kingdom principles in what he ordered his troops to do, that I must point out some illustrations.

See the enemy first. Do you know how to discern the truth from the error? Can you effectively move in the gift of discerning of spirits (1 Corinthians 12), and understand the workings of Satan and the demonic forces and their plans against you? In Section III, I wrote a portion of truth to arm you and prepare you for the Adversary's dirty tricks and his weapons of the flesh, the emotional and soulish realm, and even the dark demonic realm, which are all designed to keep you distracted and off-track, so you miss the ensuing battle itself. *Go back and reread that Section a number of times until you are walking in the disciplines outlined there.*

Tell the truth, there is an army depending on you. You must share the truths about the End to your neighbors and family and friends. You must know the truth and be fully convinced of your stance as a member of the Army of God until the end (know your identity as a son or daughter of the Almighty Father, and know your place in God's Army)! You must also LIVE the truth. Be prepared to give an answer for the hope that is within you. You must also be prepared, if need be, to die for the truth if your particular government makes the Gospel illegal (have your own Hills to Die On). It is vital that you understand correct theology and the true doctrines of the Father, Son and Holy Spirit, which are in direct opposition to the rising tide of the many doctrines of demons, which are overspreading the earth in preparation for the final conflict.

Be ready to ambush the enemy who is following you. Your enemy is not flesh and blood. You must develop strategies for persisting prayer, being led by the Spirit as a true watchman-on-the-walls, having the guts and the courage to ambush the forces arrayed against you. You must show no mercy to the realm of darkness. Be prepared at all times to bear witness to the resurrection and the light and the truth. Shine your candlelight in the darkness and so destroy the darkness with the light. Your prayers and declarations have the power and authority of the name of Jesus to dismantle Enemy territorial strongholds.

Finally, **let the enemy come close.** We can expect Jesus to do just as Rogers commanded his men. Scripture points to the end, and just when Satan thinks he has truly destroyed the witness of Christ around the world, Christ will return in triumph for His triumphal Bride (see Revelation 11:11 & 20:9-10). You must live courageously and suffer courageously. Expect that your prayers for the coming of the King will be responded to, and that Father will shorten the days of our sojourn of suffering for our own sake.

Get Ready For The Fight

I was born in July of 1970. Just one year prior to my birth, Corrie ten Boom, survivor of the Holocaust and fervent evangelist, issued a call-to-arms with a strikingly similar title to the subtitle of this book. Her book was called, "Marching Orders for the End Battle." In it she challenged the readers of her generation to develop a "stimulation to militancy" and become soldiers in God's Army. Her topics and wonderful themes included love, faithfulness, devotion in service, and even highlighted the challenge of martyrdom as our highest honor in the coming battle.[203]

I love her book!

Hers was a generation of vast atheism and the threat of Russian communism and other forces of darkness then operating. We are now part of a new generation, and as Corrie ten Boom's book does not offer any scriptural teaching specific to the Last Battle, I felt it appropriate to write this new book, which issues a fresh wake-up call to our rising generation.

We need to know the Battle is found in Scripture, and it includes persecution for God's people. Persecution of Christianity will surely spread farther and wider to the West, and all four corners of the earth, very suddenly. But also in Revelation we have the Battle Plans to be victorious!

Already we are seeing signs in nearly every culture of the gathering storm of persecution that will reach a zenith in the end. As I quoted in my Introduction, "Christians have come to be seen no longer as merely irrelevant," shared Mark Thompson, Principal of Moore College in Sydney, Australia,

203 Corrie Ten Boom, Marching Orders for the End Battle. CLC Publications, 1969

"but are seen as a threat to the culture. People are not just bored with us but angry at us."[204]

Can you see how a part of your own Marching Orders in the days to come, are to march ahead into the gathering storm of persecution for your faith? Jesus never promised a road without storms, or a battle without conflict.

"In the First Century our brothers and sisters were martyred because they maintained there was ONE God, during an age of Polytheism (defined as MANY gods in the culture surrounding Christians)." writes Roman Catholic apologist Steven Ray. "In our age, the world has been growing in their hatred of Christians due to Pluralism (defined again as MANY gods and denying Christianity's claim of ONE God, who alone defines absolute truth and true morality). Pluralism is the Polytheism of our day. The Greek word, "martyr" is the root of our word, WITNESS.

"Prepare, Church of Jesus Christ! Just as the First Century Believers suffered in the time of Polytheism, so we MUST NOW MARCH in the ever increasing persecution against followers of Jesus."[205]

To return to a special quote that my dear friend, Eric Delve, shared with me personally one day (I quoted also from Eric in the Prologue of this Book),

> "The LORD will allow the Final Battle so we, as the Church, can be weaned off of our love of the world, our contentment of what we currently have. The only way to wean us is by God in His mercy and grace, calling us to go through the pains of persecution. A dreadful thought, yes. We need to go through the tough times when we only have Jesus, and nothing else! I'm not volunteering to be a martyr, but we know that is on Satan's agenda; suffering, torture, death—I do want the LORD Jesus to return for a Bride that is passionate and full of love for Him."[206]

---

204 Mark Thompson, Principal of Moore College, in a recent address to the bible school students on the theme of the world that the new generation of ministers are facing, 2013.

205 Steven Ray, adapted from a YouTube video entitled, "The New Evangelism."

206 Rev. Eric Delve, evangelist and author. Rev. Delve is based near London and is both a mentor and friend to many evangelists and leaders in England.

The Father is after those whose hearts are fully prepared to enter this time of fear and uncertainty and counter it with faith and trust exclusively in His Son.

The earliest disciples, as recorded in the Book of Acts, did not cower in fear in their homes and build special Panic Rooms, filled with stockpiles of weapons, food and water to await some, SECRET RAPTURE (please read my Appendix 1 to learn more of why I believe in an alternative timing of the Rapture as being a part of the Second Coming of Christ).

They did just the opposite. They entered fully into the daily battle of light against darkness, and boldly witnessed throughout the cultures they were sent to. You are a part of the discerning and praying Army of Priests, and as such, you have the faith to maintain your position in the middle of the fight, and not be afraid of what is happening around you. And you can choose every single day of your faith walk to follow in the steps of Jesus who said,

> *"If anyone wishes to come after Me, let him deny himself, and take up his Cross DAILY, and follow Me"* (Luke 9:23).

The Holy Spirit Has Come To Shake The World

And what of the end of the story of Rees Howells, which I shared in the first portion of my chapter on the Advancing Army?

He died in 1950, with his final secret prayer assignment being the establishing of the Nation of Israel as a recognized homeland for the Jews.

His body was worn out through prolonged years of carrying burdens of constant prayer, intercession and fasting. But he was a giant in the faith at his passing. He shared this encouragement right before his death. "Everything in me is praising God because the Holy Ghost can say, 'I have finished the work Thou gavest me to do.' Every creature will hear the Gospel and the King will come back."[207]

---

207 Ibid, Grubb, pages 259-260.

The "Every Creature Commission" was carried on faithfully for over 50 more years through his son and a whole company of secret intercessors.

And I believe we are about to see it fulfilled in our own generation.

To share a final quote from Rees Howells, during a season of visitation from the LORD during the prayer time to see this "Every Creature Commission" happen, he once shared:

> "And looking into the future years—the darkness of the last days of this age, the final contest between heaven and hell for the kingdoms of this world—we could see only One Person who was 'sufficient for these things,' and He was the glorious Third Person of the Godhead in those whom He was able to indwell. 'Holy Spirit, you have come to shake the world.'"[208]

And His shakings continue every day!

In conclusion, always remember these words of perspective from Jesus Himself and John the Revelator.

> *"But when these things begin to take place, straighten up and lift up your heads, because your redemption is drawing near"* (Luke 21:28).
>
> *"Behold, He is coming with the clouds, and every eye will see Him, even those who pierced Him; and all the tribes of the earth will mourn over Him. Even so. Amen"* (Revelation 1:7).

The Titanic is going to sink (Judgment Day is coming). That is symbolism for the truth that the world as we know it is going to be judged, and all the works of man and of the pride of life will be burned away.

Your only hope? Allow Jesus to equip you and dress you with an **eternal life jacket and place you in an eternal life boat,** and you will be saved from the waters of judgment as the "ship sinks" (the Final Judgment comes).

208 Grubb, Ibid., pgs. 220-221.

Keep oil in your lamp! Keep it burning!

And immediately following His Return: we are transformed into the Church Triumphant for all eternity!

> *"And after these things I looked, and behold, a great multitude, which no one could count, from every Nation and all tribes and peoples and tongues, standing before the Lamb, clothed in white robes, and palm branches were in their hands; and they cry out with a loud voice, saying,*
>
> *"Salvation to our God, who sits on the throne, and to the Lamb. Amen, blessing and glory and wisdom and thanksgiving and honor and power and might be to our God forever and ever. Amen"* (Revelation 7:9-12).

Thus, you and I can shout together (and forever), CHRISTUS VICTOR!

Rev. Carl Wesley Anderson, Jr., Minneapolis, Minnesota, USA.

APPENDIX I

No One Left Behind: An Alternative Timing & Purpose of the Rapture

> *"For the Lord Himself will descend from heaven with a shout, with the voice of the archangel and with the trumpet of God, and the dead in Christ will rise first. Then we who are alive and remain will be caught up together with them in the clouds to meet the Lord in the air, and so we shall always be with the Lord"* (1 Thessalonians 4:16-17).
>
> *"Behold, I tell you a mystery; we shall not all sleep, but we shall all be changed, in a moment, in the twinkling of an eye, at the last trumpet; for the trumpet will sound, and the dead will be raised imperishable, and we shall be changed"* (1 Corinthians 15:51-52).

This Appendix challenges the modern-day theory of the Rapture, simply as it pertains to the timing of the Second Coming. In a POST-TRIB scenario, I simply believe that the Rapture happens on the very last Day of recorded history, the final Day of the LORD Scenario, at the actual time of the Second Coming, which the Book of Revelation pictures through powerful symbolism in chapter 19.

As I will show, I do believe in the Rapture. I believe it will be a very public event, instead of the potential misconception of a private or secret event. It is, instead, the awesome culmination of the redemptive power of Jesus Christ in all of history.

My intent is to open your understanding to the actual timing of this event; the "when does it happen?"

And along the way, we look at Paul's original understanding of the purpose of it. If I can help establish this event as happening at the very end of time as we know it, then this entire Book of Revelation's Battle Plans can be read the way it is meant to be read: as a relevant message for today to help prepare the Church for the Second Coming.

I believe the soldiers of God's Army are not going to miraculously disappear from the battlefield *before* the final battle is to be fought and won!

Through the modern-day success of Tim LaHaye and Jerry B. Jenkins, the "Left Behind" books and films, (the most recent appeared in theaters worldwide in 2014 starring Nicolas Cage), many Christians secretly harbor the thoughts of a soon coming great escape before the spiritual darkness has an opportunity of snuffing out the light.[209]

So for many people, the fictional content of the "Left Behind" series of books and films has turned from fiction to non-fiction, and multitudes of sincere Christians are standing by and awaiting a secret catching away event. The Pre-trib viewpoint has had the greatest popularity and most money spent through media and films, as well as many well-known writers with successful books published on the subject.

Yet, as I re-examined the apostle Paul's original intention in writing to the Thessalonians about the Second Coming, I believe it was the furthest thing from Paul's mind to conceive of a strange, two-stage timing of it. The first stage being a secret Rapture of millions of Believers, and the second stage being of those same Believers returning with Him to the earth.

I am indebted to some theological study I have made from reading some of N.T. (Tom) Wright on the subject of the apostle Paul and Jewish apocalyptic literature of the 1st century.

Where Did We Get the Modern-Day, Pop-Culture Theory of the Rapture?

This theory of the Rapture happening before the supposed tribulation of the end of days, is relatively new on the prophetic calendar. It began

209 According to Wikipedia, the 16 books in the series have sold over 80 million copies. Evangelical leader Jerry Falwell has said about the first book in the series: "In terms of its impact on Christianity, it's probably greater than that of any other book in modern times, outside the Bible."

around the year 1830 through the teachings of Edward Irving in Scotland. Prior to that, it was virtually unheard of.

"Now, be it remembered, that prior to that date (1830), no hint of any approach to such belief can be found in any Christian literature from Polycarp down," wrote Puritan theologian Robert Cameron. "Surely, a doctrine that finds no exponent or advocate in the whole history and literature of Christendom, for eighteen hundred years after the founding of the Church—a doctrine that was never taught by a Father or Doctor of the Church in the past—that has no standard Commentator or Professor of the Greek language in any Theological School until the middle of the Nineteenth century, to give it approval, and that is without a friend, even to mention its name amongst the orthodox teachers or the heretical sects of Christendom—such a fatherless and motherless doctrine, when it rises to the front, demanding universal acceptance, ought to undergo careful scrutiny before it is admitted and tabulated as part of 'the faith once for all delivered unto the saints.'"[210]

J.N. Darby popularized it soon after in his commentaries and exposed millions of people to this new theory about the timetable of the end. E. R. Sandeen wrote, "Darby introduced into discussion at Powerscourt (1833) the ideas of a secret Rapture of the church and of a parenthesis in prophetic fulfillment between the sixty-ninth and seventieth weeks of Daniel. These two concepts constituted the basic tenets of the system of theology since referred to as dispensationalism."[211]

He even influenced American evangelist D. L. Moody. In our current day, it has been popularized in the mainstream theological thinking of many Evangelical and Pentecostal denominations, particularly in America. Many seminaries and Bible Schools actively teach their students about a secret Rapture which will remove the Christians from the earth before the Antichrist appears and the Final Conflict commences.[212]

210 Robert Cameron, Scriptural Truth About The Lord's Return, Fleming H. Revell Company, 1922, pg. 72.

211 E.R. Sandeen, The Roots of Fundamentalism 1800-1930, University of Chicago Press, 1970).

212 "Until brought to the fore through the writings and preaching and teaching of a distinguished ex-clergyman, Mr. J. N. Darby, in the early part of the last century, it [Rapture theology] is scarcely to be found in a single book or sermon through a period of sixteen hundred years". [230-1830 AD] (Harry Ironside, The Mysteries Of God, 1908).

What Does the Modern-Day Pop Culture Theory Say Will Happen?

Much of the popular end-times teaching today puts the timetable of the Last Days in this order (according to Darby and others). First, a secret Rapture of all Believers, sweeping them out of the earth and away up to heaven to be with Jesus. Then, a period of either a literal and chronological three and a half years or seven years of a Great Tribulation, (varying and depending on different opinions of the Book of Daniel and Revelation). Finally, as a kind of "Second/Second Coming" when Jesus appears again, this time very publicly, and this present evil age comes to an end with the Final Judgment.

I would like to pose the following questions and propose some answers:

— Did Jesus ever teach that there would be a two-stage Second Coming? Answer: No.

— Did the Apostle Paul ever teach that there would be a two-stage Second Coming? Answer: No.

— Does any portion of the Book of Revelation clearly teach a two-stage Second Coming? Answer: No.

Let's turn to the single most hotly debated passage of Scripture about this subject, and seek to enter the heart and mind of the Apostle Paul and his original intention in writing it, and what he meant by it.

The Purpose of the "Rapture" Not "Raptured-out of" but "Transformed-into"

"Paul arrived in Thessalonica and only had 12 weeks with the new converts there," shared my mentor and friend, Chuck Porta. We were at lunch one day, and he wanted to teach me about the context of the original text. "Persecution arose against him and the early Believers, and he was forced to leave the city. It seems he did not have enough time to lay the apostolic teaching foundation of the Second Coming of Christ and the judgment to come on the pagan world. He probably started his teaching, but left them with more questions than answers."[213]

213 Chuck Porta travels around churches sharing a Seminar on the Life of Paul. He is an expert on Paul's life and New Testament theology.

So with these 12-week old baby Believers, an interesting situation has occurred. Persecution arose as Thessalonica had a largely Jewish population, and being the capital of the Roman province of Macedonia, it was an important naval base. Gentile God-fearers, as well as Jews, were among these first converts. Such a sharp jealousy among the Jews arose that they began persecuting these Believers. Some were dying, too. Paul sent Timothy to revisit these new converts as he was deeply concerned for their safety.[214]

So the audience who receives both of his letters is an audience under enemy-fire, and questions had now arisen about the truth of the Day of the LORD. What happens to those among us who have died, and what about us, who are under daily persecution for our faith in Jesus the Messiah of the world? With this context, Paul writes to answer them, having in his arsenal of understanding a strong sense of the future finality of Christ's coming to judge the world and usher in the eternal state.

The key passage in 1 Thessalonians speaks to us of what the original audience needed to hear, and what our current audience in the West needs to hear.

Both audiences, ancient and modern, are being assaulted by heresy and half-truth, and are misunderstanding Paul's heart in considering the fulfillment of Jesus Messiah's mission to both Jew and Gentile through His Body on earth. Here are some thoughts from Paul's first letter to put in your thinking.

> *"For you yourselves know full well that the day of the LORD will come just like a thief in the night. For God has not destined us for wrath, but for obtaining salvation through our Lord Jesus Christ, who died for us, that whether we are awake or asleep, we may live together with Him"* (1 Thessalonians 5:2, 9-10).

For the audience who first read those words, they were encouraged, comforted, and were taught an astounding truth: their loved ones who had died will be included in the Day to End All Days, the final day of Earth as we know it. Jesus Christ will return one specific day to finish the act of redemp-

214 The Revell Bible Dictionary, page 974. Baker Book House, 1990.

tion and justice that He began in His ministry, with His defeat of death at the cross through His resurrection three days later, and in His ascension into heaven. He is now awaiting the Father's marching orders and preparing Himself for the final battle. Paul actually employs the word, "**coming**" in various places in these letters.

> *"For who is our hope or joy or crown of exultation? Is it not even you, in the presence of our Lord Jesus at His* ***coming****?"* (1 Thessalonians 2:19).

> *"...at the* ***coming*** *of the Lord Jesus with all His saints"* (1 Thessalonians 3:13).

> *"we who are alive and remain until the* ***coming*** *of the Lord..."* (1 Thessalonians 4:15).

> *"...now we request you, brethren, with regard to the* ***coming*** *of the Lord Jesus Christ, and our gathering together to him"* (2 Thessalonians 2:1).

And now, in proper context, the famous Rapture passage.

> *"But we do not want you to be uninformed, brethren, about those who are asleep, that you may not grieve, as do the rest who have no hope. For if we believe that Jesus died and rose again, even so God will bring with Him those who have fallen asleep in Jesus. For this we say to you by the word of the Lord, that we who are alive and remain until the* ***coming*** *of the Lord, will not precede those who have fallen asleep.*

> *"For the Lord Himself will descend from heaven with a shout, with the voice of the archangel and with the trumpet of God, and the dead in Christ will rise first. Then we who are alive and remain will be caught up together with them in the clouds to meet the Lord in the air, and so we shall always be with the Lord. Therefore comfort one another with these words"* (1 Thessalonians 4:13-18).

I want to give you a fuller understanding of Paul's original intention of the rich meaning of this coming event. As he wrote this passage in his context in Roman times, I've placed a bold emphasis on two key words within this passage that are interesting to study to gain Paul's insights into his usage of them. Here are those two words and their Greek meanings.

First, the Greek word picture that Paul employs in his usage of the word, **coming**, is, **parousia**. It means, *"royal presence"* or, *"appearing."* From my study of this word, I discovered that in ancient days, whenever an important dignitary, like a Roman emperor or political leader, would approach a city, the people of the city would *come out of the city* to meet the approaching king. Then they would personally accompany him *back into* the city itself.

This is the imagery that Paul employs for his 1st century audience who knew what *parousia* meant. Amazingly, he uses the same kind of word picture to indicate that Jesus, our eternal King, will appear in the realms of glory surrounding earth, and translate us, both dead and those still alive on that day, into our eternal bodies like His.

Together, we will abide in His presence and accompany Him down to earth as phase one of the eternal events begin.

A Royal procession, King and subjects, together.

> "The close and intimate presence of the One who, for a Jewish worshipper, dwells in heaven was embodied for Paul in the close and intimate presence of the Jesus, who, now in heaven, was constantly interceding to the Father on our behalf. Our citizenship, Paul says, is in heaven, and from there we await the Savior, the Lord, Jesus the King—which means, despite many mis-readings, not that we will in the end go off to heaven, but that the One who is presently in heaven will come back and transform the earth, where we have lived as a colonial outpost of heaven waiting for that day. The point of Jesus coming from heaven is that He will change both this old world and our present bodies."[215]

A second Greek word used in this passage is, caught up, or, **harpazo**, which means, *to seize upon with force*. The Bible never uses the word, RAPTURE, but this is the word that we all base that word upon.

215 N.T Wright, Paul in Fresh Perspective (Fortress Press, Minneapolis, 2005) page 143.

This momentous seizing of the Believers who are alive on the final day of history, will actually happen! It is a real picture that Paul is teaching here that all of the elect of God, alive on that day, are transformed, *seized upon,* and wonderfully and forcefully translated into immortal beings during this event!

The dead in Christ will rise first, and then we are "caught up" and our bodies are transformed, (and not "caught away") and we then immediately return down to planet Earth as part of the redeemed created order to be with Jesus forever.

> "As Jesus returns, He shouts. Why does He shout? Because when Jesus opens His mouth and gives voice to a shout, it releases resurrection life. That shout is so powerful and creative that it resurrects the bodies of the dead saints, and transforms the bodies of the living saints into immortal bodies. It zooms around the world in a flash and resurrects the bodies of every saint who has died over thousands of years."[216]

To sum up, it appears it is all comprised as several phases of one main event, happening concurrently, and beginning on "the Last Day."

If this be true, how then should you live?

The Timing of the Rapture: NO ONE "Left Behind"

For now, let me summarize the new potential apocalyptic timetable. According to the Apostle Paul, the Rapture happens on The Last Day of recorded history, the long-awaited Day of the LORD. This will include the two elements of every single visitation scenario that has ever taken place or is prophesied about. Namely, SALVATION (for the righteous) and JUDGMENT (for the unrighteous).

The Rapture of the faithful is the final event on the prophetic horizon, as the curtain of this age closes and a new curtain rises.

216 Ibid, Bishop Hamon.

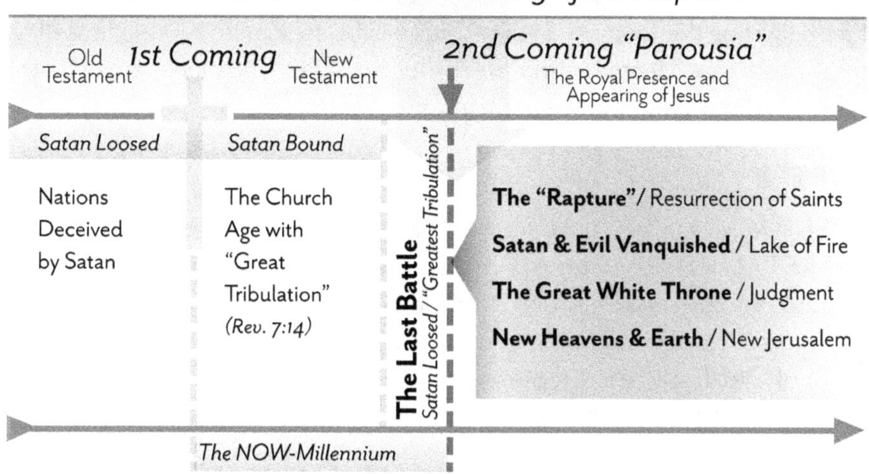

It is a very public event, not secret, and happens when *"every eye will see Him"* (Revelation 1:6).

Let us no longer expect this event to pull us out of battle. Instead, let us be reassured by Paul's words that, whether we live or die in the battle to come, we are not destined for wrath and will not experience God's justice toward the ungodly. We will indeed remain His faithful remnant and experience His grace, protection and eternal favor.

Paul's original intention in this passage goes with his fuller understanding of the Old Testament prophecies about the Messiah, and that His coming is not a SECRET RAPTURE, but instead, a very PUBLIC TRANSFORMATIONAL APPEARING, and actually takes place at the very end of time and history as we know it.

It's at the end of the story, not in the middle or near the end.

To put it another way in imagery that is found in Revelation, the Father is not calling the Son OUT of the battle to come. He is calling His Son, as the Warrior Lamb (and every Believer, Jew or Gentile, as part of that same "One New Man," the Church) to prepare to be launched INTO the battle!

In the process of this Last Battle, (which the Book of Revelation pictures behind the scenes of real spiritual conflict as an actual battle of the Warrior Lamb fighting the Dragon, Satan) Jesus will be seeking to reveal Himself as the world's true Messiah and King through it all, as Christians remain faithful to Him and even unbelievers turn their hearts to Him.

Surprise!

I believe we can better understand this event by substituting the words, SECRET RAPTURE, with the more accurate words, "PUBLIC TRANSFORMATIONAL APPEARING" of the LORD at the End. That event will begin a series of simultaneous events all-encompassing what the whole tenor of Old Testament prophets and New Testament apocalyptic writings declare as, The Day of the LORD.

This includes the fulfillment of all that the Hebrew prophets saw and proclaimed about eternal judgment and eternal redemption through the Messiah. It includes a very personal Jesus coming for all of His elect from all times, and the translation of our bodies (whether we be dead or alive at that moment) into immortal bodies to always be with him.

Here is another key thought from Paul, which relates directly to this unique and once-in-the-history-of-the-world coming event. It speaks of the believer's eternal hope in the PUBLIC TRANSFORMATIONAL APPEARING at the end of this Age.

> *"Behold, I tell you a mystery; we shall not all sleep, but we shall all be changed, in a moment, in the twinkling of an eye, at the last trumpet; for the trumpet will sound, and the dead will be raised imperishable, and we shall be changed. For this perishable must put on the imperishable, and this mortal must put on immortality. Then will come about the saying that is written, "Death is swallowed up in victory. O Death, where is your victory? O Death, where is your sting?"* (1 Corinthians 15:51-55).

As I was writing this chapter, I was stung by a wasp in my finger. I had not been stung since I was a boy of 8. I nearly cried at the feeling of that wasp sting. It hurt!

And I have stood by the graves of many of my good friends over the past few years (several of my closest friends have died suddenly). I have lost family members, friends, and ministry colleagues and mentors to that enemy: Death. He doesn't play fair. On most occasions, as I heard the news about these deaths, I would weep as I realized I never got a chance to say goodbye.

Death hurts. Death stings.

It is often a sudden reminder of the reality of eternity and the gospel that we believe.

Our hope, as Believers, lies in these several parallel passages of Scripture, and others like them. At every graveside at the burial of people whom I know walked with Jesus Christ while on earth, I remind myself that I will see each of my loved ones again. We shall actually meet together instantaneously in the PUBLIC TRANSFORMATIONAL APPEARING!

Here's how the Book of Revelation symbolizes the Second Coming in such visual power and wonder.

> *"Then I saw Heaven open wide—and oh! a white horse and its Rider. The Rider, named Faithful and True, judges and makes war in pure righteousness. His eyes are a blaze of fire, on his head many crowns. He has a Name inscribed that's known only to himself. He is dressed in a robe soaked with blood, and He is addressed as Word of God.*
>
> *"The armies of Heaven, mounted on white horses and dressed in dazzling white linen, follow Him. A sharp sword comes out of His mouth so he can subdue the nations, then rule them with a rod of iron. He treads the winepress of the raging wrath of God, the Sovereign-Strong. On his robe and thigh is written, KING OF KINGS, LORD OF LORDS!"* (Revelation 19:11-16, The Message Translation).

This is the moment that all of history stands waiting for. Death's sting will be no more. Our final enemy, defeated eternally.

We are transformed instantly and go to meet Him while He is coming towards us and on His way back to earth. How exciting! And the wicked demonic spirits and unrighteous nations are brought to justice, once and for all.

We are NOT going to be caught away to heaven while events unfold on the earth. No, we will be clothed in our eternal, immortal royal robes of righteousness, and accompany the righteous King back to earth as He ushers in eternity and judges all evil.

> *"God didn't set us up for an angry rejection but for salvation by our Master, Jesus Christ. He died for us, a death that triggered life. Whether we're awake with the living or asleep with the dead, we're alive with Him! So speak encouraging words to one another. Build up hope so you'll all be together in this, no one left out, NO ONE LEFT BEHIND"* (I Thessalonians5:9-11, The Message *Translation).*

Why It Will End This Way: The Path of Most Resistance

The understanding of the Rapture itself, and the purpose of it, and the timing of it, is a uniquely Christian idea. It encompasses the Gospel, with its redemptive purpose in history, and the culmination of that purpose in the Second Coming of Jesus the Messiah to eternally deliver all who put their faith in Him.

Other world religions do not account for an appearance of Jesus and His personal transforming power as His gift of eternal life, or for a Judgment Day itself for their own personal choices of sin and sinfulness.

The Buddhist Monk "believes after death one is either reborn into another body (reincarnated) or enters nirvana. Only Buddhas — those who have attained enlightenment - will achieve the latter destination."[217]

What about Hindus? "Life and death are both part of what Hindus call maya, a grand illusion. Hindus believe that when a soul dies, it gets born

217 http://www.religionfacts.com/buddhism/beliefs/afterlife

into a new body. The cycle of death and rebirth — samsara — ends only when a soul realizes its true nature — indistinguishable from the absolute godhead, which Hindus call Brahman. This realization — moksha — is liberation, and it may take many lifetimes of effort in a human body to attain." [218]

In world religions, there are seemingly endless ways to think about the "end," and even within Christianity itself in the pop culture of the West, it seems that the easiest way to think about it, in regards to the Rapture, is the path of *least* resistance.

Since the great world wars, devastation, and overspreading evil of the past hundred years, it is far easier to ponder an "easy out" of a Rapture of millions of Believers, than it is to consider that the opposite may be true: millions of Believers are being called *forward* in marching *towards* the battle lines, into the devastation, as the salt and light of the world.

We, as the Church of the LORD Jesus Christ, are being called into **the path of most resistance** as we face the enemies of the LORD and confront them through patience endurance, faith, hope and love.

We, the Church, endure all suffering with patience, awaiting for the true moment of Rapture on the very last day of recorded history. And JESUS Himself picks a fight, the final fight in fact, with His adversary. HE alone sovereignly allows the Enemy one Final Battle, worldwide, before returning in His majesty and destroying all evil forever.

> *"And at last, when you see how the Son of Man comes—surrounded with a cloud, with great power and miracles, in the radiance of His splendor, and with great glory and praises—it will make you jump for joy! For the time of your full transformation has arrived"* (Luke 21:27-28).[219]

218 http://classroom.synonym.com/hindu-beliefs-dying-death-afterlife-5605.html

219 The Passion Translation. NOTE on the word, "TRANSFORMATION:" The Greek word is "redemption" or "liberation." It speaks of the total transformation of our body, soul, and spirit when we see Him as He is (1 John 3:2).

Going Deeper Still

— Did you know that prior to about 1830, the theory of a secret Rapture as an end-time doctrine (to begin a two-stage Second Coming), did not exist in the history of the Christian church?

— According to the Apostle Paul, what is the purpose of the Rapture? (reread 1 Thessalonians 4 and 1 Corinthians 15).

— If the timing of the Rapture happens at the very last day of history as we know it, how does that change your personal perspective of today?

— The concept of the Rapture itself, is entirely unique to Christianity. How will the true perspective of it help you in sharing the story of Jesus with members of other religions?

— What changes will you consider making, personally, to begin preparing for the End?

APPENDIX II

The Chiastic Structure of Revelation

Did you know, besides the Seven Parallel Cycles which help us understand the unique structure of Revelation, there is also a wonderful kind of hidden, poetic structure to the Book of Revelation known to the ancients as a Chiastic or Chiasm structure?

I will help you gain a partial understanding, and show you at least three of these Chiasms in the Book, to help you begin a quest for deeper study, if you so choose.

The Book is like a colorful, inter-woven tapestry with order and poetic structure to add drama and dimension to itself. And this Chiastic structure is unique to itself, and woven through the seven parallel cycles of judgment that I defined clearly in chapter 4.

Definition of a Chiasm: It is a mirror-like pattern; a writing style that uses a unique pattern for clarification and/or emphasis; it originates from the Greek, Chi letter, or X.

When you know it is there, it provides a whole new dimension to understanding the central importance of the Book, and of the various characters in the Book. The center and/or outer edges of the Chiasm were usually the main point that the author was bringing emphasis to.

For example, did you know the very center verse of the entire Book of Revelation (and thus the central thought that the author wanted you to walk away with) is found in Revelation 12:11?

> *"And they overcame him (the Enemy) by the blood of the Lamb and the word of His (Christ's) testimony; and they loved their lives not unto death"* (Revelation 12:11).

Note: O.T. prophetic books, like the Book of Daniel (which John the Revelator draws heavily from in Revelation), were structured in this ancient (and now lost to us) form of writing.

John patterned his epistle, in many ways, after Daniel, which is organized with a mirrored pattern where key themes are presented, then revisited in reverse order. The central focus is often on Daniel's faithfulness and God's sovereignty over worldly powers. A prominent example is the pairing of chapters 2 and 7, which both present visions of future empires, highlighting the central theme of God's ultimate control over history.

Here is one of the Chiasms that form the Book of Daniel for you to study deeper, (again, note the parallelism of A vs. A', B vs. B', and C).

A. Four World Empires (chapter 2)
  B. Persecution Theme: Hebrew Children in Fiery Furnace (chapter 3)
    C. Humiliation of Nebuchadnezzar (chapter 4)
    C'. Overthrow and Death of Belshazzar (chapter 5)
  B'. Persecution Theme: Daniel in the Lion's Den (chapter 6)
A'. Four World Empires (chapter 7)

You will note the beauty and symmetry of this Chiasm of the parallel chapters in Daniel 2-7. Notice the Four World Empires are brought forth, and if you read and study those chapters, unique descriptions are included. Note also the center of this Chiasm: the enemies of God are overthrown! It's the same in the center of Revelation: the Dragon (Satan) is cast down from heaven in the moment of victory at the Cross (see Revelation 12)!

So as you begin to read Revelation, suddenly you spot different characters appearing on the scene in a specific order (the exact same technique is used in Daniel). And then later in the story, their unique destinies are assigned in a kind of reverse order (also true of Daniel). Here is a helpful Chiasm to get you excited about the study of the Book of Revelation.

Notice and compare how the themes of the original A, B, C, D, E mirror the themes of A', B', C', D', & E'.

A. The people of God depicted with the imagery of light and creation,
(12:1-2)
B. The Dragon, Satan, (12:3-6)
C. The Beast and the False Prophet, (13:1-18)
D. The bride; the people of God in the imagery of sexual purity, (14:1-5)
E. Babylon the prostitute, (17:1-6)
E'. Babylon destroyed, (17:15-18:24)
D'. The bride is blessed with marriage, (19:1-10)
C'. The Beast and the False Prophet are destroyed, (19:11-21)
B'. The Dragon is destroyed, (20:1-10)
A'. The people of God in the imagery of light and creation, (21:1-22:5)[220]

How exciting is that? Compare and contrast A-B-C-D-E with their reverse of E'-D'-C'-B'-A' and you will begin to note just one of the many ways that Revelation is a poetic tapestry, woven in intricate ways.

And can you see how John the Revelator introduces the key antagonists (evil beings) in order of: The Dragon, The Beast, The False Prophet, and Babylon the Prostitute. Then in reverse-order we see their demise: Babylon the Prostitute, The False Prophet, The Beast, and finally the Dragon is destroyed. Surrounding this spiritual darkness (in parallel chapters 12 & 21) is the beautiful imagery of the light and glory of God upon His triumphant Church!

Studying Revelation is not always a linear experience.

i.e. A----------B---------C;

(like reading chapters 4-7----8-11----12-14 and thinking those events happen chronologically and in order).

---

220 Poythress, Ibid., 63-64.

Rather, it's a bit like navigating a river, and it often looks more like this.

A
  B
    C
  B'
A'

And did you know...the Seven Churches themselves form a Chiasm?

A = Ephesus (2:5); theme: on the verge of losing their Christian identity

B = Smyrna (2:8); themes: no weaknesses! Keep up faithful witness!

C = Middle of Chiasm: three middle churches of Pergamum, Thyatira, Sardis (2:12, 2:18, 3:1); themes: mixture & challenge of faithfulness amidst temptation to compromise with idolatry.

B' = Philadelphia (3:7); themes: no weaknesses! Keep up faithful witness!

A' = Laodicea (3:16); theme: on the verge of losing their Christian identity.

Have you ever seen that before? Compare A-A' and B-B'. "C" could also be structured,

C = Pergamum
C = Thyatira
C = Sardis

"The main point in a chiastic structure lies usually on the outside parallels," writes G.K. Beale, "though sometimes the middle point receives the emphasis. The significance of the chiasm here is to emphasize that the churches in Asia Minor are in serious trouble. The chiasm is bounded by churches that could be about to lose their identity, and the churches in the middle of the pattern are in poor health. If the seven churches represent the Church universal of the 1st century and throughout the Church Age, then the significance of the Chiasm is to underscore that the Church in any generation is typically not a healthy, witnessing church. Nevertheless, there is always a small part of the church which faithfully maintains its witness (Smyrna and Philadelphia)."[221]

So, if whatever church you are currently a part of is not PERFECT, you are in good company! Reread the seven churches prayerfully, and allow the Holy Spirit to show you the healthy aspects and unhealthy aspects. I think you'll find, if you study the rise and fall of many churches, they have had parallel problems, victories, successes and failures, just like the 1st century churches in Asia Minor.

The same Enemy that they battled against is attempting to bring mixture to Leaders everywhere, and in all generations of Salvation-History, to help stop the pure witness of Christ and His People. And he is both, inside the four walls of a particular church, and outside in the culture.

Various scholars through the years have noticed various unique Chiasms hidden in the structure of Revelation. And when you study them, you glean even more insights into the unique way that John the Revelator patterned his epistle. Here is one of my personal favorites, as it highlights the spiritual warfare motif of this very book, and shows how the Book of Revelation also follows the theme of Spiritual Battle.

Study carefully the parallel numbers and how they mirror each other in poetic pattern form, A. to A', B. to B' and so on.

---

221 Ibid, Beale, pgs. 32-33.

"From the Church Militant to the Church Triumphant"
War Chiasm

Prologue: (1:1 to 1:11)
- **A.** Christophany, (1:12-20)
  - **B.** Recompense to the churches: "The CHURCH MILITANT," (2:1-3:22)
    - **C.** Throne Vision, (4:1-5:14)
      - **D.** Seven seals: rider judgments (1-4 focus on humans), (6:1-8:1)
        1. Content of the judgments, (6:1-17)
        2. Preservation of the church, (7:1-8:1)
        - **E.** Seven trumpets: angelic judgments (1-4 focus on nature), (8:2-11:19)
          1. Judgment on the nations, (8:2-9:21)
          2. Preservation of the church, (10:1-11:14) (includes the Two Witnesses of 11:3-12)
          3. Joy in heaven, (11:15-19)
          - **F.** The redeemed, (12:1-6) (with intermixed strife, 12:3-6).
            - **G**. Deceptive & destructive opponents (Satan's counterfeit trinity of the Red Dragon, (12:7-17), Beast, (13:1-10), & False Prophet, (13:11-18)

CENTER POINT OF THIS CHIASM: (12:11),
And they overcame him by the blood of the lamb, and the word of His (Christ's) testimony, and they did not love their life even to death.

- **F'.** The redeemed, (14:1-20) (with intermixed strife, 14:6-20)

E'. Seven bowls: angelic judgments (1-4 focus on nature), (15:1-19:10)
1. Judgment on the nations, (15:1-16:21)
2. End of the false "church" Babylon, (17:1-18:24)

3. Joy in heaven, (19:1-10)
D'. White horse: rider judgment
(focus on humans), (19:11-20:10)
1. Content of judgment, (19:11-21)
2. Preservation of the church, (20:1-10)
(Millennial Reign/advancement of the Gospel in the nations; Satan bound and unbound)
C'. Throne vision, (20:11-15)
B'. Announcement of recompense to the churches:
"The CHURCH TRIUMPHANT," (21:1-8)
A'. Theophany, (21:9-22:5)
Epilogue: (22:6-21).

A final thought on the CENTER POINT OF THIS CHIASM:
(12:11), *"And they overcame him by the blood of the lamb, and the word of His (Christ's) testimony, and they did not love their life even to death."*

"Revelation 12:11 tells us what hanging-in Christians can and should do to help hasten the demise of the devil.

1. It is by the sacrifice of the Lamb, His death-and-resurrection, and only by this, that the conquest takes place. This is the fundamental and necessary fact.

2. Yet, it is through the Testimony, the *martyria Jesu,* Christians make to Him that His victory is kept active and the dragon kept confronted with it.

3. And this Witness, finally, is full-powered only when it is supported by and includes the willingness "not to hold their lives too dear to lay them down."

The victory cost the Lamb everything, and He was willing to give it for our sakes; why do we think it should cost us nothing?"[222]

---

222 Ibid., Vernard Eller, page 129.

APPENDIX III

The Two Other Views of the Millennium & the Chiasm of Chapters 17-22

Question: Just what are the two common other "Millennium Views" besides the one you are advocating for in this book?

Answer: Premillennialism and Postmillennialism.

Let me describe them to you, with accompanying diagrams, and then show once again the view of the NOW-Millennium.

"*Premillennialism* holds that Jesus' physical return to earth will occur before ("pre") the 1,000 years referenced in Revelation 20. Since they believe that Jesus will have returned in His resurrection body before the 1,000 years, premillennialists typically view the millennium as a period in which Christ reigns on earth (according to their interpretation of texts elsewhere in scripture, from Jerusalem in Israel)."[223]

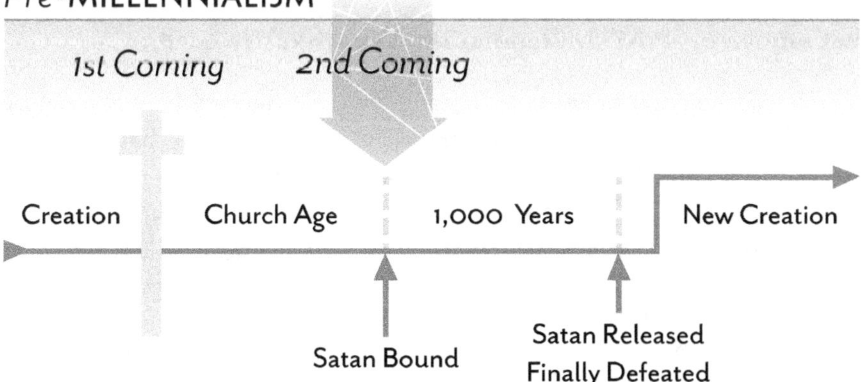

You will note that for the Premillennialist, Satan is bound at the Second Coming, (vs. the NOW-Millennialism view that he was already bound at

223 Dennis E. Johnson, Triumph of the Lamb, pg. 279. Phillipsburg, New Jersey. P & R Publishing. 2001.

the First Coming). They take the number, 1,000, and believe it is literal, not symbolic. The other areas of disagreement for me follow with the logic of Sam Storms.

1. Premillennialists believe that physical death will continue to exist beyond the time of Christ's Second Coming.
2. Premillennialists believe that the natural creation will continue, beyond the time of Christ's Second Coming, to be subjected to the curse imposed by the fall of man, and the earth will continue to be ravaged by war and sin and death.
3. Premillennialists believe that the new Heavens and the new Earth will not be introduced until the 1,000 years subsequent to the return of Christ.

I personally believe that the Second Coming encompasses the Rapture and transformation of the Church, the bowls of wrath being poured out upon the world and the demonic realms, and the Great White Throne Judgment. The New Heavens and New Earth are accomplished together as one main event happening concurrently (since time itself as we know it now is abolished at the Second Coming).

Let's move to "Post" Millennialism. What exactly is it?

"*Postmillennialism* believes that Jesus' physical Second Coming will be after ("Post") the Age given as a coming literal 1,000 years. They believe in the overwhelming fruitfulness of the evangelistic advance in the salvation of individuals and in the complete transformation of cultures, countries, and world civilizations as a whole—all before the physical return of Christ.

"The Postmillennial conception of victory is of a progressive cultural victory (which they identify with the "millennium"); in other words, Christianity's progressive victory, in time and history, into all of human life and culture."[224]

224 Sam Storms, ibid.

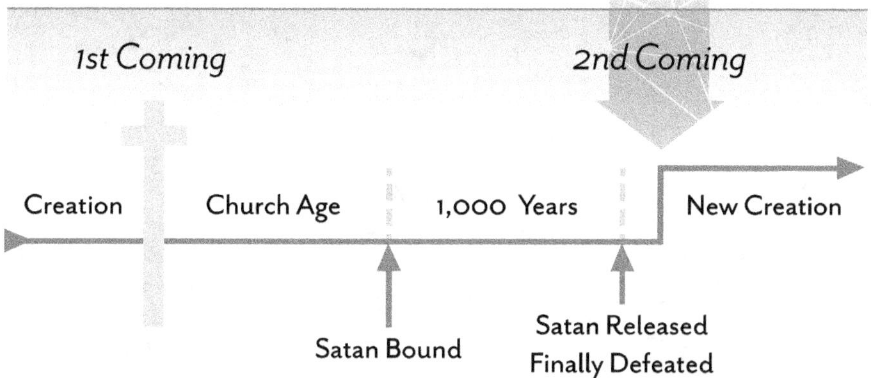

Can you see how these two other views are at odds with the NOW-Millennium and the entire progression of themes in this book? I believe that we are heading in the opposite direction of the Postmillennialist view that Christ will return to a truly Christianized world.

What are my hopes as I consider these other views? That the Gospel will continue to advance into all spheres of Society and bring continuous cultural transformation of whole regions and hearts to Christ before His Coming. Come, Holy Spirit, until the Final Battle commences! Come, Revivals! Come, mighty moves of God!

That being said, even Jesus Himself made two important observations.

1. *"Enter by the narrow gate; for the gate is wide, and the way is broad that leads to destruction, and many are those who enter by it. For the gate is small, and the way is narrow that leads to life, and few are those who find it"* (Matthew 7:13-14).

2. *"However, when the Son of Man comes, will He find faith on the earth?"* (Luke 18:8).

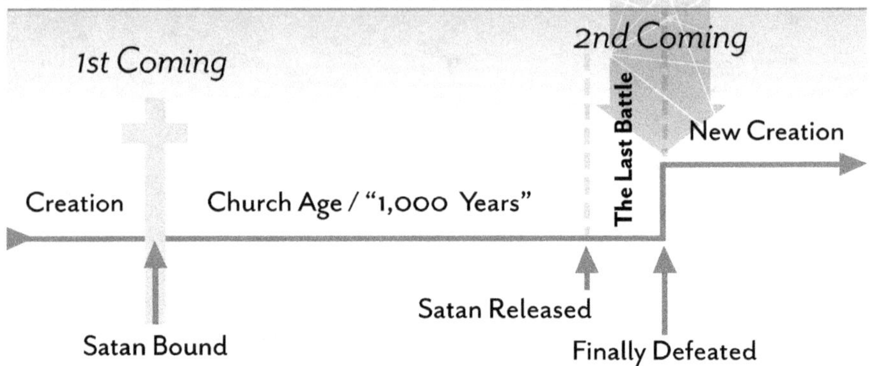

To reiterate, I believe the number 1,000 to be symbolized as a perfect cube, "10 times 10 times 10" equals a perfect period of time of God's Sovereign plan in the nations, marking the entire timeframe of the Church Age in completion.

And once again to quote Sam Storms, "Amillennialism (NOW-Millennialism) is better suited to explain the restriction placed on Satan in Revelation 20:1-3. Satan is pictured as being prevented from perpetuating the spiritual blindness of the nations and keep them in Gospel darkness. He is prevented from provoking a premature global assault on the Church, which we know to be the battle of Armageddon."[225]

And let me close this final Appendix with a final thought that John structured chapter 20 in the midst of a Chiasm, so it is a better view to note that chapter 20 is not to be considered to chronologically follow chapter 19. Thus, the NOW-Millennium makes a lot more sense, and we can apply our faith stronger to those passages. Remember as you study this, that the outside parallels and the center point of the Chiasm are usually the focus.

225 Ibid, Storms.

Implications of the Chiastic Structure in Chapters 17-22

"The broader context of chapters 17-22 forms a chiastic structure with sections exhibiting poetic parallelism, further suggesting that 20:1 DOES NOT chronologically follow 19: 11-21.

- **A.** Judgment of the Harlot (17:1-19:6)
  - **B.** The Divine Judge (19:11-16)
    - **C.** Judgment of the beast and false prophet (19:17-21; cf. Ezek. 39)
      - **D.** Satan imprisoned for 1,000 years (20:1-3)
      - **D'.** the saints reign/judge for 1,000 years (20:4-6)
    - **C'.** The judgment of Gog and Magog (20:7-10; cf Ezek. 38-39)
  - **B'.** the Divine Judge (20:11-15)
- **A'.** Vindication of the Bride (21:1-22:5; cf 19:7-9)."[226]

The significance and beauty of this particular Chiasm is in the outer parallels (the judgment of the Harlot vs. the vindication of the Bride) and the center point. While Satan has been bound for the Church Age, all saints who have died in faith have been and will continue to reign as kings with Christ Himself in Heaven until He returns. Now, that is Good News!

Thus, it is now time to prepare for the Last Battle with courage, hope and faith.

"He who testifies to these things says, 'Yes, I am coming quickly.' Amen. Come, Lord Jesus" (Revelation 22:20).

226 Ibid, Beale, pg. 983.

About the Author

I was raised as a, "good Lutheran boy." I even preached my first message from a Lutheran pulpit at the age of 17. It finally dawned on me one day, a few years later, that instead of just following Luther's teachings I needed more: I needed to follow Christ Himself!

So at the age of 20, one night during my senior year of college, I repented of my sins and gave my heart and my life to Jesus Christ.

I remember the very morning after I made that commitment in prayer. I was walking to class and suddenly it seemed my entire world was alive in new ways! Everything seemed brighter, more colorful, more vibrant and ALIVE. The Father Himself seemed to be shouting His love to me in all of His creation.

His Word became alive in me, too. I voraciously devoured the Gospel of John and soon after, the entire Bible. He has blessed me time and time again as I have followed Him, journeying into both the world of itinerant ministry and media.

My vision in equipping evangelism is to inspire passionate discipleship, and also help people of all backgrounds hear the voice of God more clearly and help equip people to share their faith in Jesus Christ. I travel extensively, bringing an inspirational preaching and teaching style to churches, seminars and conferences.

My vision in media includes being a producer of great documentary films. I even attended U.S.C. Film School for a summer in Los Angeles, California. I love to study history, and I love to bring history to life for people. I love relating stories of common Believers of all times who had extraordinary faith and did great things for God.

In personality I could be described as an "outgoing introvert." That means that I love to network and meet new people and learn all about them. It also means I love to retreat to private places to pray often in seclusion. I get recharged by being alone (even though I enjoy being with people).

In my spare time I love to go fishing, play golf, watch movies, pray, sing and worship God, and do accents and imitations.

If you are ever wanting to "test" me, just shout out, "BRAVEHEART" or, "DO SHAKESPEARE." I might just do a loud Scottish accent with the famous Braveheart speech, or even Shakespeare in an English accent.

In case you are wondering, my favorite Bible verse is John 10:10. I just love it. It is Jesus sharing this, *"The thief comes only to steal, and kill, and destroy; I came that they might have LIFE, and might have it abundantly"* (John 10:10).

I love this verse because the "thief" in context appears to be the "religious crowd" standing there. Religion, without relationship with Jesus, steals, kills and destroys. I experienced "religion" growing up, and once I found the LIFE that Jesus speaks of, it set me free. He came to set us all free and enjoy relationship!

I invite you to subscribe to my Listener Updates e-Letter so we can keep the conversation going. My blog contains sometimes *challenging* but *always inspirational* teachings, with both Scripture and practical application.

I post new devotional blogs and email them often enough, but not too often to overload your email.

Subscribe to the Listener Update e-Letter and receive my special free e-Book, "Love Speaks: Hearing the Voice of Our Father," as a free gift delivered right to your inbox.

Visit our website to subscribe at:
http://www.LoveSpeaks.Today

Enjoy instant access to all of our Love Speaks discipleship tools, including the Book, e-Book, Kindle Edition, Audio Book (read by the Author), the Love Speaks Masterclass (online training course for individuals & small group study), the Love Speaks Documentary Film Series "Video-On-Demand" Service (including Broadcast Versions and Special Director's Cuts), as well as subscribe to our latest "Listener Updates e-Letter."

I'm looking forward to hearing from you!

Scan me!

Resources for Further Study:

The Love Speaks Book

Learn to Hear God's Voice.
Experience His Love.

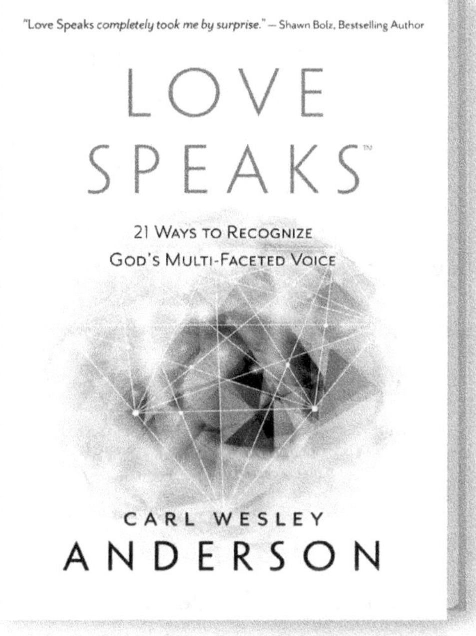

Start Listening Today!

No matter what your faith background, you can grow stronger in His eternal love as expressed through the voice of God the Father, Son, and Holy Spirit. This book is an invitation to discover that God's love is real, and He is speaking to you personally.

Visit our website to learn more — **www.LoveSpeaks.Today**

Also Available Worldwide on Amazon

Resources for Further Study:

Love Speaks Masterclass

Do you wish this wasn't the end? Are you hungry to learn more about this subject? You are not alone. Consider enrolling in the Love Speaks Masterclass (perfect for either a small group or individual study).

Join Rev. Carl in many hours of anointed teaching on the themes in this book. Your purchase allows lifetime access to all the online teaching sessions, so you can choose the ones you really like and watch them again and again, anytime, worldwide.

Delve deeper into the themes taught here, and develop new faith in expecting God to speak personally to you in His love, every week, no matter what circumstance you find yourself in.

The Masterclass includes:

— Full teaching on all 21 ways to recognize God's multi-faceted voice

— Challenging exercises to dramatically increase your contact with God on a weekly basis

— Additional inspirational stories not included in this book on several key ways of God speaking

— A Bonus Workbook & Study Guide with "dig deeper" questions, scripture verses for meditation, and a built-in prayer journal

— 5 Bonus Training Sessions of Practical Application, including themes of Fasting, Living the Revelatory Lifestyle, and How to Give a Word from the Word, and more!

Simply visit www.LoveSpeaks.Today for more info.

LOVE SPEAKS™

MASTERCLASS

RESOURCES FOR FURTHER STUDY:

The Love Speaks Documentary Film Series

The Love Speaks Documentary Film Series is a unique historical, educational, inspirational, and impartational journey for a modern generation. Based on this book, each episode focuses on a "Way" that the Father, Son, and Holy Spirit speak and shares stories of how God has faithfully spoken to every generation—plus **BONUS STORIES** from Salvation-History! If you are yearning to grow in your relationship with the LORD and recognize His voice more clearly, you will be blessed.

Season 1

- Episode 1, Way #1: The Established Word. "To the Ends of the Earth"
- Episode 2, Way #2: The Living Word. "It's Alive!"
- Episode 3, Way #3: The Inner Witness. "Follow the Witness"
- Episode 4, Way #4, The Inner Voice. "The Still, Small Voice"
- Episode 5, Way #5: The Inner Desires. "The River of God's Will"
- Episode 6, Way #6: Nature & Creation. "The Ocean of God's Love"
- Episode 7, Way #7: Providence. "Two Hearts, Strangely Warmed"

Season 2

- Episode 8, Way #8: The Preaching of His Word, "The Fire & the Hammer"
- Episode 9, Way #9: Other Believers, "Christ in Mouth of Friend or Stranger"
- Episode 10, Way #10: Visions, "Visions of the Nations"
- Episode 11, Way #11: Dreams, "I Dreamed a Dream"
- Episode 12, Way #12: Symbolic Speech, "Christ the Warrior King"
- Episode 13, Way #13: Divine Appointments, "Holy Coincidence, Batman!"
- Episode 14, Way #14: All Forms of Media, "God Goes to the Movies"

Season 3

- Episode 15, Way #5: The Gift of Prophecy, "Every Oak was Once an Acorn"
- Episode 16, Way #16: The Word of Wisdom, "Blueprints from Heaven"
- Episode 17, Way #17: Words of Knowledge, "The Revelatory Lifestyle"
- Episode 18, Way #18: Discerning of Spirits, "Spiritual Sight to Reign in Life"
- Episode 19, Way #19: Angels, "Flames of Fire"
- Episode 20, Way #20: Jesus Himself Speaking, "He Moves Among the Candlesticks"
- Episode 21, Way #21: The Audible Voice of the Father, "Some Said It Thundered"

A Gift from the Author when You visit LoveSpeaks.Today!
Use code LS20 at checkout.
Get 20% off!
LOVE SPEAKS™
A Walk Through Salvation-History: Finding God's Multi-Faceted Voice for a Modern Generation
Episodes 1 - 21
Carl Wesley Anderson
Love Speaks™ Documentaries
Historical Stories to Inspire a Listening Heart!
A Perfect Resource for Group Study!
Director's Cuts Available Streaming 24/7 as Digital Downloads for Rent or Purchase
For more Information Visit www.lovespeaks.today
Scan me!

Contact Carl

To get the latest Revelation's Battle Plans digital resources and updates, please visit, **https://revelationsbattleplans.com/**

Carl travels extensively around the world with his dynamic teaching style and brings the themes of this book to life. He can deliver an engaging 40 minute single message, a half-day, or a full training day for your church, conference, or ministry engagement. He loves to allow time also for live Q & A for people to ask him questions and respond to the material.

If you are interested in finding out more, please visit his Speaking Page here: **https://borntoblaze.com/invite-carl-booking-form/**

You can also connect with Carl here:

BLOG: http://BornToBlaze.com/blog/

FACEBOOK: https://www.facebook.com/carlwesleyandersonjunior/

TWITTER: https://twitter.com/BornToBlaze

INSTAGRAM: https://www.instagram.com/born2blaze/

Publisher's Note: *Be a sower of the Word of God and this unique message! Put a copy of this book into the hands of others who need to read it. Many people who need this message may not be looking for it.*

Consider extending this ministry by sowing 1 book, 3 books, 5 books or MORE TODAY and become an instrument of changing lives, and increasing hunger for hearing God's voice and sharing God's love around the world!

To purchase multiple copies of 'Revelation's Battle Plans' for Small Group Study or to sow to others, please Contact Carl here

Rev. Carl Wesley Anderson, Founder,
Born to Blaze Ministries, Since 1992

Find a New Way Forward in These Uncertain Times.

Every time I turn on the news, it seems the world is falling apart. Are we really getting closer to the Last of the Last Days? I can get so distracted these days and don't know if I am hearing from God. When I do hear something, I'm not sure if I am hearing God's voice, or my own thoughts? How do I tell the difference? But I DO know that consistent times set apart for listening to God build my faith, and that we can make a space for peace in this chaotic world.

Join Born to Blaze Co. – a safe, faith-filled space where you'll be equipped and encouraged to:

— Hear the voice of the Lord for yourself
— Navigate the shaking with hope and courage
— Break through obstacles that hold you back spiritually
— Experience peace that doesn't depend on your circumstances

This is new, but it's not complicated. It's powerful, but it's also personal. It's safe, because it's built on truth and grace. And it's for you.

You're not meant to walk through these days alone. Come join a growing community of people just like you—seeking clarity, courage, and the real presence of God.

Join Now for just $1!

Let's walk this out together!
https://borntoblaze.com/born-to-blaze-co-one-dollar/

BORN TO BLAZE CO.

AN INTERNATIONAL FELLOWSHIP
OF BLAZING HEARTS

Hearing God's Voice & Understanding the Book of Revelation Has Never Been Easier!

A Prayer of Consecration, Dedication and Repentance

Turning to the Lord, and Receiving His Salvation, Eternal Life, and the Voice of the Spirit Communicating within Your Redeemed Human spirit!

To begin an adventure of hearing God's Voice both internally and externally, with the Person of the Holy Spirit coming to reside within you, I have a few questions:

"Will you accept God's love for you?

Can you admit to God you have failed and are a sinner?

Will you believe that Jesus died for you?

Do these things and one step remains: a true Christian accepts Jesus as God and King forever.

Open yourself to Jesus Christ and receive Him into your life as your absolute King and Savior.

If you want to, here is a prayer to pray right now:

*'Father God, I really want to know You.
I want to be truly part of Your family.
Just as I am, I give myself to You.
I am not perfect.
I have done lots of things wrong.
I am a sinner.
Jesus Christ, I believe and trust in You.
I believe You died for me.
I give You all my sin and guilt and failure.

Thank You for forgiving me.
Thank You for making me clean.
I give myself and all I have to You, without holding anything back.
Come in now as my King and Savior forever.
Take charge of my life.
Fill me with Your Spirit.
Make me what I should be.
Thank you, Jesus Christ, Amen.'

You have just put your hand into the hand of God and He will hold you!

As Jesus has promised,

> *"I give them eternal life, and they shall never perish; no-one can snatch them out of My hand"* (John 10:28).

From now on, you belong to Jesus Christ. You have become a Christian."

**(Prayer Adapted from a writing by Eric Delve).*

Now you can return to all the Lessons and know that every single, "WAY" is available to you.

Begin recognizing God's multi-faceted voice today!

Please feel free to email any Testimonies of praying this prayer to me: **carl@BornToBlaze.com**

Are you ready yet?

New things I learned in this book:

Things I want to remember from this book:

Practical applications and strategies for my life:

Even so, come, LORD Jesus. Amen.

www.ingramcontent.com/pod-product-compliance
Lightning Source LLC
LaVergne TN
LVHW010555100826
845148LV00014B/2727

* 9 7 8 0 9 7 6 2 9 1 0 7 7 *